Case Studies in Sport Communication

Case Studies in Sport Communication: You Make the Call goes beyond the box scores by offering readers the opportunity to evaluate popular and diverse issues in sport—including management, crisis, health, ethics, gender, race, and social media. Each chapter incorporates theory and communication principles as well as topical background information and concludes with discussion questions and engaging assignments. This volume presents real-life, provocative sports cases that bring contemporary headlines into perspective and inspire critical thinking. Each chapter features scholarly evidence that will keep the conversation lively, thoughtful, and informative. Students are encouraged to challenge the ethical implications of what they have read and to "make the call." This is an invaluable resource for upper-level undergraduate and graduate students of sport communication and sport management.

Terry L. Rentner, Ph.D., Professor, teaches public relations, journalism and sports courses in Bowling Green State University's School of Media and Communication. She teaches public relations and journalism courses at the undergraduate level, including sport PR, and pedagogy, health communication, public relations, and advertising at the graduate level. She is also co-founder of the Richard Maxwell project, created to foster student participation in sport media and communication activities and events.

David P. Burns, Ph.D., Associate Professor, teaches sports reporting and other advanced journalism courses in Salisbury University's Communication Arts Department. Besides sport communication, his research interests focus on media–politics linkages that impact journalism and the communication industry. Burns serves on the editorial boards of the *Journal of Middle East Media, Central European Journal of Communication* and AEJMC's *Electronic News*.

Case Studies in Sport Communication

Communication

You Make the Call

Edited by
Terry L. Rentner, Ph.D.
David P. Burns, Ph.D.

Routledge
Taylor & Francis Group

NEW YORK AND LONDON

First published 2019
by Routledge
711 Third Avenue, New York, NY 10017

and by Routledge
2 Park Square, Milton Park, Abingdon, Oxon OX14 4RN

Routledge is an imprint of the Taylor & Francis Group, an informa business

Library of Congress Cataloging-in-Publication Data
Names: Rentner, Terry L., editor. | Burns, David P., editor.
Title: Case studies in sport communication : you make the call / Terry
    L. Rentner(ed), David P. Burns (ed).
Description: New York : Routledge, Taylor & Francis Group, 2019. |
    Includes bibliographical references.
Identifiers: LCCN 2018013262 | ISBN 9781138729520 (hardback) |
    ISBN 9781138729537 (paperback) | ISBN 9781315189833 (ebook)
Subjects: LCSH: Mass media and sports—United States. |
    Communication in sports. | Athletes—United States—Public
    opinion. | Sports—Social aspects—United States.
Classification: LCC GV742 .C38 2019 | DDC 070.4/49796—dc23
LC record available at https://lccn.loc.gov/2018013262

ISBN: 978-1-138-72952-0 (hbk)
ISBN: 978-1-138-72953-7 (pbk)
ISBN: 978-1-315-18983-3 (ebk)

Typeset in Bembo
by Apex CoVantage, LLC

Visit the eResources: www.routledge.com/9781138729537

Printed and bound in Great Britain by
TJ International Ltd, Padstow, Cornwall

To our students who inspire our teaching and inform our research.

Contents

Section II: Corporate and Organizational Identity

PART II
Clubhouse

Section III: Image Repair and Redemption

Section VI: Social Justice and Ethics   221

About the Editors

David P. Burns, Ph.D., Associate Professor, teaches sports reporting and other advanced journalism courses in Salisbury University's Communication Arts Department. Besides sport communication, his research interests focus on the media–politics linkages that impact journalism and the communication industry. He has worked for American television networks and reported for an international wire service and a Polish business newspaper. He is a past president of the Society of Professional Journalists Maryland Professional Chapter. Burns has taught media and journalism workshops in the United States, Poland, Russia, Jordan, India, the United Arab Emirates, Qatar, and Afghanistan. Burns serves on the editorial boards of the *Journal of Middle East Media, Central European Journal of Communication* and AEJMC's *Electronic News*.

Burns received his Bachelor of Science degree in television–radio from Ithaca College. His master's thesis at the University of Georgia predicts the success of worldwide technological innovations and ideas using Everett Rogers' diffusion of innovation theory. His University of Maryland doctoral dissertation explores the media–politics linkage that brought about Poland's mass media changes leading up to and after Poland's political transition from communism to a free market democracy. Burns was a member of a six-person UNESCO consulting team that helped Iraqi and Kurdish educators reform and implement a National Journalism Curriculum for every higher education institution in Iraq and Kurdistan.

Terry L. Rentner, Ph.D., a professor in the Department of Journalism and Public Relations at Bowling Green State University (BGSU), teaches public relations courses, including sport PR, and journalism courses at the undergraduate level and pedagogy, health communication, public relations, and advertising at the graduate level. She is co-founder of the Richard Maxwell project, created to foster student participation in sport media and communication activities and events. She was instrumental in launching the NFL Sport Media Boot Camp, a three-day boot camp at BGSU for current and former NFL players.

Dr. Rentner is a health communication scholar whose work as principal or co-investigator in college student health has led to more than

20 state and federal grants totaling approximately \$1.6 million. She has received several state and national awards for her health communication campaigns. Her most recent work is in international health communication campaigns and health issues in sport. She has published articles in the *Journal of International Crisis and Risk Communication Research*, the *International Journal of Communication and Health*, the *Journal of Health Communication*, *Journalism and Mass Communication Quarterly*, the *Journal of Mass Media Ethics*, and *Public Relations Review*.

Dr. Rentner served as chair of the Department of Journalism and Public Relations and Director of the School of Media and Communication at BGSU. She has twice been a top five finalist for the BGSU Master Teacher Award and served for 20 years as advisor to the Public Relations Student Society of America.

Contributors

Alisa Agozzino, Ph.D., APR, is an associate professor of Public Relations at Ohio Northern University. As the PR program head, she has taught over 16 different classes within the major and developed a social media minor at ONU. She has received numerous awards for teaching, including the international Pearson Award for Innovation in Teaching with Technology. Dr. Agozzino's current research agenda examines how social media or digital platforms impact different industries. Her work has been published in over 20 academic and trade publications.

Rebecca A. Alt is a Ph.D. candidate in the Department of Communication at the University of Maryland, College Park. Her research focuses on organizational rhetoric in the context of elite sports in the U.S. context.

Anne Bialowas, Ph.D., is an associate professor in the Department of Communication at Weber State University. She teaches undergraduate courses in communication theory, media studies, and gender in addition to graduate courses in advanced presentations, team-building, and facilitation. Her research interests encompass sport communication, rhetoric, and gender studies.

Kelli S. Boling (MMC, University of South Carolina) is a doctoral student in the School of Journalism and Mass Communications at the University of South Carolina. Her research interests include both the examination of the podcasting audience and the intersection of women and the media. She has previously had studies published in the *Journal of Radio and Audio Media* and *Visual Communication Quarterly*.

Fernando Vannier Borges, Ph.D., researcher, is involved with international research projects. He wrote a chapter for the book *Football and Supporter Activism in Europe—Whose Game Is It?*, edited as part of FREE—Football Research in an Enlarged Europe, and also collaborates with SPORT—UFRJ, in Brazil, and CPES, in Portugal. His research covers the relationship between media and football, sports journalism, and the mediatization of sports organizations. He worked at the University of Santiago, in Cape

Verde, as professor, where he co-launched the journalism undergraduate course and a master's degree in Communication Studies.

Nicola A. Corbin, Ph.D., is an assistant professor of Public Relations & Advertising in the Department of Communication at Weber State University, where she has also advised the Public Relations Student Society of America chapter and the student-run public relations firm, Ogden Peak Communications. Her research interests encompass exploring the impact of representations of black women in mass media and popular culture, and critical approaches to public relations pedagogy. Prior to academia, Corbin practiced journalism and public relations for 10 years.

Gregory A. Cranmer, Ph.D., is an assistant professor of Sport Communication at Clemson University. He teaches undergraduate and graduate courses in sport communication, theory, and research methods. His research focuses on the interpersonal interactions and experiences of athletes, including their socialization, relationships with coaches, and health decisions. This research is published in *Communication & Sport, International Journal of Sport Communication, Communication Quarterly, Communication Studies, Western Journal of Communication*, and *Communication Research Reports*—among other outlets. He currently serves as the secretary for NCA's Communication & Sport Division.

Amy Graban Crawford, Ph.D., is an associate professor in the Department of Communication at Youngstown State University. She teaches classes in television production, broadcast news, and sports media. Her research interests include rhetorical analysis of media programs, broadcast history, and the scholarship of teaching and learning in media fields.

John A. Fortunato, Ph.D., is a professor at Fordham University in the School of Business, and chair of the Area of Communication and Media Management. He is the author of *Commissioner: The Legacy of Pete Rozelle, Making Media Content*, and *Sports Sponsorship: Principles & Practices*. He has published articles in *Public Relations Review, Journal of Sports Media, Journal of Sport Management, International Journal of Sport Communication, Journal of Brand Strategy*, and multiple law reviews. Dr. Fortunato received his Ph.D. from Rutgers University in the School of Communication.

Erin E. Gilles, Ph.D., is an assistant professor who teaches undergraduate courses in public relations, advertising, and mass media research methods and graduate courses in qualitative research methods, health communication, and communication and aging at the University of Southern Indiana. Her research interests include public relations and advertising strategies, health communication technologies (mHealth, global health initiatives, and smartphone health apps), direct-to-consumer marketing of pharmaceuticals, service learning, and social support. She also advises USI's Ad Club and is the faculty advisor for the university's National Student Advertising Competition team each spring.

Ashley Grimm is the assistant director of Athletics and faculty member within the Department of Administration at Shippensburg University. Prior to starting at Ship, Ms. Grimm spent four years as a student-athlete and two years as a graduate assistant coach at Clarion University, where she earned a Bachelor of Science in Biology with an Honors Program minor before earning a Master of Business Administration. Her experience on campus and across the intercollegiate athletics landscape includes compliance, supervision, game management, advising the Student-Athlete Advisory Committee (SAAC), and various committee work within the department, on campus, and across the conference and NCAA.

Karen L. Hartman, Ph.D., is an associate professor in the Department of Communication, Media, & Persuasion at Idaho State University. She earned her Ph.D. in Rhetoric from Louisiana State University, and her research interests revolve largely around the role of sport in the United States and how language and public relations efforts frame athletes, organizations, and laws. She has authored numerous articles including research published in the *Journal of Communication Studies, International Journal of Sport Communication, Academic Exchange Quarterly*, and the edited volume *The ESPN Effect: Academic Studies of the Worldwide Leader in Sports.*

Cory Hillman, Ph.D., is an assistant professor at Ashland University, where he teaches courses in sports communication, interpersonal communication, and debate. His research centers on the neoliberal transformation of democracy and its corresponding effects on the relationship between fans and sports. Hillman has published in the *Communication and Sport Journal* and is also author of a book entitled *American Sports in the Age of Consumption: How Commercialization is Changing the Game.*

Brian Hofman, Ph.D., is a professor of Sport Management at Ohio Northern University. He teaches a variety of undergraduate courses in the sport management curriculum, as well as a course in LGBT history in ONU's Gender Studies minor. He also serves as volleyball coach at ONU and has won several national coaching awards in both men and women's volleyball. Most recently he has started to serve as a deputy coordinator of Title IX for the ONU campus with special emphasis on Title IX programming for all 23 Polar Bear athletic teams.

Kevin Hull, Ph.D., University of Florida, is an assistant professor in the School of Journalism and Mass Communications at the University of South Carolina. His research focuses on communication in the world of sports— specifically how teams, fans, media, and players interact with each other using both traditional media formats and social media. His articles have appeared in a variety of journals relating to both sports and journalism.

Jack V. Karlis (Ph.D. University of South Carolina, M.A. University of Florida) is an assistant professor of Mass Communication at Georgia College and State University. Karlis specializes in the application of social media under the strategic communication paradigm, which he incorporates into his pedagogy. He teaches Strategic Planning, Strategic Campaign Communication, Theory and Research, and Sports, Entertainment and Popular Culture. A former sportswriter in newspapers, Karlis transitioned into strategic communication by working in the public education public relations field. Karlis has more than 20 years of mass media experience.

Esen S. Koc is a Ph.D. student (doctoral candidate) in the School of Media and Communication at Bowling Green State University. He holds a master's degree in Applied Communication Theory and Methodology from Cleveland State University. As a scholar, he employs interpretive and critical perspectives to study the intersections of communication and identity, including but not limited to issues related to race, ethnicity, religion, and gender.

Kara A. Laskowski, Ph.D., is associate professor of Human Communication Studies at Shippensburg University of Pennsylvania. She teaches undergraduate courses in Interpersonal Communication, Research Methods, Conflict Resolution, Communication and Identity, and Sport Communication. She is the author of "An Athletic Director's Dilemma" (2015), in M. C. Ramsey (ed.), *Issues of Culture and Conflict: Case Studies in Organizational Communication* and conducts research in interpersonal and identity in communication. She serves as department chair and president of the Shippensburg University chapter of the Association of Pennsylvania State College and University Faculty.

Lori Liggett, Ph.D., is a senior lecturer in the School of Media and Communication at Bowling Green State University. Her teaching and research interests are critical and cultural media studies. She teaches a variety of courses, including American Broadcast History, Sport Documentary, TV & Film Criticism, Principles of Sport Broadcasting, Major Events in Sport Media, and Gender, Media and Culture. Liggett has been a faculty participant in the NFL Sports Media Boot Camp held at BGSU for five years. She serves on the Faculty Senate Intercollegiate Athletics Advisory committee and the President's Advisory Committee on Intercollegiate Athletics.

Carrie Michaels is the associate director of Athletics and senior woman administrator at Shippensburg University. She has spent 21 years in higher education working in varying roles including athletics administrator, conference commissioner, academic advisor, and coach. Her intercollegiate experience includes the overall development and management of NCAA Division II athletics with extensive knowledge of Title IX assessment, budget management, supervision, fundraising, policy creation and implementation, selection and evaluation of department personnel, game operations and promotions, and student development. She serves as the deputy Title IX coordinator on behalf of athletics and faculty chair of the Department of Administration.

Derek Moscato, Ph.D., is an assistant professor in the Department of Journalism at Western Washington University in Bellingham, Washington, where he teaches courses in public relations and journalism. Moscato's research focuses on strategic and environmental communication, public diplomacy, media ethics, and persuasion. His doctoral dissertation, completed at the University of Oregon, examined the interplay of environmental activism and rural populism during the battle over the Keystone XL Pipeline. Previous to academia, he served in senior communication roles at Simon Fraser University, the BC Lung Association, and the University of British Columbia, where he served on UBC's Vancouver Winter Olympics Communication Committee.

James Pokrywczynski, Ph.D., teaches in the Diederich College of Communication at Marquette University. He has published research in various scholarly journals as well as trade publications such as *Sports Business Journal* on sports and event marketing, couponing, job satisfaction among advertising practitioners, and product placement in movies/television. He has spoken to over a dozen marketing trade organizations on sports sponsorship and product placement. His Ph.D. is from the Grady College of Journalism and Mass Communication at the University of Georgia. He also has degrees from the University of Illinois-Urbana.

James A. Rada, Ph.D., is an associate professor and chair of the Department of Journalism at Ithaca College. He has published several scholarly pieces investigating the portrayal of African Americans in the mass media. In addition, Rada has produced five feature-length documentaries: *With INFINITE HOPE: MLK and The Civil Rights Movement* (2018); *Meet Me at Equality: The People's March on Washington (2013); Deeds Not Words: The Buffalo Soldiers in World War II (2011); Reclaiming History: The Search for the Underground Railroad* (2006); and *Brown @ 50: A New Generation of Footsoldiers* (2004).

Sada Reed, Ph.D., is an assistant professor in the Walter Cronkite School of Journalism and Mass Communication at Arizona State University in Phoenix. She teaches undergraduate and graduate courses in sports media ethics and diversity, 21st century technological issues influencing sports media practice, and intermediate sports writing. Her research focuses on sports media practices and routines. Her dissertation (University of North Carolina at Chapel Hill, 2015) examined sports journalists' conflicting roles as journalists, community members, and sports enthusiasts.

Mary Beth Reese, MBA, instructor, teaches undergraduate courses in public relations, advertising, and career and professional development at the University of Southern Indiana. Her research includes physical therapist/patient communications, fake news and identity, self-identity performance, and financial public relations theories. She serves as the Public Relations and Advertising coordinator at USI, previously working for 20-plus years in a corporate environment. Roles included leadership in merger integration teams on communications, brand identity, and the development and implementation of a new communications department. Her knowledge of the sport of swimming spanned 12 years with USA age-group swimming and high school swimming.

Kelsey R. Rentner, M.A., is the coordinator for the Detroit Red Wings Foundation, where she is responsible for fundraising and charitable giving initiatives that contribute to the growth of the sport of hockey in metro Detroit. She earned her Bachelor of Science in Journalism from Bowling Green State University (BGSU) in 2014 and received a Master of Arts in Strategic Communication from BGSU in 2017. She worked with the Detroit Lions Corporate Communication and Community Relations Departments as a post-graduate intern before obtaining her full-time position with the Detroit Red Wings Foundation.

Ryan Rogers, Ph.D., is an assistant professor at Butler University, where he teaches undergraduate courses in sports media and media production. He holds a B.A. from the University of Notre Dame, an M.A. from the S.I. Newhouse School of Public Communications at Syracuse University, and a Ph.D. from the University of North Carolina at Chapel Hill. His professional experience includes FOX Sports, ESPN, and the NFL Network. Ryan's research interests center on the psychology of human-computer interaction.

Jean Kelso Sandlin, Ed.D., is an associate professor of Communication at California Lutheran University in Thousand Oaks, CA, where she teaches courses in advertising, public relations, and campaigns. Prior to joining the university in 2007, she served as creative director for an agency in the Pacific Northwest and directed campaigns for a variety of organizations, including nonprofit, educational, government, environmental, and healthcare. Her research interests include authenticity, social media, digital storytelling, digital technologies, and users' perceptions of digital messages. Her most recent project explores viewers' perceptions of sincerity and forgiveness of social media apologies of public figures, including professional athletes.

John S. W. Spinda, Ph.D., is an assistant professor of Sport Communication at Clemson University. His research focuses largely on the roles that fans play in the consumption and perception of sport, especially mediated effects as well as technology uses and effects. This includes sports fan motives, attachment and identification with sports and teams, sports fans' responses to team victories/losses (BIRGing/CORFing), parasocial interaction, fantasy sports, and first-person and third-person media effects.

Ashli Q. Stokes, Ph.D., is an associate professor of Communication Studies at the University of North Carolina at Charlotte. Her award-winning research using rhetorical approaches to analyze public relations controversies has been published in the *Journal of Public Relations Research*, the *Journal of Communication Management*, *Public Relations Review*, and the *Southern Communication Journal*, among others. Stokes also published *Consuming Identity: The Role of Food in Redefining the South* (with Wendy Atkins-Sayre; University Press of Mississippi), *Global Public Relations: Spanning Borders, Spanning Cultures* (with Alan Freitag; Routledge), and an edited collection forthcoming from the UNC Press Office of Scholarly Services.

Chelsea L. Woods, Ph.D., is an assistant professor of Communication at Virginia Tech, where she teaches public relations courses. Her research explores the intersection of public relations and organizational communication, focusing on crisis communication, anti-corporate activism, and corporate social responsibility. Her work has been presented at national and international conferences and published in peer-reviewed journals such as *Corporate Reputation Review* and *Public Relations Review*. She received her Ph.D. from the University of Kentucky.

Richard Yeargin is an undergraduate sport communication student at Clemson University. He is a member of the 2016 national championship football team. After graduating early, he will begin pursuing a master's degree in Athletic Leadership at Clemson University. After, he hopes to pursue a career in the NFL, obtain a law degree, and work as a sports agent.

Preface

Sports departments at newspapers used to sarcastically be called the toy department; nothing serious came out of there and the content of the articles focused on fun and games. Those days are long gone. Today, professional sport and sport-related organizations are very big business, requiring huge investments to yield incredible profits. Salary caps make choosing the right player crucial, resulting in the increased use of intricate sports analytics. Non–daily fantasy sports gaming is one of the fastest growing industries in the world. So, the bounce of a ball or the juggle of a pass may constitute the margin of victory for an athlete or a team, but it may also mean millions in gambling payouts. Thus, courtside electronic line judges (known as cyclops) assist human observation, and satellites link officials thousands of miles from the playing field to confirm flags on the field. The fortunes of athletes, large corporations, and fans ride on people making the right call. It is a similar situation with sports and academia; sport communication is a relatively new but dynamic field. In this textbook, the industry and the academy come together.

Theory and research inform each of the 26 case studies in this book. At the end of each chapter, the reader is asked to review the evidence of the various sport communication cases and determine whether the major players involved made the proper decision. Then, it is the reader's turn to make the call.

This textbook is divided into three parts: Front Office, Clubhouse, and Press Box.

Front Office

The front office spotlights cases where sport management takes center stage. This is divided into two sections. The first section focuses on the role strategic communication plays in sport organizations, and the second explores corporate and organizational identities.

Strategic Communication

Two chapters focus on issues surrounding the NFL's Rams that have sparked controversy. "Coming Home" explores how the Rams framed their relocation from St. Louis to Los Angeles as a homecoming, while "There's No

Media Plan" stresses the role of proactive advocacy in the signing of the first gay player in the NFL. Both chapters consider the impact these issues have on fans, the organization, and media.

The NFL is also the topic of a case study on domestic violence among players. In "Patching a Crisis," readers are asked to put themselves in the role of the NFL commissioner and then challenged to think about what, if anything, could have been done differently in the highly publicized domestic abuse cases in the NFL.

In "Civic Recovery in the Aftermath of a Hockey Crisis," questions arise about how social media impacts the mediation of sporting riots on the part of media, spectators, and participants. The chapter asks readers to think about the role of strategic communicators working with professional sporting teams, including communication with team fans.

Fans are also at the center of a chapter on relationships between sponsors and fans. This case study, "Explaining Sports Fans' Recognition," compares the sponsorship environments for six major U.S. sports leagues—NFL, NBA, MLB, NHL, PGA, and NCAA—and seeks to understand how brands and companies can break through to stick in the consumer's mind without wasting money on expensive sponsorship packages.

Corporate and Organizational Identities

What happens to a university sports team when a controversy or scandal arises? This was the case in "Should the Team Hire the Controversial but Successful Coach?", which looks at when the University of Kentucky (UK) hired a head basketball coach with a controversial past. Controversy is also at the heart of "To Create Our Own Legacy," which examines when Penn State University (PSU) learned of the NCAA's sanctions following the Jerry Sandusky child sexual abuse scandal. At UK, it appears that Coach John Calipari's ability to win a national championship outweighed his transgressions, and fans were willing to forgive. Fans were also willing to forgive PSU, as the university turned scandal into an opportunity to create its own legacy.

Another chapter on university sports organizations, "Life After Signing," looks at how athletes transition from high school to college and questions whether current recruiting practices help or hinder student-athletes.

Taking control of one's image is at the heart of "Broadcast Yourself," a chapter on Benfica, Portugal's most successful soccer club. This chapter contextualizes the process of how creating its own TV channel helped Benfica increase its broadcast income and reestablish its place in continental soccer. What impact does such a bold move have on the future relationship between sports organizations, media companies, and journalists?

Clubhouse

The clubhouse of any sport organization can be a place of harmony or despair at any given time. It's not easy to predict if or when an athlete may be in trouble or an organization is embroiled in a controversy that gains media attention and public scrutiny. This part of the text contains two sections. The first section addresses image repair and redemption, whether it is concerning a sports figure or an entire organization. The second section digs deep into issues of gender, race, and identity, as well as political and social issues that may harm those in the clubhouse, or the clubhouse itself.

Image Repair and Redemption

How do individuals, sports organizations, and sport-related businesses survive a crisis? That is the question for both World Wrestling Entertainment, Inc. (WWE) and all NFL powerhouse institutions. "Roping Off the Ring" examines how a series of employee deaths coerced the WWE into enforcing a wellness policy. Public outcry and media scrutiny forced the NFL to address domestic violence by its players. In "Does the NFL Still Own Sundays?", the authors utilize institutional theory to demonstrate how the NFL rebranded itself as a leader in the domestic abuse crisis rather than the perpetrator.

The emerging businesses of fantasy sports are finding they are not immune to crises. "Drafting Like a King" examines the crisis communication strategies used to fight off accusations of illegal gambling and legal threats that could bring about financial ruin and embarrassment for DraftKings and FanDuel.

Embarrassment is what Olympic gold medalist Ryan Lochte faced when he admitted to fabricating a robbery story in Rio de Janeiro, Brazil, during the 2016 Olympic Games. In "What Did Ryan Lochte Do," the authors use Benoit's Image Restoration Theory to study how Lochte attempted to improve his image through social media posts and TV interviews.

Gender, Race, and Identity

Issues related to gender, race, and identity in sport are rapidly gaining media and public attention. Both sport organizations and athletes are recognizing the need to be culturally sensitive, and when they are not, major crises can erupt. Take for instance the failure of USA Gymnastics and Team USA to stand up for U.S. gymnast Gabby Douglas when she did not place her hand over her heart during the national anthem at a gold medal ceremony during the 2016 Rio Olympic Games. "A Failure to Defend" examines the cyberbullying that ensued.

Gender issues are explored in two chapters. The first, "Challenging a Boy's Club," takes a critical look at gender pay inequity in virtually all professional sports. Using reputation management as a theoretical framework, this chapter addresses pay discrepancies and the impact media rights, sponsorships, and culture have on professional sport. The chapter invites discussion of best practices and communication strategies as they relate to reputation management. A second chapter, "Gender Stereotypes in Mascot Dyads," found performances among male-female mascot duos strongly reinforce gender norms, roles, and stereotypes in society. This study further found how males are taken as the norm in sports, which in turn validates the invisible hierarchy of genders and sexes in sports and society.

Cultural sensitivity is further explored in "Topsy-Turvy Times," in which the authors study the 2017 Super Bowl LI advertisements. The authors consider the unique cultural moment when the ads aired, just weeks after the 2016 U.S. presidential election following a highly polarized political campaign and during a time when player concussion and domestic violence controversies plagued the NFL.

Press Box

We call the third and final part of the book "Press Box" because the chapters therein put the media on center stage. Digital technologies—like social media—were game changers in that they forced all stakeholders in sport to reexamine and adapt the way they communicated. The chapters in the first section deal primarily with how players and organizations use social media to connect with fans and the expectations fans have of players who use social media.

Social Media

The first chapter in this section, "A Grand Slam," examines how Major League Baseball uses social media to stay relevant while faced with statistics that show the average baseball fan is aging with fewer younger fans on deck. To attract younger fans, MLB is going where the young people are—online and on social media. By applying the Expectancy Violations Theory (EVT), the authors demonstrate how wiring stadiums and putting young people in their favorite team's locker room and dugout and even on the field itself creates a millennial buzz that may sustain the sport for another 100 years.

It's no secret fans expect a lot of their sports idols. But in the chapter called "Witness?, Lebron James, a social media maven who often weighs in on political issues, becomes the subject of a Twitter campaign which demands he literally do nothing to protest injustice. In applying attribution theory, the authors examine the media narratives created by #NoJusticeNoLeBron— a Twitter campaign where fans asked the Cleveland Cavalier to sit out a few games to protest a police shooting of a 12-year old Cleveland resident. James' refusal to sit and his online silence on the topic prompted the author to investigate how the media frame stories and to explore linkages between sports viewership and civic engagement.

Anyone who uses digital tools like Twitter, Instagram, and Facebook knows social media can be a communication minefield. One poorly chosen word or mistimed remark can cause social embarrassment or lead to accusations of being culturally tone-deaf on a topic. So, when young, social media–using

Olympians are thrust into the spotlight with little or no professional training in communicating with the masses, there is more at stake than just social awkwardness; reputations and future marketability are on the line. In both "I Was Very Intoxicated" and "Swimming Against the Tide," three very different Olympians' social media use is profiled to examine how they connect with their fans and market their personal brands. "I Was Very Intoxicated" details how one athlete masterfully used both traditional and digital media in distinct ways to handle a high-profile and high-stakes image crisis. "Swimming Against the Tide" adds to the body of literature by helpfully recommending strategies to handle crises by applying situational crisis communication theory as well as reputation management and apologia theories to crisis situations.

Social Justice and Ethics

In the final section of the book, authors address how athletes, owners, and organizations use (or misuse) the media to address pressing social issues. Then the tables are turned by putting media organizations in the spotlight by examining the ethical obligations journalists and media owners have in covering issues related to social justice.

In the chapter "Taking a Knee or Not Taking a Stand," the author explores how NFL management walked a tightrope between honoring players' First Amendment rights to protest racial injustice, retaining hundreds of millions of avid but angry football viewers and pacifying controversy-averse sponsors. By applying the Contingency Theory of Accommodation, the authors address how effectively the NFL managed the media while players took a knee during the national anthem, fans tuned out, and sponsors demanded the NFL get its house in order before underwriters took their advertising elsewhere.

In both "The Offensive Line" and "Paradigm Repair and the Hero Myth in Sports Journalism", the role of journalism and its practices are analyzed. In "The Offensive Line," the authors address the Shakespearean question, "What's in a name?" and apply it to a journalistic conundrum—using a team name even the courts agree is disparaging—the Redskins. Although the First Amendment provides wide latitude in matters of freedom of speech and freedom of the press, what responsibility, if any, do journalists have to society to refrain from using offensive team names and logos? How have other similarly named teams handled the issue? The authors provide some best practices and guidelines. In "Paradigm Repair and the Hero Myth in Sports Journalism," the author examines how sport journalists willingly used their loudest megaphone to place the seemingly age-defiant cyclist on a pedestal but failed to call their own "idol worship over objectivity" reporting methods into question after Armstrong's admission of long-term steroid use.

The final two chapters of the book ask the reader to consider the various ways in which social change can be realized through mediated action.

The "Don't Say" chapter describes how campus athletes are used to address issues like racial bias and social acceptance in campus-wide public service posters. Through the application of the Communication Theory of Identity, the chapter examines the efficacy of leveraging the power of sport to produce positive social change. "The Bathroom Bill and the Basketball Game" investigates what happened when a small school was invited onto a big stage embroiled in national controversy and what can be learned from the experience. Marist College's administration accepted an invitation to play in the NCAA men's basketball tournament in North Carolina—a state that at the time had legislation barring transgender people from using their preferred bathroom. The chapter analyzes the college's communication strategies in framing its decision and how it addressed criticisms leveled against the administration's decision by the school's faculty, students, and staff and the outside community.

Foreword

The headlines come at us so quickly, fueled by—what?

They are fueled by the constant pursuit of an audience—*any* audience—by outlets in a fragmented media industry coping with the reality of financial distress. By the democratization—for better or worse—of a social media process that can give anyone access to a very loud microphone. By agendas that set out to create spin and define a narrative, whether that spin is accurate or not.

The derisive perception of newspaper sports sections as toy departments went the way of hot type, typewriters, and reasonable deadlines long ago. But here's a truth: a similar mindset exists in the academic world to this day. When the late Myles Brand was president of the National Collegiate Athletic Association, he addressed this issue by conceiving and supporting an annual Scholarly Colloquium on College Sports, based upon a premise that the industry requires legitimate academic study. I was honored to be a part of that effort from its beginning to a premature end.

This collection extends the spirit and commitment of the Scholarly Colloquium to all levels of an industry that has expanded beyond any realistic economic expectations. The strength of these studies lies in the fact that they are not driven by an agenda of generating page views, broadcast ratings, or social media prominence. The studies are here because we have paid attention, and we care about them to the extent that it is worth taking part in a thoughtful dialogue.

I quickly discovered a very personal collection of issues. As the Knight Chair in Sports Journalism and Society at Penn State University, I tried, each day, to help student media members cope with the demands of covering the Sandusky scandal. As a reporter at the *New York Times* and *USA TODAY*, I covered domestic abuse cases before the issue generated a national conversation. I covered John Calipari's rise at the University of Massachusetts. I wrote about the struggles young athletes experience in their high-profile transitions to college. In my role at IUPUI, I observed, from a front-row seat, how Ryan Lochte's poor judgment became an international story. I supervised student coverage of Michael Sam's press conference at the National Football League Scouting Combine, and the relief he expressed when he was finally asked a question about . . . football!

You may not agree with all of the theory and research, but you have the opportunity to make your case in a way that happens too infrequently these days.

Here is the beauty of the concept: Shouting is not necessary for you to make the call.

Malcolm Moran
Director, Sports Capital Journalism
Program, IUPUI

Acknowledgments

This book would not be possible without the over 30 authors who contributed their limited time, unlimited intellect, and limitless imagination to this work. Their patience, professionalism, and persistence from the outset was both a point of pride and an inspiration to us as we inched our way through the book writing process. Often, on large research projects like this, you can grow tired of reading and re-reading the content. That did not happen with this project due in large part to the talents of our contributing fellow authors. This is their work as much as ours and a mere 'thank you' seems ludicrously inadequate.

We thank the Department of Journalism and Public Relations at Bowling Green State University and the Department of Communication Arts at Salisbury University for their generous support of this book. A special thank you to Salisbury University for granting David Burns sabbatical leave to do his part in organizing, writing, and editing this book.

Terry Rentner wishes to thank her sports-loving and supportive family, Jim (Go Blue), Jason and Kelsey, who are making their marks in the sports world, and Jessica, who sees the extraordinary in the ordinary. Thanks to my mom, who set the standard for working moms, and my dad, who is the wind beneath my wings. My love of sports began at the tender age of four where I spent summers in Bush Stadium cheering on the St. Louis Cardinals. My passion for the Cardinals led to my love of other sports and ultimately to this book. Thanks to Diane, Sue, Becky, and many other friends who always encourage and support me.

David Burns wishes to thank Christopher Callahan, dean of the Walter Cronkite School of Journalism and Mass Communication at Arizona State University, and his wife Jean for their generous hospitality. Their gorgeous, serene "writers refuge"—complete with gourmet smoker, poolside bar, and breathtaking valley views—embedded lifelong memories into these pages for me. A very special thanks to Adrienne and Debra who selflessly sacrificed evenings, weekends, vacations and holidays for this book. Your reward, or maybe punishment, is that you now have me back full-time.

Part I

Front Office

Section I

Strategic Communication

6.2/2025

- player post-season 2014
- released/1st cuts
- Dallas Cowboys signed him
  to practice squad
  - was natural

2015: signed by Montreal Alouettes
of CFL
- cut that summer/2015

did dance/Dancing with Stars
2015
- author/motivational speaker

1 "There's No Media Plan for the First Gay Player in the NFL"

A Case Study of the St. Louis Rams Drafting Michael Sam

Karen L. Hartman

This case study analyzes the public relations tactics utilized by the National Football League's (NFL) St. Louis Rams when they selected Michael Sam, the first openly gay player, in the 2014 draft. Relying on personal interviews, the study identifies and analyzes the team's response when Sam was drafted. The case study suggests the franchise was ultimately successful in its public relations efforts to manage the media and perceptions of Sam and the Rams due to three reasons: effective message framing, recognizing relevant publics, and utilizing proactive advocacy.

Introduction

249 / 25-6

During the final round of the 2014 NFL draft, the St. Louis Rams chose Michael Sam, a former University of Missouri defensive end, as the 249th pick. Sam had a successful college career from 2010–2014 and won several national awards, including the Associated Press Southeastern Conference defensive player of the year and being named first-team All-America by five different sporting organizations. While picks so late in the draft often go unnoticed, drafting Sam, the first openly gay player, put both him and the organization under a media microscope. Drafting Sam was met with mixed responses but ultimately served as a pivotal moment to question a sport often understood as "one of the most masculine sports ever" (Mazzie, 2014, p. 130). While football acts as a site of heterosexual and hegemonic masculinity, the Rams' selection arguably challenged dominant expectations of how athletes, specifically male football players, "should" act. Not only was the draft an important moment, but Sam kissing his boyfriend on national television further served to question and resist the dominant norms expected of male athletes.

Due to the historic nature of the pick, the Rams had to acknowledge and prepare for questions and responses from internal and external audiences. This case study, therefore, analyzes the public relations response the Rams organization utilized when Sam was drafted. It relies on personal interviews conducted with Artis Twyman, the senior director of communications with the team when Sam was drafted. Twyman's interviews provide perspective on what team representatives were thinking when they drafted him and how they planned to work with the media to both promote and protect Sam.

Background

The Rams have a long history in professional football, and potentially unknown to many fans, they have a record of making historic civil rights moves. Originally based in Cleveland, the team moved to Los Angeles in 1946 until they moved to St. Louis in 1995. The team stayed in St. Louis until the 2016 season, when they moved back to Los Angeles. Through the years the team was in a position to make an impact, and in 1946 owners made a historic civil rights move when they signed Kenny Washington and Woody Strode, the league's first black players in the modern era (Zeigler, 2014). Signing the players broke "the unwritten 12-year ban of African-Americans from the NFL that had been set in place by Washington Redskins owner George Preston Marshall in 1933" (Garcia, IV, 2016, para. 7). The Rams, therefore, have a reputation for tolerance and civil rights and for challenging social norms. Even today, the team's awareness of social issues largely shapes how the organization functions. For example, the Rams stress community efforts, and in 2015, community outreach was the biggest part of the organization's budget. They also incorporate monthly staff days of community service (A. Twyman, personal communication, July 24, 2015).

While the Rams value outreach and its notable part in the civil rights movement, in the larger world of sports some civil rights still remain a challenge. In particular, being openly gay in a professional sport is extremely rare. Examples exist of athletes breaking this particular barrier, such as former National Basketball Association players Jason Collins and John Amaechi, Major League Soccer's Robbie Rogers, and Major League Baseball's David Denson and Billy Bean (Kahrl, 2015), but the culture of football is seen as the most hypermasculine and resistant to challenges to heterosexual norms.

Recognizing the cultural significance of drafting Sam, the Rams needed to rely on traditional public relations tactics while also preparing for the unique media attention Sam's draft would bring. Balancing trusted PR theories and principles, while recognizing that no NFL or professional team had drafted an openly gay player, would be key to managing the media, fan, and general public attention.

The Case

The 2014 NFL draft was held at Radio City Music Hall in New York City from May 8–10. Since the first draft aired on television in 1980, it has steadily grown in popularity into its present media extravaganza. The 2014 draft "drew a combined total of 32 million viewers—a 28% increase from the previous year" ("The NFL Draft," n.d.). At its most basic, the NFL draft involves seven rounds that span three days during which each of the league's 32 teams select a player in each round. Teams spend the first few rounds selecting the most coveted players according to their scouting and team needs. Some opt for need by position; others choose the best player available at the time. In the later rounds, teams draft players who were productive in college but undersized or not as gifted athletically, or more unproductive players who demonstrate potential because of their size and athleticism. Michael Sam was a standout collegiate athlete at his position—defensive end—but by NFL standards was ill-suited for that position and, if drafted, would need to find a new niche on a professional team.

During the draft, Rams head coach Jeff Fisher, general manager Les Snead, and executive vice president Kevin Demoff made decisions for who would be drafted, cut, and signed. As the draft got closer to the seventh round, the senior director of communications for the Rams, Artis Twyman, spoke with Coach Fisher to clarify what team officials thought as the end of the draft approached. Fisher told Twyman before the seventh round that once the team's needs were met with the drafts from the higher rounds, then whoever had the highest football grade would get drafted. Entering the seventh round on Saturday, Sam had the highest grade and was drafted as the 249th pick. Immediately after the draft, Twyman spoke with Sam on the phone, and Sam emphasized that he wanted to play football and that he wanted to be comfortable with himself. He also stated that he did not want to act "as a huge civil rights person" (A. Twyman, personal communication, July 24, 2015).

Rams officials waited until the next day to start considering a media plan. Twyman spoke with Coach Fisher on Sunday morning, and they identified specific public relations strategies and tactics to follow. First, they wanted a consistent message that informed various publics about how drafting Sam was a football decision. Second, the organization wanted to educate players, staff, and fans. Third, the Rams wanted to strategically grant access to certain media outlets. Twyman believed these strategies would help keep the team and its message focused. While team representatives were confident in drafting Sam, they did not want distractions to take away from Sam's, or any other player's, ability to perform in training camp.

One of the first decisions made to educate players and staff was to invite Wade Davis, a former NFL player and gay rights activist, to speak to team personnel. Davis played in NFL Europe and spent four preseasons with NFL teams before announcing he was gay in 2012. On Monday, an all-players meeting was held, and Davis spoke about being gay in the NFL. Inviting Davis was a strategic choice for the Rams, since Davis, a former player, had immediate credibility with the players. Davis' main message focused on respect. After speaking with the players, Davis spoke with the staff, where he emphasized that Sam's draft should not be viewed as a money-making venture. Twyman and Davis worried this position might be difficult to accept for people in areas whose sole purpose was to make money, such as in marketing and sales.

Another initial contact the Rams made was with Sam's publicist, Howard Bragman. Bragman had already lined up several media commitments for Sam: An interview with *People* magazine, a *GQ* photo shoot, and an article in the LGBT publication *OUT*. In addition, Sam was receiving the Arthur Ashe ESPY award and participating in an Oprah Winfrey Network (OWN) documentary about his life. Twyman and team representatives were fine with everything except the documentary.

After speaking with Coach Fisher, who agreed that it would distract from football, Twyman spoke with Bragman and stated that the OWN documentary must not be a distraction. This turned out to be one of the more complicated components in the first few days after drafting Sam. Over a two-day period, Rams representatives spoke with people from OWN and expressed that they did not want the documentary to be done. However, days later, OWN sent out a press release stating that the network would do the documentary. This was inconsistent with how the Rams wanted to proceed, and according to Twyman, team officials were frustrated. By week's end, however, OWN's president flew to St. Louis, and all sides agreed that the documentary would be delayed. As a way to help facilitate, the Rams provided supplemental video footage (B-roll) to OWN, and the documentary did not become a distraction for players.

Beyond Sam's personal media commitments, the Rams needed to plan for media interviews, so Tuesday served as the team's news conference day. The Rams decided not to have Sam interviewed by himself, but instead they broke the day up into three parts: 1) all first-round picks; 2) second- and third-round picks; 3) all fourth-, sixth-, and seventh-round picks (the team had no fifth-round picks). Sam, therefore, was a part of the news conference day, but Twyman, staying consistent with keeping team personnel focused on football, announced that only questions about football would be taken. Afterwards Sam was available to answer any other questions, and he did so on his own. This allowed the Rams to stay consistent with their football focus but made allowances for the various types of media that attended. As the team moved past the news conference day, and the first week after the draft came to a close, the Rams continued to deny one-on-one interview requests and made Sam available to the media once per week. Twyman believed this helped maintain Sam's focus on football while minimizing media distractions.

The public relations decisions Twyman and the organization made largely utilize three PR concepts: message framing, recognition of publics, and proactive advocacy.

Message Framing

The Rams strived to present a consistent message, and Twyman's main goal was to have "one message and many messengers." Twyman's strategy fits with the message-framing theory that Entman (1993) explains as selecting "some aspects of perceived reality and [making] them more salient in a communicating text, in such a way as to promote a particular problem definition, causal interpretation, moral evaluation, and/or treatment recommendation for the item described" (p. 52). Message framing selects and emphasizes key parts of an issue, which thereby creates a social reality for how someone views the world (Hallahan, 1999).

In public relations, creating consensus among various publics is vital, and strategic message framing can help various groups view an idea or event through similar frames. The hope is that whatever strategic message is communicated will lead to consensus among the publics. The Rams utilized successful message framing by emphasizing that drafting Sam was a football decision rather than an explicit civil rights gesture. Furthermore, preventing the OWN network from filming, limiting media questions to only those related to football, and placing Sam mostly in interview situations with other players helped the Rams support their football-decision frame and messaging.

Recognition of Publics

Upon drafting Sam, the Rams had several publics that team representatives needed to address. Publics are "groups of people with shared interests related to organizations" (Kelleher, 2018, p. 2), and they can be viewed in a variety of ways depending on similarities within the group. The Rams focused largely on their internal and external publics. Internal publics are groups and individuals within an organization that have similar interests, and for the Rams, these included players, coaches, and staff. The Rams focused internally by communicating with players and staff primarily through the team meeting with Wade Davis. External publics are groups that are outside the organization that either impact the organization or are affected by the organization. The Rams primarily communicated with their external public, the media, through the news conference day and subsequent interview opportunities.

Proactive Advocacy

One final PR concept utilized was the team's ability to be proactive in its actions, especially in the first few days after the draft. According to Fortunato (2008), proactive advocacy perceives "public relations professionals [as] entrusted with the responsibility to present the organization they represent in the most positive manner to its various stakeholders" (p. 117). While team representatives emphasized that drafting Sam was a football decision, they also recognized the enormous human-interest aspect of the team's actions. For example, responses from the general public were immediate and included tweets from celebrities and even President Obama, who released a White House statement congratulating Sam. The intense spotlight and historic nature of the pick made Twyman recognize, "There's no media plan for the first gay player in the NFL" (personal communication, July 24, 2015). Therefore, establishing an immediate public relations plan was crucial, and initiating proactive advocacy, rather than ignoring the cultural importance of the draft pick, helped lead the team through a unique moment in a sport's history.

You Make the Call

Overall, it appears that team representatives successfully handled drafting the first openly gay athlete and largely controlling the message. Team representatives communicated a consistent message focusing on Sam's football abilities and new responsibilities and downplaying anything that would serve as a distraction. They communicated with internal and external audiences by inviting a credible guest speaker, allowing for controlled media access, and creating a consistent time and place for non-football specific media requests to be filled. Central tenets of public relations include recognizing relevant publics, controlling the messaging, and being proactive, which the Rams successfully executed.

Twyman believes that having the football message so deeply ingrained was particularly powerful and helped prevent a crisis or loss of message control. For example, ESPN's Josina Anderson reported on an August 26, 2014, *SportsCenter* episode about Sam's showering habits and how players in the locker room perceived his behavior. Anderson was overwhelmingly ridiculed (e.g., Wilson, 2014), and ESPN eventually suspended her. Coach Fisher also conducted an interview with the *St. Louis Dispatch* condemning the article, and his comments were picked by other well-respected sites such as nbcsports.com. Twyman viewed their "football first" message as so strong that when a reporter like Anderson tried to introduce a competing message, it ultimately was seen as inappropriate and in direct contrast to mainstream perceptions of Sam's place on the team.

It is important to consider, however, whether the organization met the needs of its fans. Educating fans was one of the priorities the organization set out to accomplish, but a communication plan with the fans was visibly lacking. The team clearly accomplished its goal of educating players and staff when Davis came to speak, but communicating to fans was largely left to the media through interviews and media reports. It is worth considering if additional tactics could have been completed to make the link to fans more direct with the team's communication efforts.

Discussion Questions

1. The Rams wanted to focus their PR efforts on players, staff, and fans. What other publics might they have overlooked? What messaging would you use to communicate with these overlooked publics?
2. Canceling the OWN documentary was a strategic decision to help eliminate distractions for players during training camp. Do you agree or disagree with this decision? Could filming the documentary have been a PR benefit to the Rams?
3. The Rams stressed proactive advocacy from the moment they drafted Sam. Were there additional proactive public relations steps they could have made? Consider this within terms of the media, fans, and organizational personnel.

4. In 2016, a report alleged that the Rams only drafted Sam to avoid being featured in *Hard Knocks*, an HBO series documenting what happens "behind the scenes" at NFL training camps. The report suggested the Rams did not want to be in the show and the NFL was worried that Sam wouldn't be drafted, so a deal was made. The Rams denied they had ulterior motives; however, Sam publicly stated he was not surprised by the report. If you were in Twyman's position, how would you respond to the allegation? What type of message framing would be appropriate to help the Rams deny the allegations?

5. The author describes the Rams' communication strategy as seemingly successful. Discuss ways in which the Rams' communication plan was successful and ways in which it was not. Is there a current example of a sports organization that had to tackle a "first" or unique situation? Assess that organization's success. What tactics did the organization use that were similar to the Rams when dealing with the Sam case? What new strategies did they employ?

References

Entman, R. (1993). Framing: Toward clarification of a fractured paradigm. *Journal of Communication, 43*(4), 51–58.

Fortunato, J. A. (2008). Restoring a reputation: The Duke University lacrosse scandal. *Public Relations Review, 34*, 116–123. http://doi:10.1016/j.pubrev.2008.03.006

Garcia, B., IV. (2016, June 30). The LA Rams played a role in the civil rights movement. Retrieved from http://ramstalk.net/the-l-a-rams-played-a-role-in-the-civil-rights-movement/

Hallahan, K. (1999). Seven models of framing: Implications for public relations. *Journal of Public Relations Research, 11*(3), 205–242.

Kahrl, C. (2015, October 27). For gay athletes, what comes after coming out? Retrieved from http://abcnews.go.com/Sports/gay-athletes-coming/story?id=34760572

Kelleher, T. (2018). *Public relations.* New York, NY: Oxford University Press.

Mazzie, L. A. (2014). Michael Sam and the NFL locker room: How masculinities theory explains the way we view gay athletes. *Marquette Sports Law Review, 25*(1), 129–162.

The NFL Draft. (n.d.). Retrieved from http://operations.nfl.com/the-players/the-nfl-draft/

Wilson, R. (2014, August 30). ESPN's Josina Anderson explains Michael Sam shower story. Retrieved from www.cbssports.com/nfl/news/espns-josina-anderson-explains-michael-sam-shower-story/

Zeigler, C. (2014, September 3). Michael Sam to wear no. 46: The year MLB and the NFL broke the color barrier. Retrieved from www.outsports.com/2014/9/3/6102169/michael-sam-46-cowboys-jackie-robinson-john-wright

2 Civic Recovery in the Aftermath of a Hockey Crisis

Analyzing a Strategic Communication Response to the Vancouver Stanley Cup Riot

Derek Moscato

2011

Vancouver's Stanley Cup riot, which saw violence and looting carried out by a mob of angry hockey fans after a championship game, left the Pacific Rim city with destruction to its physical environment and a tarnished reputation. This study examines an integrated public relations response to the event targeting city residents and businesses, and its impact in mitigating negative publicity and perceptions. Both strategic objectives and specific tactics are examined to understand the alignment between civic engagement and the role of professional strategic communication in repairing reputation and undoing the negative legacy of a sporting-related urban crisis.

Introduction

The day after the Cleveland Cavaliers' 2016 NBA championship, local media coverage focused not only on the team's superior play but also the behavior of the team's loyal fans during the post-game celebration in the city. The *Plain Dealer* reported that Cavaliers fans were simply joyful: "There were none of the typical sports-celebrations-gone-wrong. There were no overturned vehicles or dumpster fires" (Borchardt, 2016, para. 1).

The same couldn't be said for Vancouver, British Columbia, five years earlier. From the perspectives of place branding and civic public relations, the Vancouver Stanley Cup riot represented a historic low point for not only the city but also the province of British Columbia, and indeed Canada. Disturbing television footage of violent confrontations between rioting sports fans and civilians and first responders came in stark contrast to the scene of Vancouver's peaceful downtown streets just over one year previous, when the city hosted the 2010 Winter Olympic Games. Then, Vancouver's downtown core was the scene of cheerful visitors from around the world mingling with their Canadian hosts, and the uplifting, emotional spectacle of the Games.

But just over a year later, the city's post-Olympics shine was replaced with a civic darkness. Vancouver found itself at the center of another high-profile sporting event, the National Hockey League's Stanley Cup Finals.

Figure 2.1 A Hockey Fan Poses for Social Media Photos in Front of a Torched Automobile During the Vancouver Stanley Cup Riot

Source: Elopde/Wikimedia Commons

The hockey championship, featuring the Vancouver Canucks and the visiting Boston Bruins, culminated in a winner-take-all Game Seven played in Vancouver. At the conclusion of this final and deciding match, with the home side losing to Boston, a restlessness set in among some of the estimated 100,000 fans gathered downtown to watch the game at outdoor fan zones (Hutchinson, 2011, para. 1). This scene devolved into a full-blown, hours-long riot involving thousands of participants and spectators—many of whom posed for photos that were subsequently distributed across social media (see Figure 2.1).

Serious injuries were suffered by first responders, innocent bystanders, and the rioters themselves, while millions of dollars of financial costs were incurred as a result of damage to buildings, civic infrastructure, and motor vehicles. So shocking were the images from that fateful night—violence, burning cars, and the looting of stores—that media outlets broadcasted them repeatedly to international audiences on prime-time newscasts, all-news networks, and morning talk shows. Ultimately, nearly 900 criminal charges were made against 300 suspects (Crawford, 2015).

The BBC called it a scene of "wanton violence." The *New York Times* described it as "one of the worst episodes of rioting Canada has seen in decades" (Klein & Austen, 2011), while the *USA Today* warned of "angry drunken fans running wild" and a "need for traveler awareness" (Medha, 2011, para. 4).

This chapter examines the role of strategic communication in responding to a crisis borne of a sporting event—including the mitigation of negative publicity and public perceptions connected to this disturbance—and the fostering of civic engagement in its aftermath. Drawing from Guth's (1995) articulation of the role of public relations within the organizational crisis experience, this chapter examines the strategic communication response to the riot by the Downtown Vancouver Business Improvement Association (DVBIA), which was tasked with restoring the public's confidence in Vancouver as a place to live, work, and visit. The resulting "Vanlover" campaign is examined in terms of its strategic foundation and execution, as well as results emanating from the campaign. This includes an evaluation of campaign strategy and tactics. Both strategic objectives and specific actions are examined to understand the alignment of public relations with civic engagement.

Background

As an extension of sporting violence, the crowd riot sees collective violence carried out by the fans of a winning or losing sports team, often during or after a championship match (Lewis, 2007). Having long afflicted North American cities (Young, 2000), the consequences of sports rioting, and ensuing perceptions of civic disorder, have symbolic as well as actual political and economic consequences. Such rioting, or so-called "hooliganism," is also attached to the culture of European soccer, which has enjoyed longstanding attention from the media. Millward (2009), drawing from the Glasgow Rangers' 2008 loss in the Union de Associations Europeénnes de Football Cup final to the Russian club Zenit Saint Petersburg, asserts that the media played a key role in framing that riot and misrepresenting the riot's participants. In Canada, sporting riots often arise from hockey championship games, particularly in Vancouver and Montreal (Canadian Press, 2011). Montreal fans have rioted in several instances over the past three decades, while Vancouver witnessed its first major Stanley Cup riot in 1994 after the Canucks lost to the New York Rangers.

Vancouver's 2011 riot was marked both by extensive media coverage and considerable reputational impact. With a metropolitan population of three million people, the city is Canada's third largest. It ranks highly on a number of global city surveys, including the *Economist Intelligence Unit*'s most livable cities survey, the Mercer Quality of Life survey, and *Travel + Leisure*'s Top Cities list. Tourism is a major economic engine for Metro Vancouver. Clearly there is much to lose as a result of negative publicity and attention. While civic agencies work to woo visitors from abroad to visit and invest in the city, another specialized public is also a key focus of attention: the metropolitan region's own residents and businesses. Hundreds of thousands of residents of the metropolitan region regularly work, shop, and recreate in the downtown core.

Attuned to this demographic is the Downtown Vancouver Business Improvement Association (DVBIA), an agency representing 8,000 businesses in the 90-block central core of the city. For the DVBIA, the challenges stemming from the riot's aftermath invoke what Guth (1995) situates as organizational crisis, threatening the legitimacy of an industry or organization, necessitating the involvement of public relations practitioners. Coombs (2007) similarly defines a crisis as a significant threat to an organization, potentially impacting public safety, financials, and reputation and therefore requiring appropriate communication management and channels.

Confronting the reality of negative media portrayals of the downtown core in the wake of the riots—resulting in diminished retail, commercial, and recreational activity and engagement—the DVBIA needed to send a message to the city and the world that downtown Vancouver was "open for business."

The Case

Restoring the city's civic engagement and positive reputation was a central theme of the Vanlover campaign created by the DVBIA. Developed in partnership with communication consultancy FleishmanHillard, which worked with the downtown agency on a pro-bono basis, the campaign was deployed within days of the riot. In the event's aftermath, the association was hearing reports of "potential local visitors canceling reservations at restaurants with no other explanation than seeing the horrendous images being replayed on TV and online." While the city's central core was no longer the scene of rioting and looting, the images of the riot being played repeatedly on television and via Internet were creating a perception that downtown was still the scene of much civic disorder. According to the organization, changing the mood of the Vancouver public was a priority—to avoid the economic and civic losses arising from a downtown devoid of visitors:

> While citizens and media were still wallowing in the sadness of events, the DVBIA saw the window was closing to get ahead of a potential 'dead downtown' scenario where locals avoided the core out of fear of what they'd seen or experienced. For a vibrant downtown like Vancouver's with 75,000+ residents and 125,000 employees, a ghost-town situation would be devastating to both businesses affected by the riots as well as others.
>
> (DVBIA, 2011, para. 13)

The multi-tiered campaign involved several activities. It encouraged residents of the metropolitan region to come downtown for dining, shopping, or recreational purposes—and post photos of positive experiences to social media. It also invited Vancouverites to post a heart icon on their business, car, or home to show their civic pride (see Figure 2.2).

Figure 2.2 Key to the Downtown Vancouver Business Improvement Association's Vanlover
         Campaign Was Its Simple Logo, Featured on T-shirts, Stickers, Social Media
         Pages, and Store Windows

Source: Downtown Vancouver Business Improvement Association

Additionally, Facebook and Twitter accounts established originally for
the Olympic Games were reactivated to promote the Vanlover campaign. A
media kick-off event was held with Vancouver's mayor at a local business—
with Vanlover t-shirts quickly becoming a strong seller (and enjoying strong
visibility in the media). Media relations with both online and traditional
media outlets were employed, resulting in over 100 media interviews conducted within the first five days.

The Vanlover campaign was driven by four objectives: to maintain the
city's 71% "confidence in safety downtown" rating; to reduce negative online
impressions of the word "Vancouver" on Twitter to pre-riot levels; to increase
visitor/employee pedestrian counts to pre-riot levels; and to raise social media

engagement levels with the DVBIA by 10% from before the riot. Through a combination of social media tracking, surveys, and real-time pedestrian counts, the organization was able to measure significant successes in all four categories. Social media provided key evaluations of the success of the Vanlover campaign in terms of organizational engagement. The organization's existing "downtownvan" Facebook page and @downtownvan Twitter account were used to promote the campaign. The Vanlover campaign propelled Facebook followership from 1,000 to 3,800 in less than a week, with post views up by 396%. Feedback rates rose by 1610%, and likes increased by 2397%. Additionally, traffic to the DVBIA website increased by 200% (DVBIA, 2011).

You Make the Call

The DVBIA's campaign was emblematic of Guth's (1995) assertion that proactive strategic communication and an elevated role for public relations practice can minimize the worst impacts of an organizational crisis—in this case a civic organizational crisis. Working to the organization's advantage was its speed, agility, and adaptability to changing circumstances. However, as Guth (1995) notes, "this cannot happen if the person responsible for organizational public relations is not a key player in the decision-making process. It is only with management support that an appropriate program of research and gathering public feedback can be achieved" (p. 10).

Such an outcome is a testament to DVBIA's understanding of strategic communication as a central driver of positive civic engagement and reputation management. Cities are complex entities that require a nuanced understanding of multiple stakeholders and specialized communication approaches. Yet their reputation, standing, and engagement with audiences—like other organizations—benefit from an elevated role for strategic communication, including social media, media relations, and member engagement. To this end, the aftermath of the Vancouver Stanley Cup riots provides a compelling glimpse into the opportunities for a public relations response to a crisis in place branding and civic communication.

The timeliness of the Vanlover campaign was among its most important attributes. The initiative launched within days of the riot—when public sentiment was at its most negative. The Vancouver Canucks ultimately launched their own campaign to prevent fan violence—called "This is our home"—but the effort launched nearly a year after the riot and subsequently had little impact. On the other hand, the Vanlover campaign benefited from its immediacy and ability to activate and engage a local citizenry. Notably, this included the provision of over 100 interviews granted to media organizations to extol the virtues of the city and the Vanlover campaign, all within a five-day timeframe.

Other factors and events also coincided with DVBIA's campaign to produce an uptick in public sentiment—and not all of the positive media post-riot was borne of strategic communication. The dissemination of an iconic photograph by the Associated Press from the riot—showing a couple in embrace amid tear gas, hockey debris, and the baton-carrying mounted police—lightened the local and national conversation around the riot and moved the focus away from the violence and looting. Known as "The Kiss," the photo became a viral sensation that garnered significant attention from international news outlets and social media (Jones, 2011).

Even as the mood lightened post-riot, the Downtown Vancouver Business Improvement Association's practical focus on a segmented local demographic proved to be key to its campaign success. The DVBIA serves primarily local and regional stakeholders—and does not necessarily engage a national or international audience the same way that an organization like Tourism Vancouver does. While the Vanlover campaign was successful in reviving positive sentiment within the metropolitan region, its impacts on perception and reputation outside the city are far less clear.

While assessing the short-term impact of the campaign was a relatively straight-forward process thanks to social media metrics, understanding the broader and longer-term public relations implications of the riot is more difficult. It is a credit to the DVBIA that it was able to react as quickly and effectively as it did. However, its success highlights the fact that a larger stakeholder environment (citizens, tourists, investors, sporting fans) would benefit from a cohesively organized public relations response from several involved civic and commercial organizations (government, hockey franchise, business interests, tourism agencies).

Importantly, the Vancouver rioting was one of the first events of its kind to be documented in real time in the social media world. As a result, images of the city's 2011 riot are far more pervasive than the similar 1994 riot, which mostly lived on in newspaper clippings and television replays (although it has since also found an archival home of sorts on YouTube). The concern for Vancouver's civic leaders would be that the most recent riot—given the pervasiveness of its visual imagery on social media venues like YouTube—becomes the media benchmark from which future riots in urban environments are measured.

Most major North American metropolitan markets have confronted, or may one day confront, a major riot caused by a professional sporting event. Montreal, Chicago, Boston, Denver, and Detroit have all been beset by rioting or at least some degree of civic disorder in the wake of professional sporting championship games. At the same time, global sporting events like the Olympics and the FIFA World Cup present for host cities a challenging mix of athletics-fueled excitement for fans with street-level protest and activism often connected to globalization, human rights, and the environment.

Simon Anholt, a market research analyst and well-known expert in place and nation branding, asserted in *The Economist* (2011) that city reputations are built up over long periods of time and are not easily dismantled—and his sentiment extends to Vancouver's 2011 Canucks riot. Urban brands are developed over the course of decades and "don't swing around so quickly," he asserted. Furthermore, "memories are mercifully short" (The Economist, 2011, para. 2).

Yet the impacts are felt to a greater degree at the local level, as the DVBIA's research showed. Given the importance of reputation and international profile to a variety of criteria for successful cities—investment, tourism, immigration, and the invigoration of urban cores—the need for a thoughtful, timely, and coordinated strategic response to such events at wider levels remains relevant. However, it is at the hyperlocal level—from the perceptions and psychology of area residents to the viability of small businesses—where a strategic communication approach can be most effective and have its most lasting impact.

Discussion Questions

1. How has social media impacted the mediation of sporting riots on the part of media, spectators, and even participants?
2. What are other ways that city brands, which take decades or longer to build, can come undone?
3. What kind of role should be played by strategic communicators working with professional sporting teams, including communication with team fans?
4. Given the potential drawbacks of hosting events like the Stanley Cup Finals, the Super Bowl, the World Series, and global events like the Olympics and FIFA World Cup, how might communicators plan in advance for the wider civic outcomes arising from such spectacles, including the potential for fan riots?
5. Discuss any recent developments related to crowd control for large-scale sporting events. How have new developments such as social media and mobile technologies changed the nature of both staging the events and the communication surrounding them?

References

Borchardt, J. (2016, June 20). Cleveland Cavs celebration offers positive contrast to celebration following Ohio State's 2015 win. *The Plain Dealer*. Retrieved from www.cleveland.com/metro/index.ssf/2016/06/clevelands_cavs_celebration.htm

Canadian Press. (2011, June 15). Here's a list of significant hockey riots in Canada. *The Hockey News*. Retrieved from www.thehockeynews.com/news/article/heres-a-list-of-significant-hockey-riots-in-canada

Coombs, T. (2007). Institute for public relations. *Crisis Management and Communication*. Retrieved from www.instituteforpr.org/crisis-management-and-communications/

Crawford, T. (2015, November 18). Stanley Cup riot investigation winds down as last two suspects charged. *Vancouver Sun*. Retrieved from www.vancouversun.com/sports/Stanley+riot+investigation+winds+down+last+suspects+charged/10318649/story.html

Downtown Vancouver Business Improvement Association. Economic and business development: 2011 Stanley Cup Riots: The Vanlover campaign. Retrieved from www.

ida-downtown.org/eweb/docs/2011%20Awards/Downtown%20Vancouver%20
BIA,%202011%20Stanley%20Cup%20Riots%20-%20Vanlover%20Campaign.pdf

The Economist. (2011, August 27). Bouncing back. Retrieved from www.economist.com/
node/21526917

Guth, D. W. (1995). Organizational crisis experience and public relations roles. *Public
Relations Review*. Retrieved from www.dguth.journalism.ku.edu/PRJCrisis.pdf

Hutchinson, B. (2011, June 15). Transcript: Vancouver crowd chanting "Riot! Riot!
Riot!". *The National Post*. Retrieved from http://nationalpost.com/news/canada/
vancouvers-game-7-scenes-from-the-street/wcm/dcdf0e65-4bc4-4826-8a66-45a116
fe4d2d

Jones, A. (2011, June 17). Vancouver riots: A kiss amid the chaos? *BBC*. Retrieved from
www.bbc.com/news/world-us-canada-13807494

Klein, J., & Austen, I. (2011, June 16). Hockey hangover turns into riot embarrassment.
New York Times. Retrieved from www.nytimes.com/2011/06/17/world/americas/
17vancouver.html

Lewis, J. M. (2007). *Sports fan violence in North America*. Lanham, MD: Rowman & Littlefield Publishers.

Medha. (2011). International coverage of Vancouver riot tarnishes city's reputation. *Vancouver Sun*. Retrieved from www.vancouversun.com/news/World+coverage+Vancouv
er+riot+tarnishes+city+reputation/4958335/story.html

Millward, P. (2009). Glasgow Rangers supporters in the city of Manchester: The degen-
eration of a "fan party" into a "hooligan riot". *International Review for the Sociology of
Sport*, 44(4), 381–398.

Young, K. (2000). Sport and violence. In *Handbook of sports studies* (pp. 382–408). London:
Sage Publications.

Acknowledgements

The author wishes to thank Maureen Healey, former Vice President of
the Downtown Vancouver Business Improvement Association, for sharing
archived communication research and materials from the DVBIA's (2011)
Vanlover campaign for this article.

3 Patching a Crisis With CSR

How the NFL Fumbled Its Handling of Domestic Violence

Chelsea L. Woods & Ashli Q. Stokes

In 2014, the NFL faced a public relations crisis centered on domestic abuse following its mismanagement of the Ray Rice incident, in which the Baltimore Ravens player assaulted his then fiancée. Following widespread public criticism, the NFL attempted to mend its legitimacy gap (Sethi, 1975) by implementing, adhering to, and publicizing new corporate social responsibility initiatives, ranging from domestic violence education to partnerships with non-profit organizations focused on sexual assault and domestic violence. Guided by organizational legitimacy theory, this case study rhetorically analyzes the extent to which these programs successfully aided the NFL in its attempts to mend its reputation and maintain its legitimacy.

Introduction

In 2014, the National Football League (NFL) adopted a defensive stance following what many perceived to be its administration's mismanagement of a domestic violence case. On February 15, 2014, Baltimore Ravens running back Ray Rice punched his then fiancée Janay Palmer, rendering her unconscious in an Atlantic City elevator. TMZ released a video of Rice dragging Palmer out of the elevator. After pleading not guilty to the charges and completing a pretrial intervention program, Rice avoided formal prosecution but was suspended for two games and fined approximately $58,000 (Maine, 2014). Given the gravity of the situation, the public's access to video of the incident, and the league's recent crisis history, including mounting concern over player concussions, Rice's punishment generated a public outcry of disapproval. The NFL countered with a harsher policy for violent conduct, and Commissioner Roger Goodell admitted, "I didn't get it right" (Goodell, 2014a). But the NFL's troubles were not over. On September 8, *TMZ* released surveillance video of the incident from a different camera angle showing Rice striking Palmer. The event prompted the Ravens to terminate Rice's contract and forced the NFL to take overdue action, suspending Rice and altering its domestic violence policies (Brady & Corbett, 2014).

Drawing from organizational legitimacy (Sethi, 2003) and the passive style of rhetorical crisis management (Rowland & Rademacher, 1990), this chapter evaluates the NFL's crisis response by examining how the league used corporate social responsibility (CSR) in an attempt to rebuild its image and reputation. While the NFL has taken some appropriate measures, the league needs to be more proactive to ensure that its policies addressing domestic violence match its promises.

Background

Because organizations exist within a larger social environment (Hearit, 1995), they require legitimacy, which they acquire by acting in a socially desirable manner (Suchman, 1995). However, because legitimacy is granted by organizational stakeholders, it may change over time (Pfeffer & Salancik, 1978). If organizational activities and policies fail to reflect stakeholder expectations, a legitimacy gap emerges (Sethi, 1975). Legitimacy gaps develop when societal expectations change and the organization's actions no longer meet those standards, or when publics learn about the organization's irresponsible activities (Sethi, 1978). If this gap widens, an organization faces reputational damage, and its survival may be threatened (Sethi, 1977). Thus, organizations must seek to narrow this gap.

Organizations can establish legitimacy through CSR (Waymer & Heath, 2014). CSR includes voluntary activities and programs implemented to improve the well-being of organizational stakeholders, such as employees, consumers, communities, and the society at large, allowing these firms to donate their resources for the betterment of society (Coombs & Holladay, 2012). Often driven by the demands of stakeholders, CSR is not limited to creating a campaign encouraging consumers to recycle but can be found within the organization's very existence as socially responsible actions, which "constitute the essence of each organization's legitimacy" (Heath, 2006, p. 103).

Some scholars argue that sport is ideal for implementing CSR because of its prominent social and economic role in society (L'Etang, 2006; Walters, 2009), ability to foster relationships (Babiak & Wolfe, 2009; Smith & Westerbeek, 2007), and capacity to generate media exposure (Babiak & Wolfe, 2006). As Armour (2014) suggests, "Nothing commands the public's attention like the NFL" (para. 10). Sport and social responsibility are also entwined on a level that supersedes basic CSR expectations, such as charity donations, as sport organizations serve as "normative institutions" by establishing a sense of what is acceptable within society (Scott, 2001), generating questions about the obligations that organizations and players owe society (Godfrey, 2009).

To bridge its legitimacy gap, the NFL took action using CSR following the Ray Rice incident, adopting the "passive style" of rhetorical crisis management, which avoids "firm positions on controversial subjects" and emphasizes action on noncontroversial policies or on trivia (Rowland & Rademacher, 1990, p. 490). The passive style features three related elements, including an emphasis on 1) value commitments, 2) displacing blame, and 3) symbolic crisis resolution.

The Case

Reports claim domestic violence was Commissioner Roger Goodell's blind spot, as players charged with domestic violence received less severe punishment than players facing other accusations, including drug use (Pennington & Eder, 2014). Although the NFL addressed domestic violence cases before Rice's, the public release of the violent video prompted a more substantial response (Banks, 2015), igniting a discussion about the league's disciplinary problems and its response to domestic violence. Following criticism, Goodell (2014a) acknowledged the punishment was insufficient and promised the league would be getting its "house in order" (Orr, 2014, para. 5), prompting several CSR initiatives.

Internal Initiatives

Internally, the immediate response of the NFL was to alter its discipline policy. Goodell (2014a) announced a revised Personal Conduct Policy outlining "a clear set of steps" following an incident requiring review. A player's first offense resulted in a baseline suspension of six games without pay, while a second offense could generate league banishment for at least one year. The NFL hired three female domestic violence and sex crimes experts to help form its policies. It appointed Anna Isaacson to a newly created role: Vice President for Social Responsibility. Isaacson's duties: Reduce domestic violence/sexual assault incidents; increase support for affected individuals; elevate the profile of sexual violence prevention; and streamline access to resources (ESPN.com, 2014; NFL, 2015b).

The NFL implemented mandatory domestic violence and sexual assault education and awareness classes for every member of the 32 teams and its league office (Banks, 2015). Developed by domestic and sexual violence experts, the 45-minute training defined domestic violence and sexual assault and addressed warning signs and bystander intervention (NFL, 2015a, para. 10), intending to reduce the number of incidents (Jones, 2014c). In 2015, the NFL introduced a second round of training (NFL, 2015a) focused on how crimes affect victims, perpetrators, families, and teams (Jones, 2015).

The NFL expanded its educational programming to include college, high school, and youth football programs (Goodell, 2014a). Among its efforts was "A Call to Coaches," a 17-minute video about respect and the role models that athletes can be (NFL, 2015b). A digital educational program called "Character Playbook" engages students "in a conversation about critical issues," including cyberbullying and identifying warning signs (NFL, 2016a, p. 33), using self-report pre- and post-surveys to measure knowledge, attitude, and behavioral changes (NFL, 2016b).

In addition to educational initiatives, the NFL introduced Critical Response Teams in 2015. These 200 league and club leaders provide "immediate and confidential crisis assistance to anyone in the NFL family" (NFL,

2016a, para. 13) and are trained to identify risk factors (Goodell, 2014a). It also introduced the NFL Lifeline, providing confidential, free support 24/7 (NFL, 2016a).

External Initiatives

As part of its public response, the NFL relied on a public service campaign and partnerships. Its focus on public service announcements aimed to reduce incidents of domestic violence and sexual assault while elevating prevention (NFL, 2015a). The league teamed up with NO MORE, a national campaign addressing domestic violence and sexual assault, on a series of PSAs (Goodell, 2014b) to address the stigmatization of abuse and encourage victims to come forward (Maese, 2015). Approximately two weeks after Rice's suspension, the NFL aired the first series of PSAs (Jones, 2014c). Generated prior to the Rice incident, these spots showed celebrities denouncing domestic violence and the silence surrounding it (Jones, 2014a). A second series featuring NFL players aired regularly throughout the season beginning in October (Jones, 2014b) in the hopes that "NFL heroes" would inspire individuals to "step up" (Jones, 2014b, para. 4). The third round aspired to capture the difficulty in discussing domestic violence and sexual assault. The PSAs aired 12,770 times during the season (Maese, 2015), garnering around three billion impressions with an estimated $40 to $50 million in advertising airtime (Gibbs, 2015; Vranica, 2015). The NFL also aired PSAs during the 2015 and 2016 Super Bowls "to engage bystanders" in ending domestic violence and sexual assault (No More Staff, 2016).

Additionally, the NFL established multi-year, multi-million dollar partnerships with non-profit organizations (NFL, 2014a; NFL, 2015a) to increase services and access to resources (NFL, 2015a), noting the strain on organizations that resulted from the cases being dealt with in the league. Isaacson explained, "We wanted to be a partner that is interested in talking through the issues and seeing where the actual gaps are and the need we could fill" (Jones, 2016, para. 8). In the week following the release of the second Rice video, the National Domestic Violence Hotline (NDVH) experienced an 84% increase in calls, chats, and texts; more than half went unanswered due to a lack of staff (NFL, 2014a). In 2014, the NFL donated $4 million in cash and $1 million in kind (Goldman, 2015) and committed $5 million per year for five years (Armour, 2015), enabling the NDVH to handle an additional 750 calls per day (NFL, 2014a). The league made a $10 million commitment over five years to Raliance, a partnership among sexual violence prevention organizations (Gibbs, 2016), and partnered with the National Sexual Violence Resource Center to provide resources to state and local hotlines (NFL, 2014a). The league donated $1 million to be divided among 58 state and territorial anti-rape coalitions to support these hotlines (Goldman, 2015).

Following the encouragement of league executives, the 32 clubs established partnerships with more than 75 local domestic violence and sexual assault organizations (NFL, 2014b, 2015a). Teams varied in the form and extent of their initiatives, including donations to local organizations providing domestic violence education and prevention training or assisting victims, with commitments ranging from $400,000 to $1.5 million (Armour, 2015; McManus, 2014; Palma, 2015).

You Make the Call

Although there were some strengths in the NFL's response to the crisis, analysis suggests considerable room for improvement if the league intends to close its legitimacy gap. Importantly, the NFL publicly addressed the issues of domestic violence and sexual assault, nearly doubling the NDVH's operating budget, increasing its ability to help individuals (Gibbs, 2015). Further, the NFL's policy may have influenced football at lower levels, as seen when the University of Colorado indefinitely suspended defensive back Anthony Julmisse following a domestic violence arrest (Bonagura, 2017).

However, most of the NFL's actions can best be understood through the passive style. Although the passive style can help diminish the public's ability to make informed decisions about important issues, the league used it in an attempt to convince stakeholders that it took the public's concerns about domestic violence seriously. Focusing on its internal initiatives, the NFL lauded the revision of its Personal Conduct Policy as "tough, fair, clear and consistent" (NFL, 2015a). Yet many perceived the new version as ambiguous (Robbins, 2014), as the policy now relies on indeterminate language, fails to stipulate factors in determining punishments, and offers flexibility on game suspensions and league banishments to avoid taking a firm stance on admonishing personnel. Within 10 months after its implementation, nine suspensions potentially related to domestic violence occurred. In all but two cases, the league suspended players for fewer than six games, demonstrating "the NFL's hard line on consequences isn't quite as clear as it once seemed" (McManus, 2016, para. 2), making the response more symbolic as the public clamored for any sign that the NFL "takes domestic violence seriously" (Gibbs, 2016, para. 8).

Punishments consistent with the revised conduct policy, like Rice's suspension, are an anomaly rather than a regularity. In 2017, Dallas Cowboys player Ezekiel Elliott received a six-game suspension, becoming the "first high-profile suspension of its kind" since Rice (Pilon, 2017, para. 1). The punishment provoked protest from team owner Jerry Jones and incited a legal battle between the league and Elliott (Maske, 2017). Although Rice was reinstated by the NFL, he is one of very few players charged with domestic violence not playing in the league (Gibbs, 2017). Like the NFL's enforcement, its policy's effects on preventing incidents is also inconsistent. After the league introduced mandatory training in 2014, the number of NFL player arrests related to domestic violence fluctuated, increasing from five in 2014 to seven in 2015; the number dropped to two in 2016 before growing to five in 2017 ("NFL player arrests," 2017).

Other internal initiatives focused on education and critical response teams. The execution of these initiatives reflects the passive style, as the NFL tried to convince stakeholders it was serious about changing the culture. The short training sessions had little consistency, and an online video supplement dedicates only 12 minutes to domestic violence (Kogod, 2015). Documents show trainings are provided only once per year and last one hour, with no additional sessions provided on a recurring basis. Thus, the NFL demonstrates resolve to address an issue without offering a measurable impact. In doing so, the NFL focuses on the value commitments of the league in the hopes that they will pacify the public. It also offers hazy details about the content of its external educational programs and even less information about the intended outcomes and plans to gauge effectiveness of these programs offered to college, high school, and youth football organizations. Similarly, the NFL does not provide updates on its Critical Response Teams and NFL Lifeline, including whether they have been used and with what outcome. These programs exemplify the passive style by embracing a more ceremonial than considerable crisis response. The NFL makes promises to influence discourse surrounding domestic violence without offering or voicing intent to follow-up on its efforts.

The NFL also introduced several external initiatives. Its language used to publicize its PSAs and partnerships highlights the values and priorities that makes offering clear details about the level of organizational commitment crucial. These efforts are best understood through the third element of the passive style, where actions are not "designed to alter fundamentally the policy environment but merely to symbolically resolve the crisis" (Rowland & Rademacher, 1990, p. 495). The NFL expresses support for the goal of reducing domestic violence but fails to implement measurable "specific policies that carry out that goal" (p. 495). Although the voiced intent of the PSAs was to generate awareness, critics suggested they did too little to offer tangible and psychological support to victims and that messages focused on the aftermath of events rather than prevention (Davidson, 2015). A representative for a domestic violence organization suggested, "It seems to talk around the issue without actually tying it to official resources," such as local programs and shelters (Gibbs, 2015, para. 56). These forms of outreach act more as rhetorical symbols, "strengthening reassuring beliefs regardless of their validity and discouraging skeptical inquiry" (Rowland & Rademacher, 1990, p. 496). Although the PSAs featured players and expressed a strong commitment to addressing the public concern of domestic violence, they also served as a shield against skeptics analyzing the NFL's response. There was no PSA included in the 2017 Super Bowl commercial lineup, raising questions about the NFL's long-term commitment.

Partnerships with external organizations were arguably among the NFL's most substantial responses. The NFL made clear its initial steps were not "final steps" but a bridge to establishing long-term initiatives that generate awareness and prevent domestic violence and sexual assault within the league and society (NFL, 2014a). However, partnerships established with local organizations led by the teams were promoted significantly less by the NFL than its partnerships with national organizations. Team initiatives seem to vary on their level of involvement and commitment, generating inconsistency with no guidance from above.

Given the prominence of the NFL in American culture, critics argue it should allocate more than an estimated $35 million over the next five to 10 years to domestic violence organizations (Moskovitz, 2015), as it spends an estimated $10 million on its Super Bowl halftime show comparatively (Armour, 2014) and generates around $10 billion in profits annually (Isidore, 2016). Battered women's shelters were inundated nationwide following the release of the second Rice tape (Doyel, 2014); without proper resources, shelters may be unable to accommodate victims. Because the NDVH directs its callers to shelters (Gibbs, 2015), the NFL could also consider providing more assistance at a local level, rather than leaving this responsibility to its teams, with their inconsistent levels of commitment.

While the NFL suffered reputational damage as a result of the Rice case (NFL, 2015b), the long-term impact of the scandal on the NFL is unclear. Following the Rice crisis, ratings remained stable. Although sponsors spoke out about the NFL's fumbled response (Moore, 2014), none severed ties with the organization (Vranica, 2015). However, the president of the National Organization for Women compared the NFL's philanthropy to a "Band-Aid on an open, gaping wound" (Maese, 2015, para. 8), suggesting its efforts gloss over the underlying problem. Analysis largely supports this observation. Once an issue touches a large segment of the public, casting doubt on the competence or integrity of an organization or its leader to address it, the passive style is not an appropriate response (Rowland & Rademacher, 1990). From changes to its disciplinary policy to the wording used in its PSA campaign, the NFL capitalizes on creating talk about domestic violence that it does not always support with action, although Goodell (2014a) acknowledged the organization should be held to a higher standard.

The greatest concerns correspond with the NFL's ongoing struggle in responding to domestic violence when it does occur, as well as its slow approach to addressing the problem in the first place, as "it shouldn't have taken a public outcry to make the NFL realize domestic violence is a serious crime" (Armour, 2014, para. 17). The league's largely symbolic response raises questions regarding organizational culture and ethical leadership given criticism surrounding Goodell's handling of domestic violence. Previous case studies show altering organizational culture requires time, is challenging, and entails a sincere commitment (Seeger & Ulmer, 2003). By failing to actively monitor its environment for issues (Gonzalez-Herrero & Pratt, 1996) and proactively address these issues, the NFL allowed a legitimacy gap to emerge (Boyd, 2000).

The league should engage its stakeholders to determine their expectations for the league and its leadership, combining organizational goals and public concerns (Heath & Palenchar, 2009). It should implement measurable policy initiatives rather than symbolically addressing a crisis. Although the NFL acknowledged the problem, the elements of the passive style permit the league to appear committed to reforming its reaction to domestic violence. Its organizational action is not comprehensive, leaving the legitimacy gap in place.

Discussion Questions

1. Conduct an online search to identify a more recent case of domestic violence or sexual assault within the league. How is the NFL handling the case? Do its actions reflect the passive style? Why or why not?
2. Do you believe NFL commissioner Roger Goodell responded appropriately to the issues of domestic violence and sexual assault? If you were the NFL commissioner, what, if anything, would you have done differently? What should the role of organizational leaders be in cases like this one?
3. In your opinion, what obligations do sport organizations and athletes owe to society? Are these organizations responsible for establishing a sense of what is acceptable? Should we expect athletes to serve as role models?
4. View a few of the "NO MORE" campaign PSAs (www.nomore.org). Does the language used effectively address the campaign's overall goal? Do the PSAs call for any clearly measurable response by the viewer that can be quantified and used to document reach or impact?

References

Armour, N. (2014, August 29). NFL gets it right at last: Other sports must follow suit to fight domestic violence. *USA Today.* Retrieved from www.usatoday.com

Armour, N. (2015, September 7). Armour: Domestic violence hotline relies on traffic increases. *USA Today.* Retrieved from www.usatoday.com

Babiak, K., & Wolfe, R. (2006). More than just a game? Corporate social responsibility and Super Bowl XL. *Sport Marketing Quarterly, 15*(4), 214–222.

Babiak, K., & Wolfe, R. (2009). Determinants of corporate social responsibility in professional sport: Internal and external factors. *Journal of Sport Management, 23,* 717–742. doi:10.1123/jsm.23.6.717

Banks, D. (2015). Punch seen "round the world": How NFL has changed since the Ray Rice video. *Sports Illustrated.* Retrieved from www.si.com

Bonagura, K. (2017, July 28). Colorado Buffaloes DB Anthony Julmisse suspended following arrest. *ESPN.* Retrieved from www.espn.com

Boyd, J. (2000). Actional legitimacy: No crisis necessary. *Journal of Public Relations Research, 12*(4), 341–353. doi:10.1207/S1532754XJPRR1204_3

Brady, E., & Corbett, J. (2014, September 16). NFL takes action, but players return. *USA Today.* Retrieved from www.usatoday.com

Coombs, W. T., & Holladay, S. J. (2012). *Managing corporate social responsibility: A communication approach.* Malden, MA: Wiley-Blackwell.

Davidson, K. (2015, February 2). NFL's "No More" Super Bowl ad about domestic violence falls short. *The Chicago Tribune.* Retrieved from www.chicagotribune.com/news/opinion/commentary/chi-super-bowl-commercialzdomestic-violence-no-more-20150202-story.html

Doyel, G. (2014, October 31). Doyle: Ray Rice effect: More women seeking shelter. *The Indianapolis Star*. Retrieved from www.indystar.com

ESPN.com. (2014, September 15). NFL hires domestic violence advisers. *ESPN*. Retrieved from www.espn.com

Gibbs, L. (2015, October 7). After Ray Rice, the NFL pledged millions to fight domestic violence: Here's how the money was spent. *Think Progress*. Retrieved from www. thinkprogress.org

Gibbs, L. (2016, October 27). 2 years after NFL boss vowed to "get our house in order", domestic violence initiatives are a mess. *Think Progress*. Retrieved from www.think progress.org

Gibbs, L. (2017, October 3). Three years after Ray Rice, the NFL's domestic violence initiatives are still in flux. *Think Progress*. Retrieved from www.thinkprogress.org

Godfrey, P. C. (2009). Corporate social responsibility in sport: An overview and key issues. *Journal of Sports Management, 23*, 698–716. doi:10.1123/jsm.23.6.698

Goldman, T. (2015, August 12). NFL's effort to combat domestic violence may go for the long game. *NPR*. Retrieved from www.npr.org

Gonzalez-Herrero, A., & Pratt, C. B. (1996). An integrated symmetrical model for crisis-communications management. *Journal of Public Relations Research, 8*(2), 79–105. doi:10.1207/s1532754xjprr0802_01

Goodell, R. (2014a, August 28). Letter to NFL owners. *NFL*. Retrieved from www.nfl.com

Goodell, R. (2014b, September 26). Actions in support of domestic violence/sexual assault efforts. *NFL*. Retrieved from www.nfl.com

Hearit, K. M. (1995). "Mistakes were made": Organizations, apologia, and crises of social legitimacy. *Communication Studies, 46*, 1–17. doi:10.1080/10510979509368435

Heath, R. L. (2006). Onward into more fog: Thoughts on public relations' research directions. *Journal of Public Relations Research, 18*(2), 93–114. doi:10.1207/s1532754xjprr 1802_2

Heath, R. L., & Palenchar, M. J. (2009). *Strategic issues management: Organizations and public policy changes* (2nd ed.). Thousand Oaks, CA: Sage Publications.

Isidore, C. (2016, February 16). Roger Goodell's pay is cut to $34 million. *CNN*. Retrieved from www.money.cnn.com

Jones, L. H. (2014a, September 26). NFL to broadcast anti-domestic violence PSA during games. *USA Today*. Retrieved from www.usatoday.com

Jones, L. H. (2014b, October 14). NFL players join Hollywood to create anti-domestic violence PSAs. *USA Today*. Retrieved from www.usatoday.com

Jones, L. H. (2014c, November 13). Education a first step: Theme of NFL program on domestic abuse, assault is that silence is no longer a solution. *USA Today*. Retrieved from www.usatoday.com

Jones, L. H. (2015, July 28). NFL domestic violence program shifts focus. *USA Today*. Retrieved from www.usatoday.com

Jones, L. H. (2016, June 28). NFL to announce $10M in funding for coalition working to prevent sexual violence. *USA Today*. Retrieved from www.usatoday.com

Kogod, S. (2015, May 6). Players don't think the NFL's domestic violence training is working. *SB Nation*. Retrieved from www.sbnation.com

L'Etang, J. (2006). Public relations and sport in promotional culture. *Public Relations Review, 32*(4), 386–394. doi:10.1016/j.pubrev.2006.09.006

Maese, R. (2015, July 25). NFL finding its voice on domestic violence. *The Washington Post*. Retrieved from www.washingtonpost.com

Maine, D. (2014, September 10). A timeline of the NFL's and Ravens' reactions to Ray Rice incident. *ESPN*. Retrieved from www.espn.com

Maske, M. (2017, November 17). Jerry Jones vs. Roger Goodell shows just how splintered the NFL is. *The Washington Post*. Retrieved from www.washingtonpost.com

McManus, J. (2014, August 29). *Severe penalties for domestic violence*. ESPN. Retrieved from www.espn.com

McManus, J. (2016, August 28). The NFL is finding out just how complicated domestic violence punishments can be. *ESPN*. Retrieved from www.espn.com

Moore, D. L. (2014, September 15). NFL sponsors stand by, but Radisson breaks with Vikings. *USA Today*. Retrieved from www.usatoday.com

Moskovitz, D. (2015). Do the NFL's anti-domestic violence initiatives actually even exist? *Deadspin*. Retrieved from www.deadspin.com

NFL (2014a, September 15). Long-term partnerships and initial educational efforts on domestic violence/sexual assault. *NFL*. Retrieved from http://static.nfl.com/static/content/public/photo/2014/09/19/0ap3000000397111.pdf

NFL (2014b, December 5). The NFL's response to domestic violence and sexual assault. *NFL*. Retrieved from http://www.nfl.com/news/story/0ap3000000439286/article/the-nfls-response-to-domestic-violence-and-sexual-assault

NFL. (2015a, August 12). The NFL's response to domestic violence and sexual assault. *NFL*. Retrieved from www.nfl.com

NFL. (2015b, October 19). The NFL commitment: Taking action on domestic violence and sexual assault. *NFL*. Retrieved from www.nfl.com

NFL. (2016a). Beyond the game: The 2015 NFL social responsibility report. *NFL*. Retrieved from www.nfl.com

NFL. (2016b). Character Playbook. *NFL*. Retrieved from www.characterplaybook.com

NFL player arrests. (2017). *USA Today*. Retrieved from www.usatoday.com/sports/nfl/arrests

No More Staff. (2016, February 4). No More ad set to appear in Super Bowl 50. Retrieved from http://nomore.org/no-more-ad-super-bowl-50/

Orr, C. (2014, October 8). Goodell: The NFL continues work on domestic violence. *NFL*. Retrieved from www.nfl.com

Palma, B. (2015, September 16). Robert Kraft and the Patriots give $1.5 million to domestic violence. *New England Patriots*. Retrieved from www.patriots.com

Pennington, B., & Eder, S. (2014, September 20). In NFL get-tough policy, blind spot for abuse. *The New York Times*. Retrieved from www.nytimes.com

Pfeffer, J., & Salancik, G. R. (1978). *The external control of organizations: A resource dependence perspective*. New York, NY: Harper & Row.

Pilon, M. (2017, August 14). After the Ezekiel Elliott suspension, can you trust the NFL's process? *Bleacher Report*. Retrieved from www.bleacherreporter.com

Robbins, M. (2014, December 13). NFL's personal conduct policy fail. *CNN*. Retrieved from www.cnn.com

Rowland, R. C., & Rademacher, T. (1990). The passive style of rhetorical crisis management. In S. K. Foss (Ed.), *Rhetorical criticism: Exploration and practice*. Long Grove, IL: Waveland Press.

Scott, W. R. (2001). *Institutions and organizations*. Thousand Oaks, CA: Sage Publications.

Seeger, M. W., & Ulmer, R. R. (2003). Explaining Enron: Communication and responsible leadership. *Management Communication Quarterly*, *17*(1), 58–84. doi:10.1177/0893318903253436

Sethi, S. P. (1975). Dimensions of corporate social performance: An analytic framework. *California Management Review, 17*, 58–64. doi:10.2307/41162149

Sethi, S. P. (1977). *Advocacy advertising and large corporations*. Lexington, MA: Lexington Press.

Sethi, S. P. (1978). Advocacy advertising: The American experience. *California Management Review, 11*, 55–67. doi:10.2307/41165295

Sethi, S. P. (2003). *Setting global standards: Guidelines for creating codes of conduct in multinational corporations*. Hoboken, NJ: John Wiley & Sons.

Smith, A. C. T., & Westerbeek, H. M. (2007). Sport as a vehicle for deploying corporate social responsibility. *Journal of Corporate Citizenship, 25*, 43–54. doi:10.1.1.472.4859

Suchman, M. C. (1995). Managing legitimacy: Strategic and institutional approaches. *Academy of Management Review, 20*, 571–610. doi:10.2307/258788

Vranica, S. (2015, January 26). NFL brings a domestic-abuse ad to Super Bowl. *Wall Street Journal*. Retrieved from www.wsj.com

Walters, G. (2009). Corporate social responsibility through sport: The community sports trust model as a CSR delivery agency. *Journal of Corporate Citizenship, 35*, 81–94.

Waymer, D., & Heath, R. L. (2014). Organizational legitimacy: The overlooked yet all-important foundation of OPR research. *PRism, 11*(2). Retrieved from www.prism journal.org/homepage.html

4 Explaining Sports Fans' Recognition of Sponsors Using the Elaboration Likelihood Model

James Pokrywczynski

Sponsorship recognition among fans of major U.S. sports leagues is a primary goal of many corporate sponsors. The Elaboration Likelihood Model (ELM) is used to explain how avid fans will retain and respond more favorably to sponsorship efforts than casual fans. Through secondary analysis of professionally conducted surveys, data shows the official sponsors of the NFL and MLB have higher recognition on average compared to official sponsors in the NBA or NHL. Product category for a sponsorship affects a brand's recall among fans, with single and dual dominant brands in a product category likely to generate more accurate sponsorship recognition.

Introduction

Whether watching on TV, listening on the radio, or attending events, sports fans are continually bombarded with advertisements and sponsorship messages. With this cluttered message environment, how can brands and companies break through to stick in the consumer's mind without wasting money on expensive sponsorship packages? This case study will compare the sponsorship environments for six major U.S. sports leagues: NFL, NBA, MLB, NHL, PGA, and NCAA college football.

This investigation also strives to understand how sponsorships work among different levels of fans. Not all fans are alike. Avid fans—or "avids"—attend more games, follow the sport/team more often on traditional and social media, buy more team merchandise, and wear that merchandise both to games and at home (Moyer, Pokrywczynski, & Griffin, 2015). These fans respond differently to sports sponsorship efforts than casual fans—or "casuals"—and are best explained by the Elaboration Likelihood Model developed by Petty and Cacioppo (1986).

Background

Fan avidity, the intensity of the relationship between sports consumers and the team or sport they follow, is of growing interest in sports marketing as a variable to distinguish sports consumer segments. It also exists in the scholarly literature with Wann's (2006a) work on team identification. Wann defines team identification as "the extent to which a fan feels a psychological connection to a team and the team's performances are viewed as self-relevant." This coincides with the NHL's definition of avids as "fans that [sic] have an emotional connection to the game, people whose interest, enthusiasm and passion for the game defy the norm" (Syracuse, 2008). Wann (2006b) proposed that, although there are many different factors that serve as antecedents to sport team identification, the three general categories of causes are psychological, environmental, and team-related. Psychological factors include the needs for belonging and affiliation, while environmental factors include the socialization process among family members or peers. Team-related factors include organizational characteristics, team performance, and player attributes.

All of these antecedents are important because, once a fan has developed a sense of identification with a particular sport or team, the levels of sport team identification can be associated with cognitive, affective, and behavioral responses (Wann, 2006a). Bohnsack, Pokrywczynski, and Brinker (2013) tested avid fans' abilities to recall sponsors appearing in signage after viewing a short clip replaying highlights of a sports event. Compared to casual fans in the experimental condition, avid fans showed superior recall, and the stronger the team avidity, the better the recall.

Cornwell (2000) provides a theoretical explanation for the role of fan avidity in brand recall by using concepts from research on associated networks in psychology. Fans with greater knowledge of the sport or team provide more opportunities for brand linkages in the pursuit of such knowledge. The more linkages a brand has, the better its chance to be retrieved and associated with the attitudes connected to the sport or team it sponsors.

The avidity concept is well grounded in the more developed literature covering involvement. Although the involvement concept has deep cognitive roots, it also addresses the attitudinal engagement that avidity represents in consumers, whether involvement is applied in processing information, assessing products, or making purchase decisions. This includes sport and team affiliation. Audiences generally expect to engage both cognitively and emotionally when viewing sports in person or on screen, particularly those identifying as sport or team fans. At higher levels of engagement, this experience resembles the central route of Petty and Cacioppo's (1986) Elaboration Likelihood Model (ELM). It is more likely to be an enduring process, using Wann's (2006b) conceptualization, resulting in more permanent information processing. At lower engagement levels, audiences will process information peripherally, barely knowing the score of the game or who is participating at a given moment (see Figure 4.1). This is the temporal process described by Wann. These fans may be experiencing sports because they attend/view with a friend or loved one or, in today's society, media multitasking by surfing the Internet or using social media through a wireless device. This last behavior is what sports marketers today refer to as

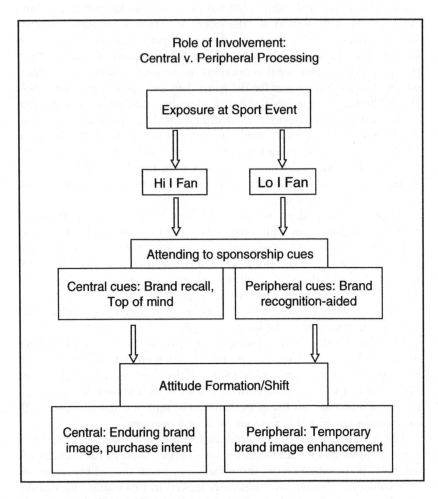

Figure 4.1 Elaboration Likelihood Model Applied to Sports Events

Source: Petty, R. & Cacioppo, J. (1986). *Communication and persuasion: Central and peripheral routes to attitude change.* New York: Springer-Verlag

"Generation Heads Down (HD)" and has teams and sponsors thinking of new ways to keep all fans engaged with the sports coverage, not the distractions (Conway, 2013).

According to the ELM, motivation to engage a message is an important factor in whether audiences dedicate significant cognitive attention to a communication. While most mass–media advertisers must constantly innovate and compete to retain this higher attentiveness, sponsors of sports can expect a certain level of personal engagement with all the content that is part of the sports presentation because it is woven so tightly into the sports event that delivers consumers in the first place. Brands sponsoring these events expect this engagement to translate into improved brand or product awareness and attitudes (Barnett, 2011). Michaelsen and Pokrywczynski (2017) elaborate on this idea by examining first how engaged consumers are with the sport, and second, the degree to which different levels of engagement lead to central or peripheral processing of brand sponsorship material that accompanies sports content. The processing outcome of focus here was brand recognition of the official sponsor. Although specific aspects of the process were not tested, the model served to explain how different types of fans, avids and casuals, react to official sponsorship efforts.

Petty and Cacioppo (1981) conceptualized involvement as the personal relevance or importance an individual attaches to an issue, a product, and in this case, a sports team. The heightened relevance of a sports team is often played out in fans of the winning team hooting, hollering, and waving pom poms or towels while fans of the losing team are pouting or shedding tears. While these are behavioral manifestations of high personal relevance, the effects on cognitive processing are more important to understand when considering sponsor recognition.

Fans either attending or following sports through media vary in terms of percent of avids as well as other key audience characteristics. Each sport below is ranked by the percent of avids according to a national sample (Simmons, 2016):

1. National Football League—With 42% of sports fans overall as avids, and 55% of males as avids, the NFL holds the highest percentage of avids among major sports leagues by a wide margin. There are no demographic distinctions between avids and casuals, with both predominantly male, 55 and older, white, and with income in the $25,000–$50,000 range. The NFL has one of the highest percentages of female fans overall, although still only 35%.
2. National Collegiate Athletic Association Football—Avids make up 31% of NCAA football fans, and 41% of male NCAA football fans. Avids tend to be slightly younger (25–44) than casuals, which may be explained by their more recent college experiences. Casuals also are in a lower average income bracket ($40,000–$75,000), which may also suggest more non-college fans are part of this college sports following.
3. Major League Baseball—-This league has 28% of its fan base as avids, and they are the oldest fan base, with the predominant group 55 and older. There are no demographic differences between avids and casuals, although league efforts are focused on drawing younger fans into the game, at least at the casual level.
4. National Basketball Association—Avids comprise 24% of its fan base. This is the most diverse fan base among the leagues analyzed, with blacks comprising 45%, whites 40%, and Hispanics about 12%. The NBA also has the youngest fan base, with one-third of its fans 18–35 compared

to most other leagues at 20% or less. No demographic differences exist between avids and casuals.

5. National Hockey League—Avids comprise 13% of its fan base. The only demographic difference between avid and casual hockey fans is that avids tend to be in a higher income bracket (avg. over $100,000). Otherwise both avids and casuals are predominantly male, 35–54, and white.

6. Professional Golf Association—Like hockey, golf has a narrow fan base, with about 12% avids. Avid PGA fans tend to be older (55+) and have higher incomes ($100K+) compared to casuals (35–50, $70,000–$100,000), a highly attractive target market for sponsors. Like the NFL, they also have a female fan base of 35%.

The Case

Turnkey Intelligence surveys reported in the *Sports Business Journal* were used to assess sponsor recognition from the following leagues: NFL, NBA, NHL, MLB, PGA, and NCAA (Which . . . NHL, NBA, NCAA, NFL, MLB, PGA, 2015). Leagues had between nine and 11 official sponsorship categories. Only about half of the product categories crossed over all leagues (e.g., soft drinks, autos, fast food), so comparisons across leagues for specific product categories were limited. Fans were categorized as "avid" if they responded "4" or "5" to "How big of a fan are you of the (Insert Professional Sports League here)?" and claimed that they looked up news, scores, and standings several times a week and watched, listened, or attended a certain number of games a season. Casuals responded "3" to the same initial question and claimed to have looked up news, scores, and standings a few times a month and attended a few games per season (less than avids).

Sponsor recognition among avids averaged from 34% to 24.7% across the six sports (see Table 4.1). For specific brands within a given sports league, percentages of avids recalling a sponsor ranged from 59% to a low of 11.5% in one case. Four sponsors across the leagues earned over 50% recognition among avids. Overall, across all six leagues the average percentage of avids recalling an official sponsor was about 29%.

For casual fans, sponsor recognition was lower, averaging from 31.4% to 16.8% across the six leagues. For specific brands, percentages of casuals recalling a sponsor were as high as 47.5% and as low as 8.5%. Six sponsors across the leagues were able to achieve 40% recognition among casuals, while 29 sponsors garnered less than 20% recognition among casuals. Overall, across all six leagues the average percentage of casuals recalling an official sponsor was about 22%, a 33% lower recall than for avid fans.

Across all six sports leagues, the NFL had the highest average percentage of sponsor recognition. An average of 34% of avid fans could correctly identify the official sponsor of the NFL. Nine of the 10 official league sponsors garnered the highest recognition among both avids and casuals with one exception. General Motors lost to Ford among casuals. Behind the NFL, the

Table 4.1 Avids and Casuals Sponsor Recall by Sports League

Avids

League	Highest recall	Lowest Recall	Overall avg	Significance
NFL	53.5%	16.5%	34%	a
NBA	55.5%	13.5%	25.4%	b
MLB	42%	19%	29%	b
NHL	30%	14.5%	24.7%	b
PGA	58.5%	17.5%	31.4%	
NCAA Football	45%	11.5%	29.7%	b

Casuals

League	Highest recall	Lowest Recall	Overall avg	Significance
NFL	47.5%	15.5%	31.4%	a
NBA	42.8%	10.4%	19.4%	c
MLB	41%	8.5%	26%	b
NHL	22%	10%	16.8%	c
PGA	43.5%	10%	20.2%	c
NCAA Football	29%	11.4%	20.3%	c

Different letters represent significant differences at p < .05

PGA had the second-highest average official sponsor recognition at 31.4%. Eight of its 10 sponsors won the recognition tourney. The hotel category lost to casuals and barely edged other brands among avids, but not with differences beyond the margin of error. The insurance category sponsorship was split three ways, with only one of the three finishing in the top three recognized brands. The NCAA and MLB topped the lower group on sponsor recognition at 29.7% and 29%, respectively, while the NBA (25.4%) and the NHL (24.7%) produced the lowest average sponsor recognition scores. For the NCAA, eight of 11 sponsors shot to the top of the recall board. Consumer electronics and delivery services failed to top its category, while the insurance category lost among avids but won among casuals. Insurance was also a loser in the MLB survey, as was a tire brand and a wireless provider.

Looking at the combined sponsor recognition for both avids and casuals, the NFL once again scores a touchdown over the other leagues, with 65% of all fans on average recalling official sponsors. A clear second tier for sponsor recognition comes from MLB, NCAA, and PGA, with average recognition scores around 50%. The bottom tier of leagues, NBA and NHL could only generate overall sponsor recognition scores in the low- to mid-40s.

Assessing the role that product category plays in sponsor recognition across leagues, the product categories having the most difficult time being recognized as the official sponsor, regardless of league, were insurance, wireless services, and auto-related products (tires, cars). Across three leagues (MLB, NCAA, and PGA), insurance companies failed to stand out across fan bases. In two leagues (MLB and PGA), this may be caused by signing multiple sponsors, splitting the category into types of insurance (auto, home, life), thereby diluting the category. For the PGA, the formula was complicated by sponsor activations, with one company sponsoring an award for best amateur golfer, while another flies blimps over select tour events providing television coverage. The most surprising violation occurred in the NCAA, where Northwestern Mutual Life (NML), a sponsor since 2012, failed to top the avids list and generated only 11.5% recall among both fan groups. This may be explained by NML's approach as a title sponsor of select events, such as the Rose Bowl in football and the Final Four tourney in basketball. For football, the playing field is cluttered with other insurance players, from Allstate sponsoring the kicking nets in many stadiums to Met Life providing blimp coverage at others.

Wireless services struggled in two (NBA, MLB) of the four leagues where wireless sponsorships are offered league-wide. Part of the challenge may be that the category has four to five major brands, all of which bought advertising time during these sports or had local sponsorship deals to confuse the consumer. For example, AT&T, not an official NBA sponsor, has naming rights to several arenas across the league, not to mention local sponsorship deals with several other teams.

This condition likely explains the one NFL sponsor (General Motors) that failed to score a touchdown among both fan groups. Despite a season-long advertising presence dating back to 2001 and activation related to the rollout of the most popular NFL video game (*Madden NFL 2015*), Ford was recalled as often as GM as an official sponsor. Ford's sponsorship of Detroit's playing field along with local sponsorship deals across the league likely led to GM coming up short of the goal line.

You Make the Call

It is not a surprise that the NFL performed best in terms of sponsor recognition since it has the highest percentage of avids among the six sports leagues. As the ELM model would predict, these avids are more likely to centrally process game information and the sponsorship information woven within that comes along for the ride. Similarly, MLB and NCAA football, with substantial numbers of avids, provide good environments for sponsors to register in fans' minds.

The PGA's strong recognition among sponsors despite the low number of avids runs counter to the ELM's prediction. Perhaps PGA avids are extremely avid in watching and attending golf events, suggesting degree of avidity may be a valuable way to segment an audience when considering sports marketing.

Official sponsor recognition is not the only measure of a successful sponsorship. Whether recognition leads to attitude formations related to brand preference and purchase intent must also be assessed. It is clear that teams and sponsors need to engage fans as much as possible to maximize their impact and maintain a desired value in their brands.

Gatorade engages fans as the official sports drink sponsor of the NFL, NBA, MLB, and NHL and has the highest average recognition compared to all other products mentioned in the surveys. Gatorade has an average avid fan recognition of 42.9%. Since 1983, Gatorade has had cups and iconic orange coolers along the NFL sidelines. Since then, Gatorade has continued to grow its presence as a staple product relied upon by NFL players. Resonating with fans are player testimonials, social media mentions, and data reporting that on average the 32 NFL teams consume 464,000 gallons of Gatorade each year and use 7.4 million branded Gatorade cups per year. But Gatorade did not want to stop at just beverages. Gatorade created Fuel Bars and tracking tools designed to keep detailed records of nutrients being consumed by athletes (Jessop, 2013). Anheuser-Busch, an official sponsor of the MLB, PGA, NHL, NFL, and NBA, only has average avid fan recognition of 29.3%. Their differences in avid fan recognition could be due to how many other competitors are present in their respective categories. Gatorade's only primary competitors are Powerade and Red Bull, while Anheuser-Busch is competing with messages from Miller-Coors, Heineken, Labatt, and Corona.

In using the ELM to explain the relationship between brands and fans, avid fans and casual fans both will have some level of recall, but due to their different involvement levels, avid fans will have a greater, longer lasting recall compared to casual fans. This case analysis suggests that what brands do around the sponsorship, including activation, ad support, and even the longevity of the sponsorship relationship, can enhance their ability to stand out for consumers. This gives marketers insights into the mind of the consumer and can help in deciding which sponsorship strategy is the best fit for them and their brand.

Discussion Questions

1. Find the most recent Turnkey Intelligence data reported in *Sports Business Journal* for one of the sports leagues discussed here and evaluate the current sponsors, their performance as recognized sponsors, and the tactics used in assessing whether the sponsorship was successful. What has occurred lately to change the relationship between sponsors and fans?
2. What other metrics for assessing sponsorship effectiveness, other than sponsor recognition, should be used? What are the advantages and disadvantages compared to sponsorship recognition?
3. How would sponsorship effectiveness be assessed differently with sports that are more international or global in nature?
4. Find an alternative theory that may better explain how sponsorships work on sports fans.

References

Barnett, M. (2011, February 6). Sponsorship: Event backers drive audience participation. *Marketing Week*, 25.

Bohnsack, D., Pokrywczynski, J., & Brinker, D. (2013, May). Sports sponsorship recall among real fans: Using fan avidity and involvement to explain effects. Paper presented to American Academy of Advertising Asia-Pacific Conference, Honolulu, HI.

Conway, M. (2013). How sports marketers can hold attention of "Generation HD". *Sports Business Journal*, 25.

Cornwell, T. B. (2000). State of the art and science in sponsorship-linked marketing. *Journal of Advertising, 37*(3), 41–55.

Jessop, A. (2013). How Super Bowl teams select their Gatorade flavor and a look inside Gatorade's NFL partnership. *Forbes*. Retrieved from www.forbes.com/sites/aliciajes sop/2013/02/03/how-super-bowl-teams-select-their-gatorade-flavor-and-a-look-inside-gatorades-nfl-partnership/#55ecfba637d7

Michaelsen, A., & Pokrywczynski, J. (2017, April). Sports In-FAN-Tuation: Casual and avid sports fans' recognition of sponsors. Paper presented to International Association of Sports Communication conference, Phoenix, AZ.

Moyer, C., Pokrywczynski, J., & Griffin, R. J. (2015). The relationship of fans' sports team identification and Facebook usage to purchase of team products. *Journal of Sports Media, 10*(1), 31–49.

Petty, R., & Cacioppo, J. (1981). Issue involvement as a moderator of the effects on attitude of advertising content and context. In K. Monroe (Ed.), *Advances in consumer research*. Ann Arbor, MI: Association for Consumer Research.

Petty, R., & Cacioppo, J. (1986). *Communication and persuasion: Central and peripheral routes to attitude change*. New York, NY: Springer-Verlag.

Simmons Market Research Bureau. (2016). Adult study: Sports league interest by key demographics. Retrieved from www.simmonssurvey.com

Sports avidity levels among the 18–34 demo. (2006, April 17). *Sports Business Journal*. Retrieved from www.sportsbusinessdaily.com/Journal/Issues/2006/04/17

Syracuse, A. (2008, November 1). The National Hockey League's power play. *Target Marketing*. Retrieved from www.targetmarketingmag.com/article/an-expanded-direct-to-consumer-portfolio-tighter-data-collection-practices-new-relational-database-400124

Wann, D. L. (2006a). The causes and consequences of sport team identification. In A. Raney & J. Bryant (Eds.), *Handbook of sports and media* (pp. 331–352). Mahwah, NJ: Lawrence Erlbaum Associates, Inc.

Wann, D. L. (2006b). Understanding the positive social psychological benefits of sport team identification: The Team Identification-Social Psychological Health Model. *Group Dynamics: Theory, Research, and Practice, 10*, 272–296.

Which of the following is an official sponsor of MLB? (2015, November 16). *Sports Business Journal*, 17.

Which of the following is an official sponsor of the NBA? (2015, July 13). *Sports Business Journal*, 17.

Which of the following is an official sponsor of the NCAA? (2015, April 27). *Sports Business Journal*, 15.

Which of the following is an official sponsor of the NFL? (2015, March 16). *Sports Business Journal*, 17.

Which of the following is an official sponsor of the NHL? (2015, June 22). *Sports Business Journal*, 14.

Which of the following is an official sponsor of the PGA? (2015, October 12). *Sports Business Journal*, 19.

Acknowledgement

The author is grateful to Allysa Michaelsen, master's degree graduate, Marquette University College of Communication, for assistance in preparing this chapter.

5 Coming Home

The Los Angeles Rams Connect to Past to Build Future

Jean Kelso Sandlin

The bumps and bruises of the NFL's Rams' move from St. Louis to Los Angeles are analyzed in this chapter. Using agenda setting and framing theories, the chapter explores how the Rams, who missed the playoffs for 11 consecutive seasons, sought to build a fan base within the entertainment capital of the world and among those who had not had a home football team in over two decades. After the record-breaking attendance at the opening game, the losing Rams faced new challenges, including the Chargers' move to LA. Initial framing strategies, however, proved successful in establishing the team in LA.

Introduction

When the National Football League approved the Rams' move from St. Louis to Los Angeles for the 2016 season, the team entered the second-largest media market in the United States (Nielsen, 2015) and a region that had been without an NFL team for more than two decades. Although the Rams had missed the playoffs for 11 consecutive seasons prior to the move, the first preseason game in LA attracted a record 90,000 fans (Figure 5.1), and season tickets sold out in just six hours (Dragon, 2016; Farmer, 2016; NFL attendance—2016, n.d.; Wang, 2016).

Successfully building and sustaining a loyal fan base, especially through a losing season, demonstrates how a high-profile media market can pose both opportunities and challenges to sports teams. This is what the Rams faced when moving from St. Louis to Los Angeles. The Rams' communication strategy focused primarily on optimizing operational decisions to leverage earned and owned media by exploiting three central frames: geographic connectedness, historical civic identity, and sport as entertainment. The theories of agenda-setting and framing were prominent in the team's approach.

Background

History Matters

A contentious historical relationship between the NFL's Rams and the city of Los Angeles complicated efforts to rebuild a fan base when the team

Figure 5.1 After the 2016 move From St. Louis to Los Angeles, the Rams first preseason
game at the Los Angeles Memorial Coliseum attracted a record 90,000 fans,
and season tickets sold out in just six hours..

Photo by Hiro Ueno, used with permission from the Los Angeles Rams.

relocated from St. Louis to LA in 2016. The Rams NFL franchise started
in Cleveland in 1937 but moved to Los Angeles in 1946 (Dufresne, 1990;
Los Angeles Rams history, n.d.). The Rams played in the LA Coliseum until
1980, when they relocated to Anaheim to take advantage of the NFL's broadcast agreement; Anaheim's smaller stadium allowed the team to sell out and
thus broadcast more games, thwarting the NFL's blackout rules and increasing advertising revenue (Hughes, 2012; Laverty, 2013). Breakdowns in negotiations over stadium improvements in Anaheim prompted the Rams' exit
from LA to St. Louis in 1994 after then owner Georgia Frontiere threatened
to sue the league if it voted against the proposed move (Dufresne, 1990;
George, 1995).

Thus, the Rams' record-breaking crowd in 2016—the largest crowd to
ever watch a preseason football game in United States history—marked the
end of a long journey for the team and was in stark contrast to the Rams'
last game in LA in 1994, when they played to a crowd of only 25,705—the
smallest crowd for an NFL game that season (Mather, 2016; Pro Football
Reference, 1994). In 1994, the fans had largely lost interest, the likely result
of consistently poor team performance and the owner's interest in relocation. However, there was a contingent of loyal fans who joined sports agent
and LA native Leigh Steinberg in a "Save-the-Rams" campaign to keep the
team in LA. During the Rams' last game of the 1994 season, some fans wore
t-shirts with the phrase, "Win or lose, stay or move, Rams fans forever"
(Mather, 2016). Two decades later, this loyal contingent would prove to be an
important public to tap into for the Rams as they staged their return to LA.

After talks broke down in St. Louis over the construction of a new stadium, the Rams filed for relocation to Los Angeles in early January 2016 (Rams file for relocation, 2016). A week later, the NFL owners voted to allow the Rams to relocate and construct a new $2.6 billion stadium (Hanzus, 2016; Los Angeles Rams history, n.d.; Pacheco, 2016). It was a victory for Rams owner Stan Kroenke, who was competing with the Oakland Raiders and the San Diego Chargers for approval to also move their teams to LA. The victory, however, gave way to three communication challenges for the Rams.

1. How does the team reach potential fans spread across a vast four-county region that includes Los Angeles, Orange, Ventura, and Santa Barbara counties and spans 9,400 square miles, in addition to parts of two adjacent counties (Riverside and San Bernardino), without being able to tap into a regional sports network (RSN) contract? (The NFL negotiates television contracts nationally.)
2. How does a team that missed the playoffs for the previous 11 consecutive seasons build and sustain a fan base in a city that had no football team for more than two decades?
3. How can the Rams successfully compete for attention in the entertainment capital of the world, the second-largest media market in the United States, and an area teeming with entertainment attractions and successful sports franchises?

The Case

Operationalizing Community

To combat the challenges of building a fan base in such a vast geographic region, the team's communication strategy focused on optimizing operational decisions. The plan relied on minimal paid advertising and focused heavily on earned and owned media (A. Twyman, personal communication, January 11, 2017).

Consistent with agenda-setting theory (Eagleman, 2008; Kiousis, Popescu, & Mitrook, 2007; Pedersen, 2013), the Rams sought opportunities for media attention to build familiarity of the players among the fans. Agenda-setting theory posits that mass media connects the events to images in people's minds, has the ability to shape the discussion of public events, and, in doing so, has the power to influence and create fans (Fortunato, 2008; Lippmann, 1922; McCombs, Shaw, & Weaver, 2014).

Framing organizes information in a way that suggests meaning and context by selecting, emphasizing, or excluding information, and these selective decisions are often made without audience awareness (Goffman, 1974; Pedersen, 2013; Tankard, 2001; Zaharopoulos, 2007). From the first announcement of the relocation, the LA Rams framed the move as a homecoming (A. Twyman, personal communication, January 11, 2017). Framing the relocation as a homecoming connected the team to the region, which is consistent with research that suggests sports consumption affirms civic identities and promotes fan creation (Kassing et al., 2004; Kolbe & James, 2000). Framing football as entertainment, with the Rams' players as celebrities, helped leverage the entertainment agenda that dominates the LA media landscape. This strategy coincides with a recent shift in sports journalism coverage that includes aspects of sport, celebrity, and pop culture (Lewis & Weaver, 2013; Schultz & Sheffer, 2010).

Framing Geographic Connections as Community

The team used three different training locations to bring the team to the people, garnering media coverage and increasing engagement in communities surrounding Los Angeles. They held mini training camp in Oxnard (west Ventura County, near Santa Barbara County's southern border); held training camp at the University of California, Irvine (Orange County near LA County's southern border); and constructed a training facility for use during the season at California Lutheran University in Thousand Oaks (east Ventura County, near LA County's northern border), all key geographical areas for attracting ticket buyers.

To further cement regional affiliation, staff from the Rams Foundation, the philanthropic arm of the organization, led a 70-stop "listening tour" of local nonprofit organizations in an effort to better understand community needs and provide organizations an avenue to seek the foundation's financial support and request player appearances (M. Higgins, personal communication, Feb 2, 2017). In addition, the Rams took advantage of opportunities to connect with local schools. For example, when a local high school's fundraising money for football equipment was stolen, the Rams provided the equipment and uniforms and delivered the gear complete with a photo opportunity that included the Rams mascot and LA Rams defensive end Robert Quinn. The event was covered by news outlets in three counties (Quan, 2016).

The Rams allocated resources for strategic events—from a draft party at LA Live, a popular downtown entertainment center, to building a playground in Inglewood (near the future stadium). In a Rams video highlighting the playground build, Kevin Demoff, the Rams chief operating officer, said, "It's great to get the players out because it tells Los Angeles, there is football here, there are players here and they are a part of the community" (Rams Inglewood playground build, 2016).

The Rams also recognized when operational decisions might impact their relationship with other LA professional teams and fans. When the Rams' trade for the first-round draft pick coincided with Lakers superstar Kobe Bryant's retirement, Rams' management delayed the announcement to "let Kobe have his day" (A. Twyman, personal communication, January 11, 2017). The first draft pick also pleased the California fans—quarterback Jared Goff, the first true freshman to start the season opener at the University of California, Berkeley.

Returning Home: Framing Historical Civic Identity

Framing the relocation as a homecoming inferred an immediate connection with the LA region and the team's past and prospective fans. This was especially important for the Rams since the team had to reach publics that grew up or moved to LA when the city was without a football team (Birkner, 2016). Using the words *return* or *home* were intentional, and a key component of the team's official communication messages (A. Twyman, personal communication, January 11, 2017).

Since the Rams' departure from LA in 1994, faithful fans created a variety of booster-type groups.

> They hold rallies, they get together in sports bars to watch football, and they show up at Dodgers, Angels, Lakers, Clippers, Kings and Ducks games . . . . And they carry a Stan Kroenke giant head with them everywhere they go.
>
> (Cole, 2016)

Fan-initiated social media efforts followed, including a "Bring Back the Los Angeles Rams" Facebook page, which started in 2009, and a Twitter account and website in 2010 (Cole, 2016). After the Rams announced their bid for relocation, hundreds of hopeful Rams supporters held a rally at the LA Coliseum (Beacham, 2016a; Suter, 2016). Among the participants was Leigh Steinberg, who had launched the Save-the-Rams campaign two decades earlier. Steinberg told a reporter,

> Rooting for the Rams in the '50s was how I fell in love with pro football. They belong in Southern California . . . . I don't like breaking the hearts of young St. Louis fans, but the Rams are ours.
>
> (Hammond, 2016)

Rally attendance included long-time Ram fans and youth who had never seen the Rams in LA (Beacham, 2016a)—a demographic mix suggesting the Rams had maintained their civic connection among loyal fans who may have influenced the next generation—a phenomenon that is supported by research (Dietz-Uler, Harrick, End, & Jacquemotte, 2000; Kassing et al., 2004; Kolbe & James, 2000). Along with the fans, former LA Rams players made appearances and rallied for the team's return—the most notable being Hall of Fame running back Eric Dickerson, whose jersey was among the most popular with fans at the rallies (Beacham, 2016a; Hammond, 2016; Suter, 2016).

On January 12, 2017, the team's website announced "Rams to return to Los Angeles" (2016). Three days later, the team's official Facebook page posted a video featuring the song "Coming Home" by Skylar Grey and P. Diddy (Los Angeles Rams, 2016). The Rams' billboard campaign featured Rams players leaping over iconic LA landmarks (Birkner, 2016). Rams executive Kevin Demoff told reporters, "When I look at the Rams' return to L.A., that's what people are excited about—it's modern NFL mixed with the team they grew up with" (Farmer & Fenno, 2016). NFL commissioner Roger Goodell announced the move by saying, "Today was an important day. We have the return of the Los Angeles Rams to their home" (Bonsignore, 2016; Hanzus, 2016), and at the press conference, owner Stan Kroenke called Rams Coach Jeff Fisher "a Southern California boy" (Los Angeles Rams introductory press conference, 2016).

Regional civic leaders and media also maintained the homecoming frame in media reports. LA mayor Eric Garcetti said, "With the return of the NFL, there is yet another reason . . . for Angelenos to love calling this city home" (L.A. Mayor Garcetti celebrates Rams' return, 2016). When the president of California Lutheran University released a statement announcing that the Rams would construct a training facility on campus, it read, "We are thrilled to be part of the return of the Rams and NFL football to Los Angeles" (LA Rams training moving to Cal Lutheran, 2016). His statement was reprinted verbatim in regional and national media, including a story by the Associated Press (Beacham, 2016c).

Although framing the message as a homecoming resonated in LA, there was a stark contrast in St. Louis, as demonstrated by the leads from two newspaper stories written on the same day. The LA story began, "The Rams' 20-year stumble into the wilderness is over. They are finally returning home to Los Angeles" (Bonsignore, 2016), while the St. Louis story began, "National Football League owners on Tuesday voted overwhelmingly to strip the Rams from St. Louis and send the team to owner Stan Kroenke's proposed $2 billion stadium in Los Angeles County" (Hunn, 2016).

Framing Sport as Entertainment

Moving into the second-largest media market provided the Rams great media reach, but there was a lot of competition for attention in a region crowded with high-profile entertainment attractions and successful sports franchises like the Dodgers (MLB), Lakers and Clippers (NBA), and Kings (NHL); two college powerhouses—USC and UCLA; and three California NFL teams—the Raiders, the 49ers, and Chargers. The team's social media ranked third to last among NFL teams (Karp, 2012) so was not a strong tactic to support the move, although the Rams did use Facebook and Twitter. Studies indicate that the sports media agenda is defined by sports news and sports broadcasts (McCombs, 2005). Recognizing the importance of earned media coverage to their strategy, the Rams held a workshop to better prepare regional sports reporters who had not had an NFL team in the city for more than two decades.

LA is known as the entertainment capital of the world, and the industry is one of the most visible and impactful parts of the economy (*The Entertainment Industry and the Los Angeles Economy*, 2012; Scott, 1996). Because of its importance, the entertainment industry is closely followed by regional media, and the LA area serves as headquarters for entertainment-focused media, such as *TMZ*, *Variety*, *Deadline Hollywood*, and the *Hollywood Reporter*. The Rams incorporated entertainment news to drive regional media coverage.

The Rams were featured on *Hard Knocks*, an Emmy Award–winning HBO reality TV show (Thiry, 2016), and, although it was unauthorized by the Rams, six players also participated in the E! reality TV show *Hollywood & Football* (Hill, 2016; Joseph, 2016). Quarterback Jared Goff appeared on the Hollywood-based late-night talk show *Jimmy Kimmel Live!* (Pedersen, 2016), and the *Hollywood Reporter* detailed which celebrities purchased Rams tickets (Lewis, 2016). The *Los Angeles Times* reported Rams' running back Todd Gurley's Hollywood Boulevard photoshoot for a men's fashion line, and the headline dubbed him "L.A.'s next marketing superstar" (Klein, 2016). To prepare the team for this added media attention, the Rams expanded their media training offerings to the players and their wives (A. Twyman, personal communication, January 11, 2017).

Once it was announced that celebrity seating would be planned in the new stadium, owner Stan Kroenke was asked in an interview, "So you want to include the entertainment industry in the stadium experience?" Kroenke replied,

> That's part of L.A. . . . . That's how you engage the community, frankly. If we're not doing that right, we're not servicing the fans of LA. . . . It's . . . a big market, there's a lot of competitive forces there.
>
> (Farmer & Fenno, 2016)

And a lot of distractions for the players.

Prior to the team's move to St. Louis, and after a dismal 1994 season which ended with a Rams' loss to the Washington Redskins for a 4–12 record, cornerback Todd Lyght told a reporter,

> We're not winning, so something has to change . . . If we move, then that might help us out. There's not a lot to do out in St. Louis, so maybe the focus would be on work and the things that need to be done, instead of what we're going to do after the game, like in this situation.
>
> (Reilley, 1994)

Although in 2016 the Rams embraced the entertainment industry and the media exposure, a former player warned the players about the unique distractions playing in LA provides. In January 2016, Hall of Famer Eric Dickerson spoke to a reporter about the move to LA.

> This is Hollywood. . . . Being in LA, there's nothing like it. It's the glitz. It's the glamour. It's the beautiful girls. It's the weather. But you've got to take your job serious, first of all. You're a football player first, and all that other stuff comes secondary.
>
> (Beacham, 2016b)

You Make the Call

The record-breaking attendance at the opening game seemed to indicate regional enthusiasm amid what one reporter wrote was "a city that embraced them, with fans who loved them, in a stadium that showcases them" (Plaschke, 2016). Yet the average attendance for the Rams 2016 season ranked 31st among 32 teams, signaling that any fan enthusiasm quickly dissipated (NFL attendance—2016). The Rams started their season with 3 wins and 1 loss, but ended it 4 and 12, winning only one game at home.

As the losses stacked up, the fans took to social media to criticize the team, particularly Coach Jeff Fisher's decision not to start rookie quarterback Jared Goff—a role Goff didn't assume until the ninth week of the season (Figure 5.2) (Mortensen, 2016).

Figure 5.2 Los Angeles Rams quarterback Jared Goff (16) drops back to pass in week 11 of the 2016 season in a game between the Los Angeles Rams and the Miami Dolphins. As early season losses mounted, fans criticized the coach on social media for not starting the rookie quarterback until the ninth week of the season.

Source: Photo by Hiro Ueno, used with permission from the Los Angeles Rams

The fans also questioned the players' off-the-field activities. "The players seem more focused on being on E!s *Hollywood & Football,*" was a tweet that reflected fan frustration (Gonzalez, U., 2016). The media also offered their negative critiques; among the team's detractors was Rams Hall of Famer Eric Dickerson. When Dickerson joined the public criticism, it allegedly sparked a response by Coach Fisher. On an LA radio show, Dickerson said Fisher called him and said he was not welcome on the sidelines if he was going to be critical of the organization (Ruiz, 2016). After Fisher's call, Dickerson vowed not to attend another Rams game as long as Fisher was the head coach (Klein & Farmer, 2016; Ruiz, 2016). One reporter called the incident "a public-relations nightmare at the worst possible time" and quoted Demoff's response:

> Everything we've done since we returned, Eric has been part of the organization, and that's what we want to make sure doesn't change . . . He's been part of our efforts to connect to the community. That's what's disappointing about any type of miscommunication, no matter how big or small. He's somebody we want around, he's somebody who sets a great example for our players, and I think anybody who's in this business has to have a thick skin to understand that when you lose there's going to be criticism.
>
> (Gonzalez, A., 2016)

Two days after the team's 42–14 loss to the Atlanta Falcons, and in the midst of the Dickerson controversy, the Rams fired Fisher and named John Fassel, the Rams special teams coordinator, interim head coach. In a press conference, Demoff said it was an effort "to finish the season with some direction and hope" (Los Angeles Rams Coach Jeff Fisher fired, n.d.).

On January 12, 2017, the same day the Chargers announced they were moving from San Diego to LA, the Rams made history by hiring 30-year-old Sean McVay, the youngest head coach in NFL history. The news of McVay's hire moved the Rams back into the media spotlight. Although the Rams said the timing of the announcement was coincidental, since the press conference for McVay had already been in the works (A. Twyman, personal communication, June 25, 2017), one reporter wrote:

> The timing was exquisite, the Rams allowing the Chargers to have the headlines for all of about a dozen hours before brashly steal-ing some thunder by hiring a celebrated 30-year-old offensive whiz to be the youngest head coach in modern NFL history. No defer-ence shown. No space given. It was the exact opposite of the Rams' approach last spring when they waited a day to announce the trade for the No. 1 overall draft pick out of respect for Kobe Bryant's final game.
>
> (Plaschke, 2017)

After the Rams' first season back in LA, Nielson ratings provided insight on the unique situation of a city that went two decades without NFL football, to having two teams relocate to Los Angeles within a span of two years:

> Fans in St. Louis seem to be sticking with the Rams despite their relocation at the start of the 2016 season. In fact, when looking at the same six games that were aired in both LA and St Louis, ratings in LA were only marginally higher than in St. Louis (9.7 versus 8.3). The Rams averaged an 8.5 rating across all games in the LA market, which is the lowest home market rating for an NFL team.
>
> (Master, 2016)

But the Rams' initial framing strategies may have established roots after all, especially among media practitioners. The same day the Chargers announced their relocation, an *LA Times* columnist who had earlier called the Rams' return "an embarrassment" and called for Coach Fisher's firing (Plaschke, 2016) wrote:

> The Rams have the digs. The Rams have the fan base. The one thing the Rams are missing is the wins, but even then, it's going to be difficult for the Chargers to quickly catch up . . . The Chargers lack the geography. They don't have any of the tradition.
>
> (Plaschke, 2017)

Discussion Questions

1. What was the risk for the Rams to frame the relocation from St. Louis to Los Angeles as a homecoming? How can you explain the stark contrast in how the relocation was framed in the LA media vs. the St. Louis media? Will this "homecoming" frame continue to serve the Rams in the future?

2. How did the Rams' strategy of framing football an entertainment impact the team's communication strategy? How has the LA region's focus on entertainment media impacted other LA-based professional teams, such as the Lakers, Dodgers, or Kings? Should the Rams continue to adapt to this entertainment agenda in the future? Why or why not?

3. Review the team's communication response during the Dickerson–Fisher controversy and determine the positive and negative aspects to the response. Did you think the team's response was appropriate? Why or why not? Did it adhere to their original strategy? What might have happened if the team handled it differently?

4. After the Chargers announced they were relocating to Los Angeles, an LA columnist commented that, unlike the Rams, the Chargers did not have "any of the tradition"—how did the columnist's perceptions relate to the Rams' communication strategy?

5. Discuss any new developments since the Rams' move to Los Angeles. How might these new developments shape the team's communication strategy for next season?

References

Beacham, G. (2016a, January 9). LA Rams fans rally at Coliseum to demand team's return. *Los Angeles Daily News*. Retrieved from www.dailynews.com/sports/20160109/la-rams-fans-rally-at-coliseum-to-demand-teams-return

Beacham, G. (2016b, January 16). Dickerson, Everett see stars lining up for Rams in LA return. *The Seattle Times*. Retrieved from www.seattletimes.com/sports/dickerson-everett-see-stars-lining-up-for-rams-in-la-return/

Beacham, G. (2016c, March 30). LA Rams finalize plan to train at school in Thousand Oaks. *Associated Press*. Retrieved from https://apnews.com/017466d25f93494ba49568 9679a66f42/la-rams-finalize-plan-train-school-thousand-oaks

Birkner, C. (2016, August 22). Here's how the Rams are promoting their return to Los Angeles. *AdWeek*. Retrieved from www.adweek.com/brand-marketing/here-s-how-rams-are-promoting-their-return-los-angeles-173079/

Bonsignore, V. (2016, January 12). NFL owners approve Rams move to Inglewood; Chargers have option to join them. *Los Angeles Daily News*. Retrieved from www.dailynews.com/sports/20160112/nfl-owners-approve-rams-move-to-inglewood-chargers-have-option-to-join-them

Cole, H. (2016, January 8). L.A. Rams advocacy group poised for team's return. *Forbes*. Retrieved from www.forbes.com/sites/howardcole/2016/01/08/l-a-rams-advocacy-group-poised-for-teams-return-to-hold-rally-saturday-at-coliseum/#14efa37a487e

Dietz-Uler, B., Harrick, E., End, C., & Jacquemotte, L. (2000). Sex differences in sport fan behavior and reasons for being a sport fan. *Journal of Sport Behavior, 23*(3), 219.

Dragon, T. (2016, August 13). Rams set U.S. preseason attendance record in L.A. *NFL.com*. Retrieved from www.nfl.com/news/story/0ap3000000685041/article/rams-set-us-preseason-attendance-record-in-la

Dufresne, C. (1990, July 3). 10 years in Anaheim: A decade of Rams memories. *Los Angeles Times*. Retrieved from http://articles.latimes.com/1990-07-03/sports/sp-817_1_anaheim-stadium

Eagleman, A. (2008). *Investigating agenda-setting and framing in sport magazines: An analysis of the coverage of major league baseball players from 2000 through 2007* (Doctoral dissertation). (Order No. 3319879). Available from ProQuest Dissertations & Theses Global. (288401138). Bloomington, IN: Indiana University. Retrieved from https://ezproxy.callutheran.edu/login?url=https://search-proquest-com.ezproxy.callutheran.edu/docview/288401138?accountid=9839

The Entertainment Industry and the Los Angeles Economy. (2012). Retrieved from Los Angeles County Economic Development Corporation http://laedc.org/reports/EntertainmentinLA.pdf

Farmer, S. (2016, July 12). Rams to inform fans they've sold out season tickets, will begin selling single-game tickets. *Los Angeles Times*. Retrieved from www.latimes.com/sports/rams/la-sp-rams-tickets-20160712-snap-story.html

Farmer, S., & Fenno, N. (2016, January 13). Stan Kroenke discusses his picture-perfect vision for the L.A. Rams. *Los Angeles Times*. Retrieved from www.latimes.com/sports/nfl/la-sp-nfl-la-kroenke-20160114-story.html

Fortunato, J. (2008). NFL agenda-setting: The NFL programming schedule: A study of agenda-setting. *Journal of Sports Media, 3*(1), 27–49.

George, T. (1995, April 13). Rams given green light for St. Louis move. *The New York Times.* Retrieved from www.nytimes.com/1995/04/13/sports/pro-football-rams-given-green-light-for-st-louis-move.html

Goffman, E. (1974). *Frame analysis: An essay on the organization of experience.* Cambridge, MA: Harvard University Press.

Gonzalez, A. (2016, November 30). Public spat between Jeff Fisher, Eric Dickerson PR nightmare for Rams. *ESPN.com.* Retrieved from www.espn.com/blog/los-angeles-rams/post/_/id/31979/public-spat-between-jeff-fisher-eric-dickerson-a-pr-nightmare-for-rams

Gonzalez, U. (2016, December 12). The players seem more focused. Retrieved from @emmayimbe at https://twitter.com/search?q=umberto%20gonzalez&src=tyah

Hammond, R. (2016, January 11). Rams fans eager for team's return. *Orange County Register.* Retrieved from www.pe.com/2016/01/11/football-rams-fans-eager-for-teams-return/

Hanzus, D. (2016, January 12). Rams to relocate to L.A.: Chargers first option to join. *NFL. com.* Retrieved from www.nfl.com/news/story/0ap3000000621645/article/rams-to-relocate-to-la-chargers-first-option-to-join

Hill, L. (2016, July 6). The Los Angeles Rams go "Hollywood" in upcoming E! Reality TV series. *Los Angeles Times.* Retrieved from www.latimes.com/entertainment/tv/showtracker/la-et-st-los-angeles-rams-reality-show-20160706-snap-story.html

Hughes, J. (2012, October 5). NFL decade-low attendance inspires new TV blackout rules. *Bleacher Report.* Retrieved from http://bleacherreport.com/articles/1360162-nfl-decade-low-attendance-inspires-new-tv-blackout-rules

Hunn, D. (2016, January 13). Goodbye, St. Louis Rams: Next stop, LA. *St. Louis Post-Dispatch.* Retrieved from www.stltoday.com/sports/football/professional/goodbye-st-louis-rams-next-stop-la/article_ae537abe-8471-5ac3-9edc-2c3174ce7fd9.html

Joseph, A. (2016, July 6). The Rams just got to Los Angeles and already have a reality TV show. *USA Today Sports.* Retrieved from http://ftw.usatoday.com/2016/07/rams-los-angeles-reality-show-e-hollywood-football

Karp, A. (2012, February 22). The usual suspects: NFL fan favorites see similar popularity on web. *Sports Business Daily.* Retrieved from www.sportsbusinessdaily.com/Daily/Issues/2012/02/22/Media/NFL-media.aspx?hl=social%20media%20rankings%2C%20Rams&sc=0

Kassing, J., Billings, A., Brown, R., Halone, K., Harrison, K., Krizek, B., . . . Turman, P. (2004). Communication in the community of sport: The process of enacting, (re)producing, consuming, and organizing sport. *Annals of the International Communication Association, 28*(1), 373–409. doi:10.1080/23808985.2004.11679040

Kiousis, S., Popescu, C., & Mitrook, M. (2007). Understanding influence on corporate reputation: An examination of public relations efforts, media coverage, public opinion, and financial performance from an agenda-building and agenda-setting perspective. *Journal of Public Relations Research, 19*(2), 147–165.

Klein, G. (2016, July 8). Rams running back Todd Gurley is primed to become L.A.'s next marketing superstar. *Los Angeles Times.* Retrieved from www.latimes.com/sports/rams/la-sp-rams-gurley-marketing-20160708-snap-story.html

Klein, G., & Farmer, S. (2016, November 29). Eric Dickerson says he will not go to Ram games as long as Jeff Fisher is the coach. *Los Angeles Times.* Retrieved from www.latimes.com/sports/rams/la-sp-rams-dickerson-fisher-20161129-story.html

Kolbe, R., & James, J. (2000). An identification and examination of influences that sh the creation of a professional team fan. *International Journal of Sports Marketing and Sponsorship, 2*(1), 14–28.

L.A. Mayor Garcetti celebrates Rams' return. (2016, January 12). *Los Angeles Daily News.* Retrieved from www.dailynews.com/sports/20160112/la-mayor-garcetti-celebrates-rams-return

LA Rams training moving to Cal Lutheran. (2016, March 30). Callutheran.edu. Retrieved from www.callutheran.edu/news/story.html?id=12331#story

Laverty, B. (2013). *Unnecessary roughness? The NFL's blackout policy and its 2012 revision* (Doctoral dissertation). Drexel University, Philadelphia, PA.

Lewis, A. (2016, September 12). Who from Hollywood got prime seats for the L.A. Rams. *The Hollywood Reporter.* Retrieved from www.hollywoodreporter.com/news/who-hollywood-got-prime-seats-926404

Lewis, N., & Weaver, A. (2013). More than a game. *Communication & Sport, 3*(2), 219–242. doi:10.1177/2167479513508273

Lippmann, W. (1922). The world outside and the pictures in our heads. In *Public opinion* (pp. 3–32). New York, NY: MacMillan Co.

Los Angeles Rams. (2016, January 15). We are proud to announce that LA's Original Team is back. Facebook post. Retrieved from www.facebook.com/Rams/videos/10154452441043484/

Los Angeles Rams coach Jeff Fisher fired. (n.d.). *Los Angeles Times.* Retrieved from www.latimes.com/sports/rams/92112209-132.html

Los Angeles Rams history. (n.d.). *TheRams.com.* Retrieved from www.therams.com/team/history.html

Los Angeles Rams introductory press conference. (2016, January 15). *TheRams.com.* Retrieved from www.therams.com/videos/videos/Los-Angeles-Rams-Introductory-Press-Conference/12992e79-7d81-4669-bda0-f2fbf39d3685

Master, S. (2016). A year in sport media report. *Nielsen.* Retrieved from www.nielsen.com/content/dam/corporate/us/en/reports-downloads/2017-reports/nielsen-year-in-sports-media-2016.pdf

Mather, V. (2016, January 13). December 24, 1994: Day of losses for Los Angeles, as Rams and Raiders fell. *New York Times.* Retrieved from www.nytimes.com/2016/01/14/sports/football/the-day-in-1994-that-los-angeles-lost-the-rams-raiders.html?_r=1

McCombs, M. (2005). A look at agenda-setting: Past, present and future. *Journalism Studies, 6*(4), 543–557.

McCombs, M., Shaw, D., & Weaver, D. (2014). New directions in agenda-setting theory and research. *Mass Communication and Society, 17*(6), 781–802. doi:10.1080/15205436.2014.964871

Mortensen, C. (2016, November 16). Rams to start rookie QB Jared Goff versus Dolphins. *NFL.com.* Retrieved from www.espn.com/nfl/story/_/id/18055763/los-angeles-rams-start-rookie-qb-jared-goff

NFL attendance—2016. (n.d.). Retrieved from www.espn.com/nfl/attendance

Nielsen. (2015). *Local television market universe estimates.* New York, NY. Retrieved from www.nielsen.com/content/dam/corporate/us/en/public%20factsheets/tv/2016-local-television-market-universe-estimates.pdf

Pacheco, A. (2016, November 22). Los Angeles Rams stadium breaks ground. *The Architects Newspaper.* Retrieved from https://archpaper.com/2016/11/los-angeles-rams-stadium-breaks-ground/#gallery-0-slide-0

Pedersen, E. (2016, April 29). Jimmy Kimmel schmoozes with L.A. Rams first overall draft pick Jared Goff. *Deadline Hollywood*. Retrieved from http://deadline.com/2016/04/jared-goff-interview-video-1201746456/

Pedersen, P. (2013). *Routledge handbook of sport communication*. London: Routledge.

Plaschke, B. (2016, December 11). Rams' return to L.A. is officially an embarrassment: Coach Jeff Fisher needs to go—now. *Los Angeles Times*. Retrieved from www.latimes.com/sports/la-sp-rams-falcons-plaschke-20161211-story.html

Plaschke, B. (2017, January 17). Rams already winning the perception fight with their new roommate. *Los Angeles Times*. Retrieved from www.latimes.com/sports/la-sp-rams-chargers-plaschke-20170112-story.html

Pro Football Reference 1994 Attendance Data. (n.d.). Retrieved from www.pro-football-reference.com/years/1994/attendance.htm

Quan, D. (2016, May 10). LA Rams surprise high school football team with equipment donation. *Los Angeles Daily News*. Retrieved from www.dailynews.com/sports/20160510/la-rams-surprise-high-school-football-team-with-equipment-donation

Rams file for relocation. (2016, January 4). *TheRams.com*. Retrieved from www.therams.com/news-and-events/article-1/Rams-File-for-Relocation/436f56d8-b5c0-4e0a-a3b2-a8bf22408c30

Rams Inglewood playground build. (2016, June 22). *TheRams.com*. Retrieved from www.therams.com/videos/videos/Rams-Inglewood-Playground-Build/705db689-215b-4835-8277-4dff1de5a479

Rams to return to Los Angeles. (2016, January 12). *Rams.com*. Retrieved from www.therams.com/news-and-events/article-1/Rams-to-Return-to-Los-Angeles/802b4e16-671e-4864-97b6-943115cdc4cf

Reilley, M. (1994, December 25). St. Louis doesn't seem too bad after mistakes put an exclamation point on 4–12 season. *Los Angeles Times*. Retrieved from http://articles.latimes.com/1994-12-25/sports/sp-12919_1_washington-redskins

Ruiz, S. (2016, November 29). A simple guide to the Jeff Fisher-Eric Dickerson feud. *USA Today*. Retrieved from http://ftw.usatoday.com/2016/11/jeff-fisher-eric-dickerson-sideline-ban-fight-feud-los-angeles-rams-nfl

Schultz, B., & Sheffer, M. (2010). An exploratory study of how Twitter is affecting sports journalism. *International Journal of Sport Communication, 3*(2), 226–239.

Scott, A. J. (1996). The craft, fashion, and cultural-products industries of Los Angeles: Competitive dynamics and policy dilemmas in a multisectoral image-producing complex. *Annals of the Association of American Geographers, 86*(2), 306–323.

Suter, L. (2016, January 9). Hundreds rally outside LA Memorial Coliseum to bring Rams back. *ABC7.com*. Retrieved from http://abc7.com/sports/hundreds-rally-outside-la-memorial-coliseum-to-bring-rams-back/1152995/

Tankard, J. (2001). The empirical approach to the study of media framing. In S. Reese, O. Gandy, Jr., & A. Grant (Eds.), *Framing public life: Perspectives on media and our understanding of the social world* (pp. 95–106). London: Routledge.

Thiry, L. (2016, September 6). Hard Knocks ends with hard realities for some Rams. *Los Angeles Times*. Retrieved from www.latimes.com/sports/rams/la-sp-rams-hard-knocks-20160906-snap-story.html

Wang, J. (2016, July 12). Rams sell out of season tickets in six hours. *Los Angeles Daily News*. Retrieved from www.dailynews.com/sports/20160712/rams-sell-out-of-season-tickets-in-six-hours

Zaharopoulos, T. (2007). The news framing of the 2004 Olympic games. *Mass Communication and Society, 10*(2), 235–249. doi:10.1080/15205430701265752

Section II

Corporate and Organizational Identity

6   Should the Team Hire the Controversial but Successful Head Coach?

A Case Study of John Calipari and the Ability to Contribute to Winning

John A. Fortunato

Should a team hire a coach who has been successful but has been involved in a crisis? The career of basketball coach John Calipari makes for an exemplary case study to debate this decision. Calipari was the head coach at two universities that had their Final Four seasons vacated due to NCAA violations. His success, however, helped him become the University of Kentucky head coach, where he won a national championship. For a sports team, fans are a critical stakeholder group. The disposition theory indicates that fans may overlook a coach's past transgressions if that person has the ability to contribute to winning.

Introduction

What are the criteria when making a decision to hire a new head coach? Certainly, the person should have a proven record of success. But what if that person's career was also marred by controversy? What transgression by the coach created the crisis? Pritchard and Burton (2014) argue that sports organizations need to apply ethical assessments to their decision-making. An ethical standard might even be more important to consider in a university setting, with these organizations widely regarded as being mission-driven and grounded in core values (e.g., Ruben, De Lisi, & Gigliotti, 2017).

The head coach of the University of Kentucky men's basketball team is considered one of the most prestigious coaching jobs in the United States, with Kentucky's eight national championships only trailing UCLA. However, for four consecutive seasons Kentucky failed to get past the round of 32 in the NCAA Tournament, and in 2008–09 Kentucky failed to qualify for the NCAA Tournament for the first time in 18 years. Those results led to the hiring of John Calipari, who at that point in his collegiate coaching career had won 76% of his games. Calipari, however, was the head coach of the University of Massachusetts and University of Memphis teams that had their Final Four seasons vacated due to NCAA violations.

Reporters' descriptions of Calipari capture the complexity of a talented head coach with a controversial past. For example, Chris Dufresne of the *Los Angeles Times* wrote,

> Calipari is what he is: a slightly slick, quotable, in-your-face coach in a sometimes unsavory sport where rules are written to be exploited and/ or broken. Is Calipari a great coach? Yes. Does he have baggage? So much that he requires his own porter.
>
> (Dufresne, 2012)

The successful, but controversial, career of Calipari was also the subject of an *ESPN 30 for 30* documentary entitled *One and Not Done*, which first aired on April 13, 2017.

Principles of crisis management provide a context for debating this hiring decision. The image restoration model attributed to Benoit (1995, 2000) offers a theoretical framework that provides a series of options for an individual or organization to pursue when confronted with a crisis. Benoit emphasizes that some corrective action is a response that is highly accepted by stakeholders. Fans are a critical stakeholder group of a sports team. Fans' enjoyment of sports is motivated by seeing their favorite team win (e.g., Wenner & Gantz, 1998; Zillmann, Bryant, & Sapolsky, 1989). Thus, fans may overlook a coach's past transgressions if that person has the ability to contribute to winning.

The Case

In his 2014 book (written along with Michael Sokolove), *Players First: Coaching from the Inside Out*, John Calipari writes,

> My credo is "Players First." It drives everything I do as a coach. Notice that it's plural, not singular. Players First. We reach our personal goals by striving together toward collective goals. During the season it's all about team. After the season it's about the individual.
>
> (Calipari & Sokolove, 2014, p. 8)

Calipari was named the head basketball coach of the University of Massachusetts in 1988, taking over a program that last had a winning season in 1977–78. His first year at Massachusetts is his only losing season ever as a collegiate head coach. In the 1991–92 season Massachusetts won 30 games and qualified for the NCAA Tournament for the first time since 1962. In 1996, Massachusetts reached the Final Four before losing to eventual national champion, Kentucky. The 1995–96 Massachusetts team later had its season vacated when it was found that the team's All-American center, Marcus Camby, accepted money and gifts from an agent (Weiss, 2009). Calipari was not implicated in the Camby investigation. By the time any penalties were imposed on Massachusetts, Calipari had become the head coach of the NBA's New Jersey Nets.

After being fired in his third season with the Nets and spending one season (2000–01) as an assistant coach with the Philadelphia 76ers, Calipari was hired as the head coach at the University of Memphis. Memphis had a losing record in its previous two seasons and had not qualified for the NCAA Tournament since the 1995–96 season. In Calipari's second season, Memphis won the National Invitational Tournament (NIT), and in his third season Memphis returned to the NCAA Tournament.

The 2007–08 season was the highlight of Calipari's nine-year tenure at Memphis, as the team reached the NCAA championship game before losing in overtime to Kansas. The 2007–08 Memphis team, however, would have its season vacated when the NCAA found that the team's All-American point guard, Derrick Rose, posted a fraudulent SAT score. After failing to reach a qualifying score on three occasions, a passing score was recorded for Rose when the Chicago native supposedly took and passed the test in Detroit, one month prior to being enrolled in classes at Memphis. It was also learned that Rose's brother received $1,735 in impermissible travel and lodging. Calipari was not implicated in the Rose investigation. Memphis was placed on probation for three years and required to pay back money it received from the NCAA for its tournament success (Weiss, 2009). Chris Dufresne would retrospectively write in the *Los Angeles Times*, "Given that Memphis' appearance was later vacated by the NCAA, it was better that Kansas won" (Dufresne, 2012).

About the controversies at Massachusetts and Memphis, Calipari states, "As a head coach, you are held responsible, but it's hard to be held accountable for things you cannot have seen or known about" (Calipari & Sokolove, 2014, p. 240). Calipari would not be at Memphis by the time the NCAA's penalties were imposed. In April 2009, he became the University of Kentucky head coach.

At Kentucky, Calipari has been criticized for his recruiting practices. Calipari persuaded star players John Wall and DeMarcus Cousins, who were planning to play for him at Memphis, to attend Kentucky instead. Their acceptance placed Kentucky over the 13-scholarship limit allowed by the NCAA. Kentucky would have five players from the previous year's team not on the 2009–10 team, as they all transferred to other schools out of concern that they would not play or would lose their scholarships (Garcia, 2010). Matt Pilgrim, who transferred from Kentucky, stated in an interview broadcast on ESPN's *Outside the Lines*,

> It hurts because I feel like I abided by the rules. I did everything I was supposed to do. I went to class every day. I didn't fail any tests. For following my part of the contract, they should follow theirs.
>
> (Garcia, 2010)

The players who transferred are never mentioned in Calipari's book.

Calipari has also been questioned about his recruiting what are referred to as "one-and-done players" (Peter, 2015; Wieberg, 2012). These are student-athletes who play one year for a college team and then enter the NBA draft.

In 2005, the NBA instituted a rule in its collective bargaining agreement with the Players Association that a player must be at least 19 years of age during the calendar year of the draft and a year out of high school to enter the NBA Draft, in response to this "one and done" practice (Wieberg, 2012).

The crowning achievement for Calipari at Kentucky was winning the 2012 NCAA Tournament. About the national championship, Mike Lopresti of *USA Today* concluded his article writing, "To some an admirable national champion. To others a symbol of bad ideas. But a wonderful team, without question. And for Calipari, validation. He deserves an upgrade on his legacy, with one caveat: This Final Four better not be vacated" (Lopresti, 2012).

In his book Calipari contends,

> At Kentucky, we follow the NCAA regulations scrupulously. It's the right thing to do, whether we like all of the rules or not. I don't want my kids or program sanctioned in any way, and I am duty bound not to embarrass the university.
>
> (Calipari & Sokolove, 2014, p. 246)

Scholarly Context

Organizations interact with stakeholder groups upon whom their success or failure depends (e.g., Freeman, 1984; Lewis, 2007). Each crisis has its own unique dynamics, but it has been emphasized that stakeholders' perceptions help define an event as a crisis, help define its severity, and evaluate the organization's crisis response (e.g., Brown, Brown, & Billings, 2015; Coombs, 2015; Fortunato, 2016). In overcoming a crisis, researchers claim that when the individual or organization accepts responsibility for the act and apologizes, there is very high acceptance by stakeholders. They also emphasize that corrective action, the individual or organization implementing steps to solve the problem and prevent a repeat of the crisis, has high acceptance by stakeholders (e.g., Benoit, 1995, 2000; Coombs, 2006; Robitaille, 2011).

The effectiveness of any crisis response is mitigated by three situational variables: (1) the nature of the transgression, with the more egregious the transgression the more difficult it is for the individual or organization to overcome the crisis (e.g., Blaney, Lippert, & Smith, 2013; Brown, 2016); (2) The individual or organization's history—with Coombs (2006) explaining that history includes whether similar crises occurred in the past and how well or poorly those crises were handled; and (3) the public allegiance to the individual or organization's products or services—with Ahluwalia, Burnkrant, and Rao (2000) pointing out that public commitment to the brand is an important concept in evaluating how the individual or organization might emerge from its crisis.

It is in the notion of public allegiance where the sports fan's perspective becomes of interest in this debate. Experiencing sports has been shown to satisfy emotional needs, resulting in consistent and enduring fan behaviors, such as attending and watching games (e.g., Earnheardt, Haridakis, & Hugenberg, 2012; Wann, Schrader, & Wilson, 1999). Wenner and Gantz (1998) claim the unknown outcome of the game is the motivation that generates the most interest and drives the behavior of the sports audience. This motivation is greatly heightened when one's favorite team is playing in the game (e.g., Wenner & Gantz, 1998; Zillmann et al., 1989).

Zillmann et al. (1989) recognize the characteristic of having favorite teams and the desire to see those teams win in their disposition theory of sports fans. The disposition theory claims that enjoyment of watching sports contests and athletic excellence

> depends to some extent at least, on the particular person displaying such excellence, and on the particular team to which this person belongs. People applaud great play on the part of their favorite athletes and teams. The same excellence, the same mastery of skills, seems to be far less appreciated, possibly even deplored, when it is exhibited by disliked athletes or resented teams.
>
> (p. 256)

This fan disposition certainly extends to the head coach. Fans of Kentucky will applaud the ability of Calipari as the Wildcats coach but deplore that same ability by a coach they once cheered. For example, this is the case with the Kentucky fans' fickle reaction to Rick Pitino, the former Kentucky head coach who coached the Wildcats to a national championship but who is also the former head coach of in-state rival Louisville.

Because of their emotional satisfaction and loyalty, sports fans tend to react differently to their favorite sports league, team, or individual being involved in a crisis (e.g., Blaney, et al., 2013; Brown et al., 2015; Lee, Bang, & Lee, 2013). More than three decades ago, Kruse (1981) articulated that while it is important for athletes in crisis to repair their image, fans are more interested in the success of their favorite teams than the character of those teams' players. Fans of Kentucky will overlook Calipari's past transgressions, especially considering the Wildcats' success. The more relevant crisis for Kentucky fans at the time of the decision to hire Calipari was the lack of the team's appearance in the NCAA Tournament in 2008–09 and the team's failure to reach the Final Four since the 1997–98 season. Conversely, fans of rival universities would find Calipari's past behavior problematic. Gary Shelton of the *Tampa Bay Times* simply described Calipari as a coach who is revered by fans and "reviled by opponents" (Shelton, 2012).

This case study recognizes a gap in the crisis management literature. Until now, researchers have failed to fully consider a person's ability to contribute to winning in relation to overcoming a crisis. Many articles studying crisis in a sports context have not emphasized the ability to contribute to the team winning variable. To illustrate, Brazeal's (2008) study of NFL player Terrell Owens applied the image restoration strategies of Benoit. The crisis surrounding Owens was that, as a member of the Philadelphia Eagles, he was belligerent to his teammates, coaches, and the media, leading to his being suspended and eventually released from the team. Brazeal (2008) argues that Owens did many things wrong in his response to this crisis and did not follow the response strategies recommended in the literature. The last sentence of the article, however, points out that three days after Owens was released by the Eagles, he signed a lucrative contract with the division rival Dallas Cowboys. Not following the repair strategies recommended in the literature was not punitive for Owens because of his ability to help another team win. As for the fans' reaction, Cowboy fans who probably disliked Owens as an Eagle were no longer concerned with his past behavior because as a Cowboy he could help their team win. In contrast, Eagle fans then despised the player they once cheered only months before.

A similar assessment could be made regarding the study by Brown, Dickhaus, and Long (2012), which documents the criticism that LeBron James received after the announcement of his decision to leave the Cleveland Cavaliers and play for the Miami Heat. "The Decision" was televised on ESPN and featured an infamous quote by James: "I'm taking my talents to South Beach." While Brown et al. (2012) debate the image repair strategies that would be the most effective, the simple conclusion was that fans in Miami would think favorably of James, while fans of other teams that James did not choose, especially Cleveland, would not root for him. Of course, the fans in Cleveland gladly welcomed James back when he returned to the Cavaliers for the 2014–15 season and when he delivered the team its first NBA Championship in 2016.

You Make the Call

For John Calipari, his ability to contribute to winning outweighed his transgressions at Massachusetts and Memphis. For Calipari, success, in essence, served as his corrective action. The importance of this case study is highlighted in the number of situations involving a controversial, yet successful, player or coach being offered another opportunity following a crisis.

As an additional example, and to further generalize about the need to acknowledge the ability to contribute to winning variable, the transgression of using performance enhancing drugs has simply not been enough to derail several baseball players' careers. For example, Chris Davis of the Baltimore Orioles was suspended for 25 games for performance enhancing drug use at the end of the 2014 season, which resulted in him not being available to play for the team in the playoffs. However, in 2016, after having led the American League in home runs in 2013 and again in 2015, Davis signed a seven-year, $161 million contract to remain with the Orioles.

Not all coaches or players receive another opportunity after their crisis. For example, Mike Rice was fired from Rutgers University after a video surfaced of him throwing basketballs at players and berating them with incendiary language during practice. Rice has yet to obtain another head coaching position. Perhaps this behavior is considered too egregious for him to obtain another job, or it may be due to Rice never having a winning record while coaching at Rutgers.

Similarly, the NFL's Ray Rice was suspended when a video surfaced of him assaulting his fiancée. No team signed Rice after the incident. The video depicted the severity of the incident, and it could certainly be the nature of the transgression that has prevented Rice from receiving another opportunity. It should, however, be noted that Rice's performance before the incident declined dramatically. After 1,143 rushing yards and 9 rushing touchdowns in 2012, Rice had only 660 rushing yards and 4 rushing touchdowns in 2013—the year the incident occurred.

It must be acknowledged that all a coach or player needs is one team (or university) willing to provide another opportunity. Balancing the ability to contribute to winning and the nature of the transgression must be acknowledged in evaluating the decision to offer a player or coach that opportunity. With fan enjoyment motivated by seeing their favorite team win, the disposition theory indicates how some segments of the audience will respond. Will college basketball fans first remember John Calipari as a championship winning coach or someone who was the coach of two universities that had their Final Four seasons vacated? For fans of the University of Kentucky, research indicates the answer is probably clear.

Discussion Questions

1. How would you weigh the nature of a transgression against the previous individual success variables when hiring a head coach?
2. Identify the stakeholder groups that you need to consider when hiring a head coach. How must you customize your message to each stakeholder group in order to address any criticism that may arise from the coach's hiring?
3. What communication strategies do you suggest if the team does decide to hire a controversial head coach or signs a controversial player?
4. Should a different hiring standard be applied for universities?
5. In 2017, Rick Pitino was dismissed as the head basketball coach at the University of Louisville for alleged recruit bribery. Investigate recent cases of similar dismissals and any other developments in this ongoing issue.

References

Ahluwalia, R., Burnkrant, R. E., & Rao, U. H. (2000). Consumer response to negative publicity: The moderating role of commitment. *Journal of Marketing Research, 37*(2), 203–215.

Benoit, W. L. (1995). *Accounts, excuses, and apologies: A theory of image restoration strategies.* Albany, NY: State University of New York Press.

Benoit, W. L. (2000). Another visit to the theory of image restoration strategies. *Communication Quarterly, 48*(1), 40–44.

Blaney, J. R., Lippert, L., & Smith, S. J. (2013). *Repairing the athlete's image: Studies in sports image restoration.* Lanham, MD: Lexington Books.

Brazeal, L. M. (2008). The image repair strategies of Terrell Owens. *Public Relations Review, 34*(2), 145–150.

Brown, K. A. (2016). Is apology the best policy? An experimental examination of the effectiveness of image repair strategies during criminal and noncriminal athlete transgressions. *Communication & Sport, 4*(1), 23–42.

Brown, K. A., Dickhaus, J., & Long, M. (2012). "The Decision" and LeBron James: An empirical examination of image repair in sports. *Journal of Sports Media, 7,* 149–167.

Brown, N. A., Brown, K. A., & Billings, A. C. (2015). "May no act of ours bring shame": Fan-enacted crisis communication surrounding the Penn State sex abuse scandal. *Communication & Sport, 3*(3), 288–311.

Calipari, J., & Sokolove, M. (2014). *Players first: Coaching from the inside out.* New York, NY: The Penguin Press.

Coombs, W. T. (2006). Crisis management: A communicative approach. In C. H. Botan & V. Hazleton (Eds.), *Public relations theory II* (pp. 171–197). Mahwah, NJ: Lawrence Erlbaum Associates, Inc.

Coombs, W. T. (2015). *Ongoing crisis communication: Planning, managing and responding* (4th ed.). Thousand Oaks, CA: Sage Publications.

Dufresne, C. (2012, March 15). His babies might be sitting pretty: Kentucky has the horses again, which means this could be Calipari's year. *Los Angeles Times,* C1.

Earnheardt, A. C., Haridakis, P. M., & Hugenberg, B. S. (2012). *Sports fans, identity, and socialization: Exploring the Fandemonium.* Lanham, MD: Lexington Books.

Fortunato, J. A. (2016). The FIFA crisis: Examining sponsor response options. *Journal of Contingencies and Crisis Management, 24*(3), 1–11.

Freeman, R. E. (1984). *Strategic management: A stakeholder approach.* Boston, MA: Pitman.

Garcia, M. (2010, March 17). Kentucky turnover: Six "Cats moved on": Calipari arrived, reshaped roster. *USA Today,* 7C.

Kruse, N. (1981). Apologia in team sport. *Quarterly Journal of Speech, 67,* 270–283.

Lee, C., Bang, H., & Lee, D. (2013). Regaining fans' trust after negative incidents: Fit between responses and nature of incidents. *Sport Marketing Quarterly, 22*(4), 235–245.

Lewis, L. K. (2007). An organizational stakeholder model of change implementation communication. *Communication Theory, 17,* 176–204.

Lopresti, M. (2012, April 3). It's time for Calipari to get his due. *USA Today,* 3C.

Peter, J. (2015, March 18). Guiding greatness: Calipari's controversial style has gone against the grain but cultivated success. *USA Today,* 1C.

Pritchard, M. P., & Burton, R. (2014). Ethical failures in sport business: Directions for research. *Sport Marketing Quarterly, 23*(2), 86–99.

Robitaille, D. (2011). Making the financial case for corrective action to management. *Global Business and Organizational Excellence, 31*(1), 20–26.

Ruben, B. D., De Lisi, R., & Gigliotti, R. A. (2017). *A guide for leaders in higher education: Core concepts, competencies, and tools.* Sterling, VA: Stylus.

Shelton, G. (2012, April 3). Calipari's constant: He wins. *Tampa Bay Times,* 1C.

Wann, D. L., Schrader, M. P., & Wilson, A. M. (1999). Sport fan motivation: Questionnaire validation, comparisons by sport, and relationship to athletic motivation. *Journal of Sport Behavior, 22*(1), 114–139.

Weiss, D. (2009, August 21). Calipari whistled for 2nd foul. *New York Daily News,* 103.

Wenner, L. A., & Gantz, W. (1998). Watching sports on television: Audience experience, gender, fanship, and marriage. In L. A. Wenner (Ed.), *Mediasport* (pp. 233–251). London: Routledge.

Wieberg, S. (2012, March 9). The one-and-done king. *USA Today,* 1C.

Zillmann, D., Bryant, J., & Sapolsky, B. S. (1989). Enjoyment from sports spectatorship. In J. H. Goldstein (Ed.), *Sports, games, and play: Social and psychological viewpoints* (pp. 241–278). Hillsdale, NJ: Lawrence Erlbaum Associates, Inc.

7 To Create Our Own Legacy

Penn State Football Players' Rhetorical Response to the NCAA Sanctions During the Sandusky Scandal

Rebecca A. Alt

The Jerry Sandusky sexual abuse scandal tarnished Penn State University's reputation and stirred debates over organizational identity. Following the NCAA's announcement of sanctions, team captains Michael Zordich and Michael Mauti delivered a joint address that sought to renew Penn State football's identity. However, their address missed important opportunities for renewal. This chapter examines Zordich and Mauti's address through the lens of crisis communication and rhetoric in the tradition of public address and suggests that analyzing communication beyond official discourse from coaches, athletic directors, and university leaders is vital for understanding the nuances of crisis communication in sport.

Introduction

On July 23, 2012, Penn State football captains Michael Zordich and Michael Mauti spoke to the press and a dozen spectators after learning about the NCAA's sanctions on the program in light of FBI investigator Louis Freeh's report on the Sandusky scandal. Regarding the $60 million fine of the university, the five-year bowl ban, the reduction of scholarships, and the relaxation of transfer restrictions, Michael Mauti said "We take this as an opportunity to create our own legacy . . . no sanction, no politician is ever going to take away what we got here." Though the Sandusky scandal era at Penn State featured a wide range of official and unofficial crisis communication, the purpose of this case study is to explore the unsanctioned, spontaneous response to the NCAA's "unprecedented" punishment in order to illustrate the nuances of organizational crisis communication in sport. For Penn State, the football sanctions were seen as a crisis within a broader crisis—for better or worse.

Much of the research on the Sandusky scandal has focused on official image management messages (Formentin, Bortree, & Fraustino, 2017; Meân, 2014). This case study, however, demonstrates the value of examining communication from a different set of organizational members during Penn State's macro and micro crises: Penn State football players. This chapter explores the following questions: How, if at all, did Michael Zordich and Michael

Mauti's spontaneous statement (1) address the particular rhetorical situation following the announcement of NCAA sanctions and (2) communicate a discourse of renewal—rather than image restoration or apologia—for Penn State football's organizational identity in the wake of the Sandusky scandal?

Background

Organizational Identity

Penn State has been called "Happy Valley" due to its campus folklore and traditions, many of which revolved around football (Foley, 2015). As a big-time, National Collegiate Athletics Association (NCAA) Division I member university, Penn State football games are often televised and played in front of crowds of 100,000 in Beaver Stadium. "We Are . . . Penn State!" is both a uni-fying cheer (Prato, 2011; Shea, 2015) and a very clear articulation of identity and pride. As Mael and Ashforth (1992) explain, organizational identification can be understood as "the perception of oneness with or belongingness to an organization" (p. 104). Members of the Penn State community—students, faculty, staff, residents, fans—identified with organizational values such as "Success with Honor," which was an expression of former coach Joe Pater-no's "Grand Experiment" (Bernstein, 1968; Stuetz, 2015). Penn State football was lauded for being a leader in collegiate sports since the program had no major NCAA infractions before the Sandusky scandal.

Essential Scandal Timeline and Rhetorical Situation

On November 4, 2011, a Pennsylvania grand jury indicted several of Penn State's highest officials (Washington Post, 2011). Former assistant football coach Jerry Sandusky was charged with sexually abusing young boys, using Penn State athletic facilities, for over a decade (Chappell, 2012). Former Penn State University president Graham Spanier, athletic director Tim Curley, and chief of police Gary Schultz were also indicted on charges of perjury in rela-tion to the case (Orso, 2011). As of June 2017, some of these officials are finally serving sentences (Hobson, 2017). Joe Paterno's role in the case con-tinues to be questioned. Media and public discourses portrayed Penn State as plagued by blind "football worship" (Mandel, 2011; Oliphant, 2012; Staples, 2011), which then stirred a debate over Penn State's organizational identity and culture both within and outside of the community.

Then, on November 8, 2011, the Penn State Board of Trustees (BOT) addressed the public after a special meeting. The BOT announced the ter-mination of both Graham Spanier and Joe Paterno. BOT vice chairman John Surma remarked that these actions were needed in order for the uni-versity to maintain a level of integrity that would satisfy the public as well as stakeholders of the institution (PSUComRadio, 2011). Additionally, Surma announced the launch of an investigation into the case. Former FBI director

Louis Freeh conducted an independent investigation of the case, and his report was released in July 2012 (Freeh, 2012). The Freeh Report concluded that Penn State administrators did not do enough to protect innocent children from Jerry Sandusky and implied that the horrific crimes *were* the result of a collegiate football culture gone awry.

Upon release of the Freeh Report, the NCAA imposed harsh penalties on the program (Hanson & Libermann, 2012; Kane, 2012). NCAA president Mark Emmert justified the sanctions by echoing the findings of the Freeh Report regarding Penn State's culture (ESPN, 2012). The sanctions included a $60 million fine, a five-year bowl ban, vacated wins, the reduction of scholarships, and the ability for any player to leave Penn State and begin playing for another university immediately (NCAA, n.d.; Stuetz, 2015). The Penn State football team—embedded within the broader organizational community—was experiencing a crisis. One foundational definition of crisis for an organization is "the perception of an unpredictable event that threatens important expectancies of stakeholders and can seriously impact an organization's performance and generate negative outcomes" (Coombs, 2012, p. 2), and the goals of a football program include achieving and maintaining cohesion and success.

The threat of not succeeding also potentially impacts the rest of the university community, since university stakeholders maintain strong emotional attachments to their alma maters and their athletic teams (Len-Rios, 2010, p. 269). As Len-Rios (2010) explains, "when a university is faced with a crisis, there is the potential that [the crisis] may affect its relationships with current students, alumni, parents, prospective students, donors, staff, faculty, residents of the local community, sports team fans, and advisory boards" (p. 269). In light of the sanctions and their material and symbolic consequences, national media pronounced Penn State football dead: Sports journalists interpreted the sanctions as being more "deathly" than the "Death Penalty" (Levy, 2012; Yanda, 2012), and the July 2012 *Sports Illustrated* cover page read in bold letters, "We Were Penn State" (Sports Illustrated, 2012). The sanctions represented a crisis within the larger crisis of the Sandusky scandal.

Scholars have written about the Sandusky scandal as a moment of organizational crisis for Penn State. For example, studies have analyzed Penn State's messaging from the perspectives of fan-enacted crisis communication (Brown, Brown, & Billings, 2015); white patriarchy and power at Penn State (Giardina & Denzin, 2012); language and ethics (Lucas & Fyke, 2014); intergroup identity (Alderfer, 2013; Grandey, Krannitz, & Slezak, 2013); and image management (Meân, 2014; Formentin et al., 2017). Though the lens of image management, specifically the typologies theorized by Coombs (1998, 2012) and Benoit (1995, 1997), is useful, it does not adequately capture or explain the nuanced discourse of this complex case involving multiple, sometimes competing, discourses within communities. Further, from a textual fragments perspective of rhetoric (McGee, 1990), an organization's official statement is only one part "of an arrangement that includes all facts, events, texts, and stylized expressions" (p. 279). Whereas official, administrative discourses focused on apologia, blame, cause, and consequence, unofficial discourses, such as the statement this case study will examine from Zordich and Mauti, had a decidedly different tone and focus.

Theoretical Content

Zordich and Mauti's address is not quite image restoration; rather it is closer to discourse of renewal. As Seeger and Griffin Padgett (2010) explain, image restoration typically focuses on issues of wrongdoing, accusations of responsibility, and questions about cause, blame, and accountability (p. 133). However, if we replace "restoration" with "recreation," as Burns and Bruner (2000) suggest (p. 30), we get closer. The discourse of renewal framework is salient where wrongdoing is not the primary or most salient exigence addressed. Instead of assessing blame or cause, organizational members "must also generate support for rebuilding and rejuvenating" relationships and community (Seeger & Griffin Padgett, 2010, p. 134).

There are four main characteristics of discourse of renewal. First, it is prospective, in that "it describes activities related to future goals, recovery efforts, and development, as opposed to retrospectively seeking to explain, justify or interpret what happened in the past" (Seeger & Griffin Padgett, 2010, p. 136). Second, discourse of renewal recognizes the opportunities inherent in a crisis, such as establishing new relationships and learning (Littlefield, Reierson, Cowden, Stowman, & Long Feather, 2009). Third, renewal discourse is a provisional rather than strategic response; it is organic and based in organizational leaders' "natural instinct to reconstitute order" and move beyond the crisis instead of a response that follows a strict communication plan (Seeger & Griffin Padgett, 2010, p. 137; Ulmer, Seeger, & Sellnow, 2007, p. 131). Finally, discourse of renewal is characterized by ethical communication grounded in core values to demonstrate a "commitment, or recommitment, to the community" (Littlefield et al., 2009; Seeger & Griffin Padgett, 2010; Seeger & Griffin Padgett, 2010; Seeger & Ulmer, 2002; Ulmer & Sellnow, 2002). The discourse of renewal reflects what rhetorical scholar Bitzer (1968) termed the "fitting response" to a rhetorical situation, which involves a specific exigence, audience, and constraints (p. 6). This fitting response must meet the requirements dictated by the situation, such as "the purpose, theme, matter, and style of the response" (Bitzer, 1968, p. 10).

The Case

Penn State football captains Michael Zordich and Michael Mauti delivered their remarks in front of a small crowd outside of the Lasch Football Building on Penn State's campus (full transcript available in the appendix). Their statement followed NCAA president Mark Emmert's announcement of sanctions, which threatened the team's cohesion and success. Thus, this response went beyond "the parameters of image restoration to address the communication exigencies associated with rebuilding, recovery, and revitalization" (Seeger & Griffin Padgett, 2010, pp. 132–133). Their statement captured the prospective focus of a discourse of renewal. Importantly, because their address was responding specifically to the sanctions—and not the larger scandal implicating the university community as a whole—rebuilding, recovery, and revitalization must be taken to mean "of the football program." Though this goal was far from the most pressing exigence of the controversy, it was, for many stakeholders, considered urgent. Their statement was also a provisional, rather than strategic, response. It is clear from the syntax that these remarks were neither planned nor rehearsed.

Though the players implicitly referenced both Sandusky and Paterno ("this program was not built by one man, and this program is sure as hell not going to get torn down by one man"), their statement centered on framing the sanctions in a positive, prospective way. This change of perspective— from a negative outlook to a positive outlook—is very important after an organization experiences a crisis (Paquette, 2015). Zordich and Mauti both emphasize the opportunity that was placed before them, reframing the crisis as good for Penn State Football:

> As a team, we don't see this as a punishment, this is an opportunity. This is the greatest opportunity a Penn Stater could ever be given. We have an obligation to Penn State, and we have the ability to fight for not just a team—not just a program—but an entire university and every man that wore the blue and white. We are going to embrace this opportunity, and we're going to make something very special happen in 2012.

Implied in this quotation is the sentiment that rather than focusing on the severity of the sanctions, the most important opportunity was to demonstrate that the current players and coaches were good people who played with honor and integrity and love for their university and community. Mauti defined Penn State Football as "every alumni, every single player that came before us, built on their backs," and sought to differentiate between the current team members, past team members, and the likes of Jerry Sandusky and other university leaders' ethical failings. Mauti emphasized the inherent opportunities in light of the sanctions when he said, "we take this as an opportunity to create our own legacy," implicitly harkening to the "old" legacy of Penn State Football that was so strongly intertwined and tangled with Paterno and Sandusky. Whereas some in the Penn State community quickly disidentified with Paterno and the football program altogether, and others clung tightly to that legacy, Zordich and Mauti expressed the desire to blaze an alternate path; post-Paterno, the organization's identity needed to be redefined and renewed:

> No sanction, no politician is ever going to take away what we got here. No, none of that is ever gonna tear us apart. We're gonna fight for Penn

State, we're gonna fight for each other, cause this is what Penn State's about—fighting through adversity, and we're gonna show up every Saturday and we're gonna raise hell.

Zordich and Mauti attempt to reaffirm a positive Penn State football identity, emphasize perseverance and corrective action in the ways possible for the team, and call for support from those who identify with the organization. Zordich later says, "We're gonna do everything in our power to make [teammates, fans, students, and families in Nittany Nation] proud, and do everything in our power to get this place back on track." This statement is focused on future goals and the opportunities presented to the team by the sanctions.

Zordich and Mauti also emphasize unity. The captains repeatedly appeal to the essence of the Penn State identity. Phrases like "we know what we're made of . . . we know what our coaches are made of, and we know what the university is made of, and we're ready and willing to fight and stick together to see this thing through to the end" reveal the players' commitment to and pride in the university. What Penn State football "is made of" can only be inferred, but it is likely—through enthymematic reasoning (Bitzer, 1959)—that the captains were speaking to characteristics like strength and perseverance in times of crisis. Zordich emphasized this call for support:

I'm personally calling out every member of Nittany Nation, all the students, faculty, fans, and family members, alumni, everybody that [sic] there is please, please come support us through this because we need you just as much as you need us, and together we're gonna get through this thing to the end.

You Make the Call

After Mark Emmert announced the NCAA's sanctions, coaches from other universities swarmed Happy Valley to "poach" Penn State players (Stuetz, 2015). However, there was no mass exodus, "despite every person on the roster being allowed to leave without penalty" (Fischer, 2012). Eleven players did transfer (Petrella, 2013), but the core of the team remained intact. Over the next five years, the NCAA ultimately relaxed some of the sanctions due to Penn State's "good behavior" (Solomon, 2014), and then in 2016 Penn State football won the Big Ten Championship and took a trip to the Rose Bowl. Many Penn State fans and media commentators mentioned the perseverance of the 2012 team led by Zordich and Mauti—some freshmen from that year were playing in 2016. Zordich and Mauti were cited as important leaders in the transition or renewal of Penn State football. That, of course, implies some causation between Zordich and Mauti's communication and the re-imagining of the Penn State football "brand"—a link that cannot be definitively made. Their statement, however, is a clear example of some successes as well as missed opportunities.

The discourse of renewal framework is not a perfect fit. For example, their statement lacked the fourth element of discourse of renewal (ethical communication grounded in core values). Given the gravity of the Sandusky scandal, players might have articulated broader values guiding the university and its football team beyond the pride that was scrutinized in the wake of the scandal. However, their subject position as young twenty-somethings speaking spontaneously in response to their specific exigence must also be considered when judging their discourse. Further, as Paquette (2015) explained, it is *how* change is communicated that can provide for renewal, healing, and "increased social legitimacy" (p. 348). The aggressive tenor of the statement ("We're gonna raise hell"), as well as ignoring the broader and horrific details of the scandal—and possibly irrelevant to some audiences—can certainly be seen as tone deaf.

Zordich and Mauti's communication was one tile of the larger rhetorical mosaic of the Sandusky scandal. Their statement was more provisional and less strategic than official discourses from the administration. It focused on the substance of the team as a symbol of community strength. Penn State administrators, in contrast, attempted to rhetorically transcend the football program, since it enabled such heinous abuse and unchecked power, and instead appeal to the broader Penn State community values and ethical concerns. This case illustrates the importance of studying the many discourses in a crisis situation and reconsidering our understanding of organizational rhetoric, echoing a call made by Liu and Fraustino (2014, p. 545). Whereas this address functions to reinforce the potential good of Penn State football, it also illustrates enduring rhetorical problems of big-time sport.

Discussion Questions

1. Imagine you had the opportunity to coach captains Mauti and Zordich on their message before they delivered their remarks. Given what you know about communication principles and practices, as well as this particular case and its exigencies, what advice would you give and why?

2. Do you think that the PSU players' communication was effective at envisioning a positive outcome for the future of Penn State football according to the theory of discourse of renewal? What about Penn State University generally? Was their statement a "fitting response," according to Bitzer's (1968) definition?

3. Take a look at the full transcript and think about this case as a whole. What communicative opportunities were missed?

4. When Zordich says, "We're gonna do everything in our power to make [teammates, fans, students, and families in Nittany Nation] proud, and do everything in our power to get this place back on track," what do you think he means? Discuss the potential and limitations of this claim.

5. Discuss any new developments in the Penn State case or other similar cases that contribute to this ongoing issue. What has occurred lately to impact the tenor of the conversation?

References

Alderfer, C. P. (2013). Not just football: An intergroup perspective on the Sandusky scandal at Penn State. *Industrial and Organizational Psychology, 6*, 117–133. doi:10.1111/iops.12022

Benoit, W. L. (1995). Sears' repair of its auto service image: Image restoration discourse in the corporate sector. *Communication Studies, 46*, 89–105. http://dx.doi.org/10.1080/10510979509368441

Benoit, W. L. (1997). Image repair discourse and crisis communication. *Public Relations Review, 23*(2), 177–186. https://doi.org/10.1016/S0363-8111(97)90023-0

Bernstein, R. (1968, November 20). "Grand Experiment" paying off for Joe Paterno and unbeaten team. *Gettysburg Times* (Sports). Retrieved from www.newspapers.com/newspage/46010015/

Bitzer, L. F. (1959). Aristotle's enthymeme revisited. *Quarterly Journal of Speech, 45*(4), 399–408. http://dx.doi.org/10.1080/00335635909382374

Bitzer, L. F. (1968). The Rhetorical Situation. *Philosophy and Rhetoric, 1*(1), 1–14. Retrieved from www.jstor.org/stable/40237697

Brown, N. A., Brown, K. A., & Billings, A. C. (2015). "May no act of ours bring shame": Fan-enacted crisis communication surrounding the Penn State sex abuse scandal. *Communication & Sport, 3*(3), 288–311. https://doi.org/10.1177/2167479513514387

Burns, J. P., & Bruner, M. S. (2000). Revisiting the theory of image restoration strategies. *Communication Quarterly, 48*, 27–38. http://dx.doi.org/10.1080/01463370009385577

Chappell, B. (2012, June 21). Penn State abuse scandal: A guide and timeline. *NPR*. Retrieved from www.npr.org/2011/11/08/142111804/penn-state-abuse-scandal-a-guide-and-timeline

Coombs, W. T. (1998). An analytic framework for crisis situations: Better responses from a better understanding of the situation. *Journal of Public Relations Research, 10*(3), 177–191. http://dx.doi.org/10.1207/s1532754xjprr1003_02

Coombs, W. T. (2012). *Ongoing crisis communication: Planning, managing, and responding* (2nd ed.). Thousand Oaks, CA: Sage Publications.

ESPN. (2012, July 23). NCAA announces PSU sanctions. *YouTube*. Retrieved from www.youtube.com/watch?v=VxlzH65ywtg

Fischer, B. (2012, August 3). Penn State transfer list. *CBSSports.com*. Retrieved from www.cbssports.com/college-football/news/penn-state-transfer-list/

Foley, A. (2015). Penn State history lesson: The origins of "Happy Valley". *Onward State*. Retrieved from http://onwardstate.com/2015/08/25/penn-state-history-lesson-the-origins-of-happy-valley/

Formentin, M., Bortree, D., & Fraustino, J. (2017). Navigating anger in happy valley: Analyzing Penn State's Facebook-based crisis responses to the Sandusky scandal. *Public Relations Review, 43*(4), 671–679. doi:10.1016/j.pubrev.2017.06.005

Freeh, L. (2012). *The Freeh report on Pennsylvania State University*. Retrieved from www.philly.com/philly/news/special_packages/162218515.html

Giardina, M. D., & Denzin, N. K. (2012). Policing the "Penn State Crisis": Violence, power, and the neoliberal university. *Critical Studies ⇔ Cultural Methodologies, 12*(4), 259–266. https://doi.org/10.1177/1532708612446418

Grandey, A., Krannitz, M. A., & Slezak, T. (2013). We are . . . more than football: Three stories of identity threat by Penn State insiders. *Industrial and Organizational Psychology, 6*, 134–155. doi:10.1111/iops.12023

Hanson, T., & Libermann, O. (2012, July 23). NCAA announces unprecedented sanctions against Penn State. *CBS Philly* (Philadelphia, PA). Retrieved from http://

philadelphia.cbslocal.com/2012/07/23/penn-state-community-awaits-ncaa-decision-on-football-program/

Hobson, W. (2017, June 2). Former Penn State president Graham Spanier sentenced to jail for child endangerment in Jerry Sandusky abuse case. *The Washington Post.* Retrieved from www.washingtonpost.com/news/sports/wp/2017/06/02/former-penn-state-president-graham-spanier-sentenced-to-jail-for-child-endangerment-in-jerry-sandusky-abuse-case/?utm_term=.bcef4a03c36c

Kane, C. (2012, July 23). NCAA punishes Penn State. *Chicago Tribune.* Retrieved from http://articles.chicagotribune.com/2012-07-23/sports/ct-spt-0724-penn-state-20120724_1_david-joyner-penn-state-ncaa-president

Len-Rios, M. E. (2010). Image repair strategies, local news portrayals and crisis stage: A case study of Duke University's lacrosse team crisis. *International Journal of Strategic Communication, 4*(4), 267–287. doi:10.1080/1553118X.2010.515534

Levy, D. (2012, July 23). Penn State scandal: NCAA smacks Happy Valley with "Death by Attrition" penalty. *Bleacher Report.* Retrieved from http://bleacherreport.com/articles/1268766-penn-state-scandal-ncaa-smacks-happy-valley-with-death-by-attrition-penalty

Littlefield, R. S., Reierson, J., Cowden, K., Stowman, S., & Long Feather, C. (2009). A case study of the Red Lake, Minnesota school shooting: Intercultural learning in the renewal process. *Communication, Culture & Critique, 2,* 361–383. doi:10.1111=j.1753-9137.2009.01043.x

Liu, B., & Fraustino, J. (2014). Beyond image repair: Suggestions for crisis communication theory development. *Public Relations Review, 40*(3), 543–546. doi:10.1016/j.pubrev.2014.04.004.

Lucas, K., & Fyke, J. P. (2014). Euphemisms and ethics: A language-centered analysis of Penn State's sexual abuse scandal. *Journal of Business Ethics, 122*(4), 551–569. doi:10.1007/s10551-013-1777-0

Mael, F., & Ashforth, B. E. (1992). Alumni and their alma mater: A partial test of the reformulated model of organizational identification. *Journal of Organizational Behavior, 13*(2), 103–123. doi:10.1002/job.4030130202

Mandel, S. (2011, November 11). Penn State tragedy shows danger of making coaches false idols. *Sports Illustrated>Inside College Football.* Retrieved from http://sportsillustrated.cnn.com/2011/writers/stewart_mandel/11/11/penn-state-joe-paterno-culture/index.html

McGee, M. C. (1990). Text, context, and the fragmentation of contemporary culture. *Western Journal of Speech Communication, 54,* 274–289. http://dx.doi.org/10.1080/10570319009374343

Meân, L. J. (2014). Managing ideologies and identities: Reporting the Penn State scandal. In B. Brummett & A. W. Ishak (Eds.), *Sports and identity: New agendas in communication.* New York, NY: Routledge.

National Collegiate Athletics Association. (n.d.). *Want to transfer?* Retrieved from www.ncaa.org/student-athletes/current/want-transfer

Oliphant, P. (2012, July 25). NCAA punishes Penn State. *Universal Press Syndicate.* Retrieved from http://thecomicnews.com/edtoons/2012/0725/pennstate/01.php

Orso, A. (2011, November 7). Sandusky charged with sex abuse: Curley, Schultz, charged with perjury. *The Daily Collegian* (State College, PA). Retrieved from www.collegian.psu.edu/archives/article_5a47a2be-3cfc-5866-94f0-7ebf2c1d250c.html

Paquette, M. (2015). Renewal or re-entrenchment? A case study of 2011 education union crisis. *Journal of Public Relations Research, 27*(4), 337–352. http://dx.doi.org/10.1080/1062726X.2015.1060130

Pennsylvania Grand Jury Report. Retrieved from www.washingtonpost.com/wp-srv/sports/documents/sandusky-grand-jury-report11052011.html

Petrella, S. (2013, September 26). Penn State football transfers: Where are they now? A look at those who left post-sanctions. *The Daily Collegian* (State College, PA). Retrieved from www.collegian.psu.edu/football/article_c8248c48-26ec-11e3-92ce-001a4bcf6878.html

Prato, L. (2011). We are . . . . cheer was years in the making. *StateCollege.com*. Retrieved from www.statecollege.com/news/columns/lou-prato-we-are-cheer-was-years-in-the-making,970985/?_ga=2.216512468.337298799.1497446986-1602099381.1495588650

PSUComRadio. (2011, November 9). *Joe Paterno Fired Press conference* [Video file]. Retrieved from www.youtube.com/watch?v=pt6d-WqIFvM

Seeger, M. W., & Griffin Padgett, D. R. (2010). From image restoration to renewal: Approaches to understanding postcrisis communication. *The Review of Communication*, *10*(2), 127–141. http://dx.doi.org/10.1080/15358590903545263

Seeger, M. W., & Ulmer, R. (2002). A post-crisis discourse of renewal: The cases of Malden Mills and Cole Hardwoods. *Journal of Applied Communication Research, 30*, 126–142. doi:10.1080=00909880216578

Shea, D. (2015). The true origins of "We Are Penn State". *Onward State*. Retrieved from http://onwardstate.com/2015/09/25/the-true-origin-of-we-are-penn-state/

Solomon, J. (2014, September 8). Mitchell report helps Penn State become bowl eligible. *CBS Sports*. Retrieved from www.cbssports.com/college-football/news/mitchell-report-helps-penn-state-become-bowl-eligible/

Sports Illustrated Covers. (2012). Retrieved from http://assets.sbnation.com/assets/1252765/image006.jpg; http://onwardstate.com/wp-content/uploads/2012/10/sports-illustrated-penn-state-cover.jpeg

Staples, A. (2011, November 10). Penn State finally puts university ahead of football by firing Paterno. *Sports Illustrated>Inside College Football*. Retrieved from http://sportsillustrated.cnn.com/2011/writers/andy_staples/11/10/joe.paterno.fired.penn.state/index.html

Stuetz, J. (2015, May 8). Surviving the sanctions: Inside the tumultuous journey of Penn State's seniors. *Bleacher Report*. Retrieved from http://bleacherreport.com/articles/2455526-surviving-the-sanctions-inside-the-tumultuous-journey-of-penn-states-seniors

Ulmer, R. R., Seeger, M. W., & Sellnow, T. L. (2007). Post-crisis communication and renewal: Expanding the parameters of post-crisis discourse. *Public Relations Review*, *33*(2), 130–134. doi:10.1016/j.pubrev.2006.11.015

Ulmer, R. R., & Sellnow, T. L. (2002). Crisis management and the discourse of renewal: Understanding the potential for positive outcomes of crisis. *Public Relations Review, 28*, 361–365. https://doi.org/10.1016/S0363-8111(02)00165-0

Washington Post (2011). *Jerry Sandusky grand jury report*. http://www.washingtonpost.com/wp-srv/sports/documents/sandusky-grand-jury-report11052011.html

Yanda, S. (2012, July 23). Penn State football punished by NCAA over Sandusky scandal. *The Washington Post*. Retrieved from www.washingtonpost.com/sports/penn-state-football-punished-by-ncaa-over-sandusky-scandal/2012/07/23/gJQAGNeM4W_story.html?utm_term=.ec914ef1ad45

Zordich, M., & Mauti, M. (2012, July 23). Address. Retrieved from www.youtube.com/watch?v=EKNhjTrU5ac&t=1s

Appendix
Transcript of the Full Statement

MICHAEL ZORDICH: We want to let the nation know that we're proud of who we are, you know, we're the true Penn Staters, you know. We're gonna stick together through this, we're gonna see this thing through, and we're gonna do everything we can for our university. We know it's not going to be easy, but um, you know, we know what we're made of, we know that through this grind there's gonna be tough times ahead, but we know what our coaches are made of and we know what the university is made of, and we're ready and willing to fight and stick together to see this thing through the end, you know. As a team, we don't see this as a punishment, this is an opportunity. This is the greatest opportunity a Penn Stater could be given. We have an obligation to Penn State, and we have the ability to fight for, not just a team—not just a program—but an entire university and every man that wore the blue and white on that gridiron before us. We are going to embrace this opportunity, and we're going to make something very special happen in 2012.

MICHAEL MAUTI: Yeah, that's right. We take this as an opportunity to create our own legacy. This program was not built by one man, and this program is sure as hell not going to get torn down by one man. This program was built on every alumni, every single player that came before us, built on their backs, and we're going to take that right now; this is our opportunity to do that.

ZORDICH: `You know, when we go out there every Saturday and suit up, for our teammates, first of all, but second of all, it's for the fans, students, and all the families in Nittany Nation that support us through all this, and you know, we're gonna do everything in our power to make them proud, and do everything in our power to get this place back on track, but I'm personally calling out every member of Nittany Nation—all the students, faculty, fans, and family members, alumni, everybody that there is—please, please come support us through this because we need you just as much as you need us, and together we're gonna get through this thing to the end.

MAUTI: Yeah, no sanction, no politician is ever going to take away what we got here. No, none of that is ever gonna tear us apart. Right now all we can do, we can put our heads down, and we're just going to work. That's all we can do. We're gonna fight for Penn State, we're gonna fight for each other, cause this is what Penn State's about: fighting through adversity, and we're gonna show up every Saturday and we're gonna raise hell.

ZORDICH: Thanks for coming out.

MAUTI: Thanks for coming out.

8   Life After Signing

The Recruiting Process as a Resource of College Football Players' Socialization

Gregory A. Cranmer, Richard Yeargin, &
John S. W. Spinda

Athletic recruiting is overlooked as a socialization process that shapes how student-athletes transition into college. This case study is composed of interviews with 15 Division I football players at a southeastern university that plays in a Power Five conference and focuses on the players' recruitment and subsequent adjustment in college. The results revealed that student-athletes were provided with information that failed to address daily commitments of athletics, the importance of academics, and the detriments of being a public figure. When this information failed to prepare student-athletes, they turned to faith, family, teammates, or an athletic department staffer for support and guidance.

Introduction

The transition from high school to collegiate athletics is one of the most difficult in an athlete's career (Wylleman & Lavallee, 2004). Division I student-athletes often arrive on campuses ill-prepared for the realities that await them (Gerdy, 1997). These student-athletes must adjust to increases in competition, role instability, and demands on their time, all while maintaining their grades and an appropriate public image to participate in collegiate athletics. It is, therefore, crucial to understand student-athletes' preparation for their collegiate careers (i.e., *anticipatory socialization*). It is during this time that student-athletes form expectations, attitudes, and motivations regarding their future, which influences their subsequent collegiate experiences (Cranmer, 2017; Cranmer & Myers, 2017).

A salient aspect of student-athletes' anticipatory socialization into their teams is the recruiting process that they endure. No recruiting process has garnered as much attention within public discourse as that of college football. The salience of collegiate football recruiting is evident in the proliferation of recruiting websites (e.g., Scout.com) and ranking systems (e.g., ESPN300), the streaming of student-athletes signing their letters of intent, and the extravagant events that celebrate signing day (e.g., Michigan's "Signing of the Stars"). Although the acquisition of talented players by universities is often a focal point, the role of recruiting in a student-athlete's transition into college is almost always overlooked. This case study examines how interactions and messages communicated during the recruiting process may prepare student-athletes to become well-acclimated students and members of their teams and communities.

Background

Collegiate football recruiting begins when coaches scour the country for promising teenagers (some as young as 13 years old) who may eventually contribute to their teams. The effort to identify young talent is often centered on regional and national sport camps or combines (e.g., Elite 11 regional camps). However, the recruitment process also includes coaches attending games and visiting homes, athletes making official and unofficial visits to universities, and lots of communication via telephone, social media, and traditional mail.

Recruiting research has focused on student-athletes' selection of a university. A range of features, including the value of scholarships, past performances, relationships with coaches, athletic facilities, academic opportunities, location, and atmosphere on campuses, contribute to student-athletes' selection of a university (Doyle & Gaeth, 1990; Klenosky, Templin, & Troutman, 2001; Magnusen, Kim, Perrewe, & Ferris, 2014; Schneider & Messenger, 2012). The importance of these features differs by sport, but football players prioritize potential athletic achievement, coaching staffs, and perceived future enjoyment in being a team member when selecting a college (Klenosky et al., 2001). Understanding the selection process is of importance to scholars and practitioners because recruiting elite athletes (based on rating systems) can predict as much as 80% of a football team's success (Caro, 2012). The desire to win can result in unethical behaviors (e.g., the provision of drugs, alcohol, sex, or payments to recruits; Perrelle, 2008) or admonishing other universities in an attempt to obtain the best talent (Fondren, 2010).

The aforementioned literature deems recruiting successful provided student-athletes select one's school. However, the existing literature provides little insight into what happens after student-athletes sign their letters of intent (Magnusen et al., 2014). Recruiting should provide teams and student-athletes the opportunity to assess their mutual fit and interest. For it is during recruiting that student-athletes gain first-hand knowledge of the workings of a football program (Fondren, 2010). Thus, recruiting serves as a foundation on which student-athletes' expectations and attitudes for college will be based. Student-athletes are highly coveted and often promised organizational realities that cannot readily be achieved (Gerdy, 1997; Ornstein, 1996). According to athlete socialization literature, unrealistic expectations hinder student-athletes' adjustment to college and may lead to dissent, resistance, absenteeism, or turnover (Cranmer & Myers, 2017). These experiences should be avoided, as student-athletes are in an important stage of their social and cognitive development that will serve them throughout their lives. As such, two research questions are forwarded:

RQ1: *How does the recruiting process prepare Division I football players for their collegiate experiences?*

RQ2: *How do Division I football players respond when the recruiting process fails to inform them of collegiate experiences?*

The Case

Interviews were conducted with 15 Division I football players from a southeastern university. The players ranged in age from 18–23 ($M = 20.87$), were primarily African American (73.33%), and played eight different positions. Participants ranged from zero-to-five-star recruits via ESPN's recruiting system ($M = 3.20$) and included two walk-ons. The second author, who was a member of the football team at the time of data collection, conducted the interviews over the course of a semester. The interviews focused on what student-athletes were told during their recruitment, how this information shaped their expectations for college, and how they responded if these expectations were inaccurate. The interviews totaled 357 minutes ($M = 23.8$) and 250 double-spaced pages of text when transcribed verbatim. Promotional materials, which are mailed to student-athletes during the recruiting process, were used to supplement the data obtained from the interviews.

A thematic analysis followed, with researchers identifying consistent themes that emerged across participants' responses. The analysis was exploratory and interpretive in nature. All three researchers reviewed the data independently and then discussed emergent themes until reaching a consensus regarding the nature of those themes. These themes were supported through the process of member validation, which featured the sharing of results with participants and providing opportunities for questions, critiques, affirmation, or feedback (Tracy, 2010). Participants confirmed that the findings of this study were consistent or plausible based on their personal experiences.

Recruiting Information

The roles of student-athletes are multifaceted, and, as such, information during recruiting is often related to being an athlete, student, or community figure. Participants reported that information about being an athlete primarily addressed future playing time and role on a team. The specifics of this information varied by student-athlete. Few high-ranking players were promised significant and early playing time or were told they were future stars in the making. Those who reported receiving such information processed it with skepticism, or as one player reported:

> Every coach would paint a picture for me regarding the defense and how I would help their team out. [But], I knew the coaches were just trying to sell me the school. I didn't want to just go somewhere because of a coach. They could leave at any time.

Most participants reported receiving information that playing time and roles are never guaranteed, and that collegiate athletics is more competitive than high school:

> They said that the rankings don't matter when you get to college. And that kind of shocked me because . . . just to see coaches say that stars don't mean anything. The three stars and two stars can be the stars of the team. It interested me to know ranking is kind of just politics.

Interestingly, little information was recalled about the day-to-day tasks and roles of being an athlete (e.g., schedule, tasks). When pressed, most participants failed to recall such information being communicated to them during recruitment.

The recruiting process also involves ensuring individuals can perform successfully as students. A minority of participants reported receiving little to no information about academics (i.e., academics was not a topic of conversation during recruiting): "They never talked about school. Just make sure you get your transcript sent. That was it about academics." Another participant suggested: "A lot of schools said academics matter, but they didn't mention potential majors or tutors. They just expressed how they wanted student-athletes to stay on course and that they would talk about that later." Perhaps the lack of verbal communication about academics with participants is because recruiting materials (e.g., brochures, letters) often tout the academic prowess of universities in question and academic support staff handles those issues. Most participants, however, recalled receiving basic information about the timeline for graduation and the types of support that programs offered (e.g., tutors, study halls, equipment). Interestingly, this support was framed as a way to help student-athletes manage their schedules and keep academics from interfering with their athletic commitments. One participant reported:

> A lot of schools talked about having an open door. You can talk about whatever is going on and they'll help manage your schedule with football. Academics can be a distraction.

The prioritization of athletics over academics was evident in participants' accounts that they were encouraged to select different majors than what they originally intended, including a student-athlete who was encouraged not to pursue engineering.

Recruiting may also touch upon the role of student-athletes as public figures. Most student-athletes, although not all, reported receiving information that emphasized the elevated status that college football players have in their communities. Yet, this information solely emphasized the adoration and opportunity to gain a second home in a new community. One player recalled: "They would tell me about the family atmosphere here. About how the fans and teammate[s] would back you up. We're all a family." Few student-athletes reported receiving information about their obligations to uphold particular standards that are valued by their universities or how their lives may be adversely affected by their membership on a team. Such limited information is consistent with researcher observations that student-athletes on high-profile teams rarely understand the social implications of their team membership prior to coming to college (Gerdy, 1997).

Failed Expectations

A few student-athletes suggested that they either purposely did not set personal expectations because of skepticism toward the recruiting process or that those expectations were fully met. One participant claimed:

> I think it was 100% what I expected. You learn how to multitask and manage football with the workload. You learn to work hard. [The coaches] were super straightforward with everything, so that was helpful when I got here.

The remaining 12 of 15 participants, however, reported that some of their expectations were not met, and they struggled at points adjusting to their collegiate experiences. For instance, student-athletes commonly cited a lack of understanding of the depth and breadth of the commitments they made:

> I thought I would have more freedom and space. [Football] takes a lot of time. It is different than high school because it is year-round and you don't get breaks. It is like a job but you do not get paid. You definitely don't get the normal college experience when you play football.

Additional expectations that were unmet included the nature of athlete-coach interactions, which were found to be more aggressive than expected, and the commonality of experiencing injuries.

When expectations were not met some participants sought support and insight from a variety of sources, including families and faith to cope with the uncertainty and stress of college athletics. However, these institutions were found to offer limited prescriptive advice given their lack of understanding of the team. Teammates and athletic department employees were most identified as beneficial sources to consult. Nearly all of the participants sought counsel from a specific athletic department employee, who played for the southeastern university, was a former team captain, won a national championship during his tenure, had a lengthy professional career, and then transitioned well into the world of business. His assigned role with the team made him responsible for the personal and professional development of student-athletes. As such, the players had a high degree of trust and respect for him:

> He is someone I go to when things get frustrating or I don't know what's going on . . . . Like, if I think I should be playing more or I don't understand why coaches are treating me a particular way. He gives good advice on how to approach those types of situations. Plus, he has been there. He went through it. And now he is here for us and in a way that [goes] beyond just making sure that we play well.

These experiences may be akin to new organizational members relying on organizational heroes or veterans to assist in their socialization (Kramer, 2010).

You Make the Call

The first research question sought to understand how recruiting prepares student-athletes for college. Results revealed some concerning trends within the information that is communicated to Division I football players during recruitment. These trends include a surprisingly limited amount of information concerning the nuances and daily requirements of athletic commitments, an academic preview that overtly prioritizes athletics, and little information about the costs of being a public figure. This suggests that student-athletes enter college with a shallow understanding of their future endeavors that overemphasizes the potential for positive experiences. In other words, Division I football players are not receiving a realistic job preview, which may impede their abilities to adapt to and successfully socialize into their athletic teams, universities, and communities (Cranmer & Myers, 2017). Although not surprising—Gerdy (1997) made similar claims over two decades ago—this study provides empirical evidence to support such assertions. This limited understanding is likely the product of the nature of recruiting. Perhaps negative aspects and experiences can be expected to be avoided during recruiting, as the onus is on team representatives to convince student-athletes to commit to their program. Likewise, academics may be deemphasized because student-athletes pay less attention to academics while being recruited (Doyle & Gaeth, 1990; Klenosky et al., 2001). To complicate the process, prospective student-athletes are provided few opportunities to observe and understand the daily routine of players because most campus visits are scheduled on weekends during games and when there are no class commitments.

The second research question sought to understand how student-athletes responded when they held inaccurate expectations for college. Although anticipatory socialization is seldom perfect, the uncertainties and stresses identified by participants can easily be traced to the ill-preparation they received during the recruiting process. One encouraging finding is that the team being studied provided student-athletes with resources to help them socialize into their teams and universities once they arrived on campus. Specifically, when student-athletes' expectations for collegiate experiences were not met they turned to a designated staff member who assisted in their professional and personal development. This finding indicates that while coaches may contribute to misunderstandings or poor job previews during recruiting, they have an interest in helping student-athletes socialize once they are on campus. In this manner, coaches' interests are served both through initially misleading or leaving student-athletes unprepared until obtaining their commitments, then aiding in their socialization once student-athletes arrive on campus. Unfortunately, student-athletes do not benefit from the former and must purposely avail themselves of the latter.

Universities spend millions of dollars on facilities and travel in an effort to recruit student-athletes (Magnusen et al., 2014). Both scholars and practitioners fail to recognize that recruiting has lasting implications for how student-athletes adjust to their collegiate experiences, as it sets their expectations for future team membership (Cranmer, 2017). Although this research may lack generalizability because it is focused on a few players from a single team and is qualitative in nature, there appears to be a need to provide incoming student-athletes with realistic job previews that include daily routines, the importance and rigor of academics, and the commitments associate with being a public figure. The functionality of these resources can be further maximized through the provision and designation of a well-respected staff member who can provide support and advice to student-athletes (Cranmer, 2018).

Discussion Questions

1. Based on the process discussed in this chapter, in what ways are current recruiting practices helping and/or hindering student-athletes? How can this process be improved? How might the process be more ethical?
2. What might be a better balance between prioritizing the acquisition of talented student-athletes and establishing realistic expectations to help in their socialization into college academics and athletics?
3. How might this case study relate to recruiting news and/or the experiences of student-athletes at your college or university?

References

Caro, C. A. (2012). College football success: The relationship between recruiting and winning. *International Journal of Sports Science & Coaching, 7*, 139–152.

Cranmer, G. A. (2017). A communicative approach to sport socialization: The functions of memorable messages during Division-I student-athletes' socialization. *International Journal of Sport Communication, 10*, 233–257. doi:10.1123/IJSC.2017-0031

Cranmer, G. A. (2018). An application of socialization resources theory: Collegiate student-athletes' team socialization as a function of their social exchanges with coaches and teammates. *Communication & Sport, 6*, 349–367. doi:10.1177/2167479517714458

Cranmer, G. A., & Myers, S. A. (2017). Exploring Division-I student-athletes' memorable messages from their anticipatory socialization. *Communication Quarterly, 65*, 125–143. doi:10.1080/01463373.2016.1197292

Doyle, C. A., & Gaeth, G. J. (1990). Assessing the institutional choice process of student-athletes. *Research Quarterly, 61*, 85–92.

Fondren, K. M. (2010). Sport and stigma: College football recruiting and institutional identity of Ole Miss. *Journal of Issues in Intercollegiate Athletics, 3*, 154–175.

Gerdy, J. R. (1997). *The successful college athletic program: The new standard.* Westport, CT: Oryx Press.

Klenosky, D. B., Templin, T. J., & Troutman, J. A. (2001). Recruiting student athletes: A means-end investigation of school-choice decision making. *Journal of Sport Management, 15*, 96–106.

Kramer, M. W. (2010). *Organizational socialization: Joining and leaving organizations.* Malden, MA: Polity.

Magnusen, M. J., Kim, Y., Perrewe, P. L., & Ferris, G. R. (2014). A critical review and synthesis of student-athlete college choice factors: Recruiting effectiveness in NCAA sports. *International Journal of Sports Science & Coaching, 9*, 1265–1286.

Ornstein, J. K. (1996). Broken promises and broken dreams: Should we hold college athletic programs accountable for breaching representations made in recruiting student-athletes. *Seton Hall Journal of Sport Law, 6*, 641–668.

Perrelle, J. (2008). An Opportunity for reform: Tennessee secondary school athletic association v. Brentwood Academy and NCAA recruiting. *Brooklyn Law Review, 74*, 1213–1252.

Schneider, R., & Messenger, S. (2012). The impact of athletic facilities on the recruitment of potential student-athletes. *College Student Journal, 46*, 805–811.

Tracy, S. J. (2010). Qualitative quality: Eight "big-tent" criteria for excellent qualitative research. *Qualitative Inquiry, 16*, 837–851.

Wylleman, P., & Lavallee, D. (2004). A developmental perspective on transitions faced by athletes. In M. R. Weiss (Ed.), *Developmental sport and exercise psychology: A lifespan perspective* (pp. 507–527). Morgantown, WV: Fitness Information Technology.

9 Broadcast Yourself and Multiply Your Revenue

Benfica TV Case Study

Fernando Vannier Borges

Benfica is Portugal's most successful soccer club. Despite their national dominance, the modernization of the game led to a big economic gap between the team and the continent's soccer elite. In an attempt to regain some of its continental glory, Benfica's board analyzed the revenue stream of the club and concluded that TV revenue had to be improved. Analyzing the Benfica case through a media economy lens and mediatization theory, this case study contextualizes how the process of creating its own TV channel increased Benfica's broadcast income from 7.5 million euros to 40 million euros per year in just a four-year period.

Introduction

Benfica is Portugal's most successful soccer club. Over its history, the team has won 36 national championships and was twice a European champion. Although it is not in one of the Big Five soccer leagues (England, Spain, Germany, France, and Italy), the club has managed to have revenues that placed them in the 27th position of the Deloitte Money League 2017 (Deloitte, 2017). Despite Benfica's national dominance, the modernization of the game led to the creation of a large economic gap between it and other continental elite teams like Real Madrid, Barcelona, Bayern Munich, and the Premier League teams. The main cause of this economic gap is Benfica's low broadcast revenue. The gap is better explained by examining the Premier League's recent TV rights contract,[1] which allows these clubs to sign and bankroll the best players in the market.

In an attempt to reclaim its past continental glory, Benfica's board analyzed the revenue stream of the club and identified a potential point of improvement—its TV rights deal. In the 2012–2013 season, Benfica received 7.5 million euros in broadcast revenue. By 2016, Benfica's new broadcast deal enabled it to ink a new deal for 40 million euros per year. From a political economy point of view, Boyle and Haynes (2004) explained that soccer clubs realized they could become less dependent on traditional media for their image rights revenue by rethinking their broadcast rights agreements. After the bankruptcy of media groups, such as Kirch Media and ISL, soccer clubs became concerned their TV revenues would decrease. Also, digital technologies allowed teams to control and manage their own image more efficiently without relying on the more traditional media channels. Manchester United was the first to create its own TV channel (MUTV), and soon other clubs followed.

As part of a larger research project about soccer club's media (Borges, 2017b), this chapter highlights the unique case of the Benfica soccer club. By first creating BTV, Benfica's dedicated sports channel, the team then took the sports channel concept a step further by exclusively broadcasting its home matches on BTV nationwide. By examining the case through a media economy lens and applying mediatization theory, this study attempts to contextualize how the process of creating its own TV channel helped Benfica increase its broadcast income and reestablish its place in continental soccer.

Background

Since the early 2000s, Benfica has undergone a massive restructuring in order to stay competitive in European soccer. A new board was elected, leading the club to economic stability and more sports victories. Benfica reorganized its administrative structure, replacing amateur directors with a full-time professional staff. An important aspect was the creation of the Benfica SAD (Sports Anonymous Society), a company which is publicly traded on the Lisbon Stock Exchange. The establishment of Benfica SAD was a way to separate the soccer structure from the rest of the club. Hence, it was possible to professionalize the administration of the soccer section of the club and maintain other less profitable sports with their amateur or semi-professional status without putting the club's finances at risk (Pereira, 2012).

Owned by Benfica SAD, Benfica TV was the first soccer club TV channel in Portugal. It was officially launched in December 2008 after an experimental broadcast the previous October. According to the club's annual report, the objective was to create a TV channel to spotlight the team's supporters and the club's sports and business activities (Benfica, 2014). Pereira (2012, p. 226) argued that the channel was the result of the president's vision to improve communications with its supporters and bolster other areas of the club. More than simply a way of increasing revenue, at its origin Benfica TV's mission was to the preserve the club's memory, which was considered by the directors as an invaluable club asset.

From its outset, Benfica TV was an exclusive channel of Serviços de Comunicações e Multimédia (MEO), a Portuguese mobile and telecommunication service provided by Portugal Telecom. As a distributor, MEO identified a demand for sports content and proposed to the club the creation of a TV channel. In practical terms, MEO was responsible for the technical aspect, and Benfica managed operations and content production. In exchange, MEO was the only company who could carry Benfica TV on its service, as a competitive asset. The Portuguese telecommunications market is dominated by three companies: Vodafone, MEO, and NOS. When Benfica

TV was launched, MEO had 55,000 subscribers; today it has more than a million. It is not possible to quantify the role Benfica TV played in MEO's growth, but it is safe to say the number of Benfica's supporters in Portugal contributed to MEO's subscriber increase.

It is undeniable that TV money has changed the professional sports landscape over the past decades. The prices for broadcast rights have exponentially increased (Andreff, 2012), being the most important source of revenue for the majority of the top-level clubs in Europe, representing in most cases more than a third of its revenue (Deloitte, 2017). Indirectly, the exposure achieved by broadcasting games also impacts commercial revenue due to the fact that ad sponsors invest in the most recognizable brands.

There is a long list of research about the relationship between media and sport. Evidence suggests a love match (Rowe, 1996), leading to the concepts of "sports/media complex" (Wenner, 1989), the "media sport cultural complex" (Rowe, 2004), and the "sport-media nexus" (Boyles & Haynes, 2009). In general, these concepts state a symbiotic or parasitic relationship exists between sport and media (Helland, 2007). Sobry (2003) makes the case that that sports provided TV the power to restructure into a media spectacle. Further, Frandsen (2015) argues that the demands of the media shape sports organizations, changing its structure and behavior.

The media-sports linkage is a good starting point when considering the impact of mediatization on sports organizations. Mediatization is defined "as the influence of media institutions and practices on other fields of social and institutional practice" (Livingstone & Lunt, 2014; Hjarvard, 2008). Thus, when Benfica leverages its reputation as a well-known brand and applies communication strategies to its message, the club starts behaving more like a media organization than a mere soccer team.

The Case

In Portugal, broadcast rights are negotiated by each individual team, and each club owns the right to its home matches. Disappointed by contract renewal talks with its players, Benfica owners decided to broadcast their games on their own BTV, instead of signing a new contract with Olivedesportos, the former rights holder. So, in July 2013, a new phase began for Benfica TV: it became a premium channel operator—meaning consumers would have to subscribe to the channel (at an extra cost of 9.90 euros per month) in order to receive Benfica games—in addition to being available on other TV packages besides MEO. This alteration was motivated by the notion that the club was not receiving a fair amount for the broadcasting rights. The arguments were that Benfica generated more audience for its matches than its rivals—Porto and Sporting—yet Benfica's contract values were similar. In all, the team felt the income was low compared with other markets in Europe; and the club deserved a 40 million euro contract, instead of the existing 7.5 million euro deal it had (Nobre & Candeias, 2012).

This change occurred so the club could renegotiate the income for the broadcasting rights contract. However, Benfica's board felt the broadcasting of Benfica's home matches (15 per season at the time) was not attractive enough to lure a desired number of subscribers (and enough revenue), so they improved the content offered by the TV channel. They already had the rights to air Greek league and MLS games, but the game changer was winning the exclusive rights to broadcast the vastly popular English Premier League (EPL).

The EPL is considered to be the best soccer league in the world and a financial boon for any media portfolio. With 10 matches spread over a week-end, game previews, results shows, and a spate of other related content, the EPL delivers an impressive level of solid programming, business sustainability, and a diverse subscriber audience of non-Benfica fans to BTV. With this new programming, Benfica created two channels—BTV1 and BTV2. BTV1's program schedule is dominated by material dedicated solely to the Benfica team brand, as this channel is authorized to be broadcast overseas, expanding its reach potential. BTV2 is dominated by the Premier League content and other sports events not related to Benfica, as the broadcasting contract restricts its reach to Portugal; thus, BTV2 is available only in Portugal.

So, with EPL and Benfica home matches, BTV has two of the most important programming lineups for football consumers in Portugal. These acquisitions worried competitive media organizations. Competitors criticized Benfica for its lack of impartiality by announcers and concern over the journalistic aspects of content production. To minimize this, BTV recruited renowned and experienced journalists to manage its news and broadcast divisions, offering guidance to young professionals and establishing credibility in the market (Borges, 2017a; Borges, 2017b).

In 2013, Olivedesportos made a final offer worth 111 million euros for a five-year contract (about 22.2 million per year). At the end of its first season commercializing its matches, Benfica earned 28.1 million euros of gross income and reach over 300,000 subscribers (Benfica, 2014). Despite the lack of discrimination on the official budget, after investigating the club's accounts and subtracting the operational costs of the TV channel, the newspaper *Público* claimed that the net profit of BTV over the first year was 17.1 million euros (Sousa, 2014a), later confirmed by Domingos Oliveira, the director of Benfica SAD, who said that the organization had a 11 million euros operating cost (Sousa, 2014b). It is a significant rise compared with the previous amount of 7.5 million euros, but less than Olivedesportos last offer of 22.2 million euros. Excluding player transfers, Benfica's broadcasting gross profits (28.1 million euros) became its main source of income, exceeding the team's UEFA prize money (22.4 million euros) and its sponsors (19 million euros) (Benfica, 2014).

After reaching 300,000 subscribers, this number remained stable. However, big changes arrived on December 2015, when Benfica announced a new deal: it sold its broadcast rights to telecom operator NOS for 400 million euros for a 10-year contract (three initial years plus seven renewable).

This deal included the rights for Benfica's home matches (75% of the total value) and the exclusivity for the BTV channel (25%). In this new scheme, BTV would no longer be a premium channel—it would once again become a Club TV channel—and BTV2 would be terminated, transferring its properties to other channels. In the end, Benfica accomplished its initial target sum for its broadcast rights.

Benfica's strategies may largely have been economically driven, but it can also be explained through the mediatization process. From a financial vantage point, BTV follows the media business models of the digital age (Ouakrat, 2012; Sonnac, 2013), profiting from subscriptions and advertisements while targeting a highly passionate and segmented audience. As the media landscape is changing, Benfica TV reflects these fluctuations. Due to the influence of the Internet, journalists increase their hybrid professional profile, and information is produced to an audience viewed more as consumers than public citizens (Estienne, 2007). This is the same logic applied in the BTV case, where professionals are focused on marketing and information strategies, and the audience is composed of avid supporters who are concerned with the well-being of the club and its victories. So, it is possible to say that Benfica TV is accepted because it presents the same characteristics that traditional media outlets have after adjustments are made to incorporate market changes.

More than positioning themselves economically in the media market, Benfica acted in part according to media logic. Based on Danish sports federations, Frandsen (2015) argued that the mediatization process has three phases: perception, structure, and behavior. First, it is perceived that media is an important factor in society. Second, the organization changes its structure, investing resources—time, money, and personnel—to improve its media capacities. Finally, everything converges into actions, and media strategies are executed by the sports organization. This was the case with Benfica: first, it perceived media and TV rights as a strategic field; second, it changed its structure, creating a TV channel; and, finally, it behaved like a media company once broadcasting started.

As much as it is hard to generalize due to great diversity among soccer clubs in the world, one of the results of the creation of soccer clubs' TV channels is that information becomes a strategic and economic asset. Club TV channels are tools to attain power: in relation to sponsors, clubs are able to foster their own relationships, creating more publicity or being able to market new campaigns to a very segmented market. In regard to traditional media, club TV channels create a competitive and cooperative relationship. On the one hand, they both battle for similar target audiences. On the other, traditional media need the content and access provided by the club. The club also needs the visibility provided by a traditional media outlet. Using their own media networks, sports organizations can create a sense of community spreading beyond the geographic limits of the stadium, where information is the link between the parts (Borges, 2017a).

You Make the Call

To discuss the success of soccer clubs is a complex subject. From a sports economy perspective, European clubs differ from American sports in that they are structured on open league formats, with promotion and relegation as their main distinctions (Andreff, 2012). Closed league organizations tend to present a profit maximization orientation, while open league organizations maximize their utility, meaning they will spend their profit margins to lure better talent to the team in order to win championships (Dobson & Goddard, 2011). In this context, success is, mostly, measured by titles and victories for European soccer clubs and not as much from a business point of view. Since Benfica won the last four national Portuguese championships (2014, 2015, 2016, 2017), and it has achieved its financial goals, the organization is happy with its current state of affairs.

BTV may be viewed as a success. It enabled Benfica to reach its goals to (1) have 300 thousand subscribers after its first year and (2) sell its broadcast rights for 40 million euros per year. Despite producing significant profits, broadcasting its own TV channel was considered a financial gamble when compared to selling its TV rights to other media companies. Broadcast rights fees are paid in advance, without the need to invest in personnel, technical infrastructure, and other costs. It is a "net" revenue, because the club does not need to spend money on anything other than what it already has, such as the match-day experience.

Unequivocally, the size of the club and the number of supporters in Portugal (somewhere around 50% of the population) were essential elements to Benfica's success. However, it was more appealing to Benfica from the outset to be part of traditional media outlets because it provided more visibility and thus better sponsorship deals. Despite the fragmentation of sports audiences, live sports still attract large numbers of spectators.

So, Benfica's decision to resell its broadcast rights is understandable in this context. However, two things must be considered: the interval of the contract and the inclusion of BTV together with the sale of its broadcast rights. On the one hand, the new contract length presents a risk: A renewable 10-year deal might offer a sense of security and stability, but if the team's value increases over those years, Benfica's main property will be undervalued. On the other hand, the inclusion of BTV in the negotiation is evidence that the club retains some of the decision power and that BTV is an important asset for its long-term strategies.

Schulz (2004) establishes four dimensions of mediatization: extension, substitution, amalgamation, and accommodation. This chapter focuses on two of these dimensions—extension and amalgamation. Amalgamation occurs when media and non-media practices become interwoven, displaying a clear influence by mediagenic symbols with respect to form, content, or organization. When a sports institution hires journalists, content producers, and technical staff and then becomes a key player in the country's national media market, adopting a media economy business model, it becomes a clear case of media logic adoption.

Extension refers to overcoming physical constraints by using communication technologies to connect individuals and groups from different geographical areas. Sports broadcasting is a way of surpassing the spatial constraints of a stadium, so when Benfica broadcasting connects with its fans and followers it extends its reach by adding fans nationwide—outside Lisbon, the team's hometown—and to its many supporters among the Portuguese diaspora and inhabitants of former Portuguese colonies in Africa.

However, BTV broadcast generates some concerns due to consequences to sports journalism. Critics say that as a club's TV channel, it offers the club's vision instead of a neutral or objective point of view. Throughout its first phase (2008–2013), players and coaches of other clubs were not given a voice. However, this situation changed when it became a premium channel and hired journalists with a national reputation. It started implementing a rigorous routine, based on journalism ethical codes, of listening to both sides before producing a piece of information (Borges, 2017b).

Despite the fact that BTV production routines and professional personnel are in consonance with the actual changes in the media market, this may have other influences on sports journalism. Access to professional sports has become more difficult, and the production of information by sports organizations may mean that some doors will be closed. The result may be a lack of independent and critical information, since media professionals are embedded with the clubs, participating in the organizations and sharing the same main objectives. This may result in a lack of objectivity and public transparency. Also, there is the concern of the separation between the marketing, or commercial, department and the information, or editorial, production. Being part of the same organization will allow marketing, PR, and media personnel to work as one cohesive group, producing content that respects the club's directives (Borges, 2017b).

Benfica's transformation was born from its desire to become more economically viable and reestablish itself as a soccer power. Yet, by adopting a media economy approach to implement its vision, the club opened itself up to a mediatization process which improved the internationalization of its brand and fostered the creation of a fan community. The collective of Benfica fans either inside or outside Portugal may never share the same space, but BTV will nevertheless play an important cultural role in producing and maintaining the memory and image of the club while simultaneously using a phatic function of communication: through Benfica's media channel, its fans can stay connected among themselves and with the club.

Discussion Questions

1. Benfica is the most popular and most successful club in Portuguese soccer; thus, it may have been relatively easier to achieve its level of success.

How might it be possible to replicate Benfica's initiatives in other organizations? What would be the main obstacles? Also, which adjustments would be necessary to apply the same strategy to other sports?

2. Benfica's actions show that sports organizations intend to take control of their own image and their rights over their product through media content. How do you see the future relationship between sports organizations, media companies, and journalists?

3. This case shows that there is a big market for media professionals within the sports industry. What is the role played by media professionals on sports organizations for the future? How does embedding journalists within an organization impact team coverage?

4. In financial terms, it was a good deal for Benfica to sign a new broadcast contract with NOS. However, taking the fan/audience perspective, since Benfica could resell the broadcast rights after three years, how would you feel as a fan who just subscribed to the new service? Might there be a better—fan-friendly—way to negotiate such contracts?

Note

1. Gibson, O. (2015, February 10). Sky and BT retain Premier League TV rights for record £5.14bn. *The Guardian*. Retrieved from https://www.theguardian.com/football/2015/feb/10/premier-league-tv-rights-sky-bt. www.espnfc.com/english-premier-league/23/blog/post/2917119/how-premier-league-record-tv-deal-will-affect-english-football

References

Andreff, W. (2012). *Mondialisation économique du Sport*. Bruxelles: De Boeck.

Benfica. (2014). *Relatório de contas Sport Lisboa e Benfica, SAD 2013/2014* [Annual Report Sport Lisboa e Benfica 2013/2014]. Lisboa: Benfica. Retrieved from www.slbenfica.pt/Portals/0/Documentos/RelatorioContasBenficaSAD201 32014.pdf

Borges, F. (2017a). Benfica TV: Taking control of the communication process. In B. Garcia & J. Zheng (Eds.), *Football and supporter activism in Europe: Whose game is it?* London: Palgrave Macmillian.

Borges, F. (2017b). *Les médias de club: nouveaux espaces de production de l'information sportive (Benfica, Botafogo et Paris Saint-Germain)* (Ph.D. Thesis). Université Panthéon-Assas (Sorbonne Universities), Paris, France.

Boyle, R., & Haynes, R. (2004). *Football in the new media age*. London: Routledge.

Boyle, R., & Haynes, R. (2009). *Power play: Sport, the media and popular culture*. Edinburgh: Edinburgh University Press.

Deloitte. (2017). *Deloitte Money League 2017*. Manchester, NH: Sports Business Group at Deloitte. Retrieved from www2.deloitte.com/uk/en/pages/sports-business-group/articles/deloitte-football-money-league.html

Dobson, S., & Goddard, J. (2011). *The economics of football*. Cambridge: Cambridge University Press.

Estienne, Y. (2007). *Le journalisme après Internet*. Paris: L'Hartman.

Frandsen, K. (2015). Sports organizations in a new wave of mediatization. *Communication & Sport*, 4(4), 385–400.

Helland, K. (2007). Changing sports, changing media: Mass appeal, the sports/media complex and TV sports rights. *Nordicom-Information, 29*(2), 105–119.

Hjarvard, S. (2008). The mediatization of society: A theory of the media as agents of social and cultural change. *Nordicom Review, 29*(2), 105–134.

Livingstone, S., & Lunt, P. (2014). Mediatization: An emerging paradigm for media and communication studies. In K. Lundby (Ed.), *Mediatization of communication* (Vol. 21, pp. 703–724). Berlin: Mouton de Gruyter.

Nobre, A., & Candeias, P. (2012, March 6). Benfica recusa 111 milhões da Sport TV. *Expresso*. Retrieved from http://expresso.sapo.pt/desporto/benfica-recusa-111-milhoes-da-sport-tv=f709520

Ouakrat, A. (2012). Le concept des modèles d'affaires: éléments de définition et état de l'art. In J. P. Benghozi (Dir.), *Entreprises culturelles et internet: Contenus numériques et modèles d' affaires innovants* (pp. 111–117). Paris: Ministère de la Culture et de la Communication, GIS Culture-Médias & Numérique.

Pereira, L. (2012). *Luís Felipe Vieira—Missão Benfica*. Lisboa: Prime Books.

Rowe, D. (1996). The global love-match: Sport and television. *Media, Culture & Society, 18*(4), 565–582.

Rowe, D. (2004). *Sport, culture and the media: The unruly trinity*. Buckingham: Open University.

Schulz, W. (2004). Reconstructing mediatization as an analytical concept. *European Journal of Communication, 19*(1), 87–101.

Sobry, C. (2003). *Socioéconomie du sport: structures sportives et libéralisme économique*. Bruxelles: De Boeck.

Sonnac, N. (2013). L'écosystème des médias. *Communication, 32*(2). Retrieved from http://communication.revues.org/5030

Sousa, H. (2014a, November 1). Benfica TV rendeu 17 milhões de euros "limpos". *Público*. Retrieved April 26, 2016 from www.publico.pt/desporto/noticia/benfica-tv-rendeu-17-milhoes-de-euros-limpos-1674862

Sousa, H. (2014b, November 21). Benfica TV prevê um "aumento interessante" de receitas no próximo ano. *Público*. Retrieved from www.publico.pt/desporto/noticia/benfica-tv-preve-um-aumento-in teressante-de-receitas-no-proximo-ano-1677056?page=-1

Wenner, L. (1989). Media, sports, and society: The research agenda. In L. Wenner (Ed.), *Media, sports and society* (pp. 13–48). Newbury Park, CA: Sage Publications.

Acknowledgements

The empirical data collected to write this text was part of PhD research financed by Capes Foundation, Ministry of Education of Brazil.

Part II
Clubhouse

Section III

Image Repair and Redemption

10 Roping Off the Ring

How a Series of Employee Deaths Coerced the WWE Into an Enforced Wellness Policy Through the Contingency Theory of Accommodation

Jack V. Karlis

From the 1980s through the early 2000s, premature deaths of talent and criminal arrests were commonplace in the media for World Wrestling Entertainment until the company began to adopt a more corporate culture, installing a Talent Wellness Policy in 2006 (WWE.com, 2017 A). The WWE was forced to harshly regulate a historically compromising culture when it came to substance abuse and wellness in both its publics' eyes. Many high-profile talents have been suspended since its creation, reassuring stakeholders that the company's image is reflective of a responsible corporation. Only "pure accommodation" on the contingency continuum of the Contingency Theory of Accommodation would work.

Introduction

World Wrestling Entertainment (WWE), the former World Wrestling Federation, has been in operation for more than 50 years. It originally started as a wrestling company based in the Northeast United States, but today is a multi-media platformed entertainment company which is publicly traded on the New York Stock Exchange and with a net worth over $1 billion. (WWE, 2017 B).

WWE "superstars" or "talent," do not have the same annual or daily schedule as other athletes. Their schedule warrants demanding travel for more than four days a week that includes multiple flights or drives to perform more than 300 times yearly as independent contractors. The mainstream media has historically associated the performers' intense travel schedules with illegal anabolic steroid use in order to gain or maintain larger-than-life physiques. The athletes admit to self-medicating injuries with alcohol, illegal narcotics, and prescription painkillers, creating a sometimes fatal and widely publicized cycle of abuse.

The company's initial public offering was on Oct. 19, 1999 (CNNMoney, 1999). Since that time, a more traditional corporate structure has been implemented. The WWE's new buttoned-up hierarchy and the organization's inherent responsibilities to stakeholders clashed with its former "laissez faire" culture, especially when it came to handling the health of its employees through the years.

Background

World Wrestling Entertainment is a publicly traded global media conglomerate that has an international audience and posted revenues of more than $729.2 million in 2016 with more than 800 employees (WWE.com, 2017 C). The company has taken the sport entertainment industry, what was once known as wrestling or "rasslin," from smoke-filled bingo halls and old gymnasiums into events at sold-out stadiums and even its own Internet-based viewer-on-demand channel, the first of its kind to provide direct-to-consumer premium content. The WWE's products are a unique mixture of theater, entertainment, reality television, and game show.

Most notably, in addition to its original programming watched by more than 650 million homes worldwide in 25 languages (WWE, 2017 B), its far-reaching social media presence helps augment its programming and enhance the experience for viewers. In 2016 alone, WWE social media had 1.14 billion engagements over 739 million different social media accounts (WWE, 2017 D), numbers that helped them achieve their financial and company goals during broadcasts. The company values raising profit margins for its stakeholders through diversification to expand its reach, but it also values society's expectation of corporate social responsibility and sustainability (Heath & Ryan, 1989). It is a delicate balancing act that the WWE and other sports entities must perform.

In the early 1990s, current WWE CEO and one-time sole owner Vincent McMahon was cleared in a highly publicized federal trial in which he was charged with distributing and encouraging the use of anabolic steroids to his performers. Despite McMahon being cleared of all charges, the trial left a lingering negative association with wrestling and steroid use among the world of sports entertainment's fans, the public, and the media. Rampant speculation of drug abuse and undiagnosed brain trauma were correlated with the deaths of performers under the age of 50 in the mainstream media, giving the company a public reputation of having little care or control of its employees' health and wellness. The mainstream media coverage put stakeholders and stockholders on notice. The company acknowledged some deaths but usually disassociated itself from others. Many characterized the performers' value to the company as simply disposable gladiators instead of human beings. The mainstream media's view was that the company didn't care about the well-being of its employees, and it didn't care about anything except its profits. Once the WWE became publicly traded in 1999, the company had to address both its inside and outside publics.

One death in particular in 2006 proved to be the "wake-up call" for the company's handling of its employees' health. Forced to take action in the face of plummeting stock value and the need for adherence to society's expectation of corporate social responsibility, the WWE was forced to abandon its practice of "avoidance" and take action. In this case, nothing short of "pure accommodation" of the Contingency Theory of Accommodation would be acceptable.

The Case

Eduardo Gory Guerrero, better known as "Eddie Guerrero," was found dead at age 38 in a Minneapolis hotel room due to heart failure on November 13, 2005 (Associated Press, 2005). Guerrero was a former world heavyweight champion, one of the company's top positions and highest honors, and was wildly popular with fans and among his fellow performers in the locker room. The company publicly acknowledged his death on its website, which was largely consistent with its previous protocol of recognizing untimely deaths of performers who, in some capacity, were still connected with the company. Five days later, during the next televised event—an episode of *WWE Smackdown!*—the WWE presented an emotional eulogy to Guerrero, showcasing his career and dedicating a part of the program solely to him. Never before had a current talent died of an overdose while playing an active role on television. It was usually former talents who had passed away due to dubious circumstances before the age of 50.

Still, the grieving company and its fan base, along with its stakeholders and investors, were left to ponder what could be done to curb the high-profile deaths of legends both past and present. The increased number of employee deaths cast the company in a negative light. The WWE faced a number of issues it had to address in order to improve its image, assuage fans, and satisfy its shareholders. Among them:

- Assure company investors the product would retain its stock value despite the negative press
- Improve its image in the mainstream media by applying corporate social responsibility principles, demonstrating its care for its employees
- Reinforce to its fan base that the company values its employees' health and is attentive to fan input

On February 27, 2006, sweeping change came to the WWE. CEO Vince McMahon announced to the WWE roster that a new Talent Wellness Policy was being implemented and would be administered by a third-party company, Aegis Sciences Corporation. Tests would be conducted to detect (PWPIX, 2016):

- Prescription medications
- Performance-enhancing drugs
- Illegal recreational drugs

The company would adopt a "three strikes" policy on violations before termination. The testing policy penalties included (WWE, 2017 D):

- First offense (other than marijuana or alcohol): 30-day suspension without pay
- Second offense (other than marijuana or alcohol): 60-day suspension without pay
- Third offense (other than marijuana or alcohol): Termination of contract with WWE; violator unable to return to WWE for at least a year, if at all

Cardiovascular stress tests would also be performed by New York Cardiology Associates to identify individuals who were susceptible to massive heart attacks, much like the one that claimed Eddie Guerrero's life. While the company informed the public via its website and through the mainstream media of its new policies, stakeholders remained uneasy about how strictly the policy would be enforced if and when a high-profile and money-making superstar tested positive for banned substances. The company assured its stakeholders that since a third-party company handled the testing, it would be impossible to cheat the tests. Thus, the WWE's new stringent policy would be on par, if not better, than other major sports leagues (WWE.com, 2017 A).

The company took proactive and reactive steps in the implementation and rollout of its policy. The WWE adopted a stringent policy that would hold up to public scrutiny. The company actively addressed questions raised by its wary publics regarding the company's commitment to employee wellness after

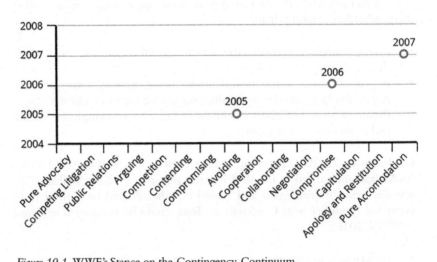

Figure 10.1 WWE's Stance on the Contingency Continuum

Source: Cancel, A.E., Cameron, G.T., Sallot, L. M., & Mitrook, M.A. (1997). It depends: a contingency theory of accommodation in public relations. *Journal of Public Relations Research, 9*(1), 31–63

years of apathy. The company's past performance of turning a "blind eye" or using "avoidance" regarding former employees' deaths—acknowledging their deaths but avoiding the larger issue—haunted the company despite the installation of the new policy. Applying the Contingency Theory of Accommodation (Cancel, Cameron, Sallot, & Mitrook, 1997), the WWE simply had to adopt a "pure accommodation" stance to satisfy its internal and external publics in order to stay financially viable as an organization (Figure 10.1).

The Contingency Theory of Accommodation helps explain the accommodation continuum for public relations practitioners' stances during crisis situations (Cancel et al., 1997). In its most simplistic terms, it is "what is going to be [the] most effective method at a given time" (Cancel et al., 1997, p. 35) considering internal and external variables within the theoretical framework for identifying why and how an entity's stance changes depending on the scope of the crisis. There are 87 different variables along a spectrum to determine which stance should be taken. The extremes of the continuum include "pure advocacy" on one side and "pure accommodation" on the other. There are two main categories of threats to consider—external and internal. On a macro level, there are five subdivisions of external variables to take into account: threats; industry and environment; general political and social environment and external culture; characteristics of the external public; and the issue under question (Table 10.1).

Multiple studies have focused on the efficacy of accommodation during crisis (Cancel, Mitrook, & Cameron, 1999; Reber, Cropp, & Cameron, 2003; Cameron, Cropp, & Reber, 2001) and have found empirical evidence to support the practical application of the theory. Under the Contingency Theory of Accommodation's framework, researchers such as Jin and Cameron (2007) examined the effects of threat types and duration on a public relation practitioner's responses to crises. Oyer and Karlis (2016) took it one step further and examined the differences in perceptions of accommodation stances among public relations practitioners, faculty, and students.

Internal variables are divided into six categories: characteristics of the organization; characteristics of the public relations department; characteristics of top management or the dominant coalition; internal threats; the individual characteristics of the public relations practitioner or managers; and characteristics of organization–public relationships.

When a case of a high-profile performer violated the new policy, the WWE had to come down hard and leave no room for favoritism. Anything short of a suspension, no matter who the violator was, would be viewed by its publics as the WWE reverting to its old ways. Society and the demands of its stakeholders had to be held with the utmost regard, thus any attempts to refute or deny any issues would not work with an already jaded public. It became evident the policy needed further refining after another high-profile death.

While Guerrero's death still haunts the company to this day, perhaps there isn't a darker cloud that hovers over the WWE than the June 2007 Chris

Table 10.1 Roping off the Ring Contingency Theory of Accommodation Set of External Variables

Threats	Industry/ Environment	Characteristics of External Public	Issue Under Question
• Litigation* • Government regulation • Potential damaging publicity • Scarring of company's reputation in business community and general public • Legitimizing activists' claims	• Dynamic or static • Number of competitors • Richness or leanness of resources in the environment	• Number of members • Degree of source credibility/ connection to powerful members • Past successes or failures of groups to evoke change • Amount of advocacy practiced by organization • Level of commitment/ involvement of members • Existence of public relations counselors or not • Public's perception of group: reasonable or radical • Level of media coverage in the past • Whether representatives of the public know or like representatives of the organization • Whether representatives of the organization know or like representatives of the public • Public's willingness to dilute its cause/ request/claim • Moves and countermoves • Relative power of organization • Relative power of public	• Stakes • Size • Complexity

Source: Cancel, A. E., Cameron, G. T., Sallot, L. M., & Mitrook, M. A. (1997). It depends: a contingency theory of accommodation in public relations. *Journal of Public Relations Research, 9*(1), 31–63.

Benoit tragedy. Benoit, Guerrero's best friend, would also have a tragic death. Benoit's murder-suicide of himself, his wife, and his 7-year-old son (Goodman, 2007) stunned the professional wrestling world. Prescription drugs and anabolic steroids were found at the crime scene, and the autopsy concluded that Benoit suffered from chronic brain damage (Science Daily, 2007) due to numerous concussions he received while performing. Doctors said his brain injury may have caused his paranoid behavior and contributed to the deaths.

In response to Benoit's death, the WWE has, to this day, erased any connection to Benoit's time with the WWE, but the issue of the long-term effects of concussions was brought to the forefront through intense media scrutiny. However, the WWE did amend its Talent Wellness Policy by adding concussion protocols to its policy (WWE.com, 2017 A). Still, the company could not control what had already been done. It needed to prove that its policy was effective.

In August of 2007, the company suspended 12 superstars, including one of its top performers, Edge (Adam Copeland). It was a bold move, but it did not convince stakeholders the company had changed its ways. The suspensions and names of the violators were reported by *Sports Illustrated* and other mainstream outlets but not the WWE (Quinn, 2007). The company still grappled with transparency issues and was mired in the "compromise" stance of the Contingency Theory of Accommodation. The WWE had to rethink its policy of not releasing the names of the offenders of the wellness policy.

Thus, on November 1, 2007, the company declared that any and all suspensions would be made public, further appealing to a stance of "pure accommodation" by making the company appear transparent to all involved (WWE, 2017 A). If someone was a risk or violated the policy, it would no longer be handled internally, and every stakeholder would be notified. While some deaths are inevitable due to years of abuse before the policy was installed, the WWE acted decisively to lessen the chance that a tragedy like the ones involving Guerrero or Benoit or any other active performer would recur. It appears the new policy is working to safeguard the company's image, as evidenced in Figure 10.2.

The WWE's most stern test recently occurred when Roman Reigns (Joseph Anoa'i), one of the company's top merchandise sellers and its top star as the "face of the company," was suspended in June 2016 for violating the WWE Talent Wellness Policy due to undisclosed reasons (Fiovarti, 2016). The 30-day suspension caused the WWE to adapt its schedule, as he was the featured performer and a contender for the WWE Title, the company's top prize. The company featured the news on its website as the top story and even retweeted Reigns' Twitter apology (Oster, 2016). The company even mentioned the 30-day suspension on its live broadcasts during his absence and used it in its storylines.

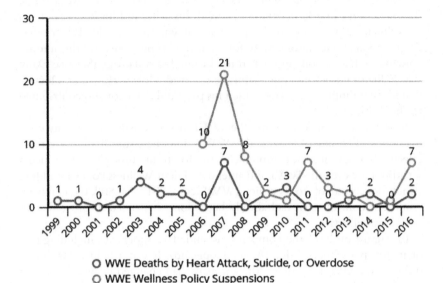

○ WWE Deaths by Heart Attack, Suicide, or Overdose
○ WWE Wellness Policy Suspensions

Figure 10.2 Effectiveness of WWE Wellness Policy: Number of Deaths vs. Number of Suspensions

Source: http://wrestlerdeaths.com

You Make the Call

The WWE, once thought of as a side show and a spectacle, chose the right path by using "pure accommodation" to implement and augment its now aptly named Talent Wellness Policy. The company also has offered and helped former employees with free rehabilitation due to substance abuse.

If the WWE tried to make special concessions, attempted to hide the violations, or refuted public criticism, the results might have been catastrophic for the company. Stockholders, employees, the media, and its fans would never view the WWE as a legitimate company worthy of financial investment instead of a P.T. Barnum–style sideshow. As much as it has sometimes put a strain on company–performer relations, the policy has worked, and the company has grown in scope, value, and profile. Without a coherent and effective wellness program, company stock would have fallen, and the WWE would lose its place as a media empire entrenched in popular culture.

While it was uncharted territory at first, by reaching the Contingency Theory of Accommodation's (Cancel et al., 1997) "pure accommodation," the WWE has enjoyed exponential success. The WWE has made good on its promise to enforce the policy no matter the status of the violator. As of this writing, more than 60 suspensions have been handed out since the launch of the policy; 12 of those suspensions came at once in August 2007 (PWPIX,

2016). The company also declared that all suspensions would be made public as of November 2007 (PWPIX, 2016).

In the 10 years since the policy was instituted in its current form, the company has grown exponentially in stock value, reach, holdings, and ability to attract and retain top international talent. The company has developed a reputation as the "premier" wrestling company in which to work. The company has also received positive and consistent mainstream media coverage from outlets like *Rolling Stone* and ESPN.

One could argue that while other sports leagues do very little or nothing to handle health issues associated with their sport, like the National Football League and its concussion issues or Major League Baseball and its steroid abuse, the WWE quickly and definitively acted when confronted with a prevalent problem. Other sports organizations would be wise to follow the WWE's example by adopting a "pure accommodation" stance by creating synergy between the human resources and public relations departments and installing a coherent wellness program with enforceable policies.

Discussion Questions

1. What did and didn't work in the WWE's use of Contingency Theory of Accommodation? Which of the 87 variables mattered the most to the WWE in regard to the situation?
2. Should the wellness policy have been installed earlier than it was? If yes, why?
3. Was there anything the WWE could have done differently with respect to changing its culture without having an official policy?
4. Since Roman Reigns' suspension in 2016, have there been any other suspensions of note? Have there been changes to the WWE policy or to the sport itself to impact the discussion on the WWE and steroids?

References

Associated Press. (2005). Eddie Guerrero, professional wrestler, dies at 38. Retrieved from www.nytimes.com/2005/11/15/sports/othersports/eddie-guerrero-professional-wrestler-dies-at-38.html

Cameron, G. T., Cropp, F., & Reber, B. H. (2001). Getting past platitudes: Factors limiting accommodation in public relations. *Journal of Communication Management, 5*(3), 242–261.

Cancel, A. E., Cameron, G. T., Sallot, L. M., & Mitrook, M. A. (1997). It depends: A contingency theory of accommodation in public relations. *Journal of Public Relations Research, 9*(1), 31–63.

Cancel, A. E., Mitrook, M. A., & Cameron, G. T. (1999). Testing the contingency theory of accommodation in public relations. *Public Relations Review, 25*(2), 171–197.

CNNMoney. (1999). WWF pins IPO. Retrieved from http://money.cnn.com/1999/08/03/companies/wrestling/

Daily, S. (2007). Wrestler Chris Benoit brain's forensic exam consistent with numerous brain injuries. Retrieved from www.sciencedaily.com/releases/2007/09/070905224343.htm

Fiovarti, T. (2016). WWE's Roman Reigns suspended for wellness violation. Retrieved from www.espn.com/espn/story/_/id/16398531/wwe-star-roman-reigns-suspended-30-days-violating-company-wellness-policy

Goodman, B. (2007). Wrestler killed wife and son, then himself. Retrieved from www.nytimes.com/2007/06/27/us/27wrestler.html

Heath, R. L., & Ryan, M. (1989). Public relations' role in defining corporate social responsibility. *Journal of Mass Media Ethics, 4*(1), 21–38.

Jin, Y., & Cameron, G. T. (2007). The effects of threat type and duration on public relations practitioner's cognitive, affective, and conative responses in crisis situations. *Journal of Public Relations Research, 19*(3), 255–281.

Oster, A. (2016). Roman Reigns suspended for wellness policy violation: Wrestling star will miss WWE draft, could be yanked from "WWE Battleground" following suspension. Retrieved from www.rollingstone.com/sports/news/wwe-star-roman-reigns-suspended-for-wellness-policy-violation-20160621

Oyer, S. A., & Karlis, J. V. (2016). Appraisal-based public relations stances in crisis situations: Conation revisited. *Public Relations Review, 42*(4), 734–738.

PWPIX. (2016). The complete list of WWE wellness policy violations. Retrieved from www.pwpix.net/wwe-wellness-program-violations/

Quinn, T. J. (2007). Top WWE names emerge in doping scandal. Retrieved from www.nydailynews.com/sports/top-wwe-names-emerge-doping-scandal-article-1.241222

Reber, B. H., Cropp, F., & Cameron, G. T. (2003). Impossible odds: Contributions of legal counsel and public relations practitioners in a hostile bid for Conrail Inc. by Norfolk Southern Corporation. *Journal of Public Relations Research, 15*(1), 1–25.

WWE A. (2017). Talent wellness policy summary. Retrieved from http://corporate.wwe.com/who-we-are/talent

WWE B. (2017). Who we are. Retrieved from http://corporate.wwe.com/who-we-are/company-overview

WWE C. (2017). Investors. Investors Overview. Retrieved from http://corporate.wwe.com/investors/investor-overview

WWE D. (2017). Key performance indicators. WWE Corporate. Retrieved from http://corporate.wwe.com/~/media/Files/W/WWE/documents/events/key-performance-indicators-q4.pdf

11 Does the NFL Still Own Sundays?

The Rebranding of the NFL Following the Domestic Abuse Crisis

Kelsey R. Rentner & Terry L. Rentner

"You're going to war with a corporation that owns a day of the week"—Dr. Cyril Wecht, (Albert Brooks) in the movie Concussion. *This chapter is a critical analysis of how the NFL is rebranding itself as a leader on domestic violence and sexual assault prevention following highly publicized media coverage of incidences involving its players. Institutional theory is the framework from which this crisis is explored, and questions are asked regarding the sincerity of the NFL's communication efforts to eradicate domestic abuse from its ranks.*

Introduction

"The NFL owns a day of the week, one the church used to own. Now it's theirs," said Dr. Cyril Wecht, played by Albert Brooks in the 2015 movie *Concussion* (Wecht, n.d.). While this may be an exaggeration, football is one of the most watched sports in the world, making the National Football League (NFL) a powerful institution. Because of its institutional power and success, the league has been able to bury cases of domestic violence for more than 14 years, but recent media attention and public outcries have made it increasingly difficult to ignore this serious social issue.

This chapter is a critical analysis of the domestic abuse crisis within the NFL and its attempts to rebrand itself as a leader on domestic violence prevention rather than a perpetrator of the problem. This chapter traces the history of domestic violence in the NFL and explores its communication efforts to regain its reputation through the lens of institutional theory and critical inquiry.

Background

Domestic Violence in the NFL

Domestic violence and sexual assault issues are not new in the NFL, but sensational stories tying the two together have gained the media and public's attention. As of January 11, 2018, 878 players have been arrested ("NFL arrests," n.d.). Among these are 98 players who were arrested for domestic violence and 74 arrested for assault, many of which were against women ("NFL Arrest.com," n.d.) The first domestic violence case was listed in the *USA Today* database in 2000 with the arrest of Rod Smith, a wide receiver arrested for choking, beating, and shoving his common-law wife near Denver ("NFL arrests," n.d.). Since then, at least 17 players have been arrested multiple times for assault or domestic abuse (Fitzsimmons, 2015).

Since 2014, the NFL has been criticized for the way it handled three highly publicized domestic violence cases among professional football players. These lawsuits created a legal case in which the league was under investigation for allegations that it was aware of an infamous video of Baltimore Ravens running back Ray Rice hitting his at-the-time fiancée in a casino elevator. This led to public outcry when the league did not react quickly enough to punish Rice. The initial punishment doled out to Rice was a two-game suspension. *Sports Illustrated* writer Chris Burke pointed out inconsistencies in penalties imposed by NFL commissioner Roger Goodell. Burke says it seems "far worse in the league's eyes to take some Adderall or smoke some marijuana than it is to, say, allegedly knock your fiancée out cold and then drag her unconscious body from a casino elevator" (Burke, 2014, para.2).

Goodell's highly respected position gives him the authority and responsibility to enforce the rules established by the NFL in circumstances that violate player conduct both on and off the field. The criticisms against Goodell included not taking appropriate action to eliminate this behavior among all professional football players. This led to Goodell reconsidering his initial decision and issuing a harsher punishment to Rice and forcing him to rethink the entire league's position. Entertainment and Sports Programming Network (ESPN) released a quote from Goodell on the issue stating,

> We allowed our standards to fall below where they should be and lost an important opportunity to emphasize our strong stance on a critical issue and the effective programs we have in place. My disciplinary decision led the public to question our sincerity, our commitment, and whether we understood the toll that domestic violence inflicts on so many families.
>
> ("Roger Goodell letter to NFL owners," 2014)

The Rice incident, along with other NFL domestic violence cases, highlighted what seems to be a well-hidden problem within the league for years prior to the most recent cases. Fifty domestic violence cases among NFL players have been pursued by law enforcement authorities since September 2006 (Schrotenboer, 2014). Numerous other cases have been reported and highlighted in the media prior to Goodell's administration in 2006, however these cases seemed to have simply faded away. According to the *Washington Post*, 77 players from the league's 32 teams have been arrested since 2000 on charges of domestic violence (Harwell & Halzack, 2014).

Arguably the most documented domestic violence case is the infamous O.J. Simpson murder trial in the mid-1990s. At the time, Simpson, a former Heisman Trophy winner and retired premier NFL running back, was accused of killing his former wife, Nicole Brown Simpson, and her friend, Ronald Goldman. In a televised media spectacle, he was tried and acquitted. The case is still talked about today, with media providing updates of Simpson's life in prison, where he served time for a different crime, and his life following his 2017 release.

Former Cleveland Browns quarterback Johnny Manziel was in the spotlight for domestic violence allegations involving his ex-girlfriend in January 2016. At the time, the former player was also in the news for other off-the-field incidents involving drugs and alcohol, which diverted attention from his domestic violence case. He was indicted by a grand jury in April 2016. The case was later dismissed.

New York Giants kicker Josh Brown was under investigation for domestic abuse and was only suspended for one game, even though he admitted to abusing his wife in his journal entries. Macur (2016) commented on how the NFL handled the case, stating the league had not adequately punished Brown, bringing into question the league's commitment to address the issue of domestic violence while asking others to take a stance.

Theoretical Foundation

Institutional Theory

Professional sport institutions have become the backbone and structure for the way a club or organization operates. Lammers and Barbour (2006) define the term "institution" as "constellations of established practices guided by enduring, formalized, rational beliefs that transcend particular organizations and situations" (p. 357). Scott and Meyer (1983) explain institutional theory as "the elaboration of rules and requirements to which organizations must conform if they are to receive support and legitimacy" (p. 140). DiMaggio and Powell (1983) added that organizational decisions must also "adhere to various institutional norms or rules to achieve a fit or to integrate into their environment" (Wang, Tseng, & Yen, 2014, p. 374). This means that the overarching institution implements mandatory rules, guidelines, and initiatives that help each member or organization reach the overall mission or goal.

The NFL can be considered an institution made up of organizations of clubs and teams within the overall institution of professional sports. The NFL can be thought of as an umbrella institution composed of smaller for-profit organizations, or teams, that agree to be governed by the umbrella institution's standards and practices. Each team has a set of standards and guidelines to follow in order to reach a common goal or support the mission of the institution. Ultimately, these help work toward the main goal of the NFL institution, which is "to provide our fans, communities and partners the highest quality sports and entertainment in the world, and to do so in a way that is consistent with our values" (NFL.com, n.d.).

Wang et al. (2014) elaborate on earlier definitions of the theory by adding that decisions made within an organization are not only driven by the mission and goals of the entire organization but also by organizational concerns, as well as social and cultural factors. Cornelissen, Durand, Fiss, Lammers, and Vaara (2015) further amplify this definition by describing it as the act of individuals gathering together to act in a complementary way under comparable circumstances by combining similar meaning and motives to these actions.

Institutional Theory in Sport

There is little research that highlights the connection between the sport industry and institutional theory. For years, institutional theory had focused on various organizational domains, such as educational systems, the radio industry, and healthcare organizations; however, it was not until recently that sport settings started integrating the theory (Washington & Patterson, 2011). In their analysis of the relationship of institutional theory to sport management, Washington and Patterson (2011) argued that there is more to this relationship than the concepts being offered in the current literature. They encouraged researchers to examine issues of institutional change and organizational dynamics and to incorporate the theory into different types of sport management questions. Washington and Patterson also argued that most institutional theory studies in sport assume that the institutions in their study are legitimate and stable (2011). In 2017, Heinze and Lu capitalized upon these recommendations in their study on concussions in the NFL. The researchers used institutional theory to explore the relationship between powerful organizations and their institutional environments (Heinze & Lu, 2017). Specifically, Heinze and Lu (2017) studied the organizational dimension of player concussions and suggested practical values from their findings that could help other sport governing bodies facing institutional pressures on concussions.

Professional sport institutions create mandatory initiatives that each of their member organizations must implement to successfully reach the mission and goal of the entire institution. For example, the NFL mandates that each member organization implements its breast cancer awareness initiative titled "A Crucial Catch" every October during Breast Cancer Awareness Month. Each organization must follow the NFL's guidelines for this campaign or face repercussions from the institution, such as fines.

The NFL institution exercises power to control how each of its 32 organizations operate. Most importantly, the institution has enough authority to control its image and self-proclaim its expertise on various internal organizational issues. This authority and control is especially crucial when dealing with high-profile social issues such as domestic violence. The NFL, not each team, serves as the official spokesperson on domestic violence and sexual assault. A weak (or no) response by the NFL may tarnish the teams under its governorship.

The Case

The 2014 domestic abuse crisis in the NFL raised questions among fans, most notably why the NFL failed to investigate other domestic violence cases prior to 2014. In USAToday.com, Schrotenboer (2014) states,

> After long being considered a private issue to be kept inside the home, domestic violence has gotten increased attention from law enforcement and policy makers in the past 40 years . . . Part of the problem is that these cases historically have been hard to prosecute, making it difficult to punish offenders, either in society or the NFL.

(para. 11)

Back in 1995, the league made its first attempt to address sexual assault and domestic violence when it developed its first personal conduct policy based on the case of Dan Wilkinson, a Cincinnati Bengals 325-pound defensive tackle accused of striking his pregnant girlfriend (Fainaru-Wada & Fainaru, 2014). This policy, however, did not result in a suspension after a 2000 domestic violence conviction (Fainaru-Wada & Fainaru, 2014). Furthermore, Fainaru-Wada and Fainaru's analysis showed that out of the 48 players who violated the league's domestic violence policy between the years 2000–2014, only 15 players were suspended for one game and 27 players received no suspension (2014). To compare, 82% of players who had substance abuse and performance-enhancing drug violations during the same time period were suspended four or more games (Fainaru-Wada & Fainaru, 2014).

The next attempt to publicly address assault and domestic violence in the NFL happened in 2014 with the Ray Rice case. Other than hosting press conferences and issuing statements to the public on their stance against the problem, the NFL waited five months before implementing its domestic violence and sexual assault prevention campaign, a series of public service announcements (PSAs) in partnership with "NO MORE". NO MORE is an international non-profit organization dedicated to reducing domestic violence and sexual assault through public awareness campaigns and partnerships with advocacy groups, service providers, governmental agencies, major corporations, universities, communities, and individuals (nomore.org, n.d.).

Since the debut of the "NO MORE" PSA at the 2015 Super Bowl, the league has taken further steps to eliminate domestic violence by updating its personal conduct policy, providing individual and family support hotlines, and creating mandatory comprehensive education and training programs. The league has also conferred with over 150 experts to review the punishments and rules for those in the NFL according to "The NFL Commitment: Taking Action on Domestic Violence and Sexual Assault" (2015). The league recently hired executives to pursue newer and stricter punishments and to review its code of conduct. Players who are under investigation for committing such acts are placed on administrative leave until the matter is investigated and conclusions are made. Ironically, in the case of Manziel, a grand jury indicted him for domestic abuse, but the NFL suspended him for four games for violating its substance abuse policy. The NFL did not address domestic abuse allegations against Manziel or take any action, despite the grand jury indictment ("Johnny Manziel reaches agreement to dismiss domestic violence charge," 2016). In the case of Josh Brown, described earlier, his one game suspension was a light punishment considering the gravity of his actions (Macur, 2016).

The problem is that the league's efforts to curb domestic violence do not appear to align with its sanctions, raising the question of the NFL's commitment to curb domestic abuse. On one hand, NFL players were arrested or charged with crimes 35 times in 2015, less than half what the league had in 2006 and the lowest annual number in the *USA Today* player-arrest data bank since 2000 (Schrotenboer, 2015). That is good news welcomed by the NFL. On the other hand, in the April 2017 draft, six players who had been accused of physical or sexual assaults "were welcomed to the NFL with little more than a shrug by their new teams" (Armour, 2017, para. 3). For example, Dede Westbrook, a finalist for the Heisman Trophy, was drafted by the Jacksonville Jaguars despite being arrested twice for assaulting the mother of his children. Even more concerning was the reaction by Jaguars general manager Dave Caldwell, who said after Westbrook's draft, "I think we all have been accused of things" (Armour, 2017, para. 4).

As of January 2018, 81 of the 1,720 active players have arrest records ("NFL arrest.com"), and since there is no penalty for signing a player who has a history of abuse, a further disconnect arises between what the NFL publicly states as its position on domestic abuse and its actions. Again, this raises the question whether the league's campaign efforts demonstrate a long-term commitment to reducing domestic violence or a quick public relations fix to protect its reputation.

You Make the Call

In each example above, the NFL has positioned itself as an institution of power, exercising control, and authority, which are tenets of institutional theory. Having documented domestic abuse cases since 2000, the NFL managed to keep this problem out of the public spotlight for nearly two decades. Once sexual assault and domestic violence gained media attention and public outrage, the NFL attempted to control the problem through light punishments and new policies. This did little to appease public criticism, forcing the NFL to try new tactics, most notably positioning itself as a leader against domestic violence. The NFL's reputation for being a family-friendly sport that positively impacts society has been severely damaged. Inaccuracies and inconsistencies in the NFL's handling of domestic abuse cases, such the Atlantic City elevator footage of Rice, were only some of the reasons advertisers considered pulling their sponsorships ("Case Analysis of the PR Scandal of the NFL," n.d.).

The NFL responded by positioning itself as an expert on domestic violence and sexual assault by partnering with NO MORE to show its commitment to reducing violence and sexual assault. As institutional theory posits, framing the NFL as the institution and the teams as the organizations allowed the NFL to speak as one voice, representing all teams, players, coaches, and owners with one powerful unified message against domestic violence. The 2015 PSAs featuring players from various teams speaking out against sexual assault and domestic violence was one example of how the NFL asserted its control and authority by positioning itself as an expert on the issue.

Though steps have been taken to repair its image, the NFL still has a long way to go before its rebranding efforts can be considered successful. Fans, including family members of NFL players, continue to speak out and create domestic violence prevention campaigns to show their commitment to reducing sexual assault and domestic violence. Many of these efforts, however, are not connected to the NFL. For example, the #NotAFan campaign includes NFL family members but is sponsored by the National Coalition Against Domestic Violence and a New York City councilwoman.

For years, the NFL flexed its muscle as a powerful and authoritative institution that bragged about owning a day of the week. It spent years ignoring documented domestic abuse cases. Instead of being forthcoming and transparent, the NFL was defiant and slow to acknowledge the crisis. Ultimately, this damaged its reputation among stakeholders and fans, creating a culture of anger and distrust of the institution. To avoid such major errors in the future, the NFL should strengthen its existing domestic abuse prevention partnerships and develop new ones, but it seems that once the domestic abuse crisis began fading from media attention, so did the NFL's efforts. Few sustainable efforts have been implemented since the launch of the "NO MORE" domestic violence awareness campaign, and there has been little progress to expand this initiative. The public service announcements are rarely aired during football broadcasts and are not present on the NFL's social media platforms. A domestic violence prevention ad did appear in the 2017 Super Bowl, and the NFL has committed $5 million a year for five years to the National Domestic Violence Hotline; however, with the NFL's revenue surpassing $13 billion in 2016, this contribution seems less impressive (Belzer, 2016).

The NFL needs to practice basic principles of good public relations. Grunig, Grunig, and Dozier (2006) provide specific tenets of excellent public relations, stating it must be managerial, strategic, symmetrical, diverse, and ethical. Specifically, the NFL should be more forthcoming, honest, and transparent in its communication efforts. It needs to better understand its target audiences and develop crisis communication plans before a crisis happens. The league should take responsibility for its actions and communicate with the public sooner rather than later. Most importantly, the NFL should revisit its institution's value statement and practice it.

The question raised throughout this critical analysis is whether the NFL has been sincere in addressing sexual assault and domestic violence or if its campaign efforts have been a move to positively rebrand itself as the solution rather than the perpetrator of the problem. The answer is not a simple yes or no but that the NFL, as an institution of power and authority, has an opportunity to demonstrate its sincerity. It is just not there yet.

Discussions Questions

1. Update the information presented in this chapter. Are domestic violence incidences in the NFL increasing or decreasing? What new domestic prevention programs, if any, has the NFL implemented?
2. How can the NFL reconcile its position of domestic violence prevention with its practice of drafting players with domestic abuse records?
3. Using institutional theory as a foundation, what other organizations are as powerful as the NFL? What makes them powerful?
4. Do you think the NFL is sincere in its efforts to reduce domestic violence, or are these efforts primarily aimed to save its reputation? Do you agree with the authors' conclusion? Explain your reasoning and provide evidence to support your position.
5. If you were overseeing communication efforts for the NFL, how would you address domestic violence involving players? What, if anything, is missing in its current messages?

References

Armour, N. (2017, May 1). NFL draft shows teams still don't care about domestic abuse. *USA Today Sports*. Retrieved from www.usatoday.com/story/sports/columnist/nancy-armour/2017/05/01/nfl-draft-domestic-violence-joe-mixon/101176656/

Belzer, J. (2016, February 29). Thanks to Roger Goodell, NFL revenues projected to surpass $13 billion in 2016. *Forbes.com*. Retrieved from www.forbes.com/sites/jasonbelzer/2016/02/29/thanks-to-roger-goodell-nfl-revenues-projected-to-surpass-13-billion-in-2016/#22d2563a1cb7

Burke, C. (2014, July 24). Lenient penalty for Ray Rice troubling proof of where NFL's priorities lie. *Sports Illustrated*. Retrieved from www.si.com/nfl/2014/07/24/ray-rice-suspension-roger-goodell-baltimore-ravens

Case Analysis of the PR Scandal of the NFL. (n.d.). *On-advertising.com*. Retrieved from http://on-advertising.com/case-analysis-pr-scandal-nfl/

Cornelissen, J. P., Durand, R., Fiss, P. C., Lammers, J. C., & Vaara, E. (2015). Putting communication front and center in institutional theory and analysis. *Academy of Management Review*, *40*(1), 10–27. doi:10.5465/amr.2014.0381

DiMaggio, P. J., & Powell, W. W. (1983). The iron cage revisited: Institutional isomorphism and collective rationality in organizational fields. *American Sociological Review*, *48*, 147–160.

Fainaru-Wada, M., & Fainaru, S. (2014. November 12). OTL: NFL didn't enforce own policies. *ESPN*. Retrieved from http://www.espn.com/espn/otl/story/_/id/11849798/outside-lines-most-nfl-players-domestic

Fitzsimmons, B. (2015, December 8). *28 NFL players who have been accused of domestic violence.* Retrieved from www.aol.com/article/2015/12/08/28-nfl-players-who-have-been-accused-of-domestic-violence/21280511/

Grunig, J. E., Grunig, L. A., & Dozier, D. M. (2006). The excellence theory. In C. H. Botan & V. Hazelton (Eds.), *Public relations theory II* (pp. 21–62). Mahwah, NJ: Lawrence Erlbaum Associates, Inc.

Harwell, D., & Halzack, S. (2014, September 12). Women are pro football's most important demographic: Will they forgive the NFL? *WashingtonPost.com.* Retrieved from www.washingtonpost.com/business/economy/women-are-pro-footballs-most-important-market-will-they-forgive-the-nfl/2014/09/12/d5ba8874-3a7f-11e4-9c9f-ebb47272e40e_story.html

Heinze, K. L., & Lu, D. (2017). Shifting responses to institutional change: The national football league and player concussions. *Journal of Sport Management, 31*(5), 497–513.

Johnny Manziel reaches agreement to dismiss domestic violence charge. (2016, December 2). *Espn.com News Services.* Retrieved from www.espn.com/nfl/story/_/id/18187426/johnny-manziel-reaches-agreement-dismiss-domestic-violence-charge

Lammers, J. C., & Barbour, J. B. (2006). An institutional theory of organizational communication. *Communication Theory, 16*(3), 356–377. doi:10.1111/j.1468-2885.2006.00274.x

Macur, J. (2016). N.F.L. shows it doesn't really care about domestic violence. *NYTimes.com.* Retrieved from www.nytimes.com/2016/10/22/sports/football/nfl-domestic-violence-josh-brown-new-york-giants.html?_r=0

NFL Arrests.com. (n.d.). Retrieved from nflarrest.com

The NFL commitment: Taking action on domestic violence and sexual assault. (2015). *NFL.com.* Retrieved from www.nfl.com/static/content/public/photo/2015/08/04/0ap3000000506403.pdf

The NFL's response to domestic violence and sexual assault. *NFL.com.* Retrieved from www.nfl.com/news/story/0ap3000000439286/article/the-nfls-response-to-domestic-violence-and-sexual-assault

NO MORE. (n.d.). *nomore.org.* Retrieved from http://nomore.org/about/our-story

Roger Goodell letter to NFL owners. (2014, August 29). *ESPN.com.* Retrieved from http://espn.go.com/nfl/story/_/id/11425532/roger-goodell-letter-nfl-teams-domestic-violence-policy

Schrotenboer, B. (2014, October 2). History of leniency: NFL domestic cases under Goodell. *USAToday.com.* Retrieved from www.usatoday.com/story/sports/nfl/2014/10/01/nfl-domestic-abuse-history-under-roger-goodell/16566615/

Schrotenboer, B. (2015, December 18). Why are fewer NFL players being arrested? *USAToday.com.* Retrieved from www.usatoday.com/story/sports/nfl/2015/12/18/nfl-arrests-personal-conduct-policy-roger-goodell/77481108/

Scott, W. R., & Meyer, J. W. (1983). The organization of societal sectors. In J. W. Meyer & W. R. Scott (Eds.), *Organizational environments: Ritual and rationality* (pp. 129–153). Beverly Hills, CA: Sage Publications.

Wang, H., Tseng, J., & Yen, Y. (2014). How do institutional norms and trust influence knowledge sharing? An institutional theory. *Innovation: Management, Policy & Practice, 16*(3), 374–391. doi:10.5172/impp.2014.16.3.374

Washington, M., & Patterson, K. (2011). Hostile takeover or joint venture: Connections between institutional theory and sport management research. *Sport Management Review, 14*(1), 1–12.

Wecht, C. (n.d.). Retrieved from www.quotes.net/mquote/987909

12 Drafting Like a King

Daily Fantasy Sports Websites in Crisis

Cory Hillman

This chapter examine the crisis communication strategies of daily fantasy sports websites such as DraftKings and FanDuel in response to allegations that they were illegal sports gambling sites engaged in false and deceptive advertising. Using Benoit's (2015) Image Restoration Theory, the study found that the substance of these allegations created a rhetorical dilemma that effectively limited their attempts at image repair. This chapter interrogates the efficacy of these choices, examines the DraftKings' and FanDuel's crisis communication plans, provides a comprehensive overview of the growth of daily fantasy sports, and outlines additional ethical issues that confront similar sports organizations and companies.

Introduction

Trevor Noah, the host of Comedy Central's *The Daily Show*, once made the following shrewd observation about the media. "These days, it feels like you can't turn on the TV without seeing one of three things: a zombie, a Kardashian, or a fantasy football ad." Referring to the 22,000 advertisements that ran on television for daily fantasy sports websites DraftKings and FanDuel between August and October of 2015, Noah remarked, "[that's] almost as many times as I've seen *Titanic* in theatres" (as quoted in Montgomery, 2015, para. 4). In fact, both sports fantasy sites managed to outspend the entire beer industry on commercial advertisements in the weeks leading up to the 2015 NFL season. This meant the average television viewer was being targeted by DraftKings and FanDuel advertisements approximately every 90 seconds, urging viewers to visit their websites in pursuit of wallet-swelling cash payouts (Alba, 2015). And then, at the height of their popularity, scandal erupted in the industry after reports surfaced that a DraftKings employee won $350,000 in a weekly fantasy football contest on rival website FanDuel allegedly using "insider information" not made available to the public (Drape & Williams, 2015). Several states, including Nevada and New York, responded by banning both companies from operating within their borders. State legislators argued that daily fantasy sites were hardly more than unregulated sports gambling operations that were cleverly exploiting a loophole in a federal law designed to prohibit online gambling. Other legal challenges followed, including a claim that DraftKings and FanDuel potentially engaged in false and deceptive advertising (Drape, 2015; Huddleston, Jr., 2016). Within a short period of time, the once promising daily fantasy sports business stood nervously on the precipice of financial ruin and public embarrassment.

The purpose of this chapter is to provide an overview of the emergence of daily fantasy sports websites while examining the crisis communication strategies DraftKings and FanDuel used to counter these legal threats using Benoit's (2015) Image Repair Theory. In particular, the chapter explores both the possible motives and the rhetorical effectiveness of their use of *denial*, *minimization*, and *compensation*. The goal of the chapter is to stimulate an informed conversation regarding the future of daily fantasy sports and discuss what, if any, productive role they might play in a fan's involvement and enjoyment of sports in the future.

Background

Fantasy sports operate through a very simple concept, one in which participants compete with one another by assembling a "dream team" of actual players who earn points based on their performance in actual games. While early forms of fantasy sports, such as rotisserie baseball, had limited appeal because of the amount of effort required to scour box scores and calculate results by hand, the Internet made playing fantasy sports much easier. Players now have access to real-time statistics that were converted into fantasy points quickly and automatically in online leagues (Hu, 2003). In 2016, an estimated 57.4 million people in the United States and Canada participated in some form of fantasy sports (Fantasy Sports Trade Association, 2017). Professional sports leagues, meanwhile, embrace fantasy sports because they encourage players to consume more sports on television, even "out of market" games they would otherwise have little reason to watch. On average, people who play fantasy sports consume an additional eight hours of sports media content per week compared to those who do not. Thus, leagues and their broadcast partners sense big money in fantasy sports because they stimulate an appetite for televised games, sports commentary, and insider coverage, translating into more lucrative advertising revenue and corporate sponsorships (Brown, Ruihley, & Billings, 2012). This has become more important as traditional sports witness a decline in younger fans (Bennett, 2014). Thus, to maximize advertising and sponsorship revenue, leagues can (1) entice existing fans to watch more sports and/or (2) attract newer—and hopefully younger—sports fans. While traditional fantasy sports may be effective at fulfilling the first condition, there is little evidence that they were productive in terms of turning younger fans on to sports. Daily fantasy websites such as FanDuel and DraftKings seem to address both issues by intensifying existing fans' relationships to sports and offering a necessary antidote against the declining appeal of sports to young people. Whereas traditional fantasy sports took place over an entire season, daily fantasy sports contests started and ended on the same day, providing the high-octane thrill of immediate gratification. As FanDuel CEO Nigel Eccles explained, daily fantasy sports were designed specifically to cater to the shorter attention spans of millennials ("This Week in Startups," 2016).

Academic research has examined the factors that motivate people to play fantasy sports, their impact on sports viewing habits, and participation on fan identity. Halverson and Halverson (2008) found that a primary appeal of fantasy sports was connected to the emergence of "competitive fandom," a mentality found among highly invested fans who use fantasy sports as a way of demonstrating their sports knowledge to their peers. Brown, Ruihley, and Billings (2012) research on the relationship between age and fantasy sports enjoyment found a similar competitive mentality to be more common among younger players. Meanwhile, Farquhar and Meeds (2007) determined that the era of fantasy sports being used to connect with family, friends, and co-workers was virtually over, suggesting that fantasy sports were becoming increasingly "*non*—or even *anti*-social." (p. 1224). They also found that highly involved participants tended to view them as games of skill, while lesser-involved players saw them as games of chance. Moreover, Billings and Ruihley (2013) concluded that fantasy sports have now become an almost obligatory ritual for anyone to be seen as a serious fan.

FanDuel launched in 2009 followed by DraftKings in 2012, each branding themselves as "daily" fantasy sports websites allowing fans to compete for immediate cash payouts and bragging rights. While they sounded like sports gambling sites, they were technically legal. In 2006, Congress passed the Unlawful Internet Gambling Enforcement Act that prohibited people from wagering money on "games of chance" online. However, an exception was made for fantasy sports because they were determined to be "games of skill" where the outcome was based on participants' accumulated knowledge of sports (Internet Gambling Prohibition and Enforcement Act, 2006). However, daily fantasy sports did not exist when the Unlawful Internet Gambling Enforcement Act was enacted. Critics argued that DraftKings and FanDuel were exploiting a loophole based on a definition of fantasy sports that did not legitimately apply to their product. Supporters claimed daily fantasy contests rewarded luck over skill, as single-game player performances were viewed as too unpredictable for any sense of strategy or knowledge to really matter at all (Kim, 2015).

Americans, however, took to the concept of daily sports almost immediately; the millions of dollars spent on advertising by daily fantasy sports sites seemed to be doing their job. In 2014, Americans paid over $1 billion in tournament entry fees as both companies saw their valuation increase to over $1 billion (Koughan & Bogdanich, 2016; Miller & Singer, 2015). The NFL, MLB, NBA, and the NHL developed partnerships with these companies, along with media heavyweights such as FOX, ESPN, Time Warner, and Google Capital (Alba, 2015). Given major professional sports leagues' strong stances against sports gambling, these relationships seemed hypocritical to fantasy site critics who argued that it was hardly different than what daily fantasy sites were offering. However, the loophole in the 2006 law allowed leagues to claim that DraftKings and FanDuel were legitimate enterprises that delivered a harmless, entertaining, and engaging way for people to enjoy sports. After all, there is sufficient evidence that wagering money on sports certainly makes them more exciting. According to American Gaming Association president Geoff Freeman, betting on tournament brackets for the NCAA's "March Madness" men's basketball tournament is uniquely responsible for making it "the big-time event that it is today" (as quoted in Moyer, 2015, para. 4). An estimated $2 billion is wagered annually on the March Madness spectacle each spring (Moyer, 2015). These numbers translate into huge sponsorship deals for the NCAA, with the 2016 men's tournament generating a record $1.2 billion in national television ad spending (Swallen, 2017).

The Case

In October of 2015, news outlets reported that Ethan Haskell, a DraftKings employee, had won $350,000 in a weekly fantasy football contest on rival website FanDuel using "insider information" that may have given him an unfair advantage (Roberts, 2015). While DraftKings and FanDuel operate similarly to traditional fantasy sports leagues, winning daily fantasy contests also involves strategically picking lesser drafted players. Because Haskell had access to information regarding the percentage of users who had selected players, he would have had a significant competitive advantage when finalizing his fantasy lineup for the week (Tepper, 2015). While an independent investigation appeared to clear DraftKings of any improprieties, lawmakers began to scrutinize the unregulated daily fantasy sports industry. The Nevada Gaming Commission, following the lead of four other states, ordered both websites to cease business in the state until they were approved for a gaming license (Drape, 2015). Meanwhile, New York Attorney General Eric Schneiderman successfully filed an injunction against DraftKings and FanDuel, contending they were illegal gambling sites engaged in false and misleading advertising (Huddleston, Jr., 2016). With legislation specifically mentioning both DraftKings and FanDuel as infamous examples, both companies had a public image problem.

Benoit's (2015) Image Repair Theory (IRT) is used to understand how individuals and organizations utilize various communication strategies to repair their damaged image or reputation after being accused of wrongdoing. According to Benoit, maintaining a positive face or reputation is a central goal of our communication behavior. Thus, when our reputation is at risk because of our perceived responsibility for an offensive act, we are often provoked to use "explanations, defenses, justifications, rationalizations, apologies, or excuses for our behavior" (p. 3). Even today, where the platitude

"I don't care what others think" is a common badge of personal authenticity, our reputations matter because they determine how we are treated by others. And, according to Benoit, threats against one's public face are quite common. This is due to the limited and unequal allocation of resources, the lack of complete control in our lives, our personal flaws, and our differing desires and wants that lead to interpersonal conflict. Even in situations where we have done nothing wrong, we may have to engage in image repair if a relevant audience holds the opinion that we have erred (Benoit, 2015).

Benoit (2015) presents a remarkable typology of communication strategies that are often used to repair one's damaged reputation. "Rhetors have five general options for self-defense: denial, evade responsibility, reduce offensiveness, corrective action, and mortification" (Benoit & McHale, 1999, p. 267). Benoit utilized IRT to analyze image repair discourses of high-profile athletes, including Tonya Harding (Benoit & Hanczor, 1994) and Tiger Woods (Benoit, 2013). IRT has also been utilized elsewhere in communication and sport research, including the Mike Leach-Texas Tech bullying scandal (Turman, Stein, & Barton, 2008) and the Lance Armstrong doping controversy (Thomsen & Anderson, 2015). Overall, this research has sought to identify the specific image repair discourses used by athletes and sports organizations as outlined by IRT and to evaluate the effectiveness of the athletes' choices.

In relation to DraftKings and FanDuel, it is important to focus on how they used *denial* and *reducing offensiveness* in response to allegations of engaging in sports gambling and false advertising. Denial involves simply claiming that one did not perform the offensive act in question or, in some cases, shifting the blame to someone or something else. Reducing offensiveness, meanwhile, attempts to highlight an individual's positive qualities and/or downplay the seriousness of the questionable act. The efficacy of any image repair strategy is constrained by the context in which it occurs, such as whether multiple parties were involved in the wrongful act, the credibility of the actor prior to the occurrence of the undesirable situation, and the knowledge and predisposition of the audience (Benoit, 2015). For example, denial would obviously represent a poor response if sufficient evidence, in the form of video, memoranda, text messages, or other credible material, publicly existed showing the actor engaged in the reprehensible act.

You Make the Call

In response to the allegations that daily fantasy sports constituted illegal gambling, both DraftKings and FanDuel relied heavily on *denial*, using previous legislative and judicial decisions to support their claim that they were legal enterprises. FanDuel CFO Matt King noted the fantasy sports exemption in the 2006 Unlawful Internet Gambling Enforcement Act as evidence that daily fantasy sports were games of skill (Koughan & Bogdanich, 2016). Meanwhile, FanDuel CEO Nigel Eccles stated that "the vast majority of fantasy sports leagues have an entry fee and a prize," adding that "fantasy sports is a game of skill" supported by an abundance of state, federal, and case law (This Week in Startups, 2016). Jason Robins, CEO of DraftKings, contended that several states had already passed legislation "clarifying that fantasy sports is a legal, skillful activity" (CBS This Morning, 2016). Overall, this approach was effective as it absolved both DraftKings and FanDuel from having to justify and explain exactly how daily fantasy sports were skill-based contests. Rather, the rationale for that determination was left to lawmakers, not FanDuel or DraftKings. The fantasy sports sites argued they were merely operating within the accepted boundaries of the law, and thus any implication that associated daily fantasy sports with illegal gambling should be shifted to elected officials and not DraftKings and FanDuel.

DraftKings and FanDuel also had to contend with allegations they engaged in false and deceptive advertising practices that misrepresented the odds of cash payouts to players. One FanDuel commercial featured Chris Prince, who claimed that "I'm just a regular guy who goes to work every day. Anybody can win." A second FanDuel ad featured a player named Scott Hanson bragging how he turned "$2 into $2 million on FanDuel" (as cited in Shen, 2016). According to New York attorney general Eric Schneiderman, who filed a lawsuit against both companies, ads like these suggested that all players, regardless of their knowledge of sports, could win big. As it turned out, Prince was a professional fantasy sports player while Hanson was employed in the sports analytics industry, facts not disclosed to viewers. Schneiderman presented evidence that nearly 90% of daily fantasy players, in fact, lost money (Shen, 2016). And, as it turned out, those who did win were not your "average Joe" but rather skilled and seasoned professionals.

One study showed that 85% of users, referred to in the industry as "fish" or "minnows," lost money on daily fantasy contests in the first half of the 2015 MLB season. Meanwhile, only the top 1.3% of players, or "sharks," regularly won money, profiting an average of $135,000 each (Miller & Singer, 2015). Minnows are recreational players who mostly construct lineups based on hunches or gut instincts. Sharks, on the other hand, devote several hours a day to constructing a fantasy team, usually with personally constructed algorithms and complicated computer software. Miller and Singer (2015) argue that "the skill element is so high that [daily fantasy sports] pros will wipe out recreational players in short order" (para. 2). Interestingly, FanDuel and DraftKings chose to ignore this evidence, which would have certainly substantiated their claims that daily fantasy sports were games of skill. However, doing so would have legitimatized the legal claims that the companies knowingly engaged in false and deceptive advertising. It is reasonable to assume that the popularity of daily fantasy sites is largely based on manufacturing the feeling that anyone can win in order to provide the kind of "gambling rush" that makes these contests appealing. Furthermore, the evidence provided by Miller and Singer (2015) would have turned off casual fantasy sports players who not only compose most of these sites' entry fees but help bankroll the large cash winnings for skilled participants.

Thus, DraftKings and FanDuel were caught in a dilemma: either acknowledge daily fantasy sports were games of skill, thereby legitimatizing the legal claims they engaged in false advertising, or state its commercials were truthful, thus undermining the skill-based argument. For monetary reasons, they opted for the former, as daily fantasy sports needed to be understood as games of skill for DraftKings and FanDuel to remain financially viable. As an example of *reducing offensiveness*, each company agreed to pay $6 million to settle lawsuits pertaining to allegations that their ads were misleading (Shen, 2016). While offering monetary compensation can be an acknowledgment of wrongdoing, it can also demonstrate that an actor is taking responsibility for their behavior, thus potentially restoring their image and credibility (Benoit, 2015).

Had DraftKings and FanDuel engaged in more truthful advertising and ensured a more level playing field in its contests by sorting players by skill level, both companies could have avoided costly legal settlements and lobbying costs. In the aftermath of their legal battles, both companies announced 60 layoffs, witnessed their market values plummet, and dealt with continuing bans in several states (Drape, 2016). FanDuel and DraftKings even desperately announced plans of a merger but opted out before the Federal Trade Commission could make a decision on the proposal (Purdum, 2017). However, the fact that 12 states, including New York, have clarified that daily fantasy sports are legal enterprises, along with an emerging globalizing strategy to secure daily fantasy sports markets outside the U.S. (Bloomberg Technology, 2017; Purdum, 2017), could mean the future survival of fantasy sports sites. Yet, ethical, existential, and regulatory questions remain. Should these websites exist at all? If so, how should they be properly regulated, and to what extent should sports leagues and media networks be allowed to partner with them?

Discussion Questions

1. Explain whether you believe daily fantasy sports leagues constitute illegal sports gambling.
2. Discuss the current status of daily fantasy sports. How have any new developments shaped the way these sites operate and impacted your opinion of the daily fantasy sports industry?
3. Explain whether you found DraftKings' and FanDuel's image restoration strategies to be effective and ethical.
4. How have DraftKings' and FanDuel's sponsorship relationship with major professional sports leagues, such as the NFL, MLB, NBA, and the NHL, impacted the sports themselves? How have they impacted the sports gambling industry?
5. Describe the ethical issues that arise when professional sports leagues and media networks partner with daily fantasy sports operations like FanDuel and DraftKings.

References

Alba, D. (2015). DraftKings and FanDuel scandal is a cautionary startup tale. *Wired.com*. Retrieved from www.wired.com/2015/10/daily-fantasy-sports-scandal-fanduel-draftkings

Bennett, R. (2014). MLS equals MLB in popularity with kids. *ESPN.com*. Retrieved from www.espn.com/soccer/news/story/_/id/1740529/mls-catches-mlb-popularity-kids-says-espn-poll.

Benoit, W. L. (2013). Tiger Woods' image repair: Could he hit one out of the rough? In J. R. Blaney, L. Lippert, & S. J. Smith (Eds.), *Repairing the athlete's image: Studies in sports image restoration* (pp. 89–96). Lanham, MD: Lexington Books.

Benoit, W. L. (2015). *Accounts, excuses, and apologies: Image repair theory and research* (2nd ed.). Albany, NY: State University of New York Press.

Benoit, W. L., & Hanczor, R. S. (1994). The Tonya Harding controversy: An analysis of image restoration strategies. *Communication Quarterly, 42*(4), 416–433.

Benoit, W. L., & McHale, J. P. (1999). Kenneth Starr's image repair discourse viewed in 20/20. *Communication Quarterly, 47*(3), 265–280. doi:10.1080/01463379909385559

Billings, A. C., & Ruihley, B. J. (2013). Why we watch, why we play: The relationship between fantasy sports and fanship motivations. *Mass Communication and Society, 16*, 5–25.

Bloomberg Technology. (2017, May 12). *DraftKings CEO focused on expansion and improving games [Video file]*. Retrieved from https://www.youtube.com/watch?v=OTT8HutzsiY.

Brown, N., Ruihley, B., & Billings, A. (2012). Exploring the change in motivations for fantasy sport participation during the life cycle of a sports fan. Communication Research Reports, 29(4), 333–342. http://dx.doi.org/10.1080/08824096.2012.723646.

CBS This Morning. (2016, June 20). DraftKings CEO on impact of New York legislation [Video file]. Retrieved from www.youtube.com/watch?v=FO64jO_pA_k

Drape, J. (2015). Gambling regulators block daily fantasy sites in Nevada. *CNBC.com*. Retrieved from www.cnbc.com/2015/10/15/draftkings-fanduel-scandal-gambling-regulators-block-daily-fantasy-sites-in-nevada.html

Drape, J. (2016). DraftKings and FanDuel agree to merge daily fantasy sports operations. *The New York Times.com*. Retrieved from www.nytimes.com/2016/11/19/sports/draftkings-fanduel-merger-fantasy-sports.html

Drape, J., & Williams, J. (2015). Scandal erupts in unregulated world of fantasy sports. *The New York Times.com*. Retrieved from www.nytimes.com/2015/10/06/sports/fanduel-draftkings-fantasy-employees-bet-rivals.html

Fantasy Sports Trade Association. (2017). Industry demographics. Retrieved from http://fsta.org/research/industry-demographics/

Farquhar, L. K., & Meeds, R. (2007). Types of fantasy sports users and their motivations. *Journal of Computer-Mediated Communication, 12*, 1208–1228.

Halverson, E. R., & Halverson, R. (2008). Fantasy baseball: The case for competitive fandom. *Games and Culture, 3*, 286–308.

Hu, J. (2003). Sites see big season for fantasy sports. *CNetNews.com*. Retrieved from http://news.cnet.com/2100-1026_3-5061351.html?tag=fd_lede2_hed.

Huddleston, T., Jr. (2016). DraftKings and FanDuel are once again legal in New York. *Fortune.com*. Retrieved from http://fortune.com/2016/08/04/draftkings-fanduel-legal-new-york/

Internet Gambling Prohibition and Enforcement Act. H.R. 4411, 109th Congress. (2006).

Kim, E. (2015). Why DraftKings, a $900 million site that allows gambling on fantasy sports, is legal. *Business Insider.com*. Retrieved from www.businessinsider.com/draftkings-not-illegal-2015-4

Koughan, F. (Writer/Director), & Bogdanich, W. (Writer). (2016). The fantasy sports gamble *[Television Broadcast]*. In F. Koughan (Producer), *Frontline*. New York, NY: PBS.

Miller, E., & Singer, D. (2015). For daily fantasy sports operators, the curse of too much skill. *Street and Smith's Sports Business Daily.com*. Retrieved from www.sportsbusiness daily.com/Journal/Issues/2015/07/27/Opinion/From-the-Field-of-Fantasy-Sports.aspx

Montgomery, J. (2015). Watch "the Daily Show" tackle dishonest daily fantasy leagues. *Rolling Stone.com*. Retrieved from www.rollingstone.com/sports/videos/watch-the-daily-show-tackle-dishonest-daily-fantasy-leagues-20151016

Moyer, C. (2015). Americans to bet $2 billion on 70 million March Madness brackets this year, says new research. *American Gaming Association*. Retrieved from http://stg.americangaming.org/newsroom/press-releases/americans-bet-2-billion-70-million-march-madness-brackets-year-says-new

Purdum, D. (2017). Planned merger between DraftKings, FanDuel is off. *ESPN.com*. Retrieved from www.espn.com/chalk/story/_/id/20002903/in-abrupt-fashion-draft kings-fanduel-merger-off

Roberts, D. (2015). Fantasy sports scandal actually helped DraftKings and FanDuel. *Fortune.com*. Retrieved from http://fortune.com/2015/10/13/scandal-helped-draftkings-fanduel/

Shen, L. (2016). DraftKings and FanDuel settle New York lawsuit for $12 million. *Fortune.com*. Retrieved from http://fortune.com/2016/10/26/draftkings-fanduel-settlement/

Swallen, J. (2017). March Madness advertising generates $1.24 billion. *Kantar.com*. Retrieved from http://us.kantar.com/business/brands/2017/march-madness-2017-advertising-by-the-numbers/

Tepper, F. (2015). Everything you need to know about the DraftKings/FanDuel scandal. *Techcrunch.com*. Retrieved from https://techcrunch.com/gallery/everything-you-need-to-know-about-the-draftkingsfanduel-scandal/

This Week in Startups. (2016, April 28). *Nigel Eccles, CEO of Fan Duel, explains why fantasy sports are a game of skill* [Video file]. Retrieved from www.youtube.com/watch?v=2kcKBbfAsYQ

Thomsen, S. R., & Anderson, H. (2015). Using the rhetoric of atonement to analyze Lance Armstrong's failed attempt at redeeming his public image. *Journal of Sports Media*, *10*(1), 79–99.

Turman, P., Stein, K., & Barton, M. (2008). Understanding the voice of the fan: *Apologia*, *antapologia*, and the 2006 World Cup controversy. In L.W. Hugenberg, P. Haridakis, & A. Earnheart (Eds.), *Sports mania: Essays on fandom and the media in the 21st century* (pp. 86–102). Jefferson, NC: McFarland.

13 What Did Ryan Lochte Do?

Bouncing Back From an International Crisis

Nicola A. Corbin & Anne Bialowas

This chapter analyzes the image restoration strategies undertaken by U.S. swimmer Ryan Lochte and his management following Lochte's misbehavior during the 2016 Rio Olympics, which resulted in a derogatory #lochtegate Twitter campaign. Lochte promptly lost four sponsors and was suspended from international swimming for 10 months. However, within the span of five months, he picked up new sponsorships, including one with a major swimming apparel company, Tyr, and competed on ABC's Dancing with the Stars. Using Benoit's (1995) theoretical typology, this chapter establishes the case as a public relations crisis and examines the image restoration strategies Lochte employed.

Introduction

On August 14, 2016, U.S. Olympic swimmer Ryan Lochte confirmed a rumor with former NBC television presenter Billy Bush that he, and three of his American swim teammates, had been robbed at gunpoint at a gas station in Rio de Janeiro, Brazil, during the 2016 Olympic Games. Soon after, when the Brazilian police cast significant doubt on the allegations, Lochte's story began to fall apart, and in a television interview with then NBC anchor Matt Lauer, he said that he "over-exaggerated" the details of the incident. The Brazilian police charged him with filing a false police report, USA Swimming suspended him for 10 months, and he was required to complete 20 hours of community service (Drehs, 2016).

Within eight days of the first reports, all four of his named corporate sponsors, Speedo, Polo Ralph Lauren, Gentle Hair Removal, and Airweave, cut ties with the swimmer (Bonesteel, 2016). However, despite public castigation both within legacy and social media, Lochte was allowed to compete on the television program *Dancing with the Stars*. By January 2017, he had new sponsorships from Pine Bros. Softish Throat Drops, alarm company Robocopp, and major swimming apparel company Tyr. Additionally, he had starred in commercials for PowerBar and Debt.com. The following case examines the steps Lochte undertook to re-establish himself as an acceptable spokesperson for a major brand within his sport of swimming and more within just five months of a career-damaging event.

Background

Ryan Lochte's Brand

Ryan Lochte is a U.S. swimmer who competed at the 2004, 2008, 2012, and 2016 Olympic Games, earning a total of 12 medals. Lochte, a well-decorated Olympian, was often presented as the supporting cast member to swimming phenom Michael Phelps. Lochte was the affable, easy-going, uncomplicated training partner who possessed the stone-cold opposite traits to Phelps' intensity and drive (Crouse, 2016). Outside the pool, the Lochte brand was even more carefree. In public appearances and interviews, Lochte appeared as the white (he claims Cuban in his heritage), handsome athlete who was lovable and adorably clueless. His answers to questions often seemed vacuous and devoid of consistent coherency (Boren, 2016). In fact, in 2013, cable television station E! aired a short-lived (eight-episode) reality series called *What Would Ryan Lochte Do?* that "featured Lochte at his Lochte best: Swimming, partying, dating, hanging out with his family, yelling 'Jeah!' and hanging out with his Lochterage" (Yahr, 2016, para. 3). However, the series really shone when it capitalized on Lochte's seeming lack of depth in the on-camera interviews. According to Yahr (2016), "producers didn't care if Lochte actually made sense—the more stuttering or blank looks or long pauses, the better" (para. 4). His conventional good looks and athletic talent combined with his seeming cluelessness aligned with the longstanding, cultural narrative of the loveable "dumb jock," one that Lochte embraced and perpetuated.

Crisis: Incident in Rio

On Sunday, August 14, 2016, at the beginning of the second and final week of the Olympic Games, Ryan Lochte confirmed a rumor that was first attributed to his mother, Illeana Lochte, that he and three of his American swim teammates had been robbed at gunpoint near a gas station in Rio. In a camera phone–recorded interview on Ipanema Beach, Lochte recounted a version of events to former NBC correspondent Billy Bush. Lochte said that, as they were leaving a party at dawn, the taxi in which he and his teammates were traveling was stopped by armed men who pretended to be police officers and who made them exit the vehicle and get on the ground. Lochte claimed to have refused to get on the ground because "we didn't do anything wrong." At this point, he said one of the men "pulled out his gun, he cocked it and put it to my forehead," and took his money and wallet (Bush, 2016).

This version of events quickly captivated international media and became the dominant story for the day, overshadowing normal coverage of the games. However, there were rumblings skeptical of Lochte's original account to Bush. On Wednesday, August 16, then NBC network anchor Matt Lauer said that Lochte had "softened some things, or stepped back" and changed the details about the gun being pointed at his head. Instead, he said the gun was pointed in his direction (Lauer, 2016).

Controversy over this revised account escalated on Thursday, August 17, when the Brazilian police disputed Lochte's version of events and accused the swimmer of fabrication (Romero, 2016). As the authorities put it at an internationally televised news conference, the athletes stopped at a Rio gas station that morning to use the bathroom and vandalized the premises. They broke a soap dispenser, tore a sign, urinated on the premises, and damaged a door (Romero, 2016). During the event, off-duty Rio police officers, working as security guards at the gas station, demanded remuneration for the damages. At some point, one of the guards brandished a gun, though not pointing it directly at anyone. The Rio police chief pushed back against Lochte's claim of victim, calling the swimmers vandals instead (Lauer, 2016).

These new details, presented by the Rio police, sent the incident into an even larger international crisis, with coverage being tracked at 18,689 stories on Thursday, August 18 (Den, 2016). Agilitypr.com reported that public sentiment shifted from being 90% positive in the August 14–16 period, buoyed by relief that the athletes were safe. to 70% negative by the August 17–18 period in demonstrated outrage and embarrassment (Den, 2016). #Lochtegate began trending on Twitter. U.S. national media carried headlines like the *New York Post*'s "Liar, Liar, Speedo on Fire: The Ugly American" (Serjeant, 2016).

The Case

Image Restoration Frameworks

According to Coombs (1995), the primary goals when responding in a crisis are to maintain the reputation of the person or organization and to reestablish legitimacy. From a theoretical standpoint, Coombs (1995) and Benoit (1995) offer useful frameworks to help crisis communicators produce effective responses and construct strategies to restore reputations and reestablish legitimacy. While these frameworks have been adapted and expanded upon in recent years, they form the bedrock of academic considerations for evaluating crisis communication responses (see e.g. Frederick, Burch, Sanderson, & Hambrick, 2014; Holdener & Kauffman, 2014).

Benoit's (1995) formative image repair typology will guide the assessment of the effectiveness of Lochte's deliberate attempts to restore his image. This typology has been used to analyze the image repair of other athletes such as Olympic ice skater Tonya Harding (Benoit & Hanczor, 1994), NFL star Terrell Owens (Brazeal, 2008), and Olympic swimmer and Lochte rival Michael Phelps (Walsh & McAllister-Spooner, 2011). Benoit's (1995) typology revolves around the following themes: denial, evasion of responsibility, reduction of offensiveness, corrective action, and mortification. Mortification requires the person to admit to wrongdoing, apologize, and ask for forgiveness. Adding complexity, Benoit (1995) expands upon the reduction of offensiveness category into subcategories to include bolstering (spotlighting a person's positive traits); minimizing the magnitude of backlash; differentiating the act from other similar, offensive acts; and compensation.

Additionally, this case study lends support to such best practices as considering the medium in the delivery strategies, maintaining authenticity in the actor or organization, and considering the pre-crisis reputation of the actor. Further, it examines the impact of unscripted events. The following is an analysis of Lochte's major communication interactions regarding this crisis from August through September 2016.

Social Media Apology

On the morning of Friday, August 19, an apology was posted to Lochte's Instagram account and was quickly picked up by news outlets and shared via Twitter (Winsor, 2016). This apology was widely panned for its failure to clearly demonstrate acceptance of responsibility. The post read:

> I want to apologize for my behavior last weekend—for not being more careful and candid in how I described the events of that early morning and for my role in taking the focus away from the many athletes fulfilling their dreams of participating in the Olympics.

In form, this apology represents mortification in Benoit's (1995) typology. However, the actual text of the apology fails to rise to this level completely and engages with other strategies. Lochte evaded responsibility. There is no admission to specific acts committed by him or the other swimmers. Instead, with his "not being more careful and candid," he refocused the apology on the way he describes the event rather than his role in the acts that landed him in the situation in the first place. In fact, he hinted that others behaved poorly as well and still managed to cast himself as a scared, hapless American victim in a foreign land. He added:

> It is traumatic to be out late with your friends in a foreign country—with a language barrier—and have a stranger point a gun at you and demand money to let you leave, but regardless of the behavior of anyone else that night, I should have been much more responsible in how I handled myself.

Lochte also used bolstering strategies intended to focus on positive aspects about himself and relevant stakeholders by highlighting his own pride in representing his country, recognizing his teammates and his fans, and the "effort of the IOC, the Rio '16 Host Committee and the people of Brazil who worked so hard to make sure that these Olympic Games provided a lifetime of great memories."

However, because Lochte primarily evaded responsibility, this apology fell flat. The public media narrative had been widely established that he was more intricately involved in the incident than his apology acknowledged. His post about not "being more careful and candid" reinforced the idea of evasion in its attempt to minimize his actions.

Additionally, the use of Instagram, and only that medium, to make the apology is problematic, as using multiple platforms in an apology is tremendously useful (Schweitzer, Brooks, & Galinksy, 2015). The medium certainly matters in the delivery of a message. Lochte would have been better served in making this apology "in front of a camera or at a press conference" as his initial description of the events was done in front of a camera with Billy Bush (Heath, 2016, para. 3). Further, authenticity and sincerity are two factors that contribute heavily to believability and the eventual acceptance of public apologies. In this case, the very polished and deliberate word choices in the Instagram post screamed "prepared PR-speak" in contrast to Lochte's established brand image as the vacuous "dumb jock."

Interviews and Television Appearances

On Saturday, August 20, Lochte taped two video interviews, one with former-NBC anchor Matt Lauer, and Felipe Santana of Brazil's TV Globo. In both cases, Lochte appeared on screen attempting to look contrite in freshly dyed brown hair, a change from the platinum blond he sported at the Olympics. In both interviews, he was asked why he made this "over-exaggeration." He responded that he was intoxicated at the time and still did not know why he behaved the way he did. His general tone in the interviews expressed some measure of regret but rhetorically functioned within the realm of Lochte's "dumb jock" brand image and the larger cultural narrative of the attractive, all-American male who occasionally gets into harmless mischief. Lochte frequently used words like "immature" and "shenanigans." Here again, Lochte attempted to evade responsibility for his specific actions of that night and reduce the offensiveness of the way in which he re-told the incident to Bush by minimizing his intent. He only apologized for his "over-exaggeration" of the events and invoked the spirit of the "boys will be boys" narrative even while saying he did not want to be seen as a "drunk frat boy." In short, he sought to evade responsibility by blaming his actions on the alcohol. In the NBC interview, Lochte said:

> And that's why I'm taking full responsibility for it, because I over-exaggerated that story. And if I never had done that, we wouldn't be in this mess . . . . And it was my immature behavior. You know, we just finished. We were wanting to celebrate . . . . And I definitely had too much to drink that night. And I was very intoxicated. And none of this would have happened if I didn't do that.

> (Lauer, 2016)

Schweitzer et al. (2015) state that, in addition to the who and the what, the where, when, and how of an apology matter. Lochte specifically asked to speak with NBC's Matt Lauer and not Billy Bush. He also timed his apology interview with Santana on Brazil's TV Globo to appear following a nationally televised soccer match, when the viewing audience was presumably high. The use of television as a delivery medium worked in Lochte's favor. The two interviews allowed nonverbal cues, such as Lochte becoming emotional when discussing his teammates—demonstrating Benoit's mortification strategy. As he bumbled through his attempt to explain himself and express regrets, the viewers were reminded that this is precisely Ryan Lochte's persona. These cues dovetailed with his larger cultural narrative claim of clueless, boyish behavior.

The immediate results of these apologies were negative. His four sponsors promptly announced they were dropping him on August 22 following the airing of these interviews. Lochte's failure to fully admit fault hampered the effectiveness of his mortification strategy. Instead, by blaming alcohol, he continued to evade responsibility.

Dancing With the Stars

On August 30, the ABC television network announced Lochte was a cast member on *Dancing With the Stars (DWTS)*. Upon his first outing, two men rushed the stage in protest of Lochte's "shenanigans" at the Olympics. Other protesters were removed from the crowd. This unscripted incident unintentionally worked to push public sentiment back into Lochte's favor. The framing of the protesters as deliberate bullies who would not let an issue go collided with the clueless, boyish Lochte brand that he cultivated prior to the scandal and evoked during his apology tour. Without having to say the words this time, this incident cast Lochte as a victim and a sympathetic character. As one Twitter user posted, "Lochte's a pretty crappy person, but somehow these protesters are somehow worse" (@SeanathonTXST, 2016).

The support he received from the *DWTS* cast and ABC connected him and his brand to a non-threatening and popular show, which eased the sting of his actions in Rio. Professional dancer and show competitor Witney Carson said on CNN that she was saddened and disheartened "because this is such a positive show and we're all about putting people in a positive light . . . . For somebody to want to ruin that for Ryan is just really, really hard" (Park & Gonzalez, 2016).

Recovery: New Sponsors and Second Chances

Following the season finale of *DWTS*, Lochte announced his marriage engagement and expected baby. He gained new sponsorships with Pine Bros. Softish Throat Drops, Robocopp, and major swimming apparel company Tyr.

PowerBar hired him to pitch its Clean Start product in January 2017, while Debt.com commercials touted that "Even Ryan Lochte deserves a second chance." In these second chance–themed commercials, the pre-scandal brand of Lochte's goofy boyishness was invoked. His image was restored enough for sponsors to feel comfortable being aligned with him. Most importantly, these sponsors capitalized upon the scandal by playing up the second chances narrative. On June 6, 2017, ESPN ran an in-depth story catching up with the swimmer during his 10-month suspension, asking "Do You Still Really Hate Ryan Lochte?"(Gock, 2017). Perhaps not.

You Make the Call

This case of Ryan Lochte suggests there is space for redemption even when the actor's deliberate image restoration strategies are not fully effective. From selecting Instagram as the first way to apologize to failing to own up completely to all of his actions in Rio, Lochte initially inhibited his ability to present himself as a person who demonstrated contrition, understood the magnitude of his actions, and was worthy of forgiveness. These considerations more than likely contributed to him being dropped by his sponsors. This result is in line with historical trends. In a meta-analysis of image repair strategies from 1986 to 2016, evasion of responsibility and reduction of offensiveness were listed among the least effective, while corrective action when paired with bolstering was very effective (Arendt, LaFleche, & Limperopulos, 2017).

However, Lochte benefited from unscripted actions, emotional connections, and cultural narratives to make the case that he deserved a second chance. Through televised interviews, audiences were reminded of his bumbling "dumb jock" brand image, and his repetition of words such as "immature," "shenanigans," and "over-exaggerated" and claims of intoxication functioned to reinforce this nonverbal performance during the interviews. Therefore, when the unscripted incident occurred on *DWTS*, the groundwork was laid for acceptance that he and his brand were deserving of forgiveness. As one Twitter user posted, "Watching #DWTS and kinda forgiving Lochte now, not cuz of his dancing but I just think he's clinically dumb enough to make #lochtegate OK" (@nanoyaBusiness, 2016).

Another crucial lesson in this case is the need to consider and maintain authenticity of the actor when crafting crisis communication strategies. Before the crisis, Lochte cultivated and perpetuated a brand of being a dumb but gifted athlete. The purpose of crisis communication is to reestablish legitimacy to the organization or person (Coombs, 1995). In the case of Lochte, he only had to be seen again as the clueless, vacuous jock to be relegitimized. He did not have far to rise. The pre-crisis reputation can dictate the effectiveness and length of time for image restoration. Luckily for Lochte and his crisis management team, he was known more for his swimming accolades at the University of Florida than his academic achievements.

Discussion Questions

1. Compare the two interviews Lochte conducted with Matt Lauer (NBC) and Felipe Santana (TV Globo).

    a. What were the key messages?
    b. Were the messages consistent?
    c. What, if any, was the impact of the network's audiences of each interview?
    d. What crisis strategies were actively present in the interviews?

    > TV Globo interview clip: www.reuters.com/article/us-olympics-rio-lochte-idUSKCN10V0IO
    > NBC interview: www.youtube.com/watch?v=-1ClJ-r5dGA

2. Consider if the Olympic Games were held in a U.S. city and a top Brazilian athlete had made the same claims against American police officers. Discuss the ways in which you believe the narrative might have developed. What are some of the sociocultural factors that enabled easy acceptance of Lochte's initial version of events?
3. In addition to the strategies discussed in the chapter, what other American socio-cultural values and discourses might have provided a hospitable environment to aid Lochte's image restoration?
4. In October 2016, the #lochtegate hashtag was invoked again on Twitter as reality star Kim Kardashian was robbed abroad, and NBC Billy Bush became embroiled in a scandal with then presidential candidate Donald Trump. What lessons might PR practitioners take about social media and crisis?
5. How would you update this case to reflect any changes to the public stature of the key actors named here, shifts in relevant popular cultural narratives, or changes in the media landscape?

References

Arendt, C., LaFleche, M., & Limperopulos, M. A. (2017). A qualitative meta-analysis of apologia, image repair, and crisis communication: Implications for theory and practice. *Public Relations Review, 43*(3), 517–526.

Benoit, W. L. (1995). *Accounts, excuses, and apologies: A theory of image restoration strategies.* Albany, NY: State University of New York Press.

Benoit, W. L., & Hanczor, R. S. (1994). The Tonya Harding controversy: An analysis of image restoration strategies. *Communication Quarterly, 42*(4), 416–433.

Bonesteel, M. (2016, August 22). Ryan Lochte loses all four commercial sponsors after Rio Olympics incident. *The Washington Post.* Retrieved from www.washingtonpost.com/news/early-lead/wp/2016/08/22/speedo-drops-ryan-lochte-after-rio-olympics-incident/?utm_term=.10cb4699e8c8

Boren, C. (2016, August 18). Just who is Ryan Lochte? A look at the public persona the swimmer has built. *The Washington Post.* Retrieved from www.washingtonpost.com/

news/early-lead/wp/2016/08/18/just-who-is-ryan-lochte-alook-at-the-public-per sona-the-swimmer-has-built/?tid=a_inl&utm_term=.c699ef84cade

Brazeal, L. M. (2008). The image repair strategies of Terrell Owens. *Public Relations Review*, *34*(2), 145–150.

Bush, B. (2016, August 15). *Today*. Retrieved from www.youtube.com/watch?v=Ixr Yj0yCyLE

Coombs, W. T. (1995). Choosing the right words: The development of guidelines for the selection of the "appropriate" crisis-response strategies. *Management Communication Quarterly*, *8*(4), 447–476.

Crouse, K. (2016, August 18). For the spotlight? Ryan Lochte was ready to do anything. *The New York Times*. Retrieved from www.nytimes.com/2016/08/19/sports/olym pics/eccentric-everyman-ryan-lochte-profile.html

Den, D. (2016, August 19). Lochte and the boys: Timeline of an Olympic contro-versy. Retrieved from www.agilitypr.com/pr-news/analysis/lochte-boys-timeline-olympic-controversy/

Drehs, W. (2016, September 8). Swimmer Ryan Lochte reportedly suspended 10 months. *ESPN*. Retrieved from www.espn.com/olympics/swimming/story/_/id/17493633/ ryan-lochtesuspended-10-months-united-states-olympic-committee-usa-swimming

Frederick, E. L., Burch, L. M., Sanderson, J., & Hambrick, M. E. (2014). To invest in the invisible: A case study of Manti Te'o's image repair strategies during the Katie Couric interview. *Public Relations Review*, *40*(5), 780–788.

Gock, A. (2017, June 6). Do you really still hate Ryan Lochte? In consideration of fire-works, massages, Olympic gold, reality TV, marriage, fatherhood: And that incident in Rio. *ESPN*. Retrieved from www.espn.com/espn/feature/story/_/id/19506033/ will-hate-ryanlochte-end-story

Heath, T. (2016, August 19). Ryan Lochte's image hit will make endorsement deals harder after Rio. *The Washington Post*. Retrieved from www.washingtonpost.com/ business/capitalbusiness/ryan-lochtes-image-hit-will-make-endorsement-deals-harder-after-rio/2016/08/19/85d794aa-663d-11e6-96c0-37533479f3f5_story. html?tid=a_inl&utm_term=.135db4130e5d

Holdener, M., & Kauffman, J. (2014). Getting out of the doghouse: The image repair strategies of Michael Vick. *Public Relations Review*, *40*(1), 92–99.

Lauer, M. (2016, August 22). *Today*. Retrieved from www.youtube.com/watch?v=-1ClJ-r5dGA

[@nanoyaBusiness]. (2016, September 27). Watching #DWTS rn and kinda forgiving Lochte now, not cuz of his dancing but I just think he's clinically dumb enough to make #lochtegate OK [Tweet].

Park, M., & Gonzalez, S. (2016, September 13). Audience members crash Ryan Lochte's debut on "Dancing with the Stars". *CNN*. Retrieved from www.cnn.com/2016/ 09/12/entertainment/ryan-lochte-dancing-with-thestars/index.html

Romero, S. (2016, August 18). U.S. Swimmers' disputed robbery claim fuels tension in Brazil. *The New York Times*. Retrieved from www.nytimes.com/2016/08/19/sports/ olympics/police-say-ryan-lochte-lied-about-gunpoint-assault.html

Schweitzer, M. E., Brooks, A. W., & Galinksy, A. D. (2015, September). The organi-zational apology. *Harvard Business Review*. Retrieved from https://hbr.org/2015/09/ the-organizational-apology

[@SeanathonTXST]. (2016, September 14). Lochte's a pretty crappy person . . . but these protesters are somehow worse #DWTS #LochteGate [Tweet].

Serjeant, J. (2016, August 19). Ryan Lochte dubbed "Ugly American" as Rio robbery tale collapses. Retrieved from www.reuters.com/article/olympics-rio-lochte-reac tion/ryan-lochte-dubbed-ugly-american-as-rio-robbery-tale-collapses-idUSL1N 1B00U4

Walsh, J., & McAllister-Spooner, S. M. (2011). Analysis of the image repair discourse in the Michael Phelps controversy. *Public Relations Review, 37*(2), 157–162.

Winsor, M. (2016, August 19). Ryan Lochte apologizes "for not being more careful" in explaining "traumatic" Rio incident. *ABC News*. Retrieved http://abcnews.go.com/ US/ryan-lochte-apologizes-behavior-rio/story?id=41511737

Yahr, E. (2016, August 19). Now you can watch Ryan Lochte's gloriously terrible reality show. *The Washington Post*. Retrieved from www.washingtonpost.com/news/arts-and-entertainment/wp/2016/08/19/now-you-can-watch-ryan-lochtes-gloriously-terri ble-reality-show/?utm_term=.94f2e3d3df28

Section IV

Gender, Race, and Identity

14 Challenging a Boy's Club

Reputation Management and the Case of Women's Pay Inequity in Professional Sport

Terry L. Rentner & David P. Burns

Media attention regarding the 2015 FIFA Women's World Cup Championship and the U.S. women's hockey team boycott have put pay inequity in sports in the spotlight. While the debate itself is not novel, it is clearly unsettled. This chapter explores how sport organizations may face a reputation crisis due to growing equal pay demands. Using reputation management as a theoretical framework, the chapter addresses pay discrepancies and the impact that media rights, sponsorships, and culture have on professional sport. The chapter invites discussion of best practices and communication strategies as they relate to reputation management.

Introduction

A 2015 Pew Research Center study found that women earn 83% of what men do. As dismal as that is, it is a sum which might provoke envy among many professional female athletes in the United States, whose earnings are far below that national percentage compared to their male counterparts. That fact led one writer in the *New Yorker* to call professional sports "one of the last boys' clubs in mainstream culture" (Thomas, 2016). The evidence to support this claim is strong.

This chapter is a critical analysis of the gender pay gap in professional sports. Critical analysis, or critical inquiry, is a method that suggests theories of being and knowledge are based on issues of power and its distribution. According to Lather (2004), doing critical inquiry means "taking into account how our lives are mediated by systems of inequity such as classism, racism, sexism, and heterosexism" (p. 205). This method is useful in helping researchers study and evaluate social phenomena such as gender pay inequality.

While the debate itself is not novel, it is still unsettled. This chapter explores how professional sport organizations are facing a reputation management crisis as a result of growing demands for equal pay among female athletes. The chapter addresses these discrepancies in specific professional sports and discusses the impact media rights, sponsorships, and culture are having on female athletes' pay.

Background

Capitalizing on their 2015 FIFA Women's World Cup championship, top-tier members of the U.S. women's national soccer team are suing their employer—the United States Soccer Federation—for wage discrimination. The plaintiffs contend the U.S. women's team outperformed their national male counterparts, generated tens of millions of dollars more in revenue than the men, but were paid in multiples of 10 less than the underachieving male team players.

In spring 2017, the sports juggernaut that is the U.S. women's hockey team (they have won seven of the past nine world championships) announced it would not defend its championship title and boycott the upcoming International Ice Hockey Federation tournament—played on U.S. soil nonetheless—unless a wage dispute with its parent organization—USA Hockey—was settled. According to the law firm representing the players, in the past USA Hockey has only paid players $1,000 a month during the players' six-month Olympic residency period and nothing the rest of the time. If you are keeping score, that's six months of pay for 48 months of work. Players faced off against management and demanded a deal that compensates them in all years, not just Olympic years (Whyno, 2017). After courting replacement players to no avail and threats from the U.S. men's hockey team to join the walkout, USA Hockey relented mere hours before the women were to take the ice (Allen & Perez, 2017).

Yet, professional female sports are still caught in what Australian economics professor Ross Booth calls a "circular problem"—low media coverage contributes to low popularity which in turn leads to weak corporate sponsorship of the sport (Booth, 2014, p. 423). If women's sports are still caught in the media doldrums, men's sports have broken out of this vicious cycle and into commercial and financial prosperity. Seemingly this has allowed organizational leaders of unisex sports to act both tone deaf and blind to social changes and to use their economic bottom line as justification for underpaying female players.

Raymond Moore, the former director of the Indian Wells tennis tournament, stated in March 2016 that female players "ride on the coattails of men" and they should "go down every night on their knees and thank God that Roger Federer and Rafael Nadal were born because they have carried the sport" (Wagner-McGough, 2016, para 1). Following an outpouring of criticism on social media, Moore was forced to resign. While Moore's resignation may be seen as a positive step in addressing gender pay inequity in professional sports, the huge gap continues, a problem that the 2016 Gender Balance in Global Sport Report concludes is not likely to close soon (Tranter, Medd, & Braun, 2016).

Reputation Management as a Theoretical Framework

Reputation management is one of the most important functions in public relations within a sports organization. Put simply, it is the function that moderates the relationship between the organization and its stakeholders. Fombrun defines it as the "overall estimation in which a company is held by its constituents" (1996, p. 37), while Power (2007) describes it as an institutionalized prescription with which modern organizations must cope. Similarly, Smith (2013) defines reputation management as the part of the organization's external environment that deals with how stakeholders evaluate the information they have about any organization. Smith further offers that reputation management includes research, strategic planning, implementation, monitoring, and evaluation (Smith, 2013). According to Elsbach (2012), reputation management thus becomes the means to systematically influence the perceptions that form this evaluation.

Reputation management does not occur by chance and requires strategic management of the relationship among stakeholders (Melewar, 2008). The NFL is a good example. At the individual level, reputation management is essential in managing player images such as the Ray Rice domestic violence incident or the Michael Vick dogfighting scandal. At the team level, reputation management became critical for the New England Patriots during the infamous "deflategate" scandal, creating an image problem among top players, management, and the team itself. At the institutional level, the NFL's denial of the seriousness of concussion-related injuries sparked a class-action lawsuit by players and spawned a PBS documentary series and the feature film *Concussion*. In the above cases, the individual athlete's brand was negatively impacted and the NFL's public reputation suffered a bit, but the NFL's overall brand did not suffer financially.

The recent news coverage of gender pay inequity in professional soccer, tennis, and other sports has created a reputation crisis for the governing bodies of these sports. Reputation management serves as the model for a critical analysis of why professional sport must address pay inequity.

Case Study

According to *Forbes* magazine, Portuguese professional footballer Cristiano Ronaldo was the world's highest paid athlete in 2017, with a reported salary of $58 million and earnings of $93 million (Badenhausen, 2017). The world's highest paid female athlete in 2017 was Serena Williams, who earned a reported $8 million in salary and $27 million in overall earnings, 71% lower than Ronaldo (Badenhausen, 2017). Ironically, tennis is one of the few sports where women are compensated more comparably to their male partners, but the gap mirrors the pay gap of the American workforce, with women tennis players making roughly 80 cents on each dollar men earn (Rothenberg, 2016).

In soccer, one analysis of the federation's financial documents compared two male players and two female players of similar seniority in their respective World Cup years. The comparison showed that the men made almost twice as much as the women (Carroll, 2016). Pay discrepancies in golf showed total prize money for the 2014 men's PGA tour was five times more than the prize money for the 2015 women's LPGA tour (Women's Sports Foundation, 2015). In the WNBA, the maximum salary in 2015 was $109,500, whereas the maximum salary in the NBA was $16.407 million (Women's Sports Foundation, 2015).

The pay gap crosses international borders. For example, for winning the 2015 Women's World Cup, the U.S. women's national team won $2 million, whereas Germany took home $35 million for winning the 2014 World Cup (Women's Sports Foundation, 2015). This was also the case for cricket, where men and women simultaneously played in the World Twenty20 Competitions, but the total prize money for the men's event was 16 times that of the women's event (Wigmore, 2016). An even greater insult was that the International Cricket Council paid for men's teams to fly business class to India for the competition but only paid for the women players to fly economy class (Wigmore, 2016).

Overall, it is very difficult to get an apples-to-apples comparison of men's and women's salaries in sports because compensation agreements can drastically differ (Carroll, 2016). Critics argue pay differences occur because men's and women's sports are not the same in their style of play, officiating, and the way they are regarded by fans (Smallwood, 2016).

Media Rights and Sponsorships

Coverage of women's sports can be compared to the chicken-or-egg debate. Is there little coverage of women's sports because there is so little demand or is the demand so low because there is little mainstream coverage? Either way, media rights and sponsorships are largely to blame for the imbalance in pay. According to Fiona Hathorn, the Women on Boards UK's managing director, "It is not about how much an athlete is paid necessarily, it is about how much the sport is sponsored, and the sort of sponsorship deals one athlete can get" (Broadhurst, 2016, para. 8). Simply put, right now men outdraw women in viewership in massive numbers. Companies shelled out over $600 million for about 450 thirty-second TV commercials during the 2014 FIFA Men's World Cup compared to about the $40 million the 2015 FIFA Women's World Cup drew (Smallwood, 2016). And those sponsors were rewarded with viewers. When comparing viewers of men's and women's send-off games in 2014 and 2015 respectively, the men drew 87% more viewers than the women. Even when you factor in the 25 million viewers who watched the 2015 U.S. women vs. Japan final, the U.S. men outdrew the women in viewers by 74% (Kennedy, 2016).

Media coverage of sports helps introduce, incubate, and sustain interest in a sport. In this regard, the U.S. media have done a woeful job in covering women's sports. Cooky, Messner, and Musto (2015), in a 25-year longitudinal study of gender in televised sports news and highlight shows, examined coverage of women's sports by large-market local network affiliates and cable behemoth ESPN in 2014. The result was that, even considering the proliferation of channel choices today, coverage of women's sports was the lowest it has been in 25 years.

In examining 934 local network affiliate news stories from 2014, only 32 segments (about 23 minutes of coverage) were dedicated to women's sports. In contrast, 880 stories featured men's sports and 22 segments were non-gender specific sports. ESPN's *SportsCenter* covered 376 stories on men's sports versus 13 segments for women's sports (Cooky et al., 2015). "Moreover, women's sports continue to be covered in ways that convey the message to audiences that women's sport is less important, less exciting and, therefore, less valued than men's sports" (Cooky, Messner, & Hextrum, 2013; Greer, Hardin, & Homan, 2009).

In a 2013 study on college coaches, Von Allmen found that "aggregate data indicate coaches of women's programs earn less than coaches of men's programs at both the head and assistant coach levels" (p. 286). The pay disparity is especially noted at college institutions with large, revenue-producing sports like football and basketball where coaches negotiate huge contracts (see Berkowitz, Schnaars, & Wolken, 2017). Von Allmen also reported that women were no less skilled than men at coaching Division I women's softball. Von Allmen's research showed women coaches perform just as well as their male counterparts in that sport (p. 286). But women coaches are underrepresented in women's collegiate sports; women coach less than half the women's teams. And, that percentage is falling (Von Allmen, 2013).

Cultural Influences

Fraser (2007) offers the concept of gender justice in terms of "participatory parity" as a measure of material and cultural equality for women. Gender injustice occurs when women "are denied participatory parity by being culturally devalued and economically marginalized" (Travers, 2008, p. 78). Other scholars refer to a sports nexus that combines economic and cultural influence to reinforce and perpetuate gender injustice (see Travers, 2008; Heywood & Dworkin, 2003; and Burstyn, 1999). In her work, Travers describes the role of the sports nexus in "promoting and perpetuating gender injustice through the cultural and economic marginalization of women and the non-normatively gendered" (Travers, 2008, p. 80). Travers (2008) further argues that sport reinforces masculinity and perpetuates sexism while failing to challenge the sex-segregated structure of the sport itself. In other words, sport enthusiasts simply accept the disparity in pay as the norm.

On the other hand, Bruce (2015) sees a cultural change occurring in the way the media frame women athletes and, maybe more importantly, the way the audience accepts women in sports. He suggests there is a new form of femininity arising "that refuses to cede physical strength and sporting excellence to men and thus represents an important rupture in the articulation of sport and masculinity" (p. 372). Bruce credits in part the "globalized and unbounded media landscape" for framing female athletes in a multiplicity of ways.

Communication and Structural Challenges

One problem, according to the Gender Balance in Global Sport Report (Tranter et al., 2016), is that pay equity is not being addressed directly and in a timely fashion. Instead, change is coming about at a snail's pace through emphasis on increasing the number of women who sit on boards and committees, increasing the number of women in sport from early ages through the elite levels of sport, and fostering better sponsorship deals (2016). While addressing structural issues like these is important, more direct, timely, and permanent solutions are needed to address the pay gap.

One of the main structural issues blocking progress in pay equity lies in the lack of women governing sport. For example, a 2014 study showed that while the number of women in Olympic sports is growing steadily, female representation on boards of sport organizations is below 30%, a commendable but modest increase from 21% in 2009 (Hutt, 2016). Even more vexing is that almost half of National Olympic Committees have fewer than 20% of women on their executive boards, including 10 nations who had no women at all (Wigmore, 2016).

Another structural problem lies in how non–profit sport organizations structure their player pay. Walters, in his article on gender pay gaps, poses two thought-provoking questions. The first concerns why non–profit organizations such as the U.S. Soccer Federation base payroll decisions on potential revenue rather than on actual performance (Walters, 2016). His second question challenges why, in a post–Title IX country, discrimination between men and women occurs at all (Walters, 2016).

In 1973, Billie Jean King took a very public stance to address the pay gap in her sport. At the height of her popularity and competitive domination, she threatened not to play anymore, and it worked. Unfortunately, for female athletes, this all or nothing approach necessitates a willingness to walk away if their terms are not met. Berri, an economics professor at Southern Utah University, says this is a traditional worker versus management conflict. He said the WNBA owners are telling players "they are paying them the best they can, and that is exactly the same story that sports owners have told athletes since the 19th century" (Littlefield, 2016, para 21). Berri equates this to Major League Baseball, where players were underpaid until they unionized. But, he notes, pay equity will not happen in the WNBA until women "call their employer's bluff" (Littlefield, 2016, para 22). This, of course, can be very risky when one's livelihood is tied to the sport.

The growing commercialization of sport in general is a factor contributing to the pay discrepancy. For example, Hutt, (2016) points out that while the Grand Slams pay the same prize money to both male and female tennis champions, the male player consistently earns more in endorsements and sponsorships.

Only two women have recently broken barriers in male-dominated sports. While never winning an IndyCar or NASCAR event, Danica Patrick earned more than $13 million last year, half coming from endorsements, while endorsements helped pro golfer Stacy Lewis become one of the world's 10 highest paid female athletes in 2015 with $4 million (Walters, 2016). Compare this to NASCAR driver Dale Earnhardt, Jr. who made an estimated $23.5 million in 2015 and pro golfer Phil Mickelson who earned $44 million in endorsements (Walters, 2016). Interestingly, female Ultimate Fighting Championship (UFC) fighter Ronda Rousey became the second-highest paid fighter last year earning $3.3 million, while UFC fighter Conor McGregor, who ranked number one, had earnings that topped $7.77 million (Cole, 2017). These figures clearly show that even when women are at the top of their sport, especially traditionally male-dominated sports, their salaries and endorsements are significantly lower.

Overall, the argument that women should be paid the same as men, regardless of revenue, has not gained much traction over the years. Yet, this argument ironically prevailed in men's figure skating, where top male athletes argued that the prize money should be distributed equally between male and female figure skaters, despite the fact the women in figure skating produce more revenue than the men. The end result: The prize money in this sport is now equally distributed between the sexes (Wahl, 2016).

You Make the Call

Though few, examples of pay equity, successful media coverage, and profitable sponsorship exist and should be used as prototypes. The Women's Sports Foundation (2015) summarizes a list of equal pay sports. For example, the World Major Marathon series pays the leading man and woman a half-million dollars each. Professional tennis pays equally in all Grand Slam events, and in 2015, the WNBA inked a six-year extension with ESPN worth about $12 million dollars a year, making it the most profitable women's professional league (Clarke, 2015).

While these are admirable steps, the challenge continues to be to get sports organization owners to listen, particularly challenging the message that management is paying them the best they can given the circumstances. It recently worked for U.S. women's hockey, as the players won a "who will blink first" standoff against management. After using typical strong-arm tactics with the women—threatening to use replacement players, giving the players a "do or die" deadline—USA Hockey capitulated on player demands in what can only be described as a rout. U.S. player Hilary Knight said of the negotiation's result, "this empowered women all over the world—and not only those involved in sports" (Allen & Perez, 2017).

Reputation is manageable and it can be enhanced by the way sport organizations actively and strategically interact with its target audiences (Smith, 2013). In applying reputation management functions to sports organizations, the USA Hockey negotiations may serve a cautionary tale.

Discussion Questions

1. Update the information presented in this chapter. Where does the state of professional sport pay currently stand? Which sport organizations are addressing this issue now? What lessons in reputation management can other sport organizations learn from the U.S. women's national hockey team case?

2. Of the 15 biggest athlete endorsement deals in sports history, 11 of these are endorsed by Nike. The first woman on this list, tennis player Maria Sharapova, ranks no. 15, with a $70 million deal over eight years (Biggest Athlete Endorsement, 2016).

    Investigate Nike's corporate philosophy and its differences in corporate sponsorships between male and female athletes. To what extent, if any, would they benefit from paying female athletes more in the future? What corporate entities are at the vanguard of pay equity? How might corporations enhance their public image by focusing more on female athletes?

3. Is pay inequity in professional sports a natural result of market demands? Do governing bodies hold any responsibility for the sexual disparity in pay? Are media organizations that pay millions in broadcast rights at all culpable? Explain your reasoning and provide evidence in support of your positions.

4. What communication strategies could increase attendance at women's sporting events at all levels? How can the power of social media be instrumental in creating an interest in the pay equity issue and facilitating a national and worldwide conversation?

5. Market estimates place women's purchasing power in the $5–$15 trillion dollar range annually, and experts predict that women will control two-thirds of the consumer wealth in the U.S. over the next decade or so (Nielsen, 2013). How would pay equity in sports translate to good business practice?

References

Allen, K., & Perez, A. J. (2017, March 28). U.S. women agree to new deal with USA Hockey: Will play at world championships. Retrieved from www.usatoday.com/story/sports/hockey/2017/03/28/usa-hockey-women-dispute-world-championships/99538056/

Badenhausen, K. (2017, June 7). Ronaldo, LeBron top the world's highest-paid athletes of 2017. Retrieved June 13, 2017, from www.forbes.com/sites/kurtbadenhausen/2017/06/07/ronaldo-lebron-top-the-worlds-highest-paid-athletes-of-2017/#78537ca84a1c

Berkowitz, S., Schnaars, C., & Wolken, D. (2017, March 30). College basketball coaches enjoy record compensation. Retrieved from www.pressreader.com/usa/usa-today-international-edition/20170331/281496456123480

Biggest athlete endorsement deals in sports history. (2016, January 27). Retrieved from www.totalsportek.com/money/biggest-endorsement-deals-sports-history/

Booth, R. (2014). Media coverage and pay in women's basketball and netball in Australia. In *Handbook on the economics of women in sports* (pp. 410–425). Cheltenham, UK: Edward Elgar.

Broadhurst, C. (2016, September 16). New study reveals gender pay gap in sport isn't closing. Retrieved from http://en.rfi.fr/sports/20160915-new-study-reveals-huge-gender-pay-gap-sport-isn-t-closing

Bruce, T. (2015). New rules for new times: Sportswomen and media representation in the third wave. *Sex Roles*, 74(7–8), 361–376. doi:10.1007/s11199-015-0497-6

Burstyn, V. (1999). *The rites of men: Manhood, politics and the culture of sport.* Toronto: University of Toronto Press.

Carroll, L. (2016, April). Facebook post exaggerates discrepancy between U.S. men's and Women's Soccer Teams. Retrieved from www.politifact.com/punditfact/statements/2016/apr/06/other-98/facebook-post-exaggerates-discrepancy-between-us-m/

Clarke, L. (2015, June 26). Five myths about women's sports. Retrieved March 17, 2017, from www.washingtonpost.com/opinions/five-myths-about-womens-sports/2015/06/26/8dee2470-1b5b-11e5-93b7-5eddc056ad8a_story.html

Cole, R. (2017, January 1). Top 10 highest paid UFC fighters of 2016. *LowKick.* Retrieved from www.lowkickmma.com/UFC/top-10-highest-paid-ufc-stars-of-2016/

Cooky, C., Messner, M. A., & Hextrum, R. H. (2013). Women play sport, but not on TV. *Communication & Sport*, 1(3), 203–230. doi:10.1177/2167479513476947

Cooky, C., Messner, M. A., & Musto, M. (2015). "It's dude time!": A quarter century of excluding women's sports in televised news and highlight shows. *Communication & Sport*, 3(3), 261–287. doi:10.1177/2167479515588761

Elsbach, K. D. (2012). A framework for reputation management over the course of evolving controversies. In *The Oxford handbook of corporate reputation* (pp. 466–486). Oxford: Oxford University Press. doi:10.1177/0149206316680030

Fombrun, C. J. (1996). *Reputation: Realizing value from the corporate image.* Watertown, MA: Harvard Business School Press.

Fraser, N. (2007). Feminist politics in the age of recognition: A two-dimensional approach to gender justice. *Studies in Social Justice*, 1, 23–25.

Greer, J. D., Hardin, M., & Homan, C. (2009). "Naturally" less exciting? Visual production of men's and women's track and field coverage during the 2004 Olympics. *Journal of Broadcasting & Electronic Media*, 53(2), 173–189. doi:10.1080/08838150902907595

Heywood, L., & Dworkin, S. (2003). *Built to win: The female athlete as cultural icon.* Minneapolis, MN: University of Minnesota Press.

Hutt, R. (2016, September 15). Sport has a huge gender pay gap: And it's not about to close. *World Economic Forum.* Retrieved from www.weforum.org/agenda/2016/09/sport-has-a-huge-gender-pay-gap-and-it-s-not-about-to-close-soon/

Kennedy, P. (2016, April 1). Soccer America Daily: TV viewers: U.S. men vs. U.S. women. Retrieved from www.socceramerica.com/article/68281/tv-viewers-us-men-vs-us-women.html

Lather, P. (2004). Critical inquiry in qualitative research: Feminist and poststructural perspectives: Science "after truth". In K. deMarrais, K., & S.D. Lapan (Eds.), *Foundations for research: Methods of inquiry in education and the social sciences* (pp. 203–215). Mahwah, NJ: Lawrence Erlbaum Associates.

Littlefield, B. (2016, April 16). No matter the sport, women athletes are always paid less. Retrieved from www.wbur.org/onlyagame/2016/04/16/pay-gap-female-sports

Melewar, T. C. (2008). *Facets of corporate identity, communication, and reputation.* Abingdon, UK: Routledge.

Nielsen. (2013, April 2). U.S. women control the purse strings. Retrieved from www.nielsen.com/us/en/insights/news/2013/u-s—women-control-the-purse-strings.html

Power, M. (2007). *Organized uncertainty: Designing a world of risk management.* Oxford: Oxford University Press.

Rothenberg, B. (2016, April 12). Roger Federer, $731,000: Serena Williams, $495,000: The pay gap in tennis. Retrieved from www.nytimes.com/2016/04/13/sports/tennis/equal-pay-gender-gap-grand-slam-majors-wta-atp.htm

Smallwood, J. (2016, April 6). You can't equate men's and women's sports. Retrieved March 18, from www.philly.com/philly/blogs/pattisonave/You-cant-equate-mens-and-womens-sports.html

Smith, R. D. (2013). *Strategic planning for public relations* (4th ed.). Abingdon, UK: Routledge.

Thomas, L. (2016, July 25). Equal pay for equal play: The case for the Women's Soccer Team. Retrieved from www.newyorker.com/culture/cultural-comment/the-case-for-equal-pay-in-womens-sports

Tranter, R., Medd, R., & Braun, C. (2016). Gender balance in global sport report (Rep.). Retrieved from www.bing.com/cr?IG=4815A3BF29474AF9AA3A2A4D82BAA49F&CID=3362152117516D0000DF1F6E16606C1C&rd=1&h=HBwhSGvna_v26X3vjpJFiT1Z_DAhQD1mhmWUjQmfBW0&v=1&r=www.womenonboards.net/womenonboards-AU/media/AU-Reports/2016-Gender-Balance-In-Global-Sport-Report.pdf&p=DevEx,5060.1

Travers, A. (2008). The sport nexus and gender injustice. *Studies in Social Justice, 2*(1), 79–101.

Von Allmen, P. (2013). Coaching women and women coaching: Pay differentials in the Title IX era. In E.M. Leeds & M.A, Leeds (Eds.), *Handbook on the economics of women in sports* (pp. 269–289). Cheltenham, UK: Edward Elgar.

Wagner-McGough, S. (2016, March 20). Serena Williams rips Indian Wells CEO after sexist comments. *CBS Sports.* Retrieved from https://www.cbssports.com/general/news/serena-williams-rips-indian-wells-ceo-after-sexist-comments/

Wahl, G. (2016, April). Revenue generation a key matter in USWNT, US Soccer wage dispute. Retrieved from www.si.com/planet-futbol/2016/04/06/uswnt-us-soccer-wage-discrimination-revenue-unequal-pay

Walters, J. (2016, April 1). Taking a closer look at the gender pay gaps in sports. *Newsweek.* Retrieved from www.newsweek.com/womens-soccer-suit-underscores-sports-gender-pay-gap-443137

Whyno, B. S. (2017, March 15). US women's hockey players threaten boycott over wages. *AP Online.* Retrieved from www.highbeam.com/doc/1A1-cac4b959fac248629ba637676d83cce0.html?refid=easy_hf

Wigmore, T. (2016, August 5). Sports gender gap: Why women are still paid less than men? Retrieved from www.newstatesman.com/politics/sport/2016/08/sport-s-gender-pay-gap-why-are-women-still-paid-less-men

Women's Sports Foundation. (2015, July 20). Pay inequity in athletics. Retrieved from www.womenssportsfoundation.org/research/article-and-report/equity-issues/pay-inequity/

15 A Failure to Defend Against Cyberbullying

Examining the Organization's Competency in Standing Up for Its Members

Anne Bialowas & Nicola A. Corbin

During the 2016 Rio Olympic Games, U.S. gymnast Gabby Douglas was bullied via social media for her appearance, perceived lack of support of team-mates, and her failure to place her hand over her heart during the national anthem at a gold medal ceremony. Supportive responses from the official associated organizations, USA Gymnastics and Team USA, were paltry at best. This chapter considers the organizational competency in handling culturally sensitive issues about crises that involve culture, ethnicity, and/or race; provides a textual analysis of Douglas' response; and examines the complexities of race and gender issues in sport.

Introduction

Gold-medal winning Olympic gymnast Gabby Douglas faced unprecedented criticism during the 2012 London Games and the 2016 Rio Games. The criticism on social media in 2012 primarily revolved around the condition of her hair (Whiteside, 2012). She went on to become the first African American to win the gold medal in the women's individual all-around event. Douglas returned to the 2016 Rio Games and was soon engulfed in media criticism that could be categorized as bullying. She was criticized for a per-ceived negative attitude or "saltiness" toward her teammates and for her hair. In addition, she was accused of bleaching her skin, and most significantly, her patriotism was called into question for her failure to place her hand over her heart during the playing of the U.S. national anthem at the team event medal ceremony (Rogers, 2016). She was nicknamed "Crabby Gabby" (Boren, 2016). At its peak, Douglas broke down in tears during an on-camera interview while attempting to respond to a reporter's question about the vit-riol (Howard, 2016).

Examples of U.S. athletes abound who have not followed the advised pro-tocol[1] of hand placement during the national anthem. For example, members of the 1992 U.S. Olympic men's basketball "Dream Team" failed to place their hands over their hearts, to no public outcry. Also, Michael Phelps faced mild "flag flap" for his laughter at the games in Rio; he explained he was laughing at his friends who were following the tradition of the Baltimore

Orioles baseball fans by shouting the word "O" (Plaschke, 2016). No official response from Team USA, the official body governing American Olympic athletes, was warranted.

However, the criticism of Douglas is unparalleled in scope for the perceived offense and perhaps highlights a double standard when evaluating the behavior of women. USA Gymnastics and Team USA were mostly short on open support for Douglas. She received most initial public support from her mother and comedian Leslie Jones, who coined the hashtag #LOVE4GAB-BYUSA on Twitter (Andrews, 2016).

Background

The Olympic games as a "media event" is a major area of sport research that exemplifies the relationship between sport and culture (Katz, 1980). The telecast of the two-week games provides a prominent display of national and cultural ideologies. The case of Gabby Douglas at the 2016 Rio Games presents one possible opportunity to interrogate cultural issues of race and gender within U.S. society.

Sport and gender research typically examines the amount of news coverage and highlights the dearth of serious and respectful reporting about women's sport. For example, Cooky, Messner, and Hextrum (2013) note that women's sport in 2009 "received 1.3% of the coverage on TV news, and 1.3% on *ESPN's SportsCenter*" despite increased women's participation (p. 221). This trend was upended during recent Olympic games when women's media coverage increased. Billings, Angelini, MacArthur, Bissell, and Smith (2014) found that women received the majority of clock time and on-air mentions, for the first time, during the 2012 London Games. However, while increased media attention can be positive, the stories told and the images shown with such coverage must be critically analyzed.

Often, the focus of many studies has primarily centered on race, and specifically on black men and issues of masculinity (Bruening, 2005). However, scholars argue that it is important to understand how race and gender intersect within media representations (e.g., Crenshaw, 1991, 1997). As Carter-Francique and Richardson (2016) note, "Black sports women have faced the most (in)visible journey and are marred by their omission and/or image representation in the media" (p. 7). When they are shown in the media, black women athletes are often represented using negative stereotypes that dehumanize (Cahn, 1994; Carter-Francique, 2014) or sexualize their bodies (Hobson, 2003). For example, Schultz (2005) noted the media coverage and focus on Serena Williams' buttocks while she wore a catsuit was more than a case of heterosexualization that is typical in media coverage of women athletes, but "rather that her catsuit was indicative of deviant sexuality" (p. 350), which set her apart from white players on the tennis tour, who were not similarly depicted.

Black women athletes have largely been rendered both invisible and hypervisible (in negative representations), leaving them open to more vicious criticism than their white counterparts. Such criticism not only affects the athlete but has implications for athletic organizations. When the criticism actively involves issues of race and gender, Liu and Pompper (2012) argue that the stakes are more elevated for the organization, as such crises are prone to be sensationalized. The scholars draw on complexity theory to recommend best practices for crisis communication that involve issues of culture, ethnicity, and/or race. They argue that this approach attempts to avoid oversimplifying and overgeneralizing "complex issues out of context" (Liu & Pompper, 2012, p. 129). In fact, "concerns or events with potentially negative culture, ethnicity, and/or racial implications may constitute the most painful and volatile threats faced by organizations and individuals" (Liu & Pompper, 2012, p. 142). When handling crises with such implications, they urge managers to consider that these events are often dynamic, that they require a focus on both internal and external stakeholders, and that they are affected by historical and present cultural environments. To this end, the scholars make three recommendations: (1) recognize historical influences; (2) employ emotional intelligence by demonstrating compassion, concern, and empathy; and (3) pay close attention to media scrutiny as the crisis will become sensationalized and spread quickly on social media. Through a textual analysis of the organizational response to the bullying of Gabby Douglas, this case study evaluates USA Gymnastics' and Team USA's competence in handling culturally sensitive issues.

The Case

The U.S. women's gymnastics team, dubbed the "Final Five," was shaping up for a dominant performance at the 2016 Rio Olympics. The team, with members Simone Biles, Gabby Douglas, Laurie Hernandez, Madison Kocian, and Aly Raisman, ultimately captured the United States' second consecutive Olympic team gold medal. Spread over a week, the four-day competition was televised during primetime NBC coverage.[2] The team-qualifying round was held on Sunday, August 7, during which each country competed for a spot in the team finals. The team finals competition was held on Tuesday, August 9. Also, during the team-qualifying competition, the top two gymnasts from each participating country were selected to compete in the individual all-around finals based on their total event scores. The individual all-around competition was held on Thursday, August 11. Douglas was the first reigning Olympic all-around gymnast to defend her title since Nadia Comaneci in 1980. U.S. Olympic legends Mary Lou Retton (1984 gold all-around) and Nastia Liukin (2008 gold all-around) praised Douglas for having the physical strength and mental toughness to not only make a second Olympic team but also defend her title (Axon, 2016). However, Douglas had the third-highest qualifying score, coming in behind her own teammates, Simone Biles, first, and Aly Raisman, second. Thus, Douglas was only able to compete for a team gold medal and an individual event medal for the uneven bars, which was held on Sunday, August 14.

Obviously, Douglas was disappointed. However, she was part of the successful effort to win the team gold medal. It was during this medal ceremony on Tuesday, August 9, that media, and social media in particular, reacted harshly to her physical stance and overall demeanor. Some accused her of being unpatriotic posting, that she "had no excuse not to honor the flag of the country that gave her the opportunity to compete" (Plaschke, 2016). One tweet said "NOT DEALING! QUIT TEAM TRAITOR! U EITHER COVER YOUR HEART OR QUIT! U ASHAMED TO COVER? U R TRAITOR!" (Perez, 2016). Douglas responded on Twitter:

> In response to a few tweets I saw tonight, I always stand at attention out of respect for our country whenever the national anthem is played. I never meant any disrespect and apologize if I offended anyone. I'm so overwhelmed at what our team accomplished today and overjoyed that we were able to bring home another gold for our country!
>
> (Douglas, 2016a)

The negative reaction to Douglas only intensified when she was further criticized for not giving teammates Biles and Raisman a standing ovation when they claimed gold and silver, respectively, in the individual all-around competition on Thursday, August 11. The hashtag #CrabbyGabby started trending on social media for her perceived "saltiness" (Sarkar, 2016). Douglas posted her congratulations to Biles and Raisman via Twitter the next day. Finishing seventh on the uneven bars in the individual finals competition on Sunday, August 14, Douglas reflected on the week of gymnastics and media attention:

> I tried to stay off the Internet because there's just so much negativity . . . . Either it was about my hair or my hand not being over my heart [on the medal podium] or I looked depressed . . . . It was hurtful. It was hurtful. It was. It's been kind of a lot to deal with . . . . I've been through a lot. A lot. Sometimes I sit back and say, 'Wait. What did I do to disrespect people? What have I done to disrespect the USA?
>
> (Howard, 2016)

During this competition week, there was little public support for Douglas from USA Gymnastics or Team USA. Douglas was put in the position of being the primary, and almost only, defender of her person, reputation, and brand. She apologized via Twitter and again during a tearful, impromptu press interview when a reporter asked about the negative online comments. On one level, Douglas responded to these online attacks with the very human response of attempting to defend her person from remarks that attacked many aspects of her identity—her race, her gender, her American-ness. It is precisely the intersection of these embodied identities, as described by Crenshaw (1991), that calls for the application of complexity theory (Liu & Pompper, 2012) to this case. From an organizational standpoint, alert officials should have recognized and acknowledged the dynamic and changing nature of the attacks over the course of the competition, the assault on her physical appearance as a black woman, and the historical, racial implications of attacking her American-ness.

USA Gymnastics and Team USA did not specifically address any of these issues. Instead, an official news release from Team USA quoted Douglas as saying of her team gold medal while laughing: "It's one more big sparkle. It feels good, really, really good" (McCarvel, 2016). This description of laughter and responding to sparkly leotards and winning a sparkly gold medal contrasts with her comments on Twitter and her tears. Steve Penny (2016), USA Gymnastics president and CEO, released the following statement on August 16, a full week after the team gold medal stand ceremony:

> Gabby Douglas has been and continues to be an inspiration to many people and her achievements have been instrumental to our program's success over the past five years. Since emerging on the world stage in 2011, Gabby has met every expectation of success and continues to be an outstanding ambassador for our country and USA Gymnastics. Her return to gymnastics after winning the all-around in 2012 has been remarkable and she is one of the most gracious people I have ever known.

This statement is vague in its response to character attacks on Douglas, only noting that she is an "outstanding ambassador" (Penny, 2016). Also it lacks explicit demonstration of emotional intelligence, as informed by Liu and Pompper (2012), and shows little concern or compassion for Douglas in the face of the media attacks. Further, the statement showed no consideration for Douglas' complex, intersecting identities that carried historical significance and which were explicitly attacked in some of the comments. A condensed statement was also posted to Twitter. However, neither post was picked up in mainstream media coverage. In a conventional sense, releasing this statement via its website and Twitter seemed logical, as the controversy was magnified on social media. But the posts came too late. Speed in a response amplifies sincerity and quells speculation that the organization is uncertain in its decision (Schweitzer, Brooks, & Galinksy, 2015). This too-late and tepid support reflected poorly on USA Gymnastics and Team USA in handling culturally sensitive issues.

In fact, the only initial, explicit support came from Douglas' mother, Natalie Hawkins, and comedian Leslie Jones. Hawkins reflected on how she and Douglas have "been brought to many tears because I don't know what she's done to warrant such an attack. To me it looks like she is being bullied" (Sarkar, 2016). Furthermore, Hawkins addressed the racial undertones in the attacks. She said:

> Many people are telling me that all the time. And that's from white people and black people. I don't want to believe (it's a race attack) as I want to have more faith . . . But when I go on Twitter, I can't help but see

all the blacks are saying: 'was it just the white people that are saying this against us?'. . . . Maybe people are very frustrated. Our country has a lot of unrest and turmoil recently and people are frustrated and maybe they want to vent and they just see someone innocent and . . . bully them.

(Sarkar, 2016)

Jones has her own history of being cyberbullied and a reputation for publicly calling out perpetrators. She defended Douglas by tweeting "Yo I just heard Gabby getting attacked on her page show her the love you showed me #LOVE4GABBYUSA send to @gabrielledoug" (Andrews, 2016). Other black celebrities, like Shonda Rhimes, Terry McMillan, and Kerry Washington, along with other Twitter users, joined Jones in tweeting support such as "Know you are supported and loved" (Andrews, 2016). Douglas responded with "Thank u so much for all the love! My heart is full! @Lesdoggg I love you guys!" (Douglas, 2016b).

You Make the Call

In this case, Gabby Douglas had a personal stake in maintaining her brand for post-Olympic marketing and image-building opportunities. Her action on the medal stand went against prescribed protocol and might have imperiled her brand. According to Mark Dyreson, author of *Making the American Dream: Sport, Culture, and the Olympic Experience*, "When it comes to Olympic athlete celebrities, a word to the wise—be careful what you do on the medal stand, you can alienate a lot of your customer base" (Plaschke, 2016). Douglas made ample apologies and expressed support for her team. Additional public communications from Douglas, such as discussing the issue during the "Final Five" interview with Bob Costas, might have been perceived as attention grabbing from the rest of the team. There was little space for more personal communication from Douglas.

It is within this space that organizational support might have mattered. But Team USA and USA Gymnastics remained distant. Additionally, they did not explicitly engage any of the racial bias speculations noted by Douglas' mother. By concentrating on Douglas' overall accomplishments ("Her return to gymnastics after winning the all-around in 2012 has been remarkable") and praising her overall disposition ("she is one of the most gracious people I have ever known"), the organizations showed some support for her as a person but failed to call out the problematic behaviors in the media. This distance appeared strategic because, on the one hand, it buffered the organizations from chatter and coverage involving complex race issues and inoculated them against possible charges of race-baiting. However, on the other hand, the organizations appeared ill-equipped to craft an adequate response. One might also assume that given the underlying tone of race and gender in the attacks, and the potential cultural minefield, their lack of preparedness caused them to "freeze like deer in headlights." Such ineptitude might have created a barrier to a more supportive response. In the end, since Douglas was the solo target of the criticism, the organizations were absolved of being responsible for the perceived poor behavior.

However, Team USA and USA Gymnastics missed an opportunity both to speak up about issues of diversity and to support a past champion. In a feature article leading up to the Rio 2016 games, USA Gymnastics detailed the extensive support of the renowned U.S. women's national team coordinator Marta Karolyi for Douglas (Barnas, 2016). However, that organizational support seemed to disappear once controversy surrounded the athlete at the games. ESPN senior writer Johnette Howard (2016) described a visual of Douglas crying alone in a corner, facing a wall:

> It was hard to watch. Every now and then, a Team USA worker took a look at her. Finally, a woman walked over and handed Douglas what appeared to be a Kleenex. The woman wrapped an arm around Douglas' shoulder and patted her a couple of times, then left the gymnast alone once more.

Liu and Pompper (2012) note that issues of culture, ethnicity, and/or race are "rooted in history and are cyclical" and that historical consequences exist (p. 133). For the first time in the history of elite gymnastics, the U.S. was able to send a diverse team, with two African Americans, a Latina, a Jewish woman, and a Catholic (Gregorian, 2016). Such a composition presented a unique opportunity for the organizations to give due attention and celebrate this complexity. By highlighting this part of the story, Team USA and USA Gymnastics would have gracefully accomplished a few goals: (1) promoted the team spirit of the games; (2) explicitly highlighted that each team member, including Douglas, brought her own unique, intersecting American identity while winning the gold medal on behalf of the United States; and (3) sent a sincere and nuanced message against online bullying while demonstrating support for the emotional wellbeing of athletes, not just the physical. Such a move would have demonstrated organizational compassion and concern for their stakeholders and embodied strategies, laid out by Liu and Pompper (2012), of accounting for cultural historical context while responding in an emotionally intelligent manner.

Discussion Questions

1. Conduct an Internet search of images using the following terms "Gabby Douglas medal stand" and "1992 Dream Team medal stand" to analyze some of the images in the case study. How much of a role do you believe Gabby Douglas' race and gender played in the dynamics of this crisis? What are some other historical and present examples of the ways in which the U.S. media and public respond to an athlete's race and/or gender in a sports crisis, or sports coverage in general? Reflect on the case study in Chapter 13 about Ryan Lochte. How were Lochte and

Douglas treated differently? How was this difference based on gender and/or race? What cultural narratives (like "boys will be boys") allow for such differences?

2. What other messaging strategies might the organizations (Team USA and USA Gymnastics) have used to respond to this issue in a culturally competent manner?

3. Discuss particular instances (or current examples) in which an organization is ethically obligated to defend an employee or team member. What are some instances when it absolutely should not?

4. In a continuation of a long saga regarding black women and the state of their hair, U.S. Olympic gymnast Simone Biles was cyberbullied after she appeared as an honorary cheerleader at the Houston Texans football game on December 10, 2017. Read the following story that includes some of the tweets: www.yahoo.com/lifestyle/simone-biles-gets-hair-shamed-cheerleading-cameo-need-black-friends-181118314.html

    Why does this trend continue? Identify the similarities and differences between this and the Gabby Douglas case. Discuss any new developments in this ongoing issue of online bullying and commentary about African-American women.

5. USA Gymnastics has come under attack for its response to another crisis—the sexual abuse scandal involving former team doctor Larry Nassar. Nassar ultimately pleaded guilty and was sentenced to 60 years in prison on December 7, 2017. Many Olympic gymnasts have spoken out about the abuse. Read the following two articles about Aly Raisman and McKayla Maroney:

    1) www.usatoday.com/story/sports/2017/08/19/aly-raisman-crit icizes-usa-gymnastics-usoc-response-sex-abuse-scandal/58369 5001/

    2) www.cnn.com/2017/10/18/us/mckayla-maroney-me-too-abuse/ index.html

        Evaluate the released statements by USA Gymnastics for their ability to show emotional intelligence.

        —First USA Gymnastics response regarding story about Larry Nassar:https://usagym.org/pages/post.html?PostID= 19219&prog=h
        —Second response after Olympic gymnast McKayla Maroney's post on Twitter: https://usagym.org/pages/post.html?Post ID=20939&prog=h
        —Third response after Larry Nassar's guilty plea: https://usa gym.org/pages/post.html?PostID=21064&prog=h

Notes

1. A 2008 amendment to U.S. Code 301 made official a normative expectation that "all other persons present should face the flag and stand at attention with their right

hand over their heart" during the playing of the national anthem. However, the First Amendment protects a person's right to refrain from doing so.

2. The evening primetime telecast is the most important part of the network coverage as it drives the bulk of ratings and advertising revenue (Billings, Angelini, MacArthur, Smith, and Vincent, 2014).

References

Andrews, T. (2016, August 16). Leslie Jones took on Twitter trolls and won: Now, she's launched an outpouring of love for Gabby Douglas. *The Washington Post*. Retrieved from www.chicagotribune.com/sports/international/ct-leslie-jones-gabby-douglas-twitter-olympics-20160816-story.html

Axon, R. (2016, July 15). Gymnasts Gabby Douglas, Aly Raisman beat odds by making second Olympic team. *USA Today Sports*. Retrieved from www.usatoday.com/story/sports/olympics/2016/07/11/gymnatics-gabby-douglas-aly-raisman-rio-summer-games/86967254/

Barnas, J. (2016, August 5). Douglas: "Martha pulls the best out of me". *USA Gymnastics*. Retrieved from https://usagym.org/pages/post.html?PostID=19009&prog=h

Billings, A. C., Angelini, J. R., MacArthur, P. J., Bissell, K., & Smith, L. R. (2014). (Re)calling London: The gender frame agenda within NBC's Primetime broadcast of the 2012 Olympiad. *Journalism & Mass Communication Quarterly*, *91*(1), 38–58.

Billings, A. C., Angelini, J. R., MacArthur, P. J., Smith, L. R., & Vincent, J. (2014). Fanfare for the American: NBC's Primetime broadcast of the 2012 London Olympiad. *Electronic News*, *8*(2), 101–119.

Boren, C. (2016, August 15). Crabby Gabby? Douglas makes peace with her critics. *The Washington Post*. Retrieved from www.washingtonpost.com/news/early-lead/wp/2016/08/15/crabby-gabby-douglas-makes-peace-with-her-critics/?utm_term=.179997666965

Bruening, J. E. (2005). Gender and racial analysis in sport: Are all the women white and all the blacks men? *Quest*, *57*, 330–349.

Cahn, S. (1994). *Coming on strong: Gender and sexuality in twentieth-century women's sport*. New York, NY: Free Press.

Carter-Francique, A. R. (2014). "Re"presenting "Gabby": Examining the digital media coverage of Gabrielle Douglas at the 2012 London Olympic games. *International Journal of Sport Studies*, *4*(9), 1080–1091.

Carter-Francique, A. R., & Richardson, M. F. (2016). Controlling media, controlling access: The role of sport media on black women's sport participation. *Race, Gender & Class*, *23*, 7–33.

Cooky, C., Messner, M. A., & Hextrum, R. H. (2013). Women play sport, but not on TV: A longitudinal study of televised news media. *Communication & Sport*, *1*(3), 203–230.

Crenshaw, C. (1997). Women in the Gulf War: Toward an intersectional feminist rhetorical criticism. *Howard Journal of Communications*, *8*, 219–235.

Crenshaw, K. W. (1991). Mapping the margins: Intersectionality, identity politics, and violence against women of color. *Stanford Law Review*, *43*(6), 1241–1299.

Douglas, G. [@gabrielledoug]. (2016a, August 9). First I want to say thank you everyone for all your support! It's a huge honor for me to be able to represent #TeamUSA: In response to a few tweets I saw tonight, I always stand at attention . . . . [Tweet]. Retrieved from https://twitter.com/gabrielledoug/status/763173304228249600

Douglas, G. [@gabrielledoug]. (2016b, August 15). Thank u so much for all the love! My heart is full! @Lesdoggg I love you guys! [Tweet]. Retrieved from https://twitter.com/gabrielledoug/status/765309307093155842

Gregorian, V. (2016, August 10). Dominant U.S. gymnastics sets an example: And not just in sports. *The Kansas City Star*. Retrieved from www.kansascity.com/sports/spt-columns-blogs/vahe-gregorian/article94741812.html

Hobson, J. (2003). The "batty" politic: Toward as aesthetic of the black female body. *Hypatia, 18*(4), 87–105.

Howard, J. (2016, August 16). Gabby Douglas calls social media critics "hurtful" after ending Olympic career. *ESPN.com*. Retrieved from www.espn.com/olympics/summer/gymnastics/story/_/id/17303885/gabby-douglas-cals-social-media-critics-hurtful-ending-olympic-career

Katz, E. (1980). Media events: The sense of occasion. *Studies in Visual Communication, 6*(3), 84–89.

Liu, B. F., & Pompper, D. (2012). The crisis with no name: Defining the interplay of culture, ethnicity, and race on organizational issues and media outcomes. *Journal of Applied Communication, 40*(2), 127–146.

McCarvel, N. (2016, August 9). U.S. women's gymnastics team earns Rio Olympic gold in sparkling fashion. *Team USA*. Retrieved from www.teamusa.org/News/2016/August/09/US-Women-Gymnastics-Team-Earns-Rio-Olympic-Gold-In-Sparkling-Fashion

Penny, S. (2016, August 16). USA Gymnastics: Gabby is outstanding ambassador. *USA Gymnastics*. Retrieved from https://usagym.org/pages/post.html?PostID=19153&prog=h

Perez, R. (2016, August 15). How the internet ruined the Olympics for Gabby Douglas. *New York Post*. Retrieved from http://nypost.com/2016/08/15/how-the-internet-ruined-the-olympics-for-gabby-douglas/

Plaschke, B. (2016, August 10). Gymnast Gabby Douglas resurrects the debate over how to act during the national anthem. *Los Angeles Times*. Retrieved from www.latimes.com/sports/olympics/la-sp-oly-rio-2016-gabby-douglas-and-podiumdecorum-become-1470892038-htmlstory.html

Rogers, K. (2016, August 15). Gabby Douglas defends herself against the wrath of social media. *New York Times*. Retrieved from www.nytimes.com/2016/08/16/sports/olympics/gabby-douglas-defends-herself-against-the-wrath-of-social-media.html?mcubz=2

Sarkar, P. (2016, August 14). Gymnastics: Bullies are tormenting Douglas, says mother. *Reuters*. Retrieved from www.reuters.com/article/us-olympics-rio-agymnastics-douglas-bull-idUSKCN10P0M6

Schultz, J. (2005). Reading the catsuit: Serena Williams and the production of blackness at the 2002 U.S. Open. *Journal of Sport & Social Issues, 29*, 338–357.

Schweitzer, M. E., Brooks, A. W., & Galinksy, A. D. (2015, September). The organizational apology. *Harvard Business Review*. Retrieved from https://hbr.org/2015/09/the-organizational-apology

Whiteside, K. (2012, August 6). Don't like Gabby Douglas's hair? Too bad. *USA Today*. Retrieved from https://usatoday30.usatoday.com/sports/olympics/london/gymnastics/story/2012-08-03/London-Olympics-Gabby-Douglas-Rochelle-Riley-hair-debate/56760470/1

16 Topsy-Turvy Times

The Impact of Political and Social Issues on Super Bowl LI Ads

Lori Liggett & Terry L. Rentner

This study is a cultural content analysis of the national TV commercials that aired during the 2017 Super Bowl. It considers the unique cultural moment in which they aired, occurring just weeks after the 2016 U.S. presidential election following a highly polarized political campaign. The evaluation is framed amid recent controversies plaguing the NFL, including player concussions and domestic violence. Did advertisers either explicitly or implicitly address issues or avoid specific topics on the left-right socio-political spectrum? The findings reflect on the potential pitfalls, economic or public relations, of corporations aligning with certain viewpoints or causes in Super Bowl commercials.

Introduction

To be watched, streamed, blogged, liked, snapped, and tweeted—that is the main goal of advertisers, marketers, and branding professionals every year on one special Sunday. While the audience perceives Super Bowl commercials to be an important part of the overall entertainment spectacle, scholars show the ads significantly influence attitudes and behaviors. With that in mind, the authors reviewed the content of the 67 national commercials that aired during Super Bowl LI between the New England Patriots (34) and the Atlanta Falcons (28) to see how they reflected the current political and social environment and to ascertain if they addressed any of the public relations challenges currently facing the National Football League (NFL). It is important to reflect on how the sales messages inserted into the main entertainment content of the game contribute to, address, or reflect the external narrative of the political and social climate during that time.

Background

The Super Bowl represents an American tradition, indeed a global ritual of nearly mythical proportions, in which rabid football devotees and even fans-for-a-day come together to watch the biggest sporting event of the year. This shared cultural experience presents an unprecedented opportunity for domestic and international corporations to publicly showcase and shape their brand image.

> A spot on Super Bowl Sunday—just one—makes a huge public state-ment. It says you're part of a special culture. It says you've arrived . . . [But] you've got to spin some magic. And that's what separates the real players, the all-stars, from the rest of the league.
>
> (Kanner, 2004)

Annually, the Big Game represents lucrative opportunities for consumer brands to reach a concentrated global viewership of millions—the largest television audience of the year. And the messaging is influential. But the price is steep—and ever-increasing.

Given the discordant political times and the NFL's public relations chal-lenges, the 2017 spots are of particular interest. While the election of a new U.S. president and the operational challenges of the NFL are not related, the fact that they exist within the same controversial cultural moment provides a uniquely politicized backdrop for those eagerly watching the Super Bowl commercials. The recently concluded presidential election left advertisers "a little more careful in terms of taking a position on one issue, because they will have an equal number of [viewers] on the other side" (Steinberg, 2017, para. 3). Erik Brady noted in a *USA Today* essay that Donald Trump appeared in a Super Bowl ad five years ago, "but this time you won't find President Trump in the ads, though his unmistakable shadow will loom over them" (Brady, 2017, para. 1).

Also relevant to the 2017 ads is media criticism of the NFL's handling of domestic violence and the prevalence of players' concussions, specifically chronic traumatic encephalopathy (CTE), a degenerative disease found in many who suffered repeated blows to the head. These issues continue to impact soci-ety's perception of the game, which could eventually influence advertisers' willingness to spend. According to Robert Thompson, director of the Bleier Center for Television and Popular Culture at Syracuse University, the relation-ship between advertisers and the Super Bowl could be negatively impacted if the NFL's reputation is sullied. "The future of the primacy of Super Bowl ads in our consciousness . . . is dependent on the continued power of the NFL" (Brady, 2017). For the present, Thompson believes the Super Bowl is secure in its cul-tural dominance: "Even with a ratings drop, football is still the most important regularly scheduled programming type in the country" (Brady, 2017).

The case

The research methodology was a culture-based content analysis guided by the survey findings of the *USA Today* Ad Meter ratings (http://admeter. usatoday.com/results/2017) and informed by the previous work of scholars in visual communication studies, rhetoric, and cultural studies (Olson et al, 2008; Schirato & Webb, 2004; Rose, 2007).

To evaluate each spot, categories were determined to address the visual techniques and narrative devices created by advertisers. These strategies determined what viewers saw in the commercials, which presumably influenced how they responded. The categories included product/service type; depictions of alcohol or sexualized situations; appearance of celebrities or animals; and the overall tone or feeling elicited by the narrative. Characters depicted were evaluated to determine how they were likely perceived by the audience: gender identity, gender roles, and sexuality/sexual preference. Finally, the researchers attempted to ascertain if the ads implicitly or explicitly addressed political or social issues. Within that framework, the authors also endeavored to determine if the current contentious political climate was depicted and if the NFL's public relations challenges were a factor. If so, what recognizable cultural markers were filtered through a societal lens? It was decided that those were indicated by images, symbols, dialogue, music, and the narrative itself—all intended to grab viewer attention and make lasting brand impression.

Before reporting the findings, it was necessary to address which Super Bowl commercials were deemed by viewers to be their favorite and thus the most successful. In other words, which ads resonated with the audience? While there is not one definitive list of favorites, certain commercials rated high among viewers and media critics alike. The top 20 rated ads according to *USA Today* Ad Meter can be found in Appendix A.

The list shows which spots made a positive impression on the audience. Automobile companies have created Super Bowl ads since it began, so not surprisingly they took the top three spots: Kia's "Hero's Journey," Honda's "Yearbooks," and Audi's "Daughter." Overall, carmakers took seven out of the 20 top spots as rated by viewers. What perhaps is unusual is that none of the top three car commercials were overtly male-oriented. The Kia spot starred Melissa McCarthy in a comedic role that relied on a cartoonish physicality and her likable personality to perform tasks highly athletic in nature. She was the heroine of the "Hero's Journey" in a socially conscious albeit unsuccessful effort to save the planet. On the other hand, Honda's spot "Yearbooks" relied on the universal trope of teenage awkwardness, whether male or female. The combination of comedy and celebrities provided a narrative of hopefulness in a visually innovative commercial.

A longing for bygone youth was a theme that appeared in several spots, including Mercedes-AMG's ode to baby boomers "Born to Be Wild," Buick's "Peewee," Alfa Romeo's "Riding Dragons," and to a lesser extent Bud Light's "Ghost Spuds." There was also an element of this leitmotif in the Audi commercial that took the third-favorite spot—"Daughter," a tale of untarnished youth, hometown sport, and the father-daughter bond. As his fearless female child wins a fierce go-cart race against a determined male opponent, the dad wonders about her future, especially gender-related issues such as pay equity and economic opportunity.

Another theme that emanated was family, friends, and human connection in general. The NFL aired the well-received PR-type spot "Inside These

Lines" during the fourth quarter. Dramatic voiceover narration and emotive football imagery created a powerful backdrop for the league to address ethical conduct and comradery in competitive sport. That concept of human connection was utilized to market a wide variety of brands, from beer and bottled water to technology. Budweiser's historical immigrant drama "Born the Hard Way" and Mercedes-AMG's "Born to Be Wild" received high marks in their depiction of human drama, both serious and comedic. But CenturyLink's "Coast to Coast," Michelob's "Our Bar," Google's "Coming Home," and Lifewtr's "Inspiration Drops" (featuring another father-daughter duo) did not resonate with viewers even though human connection was the general theme. Similarly, connecting human experience through virtual reality—Samsung Mobile's "Feel the Raid"—did not make a lasting impact on viewers.

Related to the theme of family, friends, and human connection, the most popular location setting was home. Domestic settings dominated, whether the tone was comedic, somber, silly, or poignant. Five of the top favorites substantially featured a home setting in their narrative. Mr. Clean's "Cleaner of Your Dreams" took a silly-sexy approach to a woman's need to liven up her household chores with a fantasy version of Mr. Clean. In the Skittles spot "Romance," the family home became a comedic barrier to young love like the balcony scene in Romeo and Juliet. But, it is important to note, within the 2017 commercials males dominated the home mise-en-scène. A couple of guys and their two sons humorously connected through the "false cabinet" where they hid their secret stash of King's Hawaiian rolls. And Bud Light's advertising icon and public service-pooch, Spuds MacKenzie, came out of retirement to lure a young guy out of his solitary home environment, encouraging him to socialize with friends again.

Eschewing the raunchiness of previous Super Bowls, website domain registrar GoDaddy chose home as its setting to show what the life of the Internet would look like—if the Internet were a man. Even Intel 360's "Everyday Brady" spot featuring quarterback Tom Brady took place in what supposedly was his home—or in this case his bachelor pad since his supermodel wife Gisele Bundchen was nowhere to be found. All three Amazon Echo spots were located in the living/TV room. Only the "Big Game Buster" spot with a naughty Boston terrier devouring a plate of nachos made the Ad Meter Top 20, and it featured a male dog and a male human voice.

It is noteworthy that another Amazon Echo's other ad, "My Girl," featured a father with his young football-fanatic daughter watching the game together. While the father-daughter pairing was seen several times, mothers did not fare so well. The video game "World of Tanks" aired two commercials, both with tangential domestic themes and a nod to reality TV. In "Real Awful Moms," four "bad mothers" got into a cat fight so vicious it destroyed the house around them (with the help of a video-game tank). The effort to capitalize on the notoriety of the "The Real Housewives" reality franchise did not work with viewers, who rated it the Super Bowl's worst commercial (Siegel, 2017).

The American Petroleum Institute showed viewers a more positive depiction of women when it got into the game in the first quarter. In an effort to shape public opinion about America's dependency on oil in the twenty-first century, "Power Past Impossible" was a visually stimulating futuristic-looking commercial that featured strong women demonstrating unique non-polluting uses for oil. But the pro-woman visuals were undercut by the slogan "This Ain't Your Daddy's Oil"—a nod to generational perceptions about oil, but the impression viewers were left with was that the slogan was too closely referencing (and undercutting) the women in the ad.

However, mothers were not altogether forgotten by advertisers. In the most politically explosive and talked about commercial, a mother and daughter were seen embarking on a treacherous journey to leave their homeland (presumably Mexico) and cross the border into America (presumably illegally). The original commercial for 84 Lumber was six minutes long but was rejected by Fox for being too politically controversial, a charge denied by the sponsor. "'The intent of the Super Bowl commercial . . . was to show that 84 Lumber is a company of opportunity,' said the company's CEO Maggie Hardy Magerko" (Payne, 2017). Before the shortened version even aired during the live broadcast, Trump supporters called for a ban of the family-owned company, and critics of the current administration lauded it for calling attention to immigration policy disputes (Payne, 2017). Viewers rated the more traditional and temporally removed immigrant story from Budweiser ("Born the Hard Way") as their fourth-favorite commercial. 84 Lumber's "The Journey Begins" rated significantly behind as the 29th favorite commercial overall. Even so, curiosity compelled so many people to go online after the 84 Lumber ad aired its website crashed (Payne, 2017).

Several advertisers opted to forego traditional sales pitches in favor of social issues messaging (Krygowska, 2017). In addition to 84 Lumber, other commercials interwove social consciousness and activism into their messaging, most notably the aforementioned "Hero's Journey" by Kia, "Daughter" by Audi, and "Born the Hard Way" by Budweiser. The tourist hosting service Airbnb received positive attention for its message of diversity and inclusivity in "We Accept," which led to its ranking of 16, but the ad was prompted by prolonged public criticism. The commercial was in direct response to media reports the company had engaged in biased and discriminatory practices against people of color, the differently abled, and transgender travelers (Bowles, 2016). The commercial received a positive response from the audience, but only time will tell how the brand continues to perform.

Perhaps "sex sells," but not this year. Blatant sexuality, sexualized situations, and sexiness in general were nearly absent from 2017 commercials. Given the lack of ads featuring raucous beer parties and sexually explicit images, it appeared that advertisers played it safe to avoid offending major segments of the audience. In "Restaurant" by website builder Wix, starring celebrity actors Jason Statham and Gal Gadot, the woman was dressed as a stereotypical sexy spy/assassin character, while the man was wearing a suit and turtleneck shirt. But the action-packed mini-movie steered clear of a sexualized situation. The choices of advertisers seemed almost chaste when compared to previous years. There was a bikini-clad model in the Yellow Tail wine "Kangaroo" spot and a split-second shot of a long stiletto-heeled leg in one of the car commercials. In the trailer for the "Baywatch" movie, Dwayne "The Rock" Johnson flexed his bare muscles, and Zac Efron showed too much of his red-white-and-blue mankini—sexually tame by today's standards. With recent cultural shifts in attitudes about gender and more nuanced forms of gender identity readily available in media and popular culture, perhaps so too the content of Super Bowl commercials has begun to evolve.

It should be noted that the commercials which did imply sexual intimacy positioned the characters in traditional heterosexual relationships with none as the primary focus of the ad. Advertisers steered clear of images and narratives that went beyond mainstream gender roles, gender identities, and sexuality. None of the ads overtly referred to the LGBTQ community. However, if one were to select the Super Bowl ad that spoke most directly to the gendered political environment of 2017, easily it was the trailer for HULU's dark dystopian series *The Handmaid's Tale*—a grim reminder that authoritarian regimes always subjugate women politically, economically, and sexually.

It is undeniable that two ads blatantly went for the sex angle: Mr. Clean's "Cleaner of Your Dreams" and T-Mobile's "Punished." Initially, the first ad reinforced stereotypical gender roles by depicting a woman doing household cleaning. But that was disrupted when an animated boy-band-singing-booty-shaking Mr. Clean began doing the dirty work for her. She became so enraptured by the sight of a man sexily doing chores that she lustily "attacked" her average-Joe husband who was sheepishly holding a bucket and mop. In the T-Mobile commercial, comedic actor Kristen Schaal discussed cell phone options in a situation rife with sadomasochistic innuendo and imagery played for comedic effect. "Punished" aired twice during the Super Bowl, but it was not provocative—only rather weird and out of place. Viewers seemed to agree and ranked it 53rd. If we are to view these sexually direct ads through a feminist lens, it is worth noting that in both spots the woman was the primary character and the subject in control of the sexualized situation. She was not the objectified woman of countless previous Super Bowl commercials but rather a sexual being in pursuit of her own desires. Even so, both commercials represented commodification of female sexuality in service to a consumer product.

You Make the Call

There were a few commercials that attempted to speak more explicitly to the current social and political environment. For example, It's A 10 Hair opted for a comedic approach to the political climate in its spot "Four More Years." In a satirical manner, the commercial claimed that America is facing four more years of bad hair—a direct criticism of the U.S. president's questionable coif—and then it proceeded to encourage Americans to stick together. "America, we're in for at least four years of *awful* hair. So it's up to you to do your part by making up for it with great hair. And we mean *all* hair . . . Do your part." The unusual ad ranked 26th favorite by Ad Meter respondents (www.youtube.com/watch?v=rjS3xKfj42E).

In some of its own spots, the National Football League addressed public concerns about the dangers of playing football. While "Super Bowl Baby Legends" played for laughs and "Inside These Lines" emphasized family, comradery, and ethics, its PR spots overtly made the issue of player safety the central theme: "Virtual Player," "Future of Football: Impact," and "Shoes" focused on injury-deterrence measures being taken by the league to make football less dangerous. Interestingly, no domestic violence ads aired this year, despite the NFL's partnership with NO MORE and the airing of anti-domestic violence ads during the 2015 and 2016 Super Bowls.

By closely analyzing the content of Super Bowl commercials, the researchers were able to determine if advertisers elected to address or avoid certain issues dominating the 2017 socio-political American landscape. The decision to address social issues such as diversity, environmental justice, and gender equality in Super Bowl commercials warrants more study. Were the 2017 attempts to reflect current national conversations or to mitigate the different points of view of football fans? Or, simply, do the ads represent corporate commodification of social and political issues? Did advertisers exploit hot topics by creating emotionally charged messaging in order to reach a specific target audience or only to generate sales?

Summary

In this study, the researchers reflect on the content of 2017 Super Bowl commercials and ask readers to critically consider the potential short-term and long-term benefits and drawbacks of corporations aligning with certain political points of view or social causes. Future comparative studies of this nature are warranted, keeping in mind that the Super Bowl will continue to reign supreme in its ability to reach a large, global audience, to entertain and influence viewers, and to generate lucrative advertising revenue well into the future.

Discussion Questions

1. After watching the 2017 Super Bowl commercials, discuss whether advertisers explicitly or implicitly attempted to speak to controversial issues or tried to avoid them.
2. What are the potential pitfalls, economic or public relations, of aligning with a certain political point of view or taking up the cause of a specific social issue in a Super Bowl commercial?
3. How might we determine the "success" of the messaging presented in the commercials?

4.   Update this chapter by comparing Super Bowl ads from this year to the 2017 ads, using the categories of analysis in this study. What similarities did you find? What differences emerged?
5.   Have there been any new developments that would contribute to a different focus in subsequent Super Bowl commercials? Have perspectives changed? What has occurred lately to impact the tone of the discussion?

References

Bowl. (2017, February 7). It's a 10 hair care Super Bowl commercial 2017. Retrieved from www.youtube.com/watch?v=rjS3xKfj42E

Bowles, N. (2016, June 6). Airbnb faces outcry after transgender guest was denied stay by a host. *The Guardian.com*. Retrieved from www.theguardian.com/technology/2016/jun/06/airbnb-criticism-transgender-guest-denied-super-host

Brady, E. (2017). Super Bowl ads toned down by Trump's shadow? *USA Today*. Retrieved from www.usatoday.com/story/sports/2017/01/31/donald-trump-impact-super-bowl-51-commercials/97295674/

Kanner, B. (2004). *The Super Bowl of advertising: How the commercials won the game*. Princeton, NJ: Bloomberg Press.

Krygowska, J. (2017, February 6). Seven Super Bowl commercials aim to increase awareness, not sales in 2017. Retrieved from https://andrewgoodman.org/news-list/seven-super-bowl-commercials-aim-increase-awareness-not-sales-017/?gclid=CjwKEAjw4IjKBRDr6p752cCUm3kSJAC-eqRt5BEEyMcbq2pOmMj2v1lhVQ44VRLOKYRZE9h6a1vVzxoCqqXw_wcB

Olson, L. C., Finnegan, C. A., & Hope, D. S. (2008). Visual rhetoric in communication: Continuing questions and contemporary issues. In L. C. Olson, C. A. Finnegan, & D. S. Hope (Eds.), *Visual rhetoric: A reader in communication and American culture* (pp. 1–14). Thousand Oaks, CA: Sage Publications.

Payne, M. (2017, February 7). 84 CEO: Super Bowl ad showing Trump's wall wasn't intended to be political. Retrieved from www.washingtonpost.com/news/early-lead/wp/2017/02/04/company-re-tools-rejected-super-bowl-ad-but-you-can-still-see-the-original/?utm_term=.77b158db2762

Rose, G. (2007). *Visual methodologies: And introduction to the interpretation of visual materials* (2nd ed.). Thousand Oaks, CA: Sage Publications.

Schirato, T., & Webb, J. (2004). *Understanding the visual*. Thousand Oaks, CA: Sage Publications.

Siegel, A. (2017, February 6). The 5 worst Super Bowl LI commercials on ad meter. *USA-Today.com*. Retrieved from http://admeter.usatoday.com/2017/02/06/the-5-worst-super-bowl-li-commercials-on-ad-meter

Steinberg, B. (2017, January 19). Donald Trump's election puts Super Bowl advertisers on tricky playing field. *Variety.com*. Retrieved from http://variety.com/2017/tv/news/super-bowl-commercials-donald-trump-advertising-1201963791/

USA Today Ad Meter. (n.d.). *USA Today*. Retrieved from http://admeter.usatoday.com/results/2017

Appendix A

USA Today Ad Meter
(2017 Super Bowl Ads)

Listed in Alphabetical Order

Airbnb (tourism rental service) "We Accept" took an artistic approach during the first quarter to visually portraying a corporate attitude of inclusivity toward all people regardless of race, ethnicity, gender, age, or ability.

Alfa Romeo (automobiles) "Riding Dragons" created an emotional tale during the second quarter about the hopes and dreams of boys and girls evolving into adult strength and courage.

Amazon Echo (technology) "Big Game Moments/Buster" ended the game as the final spot of the night as it brought together one dog, football, and a plate of nachos for comedic effect.

Audi (automobiles) "Daughter" depicted a heart-rending bond between father and daughter at a go-cart race as the dad questions his daughter's economic future during the third quarter of the game.

Bai (bottled water) "Jentleman" brought back the audience's affinity for 90s boy bands with former NSYNC front man Justin Timberlake and quirky actor Christopher Walken sharing an awkward moment together on a leather couch in the second quarter.

Budweiser (beer) "Born the Hard Way" relied on historical narrative in the third quarter to tell the poignant story of the German immigrant who founded Anheuser-Busch and his perilous journey to America in the 1800s.

Bud Light (beer) "Ghost Spuds" revived the superstar pitchdog during the fourth quarter in a Dickensian tale warning of isolationism and what can be lost when one does not engage.

Buick (automobiles) "Peewee" did well in the first quarter as it inserted football superstar Cam Newton and Victoria's Secret model Miranda Kerr into the story of a hometown peewee football game.

Ford (automobiles) "Go Further" showed in the first quarter how the Ford Corporation is developing ways to help people (and animals) get unstuck from frustrating situations.

Honda (automobiles) "Yearbooks" brought to life high school photos of noted celebrities such as Steve Carell, Tina Fey, Jimmy Kimmel, and others, as it gave hope to all geeks and nerds during the second quarter.

Kia (automobiles) "Hero's Journey" relied on the popularity and likability of comedic star Melissa McCarthy as well as the current trend of average-citizen activism in its eco-warrior tale during the third quarter.

King's Hawaiian (bread) "False Cabinet" showed during the fourth quarter that men willbe men and boys will be boys when it comes to their love of food.

Mercedes-AMG (automobiles) "Born to Be Wild" went for baby boomers in the fourth quarter with its action-packed biker-bar brawl while Steppenwolf's anthem played on the jukebox—only to be quelled by *Easy Rider* star Peter Fonda.

Mr. Clean (household cleanser) "Cleaner of Your Dreams" depicted a woman finding relief from household chores when an ultra-sexy boy-band gyrating animated Mr. Clean comes to life in her living room in the third quarter.

NFL "Inside These Lines" made an impression during the fourth quarter with dramatic voiceover and historical footage of emotional NFL moments to weave a trope of sportsmanship and unity.

NFL "Super Bowl Baby Legends" scored during halftime in a spot that dressed up toddlers like Super Bowl superstars of the past such as Mike Ditka replete with bushy moustache, bouffant hair, and sunglasses.

Skittles (candy) "Romance" made an impression during the first quarter with its tale of love gone wrong, a beaver, and inter-generational opportunism.

Tide (laundry detergent) "Bradshaw Stain" aired in two parts (second and fourth quarters) and starred former quarterback Terry Bradshaw on a journey to get a stain out of his shirt.

Tide (laundry detergent) "Get Your Own" during the fourth quarter proved that Tide chose its pitchman well, with another Terry Bradshaw score.

TurboTax (tax service) "Humpty Hospital" in the second quarter reimagined a children's fairytale intertwined with contemporary media coverage of sensational incidents.

(http://admeter.usatoday.com/results/2017)

17 Gender Stereotypes in College Mascot Dyads

Esen S. Koc

This chapter provides an analysis and critique of college mascots in regard to performing and reinforcing gender stereotypes. In total, nine college mascot dyads are examined in categories such as size, physical features, clothes and accessories, and nonverbal language. A very salient form of gender stereotyping was found in all mascot dyads. This is problematic, as these gendered performances strongly reinforce gender norms, roles, and stereotypes in the society. The analysis also contributes to the literature by demonstrating how males are taken as the norm in sports, which in turn validates the invisible hierarchy of genders and sexes in sports and society.

Introduction

Mascots are everywhere, whether they are called icons, images, characters, or logos. They have the ability to communicate across audiences; GEICO's gecko, for instance, targets an audience of adults, yet, Tony the Tiger (of Kellogg's Frosted Flakes) targets children (Hayden & Dills, 2015). In this chapter, the focus is on university (or college) mascots, most of which are animated by costume–clad college students, mainly based on the appearance of a certain animal.

Research in sport communication becomes controversial when it presents evidence that supports a need for change in the structure of society and the organization of sports. Studying sport is significant, as it has been integrated into various levels of social life, including the family, education, economy, politics, and media. Thus, sport plays a highly important role in many people's lives and serves to reinforce cultural and societal beliefs and ideas (Coakley, 2009).

Following Coakley's argument (2009) which claims that "good research always inspires critical approaches to the social conditions that affect our lives" (p. 15), this chapter takes a critical look at the gendered performances of nine college mascot dyads, which both portray and reinforce society's gender norms and stereotypes. Studying mascots is important not only because of their ubiquity in sports but also because of the historical, social, and cultural meanings and messages they convey. Currently, most research on mascots focuses on the controversial topic of Native American images and portrayals, focusing on the racial and historical aspects. However, the number of studies that investigate gender in mascots (of colleges and/or professional sports teams) is extremely limited.

Background

Mascots made their first appearance in sporting events in the 1950s. Initially, their only function was to entertain the audience during lulls and breaks. Today, however, mascots serve a broader and more important role. Today, team mascots participate in community outreach by appearing at national events and promotional and marketing functions. They also help create brand recognition and build team spirit (Dane-Staples, 2012; Deveney & McNeal, 2002; Egan, 2002; Robinson, 2003; Svoboda, 1998). Furthermore, mascots help generate fan interest and devotion while also providing an ancillary source of income (Jacobsen, 2013).

A mascot of a university is a symbol and a unifying image with which students can identify. Even after graduation, many alumni still identify with their school's mascot and call themselves a buckeye, a falcon, a badger, etc. and thus continue their affiliation with their alma mater through these mascots (Baranko, 2011). In some colleges, for instance, the identities of the students who were selected to be mascots (for that year or semester) are kept secret and only revealed at a special ceremony, usually after a certain sports event. In short, mascots are not a frivolous part of college sports. On the contrary, they are a key element in creating a unifying spirit for students as well as for faculty, staff, and alumni.

Gender and Gender Ideology

Femininity and masculinity stem from one's gender rather than one's sex. In other words, femininity and masculinity are social rather than biological constructs. Although males mostly define themselves as masculine and females as feminine, it is important to note that, since these are mere social constructions, it is possible for a female to see herself as masculine, and vice versa. Culturally defined and constructed physical attributes, abilities, personal traits, occupational preferences, and many other things contribute to an individual's gender identity (Stets & Burke, 2000).

Coakley (2009) suggests that gender ideology is a web of ideas and beliefs about male-female relationships, including masculinity and femininity in the structure of social worlds. Individuals often employ gender ideologies as a guide to interpret what it means to be a man or a woman, how they perceive and evaluate other people and their relationships, and how to make sense of "what is 'natural' and 'moral' when it comes to performing gender in their lives" (Coakley, 2009, p. 19).

The traditional (and dominant) gender ideology sees men as superior to women in physical activities and in controlling one's emotions. Subsequently, most athletic traits and qualities are shaped to match the traditional male gender role much better than the female gender role (Eitzen & Zinn, 1989, 1993). This can cause female athletes to be seen as unfeminine (and/or masculine) and their interest in sports as "unnatural" and perhaps even "immoral" (Griffin, 1998). For instance, it is common for people to make comments such as "throws it like a man" when the action of throwing is done "correctly"; however, when it is done "incorrectly," one might say, "don't throw it like a girl." In fact, coaches of men's teams have used similar statements, such as telling players they are "playing like a bunch of girls" as motivation for them to play more aggressively (Coakley, 2009). Therefore, it is not surprising that females, particularly those in poor and working-class families, have lower participation rates in sports compared to other demographic groups (Coakley, 2009; Donnelly & Harvey, 2007; Hargreaves, 1994, 2000; Tomlinson, 2007).

Gender norms and stereotypes are mostly subtle, invisible, and deeply embedded in the society; therefore, people often fail to recognize them. Yager and Baker (1979) identified the Masculine Supremacy Effect, which suggests that masculinity and its traits have greater social utility in the American culture, which creates a culture bias towards masculinity. Highly masculine males benefit from this bias; they not only receive more positive reinforcement from people but also develop higher levels of self-esteem. Burnett, Anderson, and Heppner (1995) found supporting evidence for the Masculine Supremacy Effect suggesting that people with more masculine characteristics (i.e., decisiveness, competitiveness, independence) have higher self-esteem levels than those who possess fewer of these traits.

The portrayal of important icons, such as the mascot dyads in this chapter, are significant, as they can influence how people act by reinforcing gender stereotypes and norms. From a cognitive development perspective, children look for gender cues in order to help them interpret the world around them (Martin & Ruble, 2004, 2009). Similarly, social learning theory suggests that people learn how to act by first seeking and attending to the actions of others and then modeling those actions (Bandura, 1977). Bem (1983) agrees that environmentalist cues shape gendered behavior in children as young as four or five years of age. Eccles and Harold (1991) suggest that gender stereotypes and gender role beliefs can affect children's self-images, self-concepts, and the perceptions of activity values, as well as their expectations and perceptions of success in various tasks. It was found that as early as grade one, girls saw themselves as less able in both math and sports than boys. Interestingly, girls felt least competent in sports; in contrast, boys perceived themselves most competent in the sports domain (Eccles & Harold, 1991). It seems evident that gender differences in children's attitudes and perceptions, at least in terms of sports, are fairly strong and emerge and develop at a very young age. Not surprisingly and consistent with this chapter's perspective, the found gender differences were related as a consequence of socially constructed gender roles and not natural biological differences.

Individuals' gender performances are also refined by reinforcement from families and friends. Additionally, children are exposed to countless images and messages in the media, which is another important source of identity formation (Coakley, 2009). When attending sports games or promotional activities, mascots can serve as active agents in socialization and have the ability to influence children as well as adolescents and young adults (Dane-Staples, 2012; Martin, Richardson, Weiller, & Jackson, 2004).

The Case

Most research on sports mascots is focused on the use of images of Native Americans (e.g., see Bever, 2011; Burkley, Burkley, Andrade, & Bell, 2016; Davis-Delano, 2007; Deveney & McNeal, 2002; Eitzen & Zinn, 1993; Freng & Willis-Esqueda, 2011; Fryberg, Markus, Oyserman, & Stone, 2008; Laveay, Callison, & Rodriguez, 2009; Morris, 2015). While some have looked at the issue of using live animals as mascots (e.g., see Baranko, 2011; Wells, 2017), only a few research studies focused on the naming of sports teams and mascot interactions in terms of gender differences. The naming of college teams is important and directly related to the mascots. Especially in the United States, mascots are generally based on the team's location and its local or regional traits, and some adopt qualities of a predatory animal (Jacobsen, 2013).

According to Eitzen and Zinn (1993, 2001), naming a sports team is not a neutral process, as names chosen for teams are mostly badges of femininity and masculinity, hence of inferiority and superiority. To put it differently, naming of sports teams reinforces gender roles, creating a hierarchy. In a different study, Eitzen and Zinn (1989) found that over half of the colleges and universities in the United States used sexist names and/or logos for their athletic teams. A few examples drive home the point. The Washington and Jefferson College men's team is called the "Presidents," whereas its women's team is called the "First Ladies," directly labeling women as inferior to men. Another example is Angelo State University's athletic teams. The men's teams are called the "Rams," and women's teams are called the "Rambelles." This is problematic for a few reasons: First, according to both the Merriam-Webster and Oxford dictionaries, a male sheep is called a ram, but a female sheep is called a ewe, not a rambelle. Angelo State University invented the word "rambelle" so as not to deviate from their androcentric stance in sports. Secondly, the name of the university's mascot, Dominic the Ram, blatantly demonstrates this male–centric perspective.

Other examples demonstrate that men's teams are taken as the norm in athletics and thus do not need a gender indicator, unlike their female counterparts. For instance, Alcorn State University's men's and women's teams are called "Braves" and "Lady Braves," respectively; Louisiana State University's men's teams are "Tigers," whereas women's teams are "Lady Tigers"; and finally, Dillard University's men's teams are the "Bleu Devils," while the female athletes and teams are called the "Lady Bleu Devils." These examples clearly show that men's teams do not need a gender indicator, as they are the norm; however, women's teams almost always require a gender indicator. Furthermore, adding "lady" to team names reinforces the gender stereotype, as the word "lady" evokes elegance, propriety, and correct behavior (Miller & Swift, 1988). To sum, it can be argued that these types of practices reinforce the gender stereotypes while maintaining male dominance in college athletics (Eitzen & Zinn, 1989, 1993, 2001; Miller & Swift, 1988).

For the current analysis, nine universities were identified with the following mascot dyads: Albert and Alberta Gator (University of Florida), Aristokat and Mrs. Aristokat (Tennessee State University), Big Red and Sue E. (University of Arkansas), Wilbur and Wilma Wildcat (University of Arizona), Pete and Penny (Youngstown State University), Mr. Wuf and Mrs. Wuf (North Carolina State University), Joe and Josie Bruin (University of California, Los Angeles), Freddie and Frieda Falcon (Bowling Green State University), and lastly Lobo Louie and Lucy (University of New Mexico). These institutions were selected for study based on scarcity; there is a limited number of universities that feature mascot dyads. In fact, an extensive web search resulted in a total number of 10 universities that used mascot couples. Yet, even then, the number of images found online were fairly limited since some of these universities do not feature their female mascot in all events. For instance, the University of Alabama's Big Al and Big Alice were excluded, as they were not actually a dyad since the female mascot (Big Alice) only joined the other mascot occasionally, resulting in a limited online presence.

After an online Google Images search that included both mascots in the same picture, a total number of 51 images were found. The fewest number of photos per dyad was two, and the maximum was 10; on average, five photos per dyad of mascots were identified. The next step involved the analysis of the images, in which the visibly salient differences were taken into account. In the end, differences between individual mascots in each of the dyads were divided into the following categories: *size, physical appearance, nonverbal language,* and *clothes and accessories.* These differences established the categories for the analysis, mainly due to the visible salient differences on the images analyzed. This is also the rationale for using photos that have both members of the dyad at the same time—to avoid mistakes in the analysis that may be caused by the image quality, size, perspective, and so on.

Size

The size of the mascots and/or their costumes were consistent with the difference (mostly assumed to be biological) between males and females, in that females are smaller and shorter compared to men (i.e., on average). For instance, in the U.S., the average height for an adult female is 161.8 cm (63.7 inches), whereas an adult male's height is 175.7 cm (69.7 inches) (NCHS, 2016). In the current analysis, eight male mascots were taller than female mascots, and one of the dyads were the same height.

The other significant difference among the mascots in terms of physical size was the size of the mascot's head: Three of the male mascots had larger heads than their female counterparts. This may be interpreted using the size difference between a male and a female body; yet, since costumes are much more exaggerated than real clothing, these differences made the implied nonverbal messages and characteristics much more salient and significant (e.g., assertiveness, dominance, etc.—discussed below under nonverbal language).

Physical Features

In this category, facial and bodily features of the mascots were examined in terms of physical appearance. The most prominent difference between the two genders in the dyads was the absence or presence of *eyelashes* on mascots: Six female mascots had eyelashes, whereas none of the male mascots had eyelashes at all. The second most prominent difference was the *lips*. Male mascots did not have lips; however, three of the female mascots had prominent red lips, as if they were wearing lipstick. The third most salient difference was the *teeth*. Three of the male mascots had larger teeth than their female counterparts. The final significant difference between male and female mascots was the size of the *eyebrows*. Two of the male mascots had significantly thicker eyebrows compared to the eyebrows of the female mascots.

Clothes and Accessories

Of the 51 photos analyzed in this study, male mascots were wearing a jersey in 33 of the photos (male mascots were not wearing jerseys in only 18 of the 51 photos). For example, male mascots were wearing baseball, football, and basketball jerseys. Only two male mascots did not wear jerseys: Pete of Youngstown State University and Albert of the University of Florida. The other male mascots were featured in at least three photos with a jersey on. Female mascots on the other hand, wore significantly fewer jerseys; Frieda (Bowling Green State University) and Wilma (University of Arizona) were the only female mascots who had photos with a jersey on. Even then, the number of the photos in which these mascots were wearing a type of jersey was three out of 51 photos.

The most common clothing item worn by female mascots was a *dress*. In most of the images, six out of nine female mascots were wearing dresses similar those of cheerleaders' attire. Even when wearing a jersey or some other type of top part, the female mascots always had a skirt on. In other words, all female mascots either did not wear any additional clothing piece on top of their costumes (such as Penny of Youngstown State University), or they wore a dress or a skirt.

In 33 images, the male mascots either wore shorts or (knee-long) pants or did not wear any additional clothing piece. However, it is important to note that Albert of the University of Florida and Pete of Youngstown State University did not wear any type of bottoms (e.g., pants, shorts, etc.) in the pictures under study.

One of the most interesting findings were the accessories worn by the female mascots. All the female mascots wore at least one accessory. The most prominent accessory was a *bow* on the heads of the female mascots. Eight out of nine female mascots had a bow or a ribbon on their heads, and the other one mascot had a hair band. The male mascots, on the other hand, mostly did not have any accessories, other than two mascots wearing hats and one wearing a scarf. The other accessory that stood out were cheerleading pom-poms: two female mascots had pom-poms in their hands in a total of eight images. Finally, one of the female mascots, Penny of Youngstown State University wore a headscarf in all of the dyad's photos.

Nonverbal Language

The most prominent nonverbal difference was a forward bent knee among female mascots in 23 of 51 photos. In three additional photos, the female mascots had one of their knees bent, and the leg was lifted towards the back. In other words, almost all female mascots looked like they were curtsying, which is generally accepted as a feminine gesture (Giersdorf, 2006). The second most salient nonverbal feature seen in female mascots in 20 photos portrayed them standing with their hand(s) on their waists. The male mascots, on the other hand, were standing straight and looked more assertive (e.g., pointing at the camera, showing muscles, or other intimidating postures) compared to female mascots that mostly showed a somehow bent body. Overall, the male mascots portrayed a very straight, stiff, and assertive body language, whereas the female mascots always showed bent, curved, and flexible body postures.

You Make the Call

As stated earlier, gender norms and stereotypes are subtle, invisible, and deeply embedded in the society; therefore, people often fail to recognize them. This chapter analyzed and demonstrated how college mascots portray and reinforce gender stereotypes through their physical appearance and physicality. This is important because people of all ages associate themselves with these mascots as a part of their identity journey, mainly as a part of the team spirit built around their university's identity. Nonetheless, the reinforced gender stereotypes by these mascots strengthen the already dominant and powerful gender roles and norms of hegemonic masculinity (i.e., the status-quo). Considering these factors together with other elements of power dynamics in the society (e.g., pressure to conform to society's rules, norms, etc.) can be helpful, especially to see its significance and its broad scope and, thus, why it should be widely discussed and critiqued in all possible occasions.

Discussion Questions

1. After reading this chapter, in what ways would you change how mascots are portrayed in terms of gender stereotypes?

   a. How can they be changed considering the popularity of these mascots?

    b.   How might an institution rationalize that it is appropriate for colleges to maintain and reinforce the status quo in terms of stereotypical gender roles and performances?

2.   Can you find other examples in sports where males are the primary, and females the secondary, mascot? Can you find examples of the opposite dynamic? What does this say about the situation?

3.   What are some of the positive or negative consequences for males to be the norm in sports?

4.   Does your own school (or sports' team) have a mascot? What do you think in terms of their portrayal of gender stereotypes and performances? Find a different mascot dyad and conduct a similar study to the one done in this chapter on that dyad. Share your findings with the class.

References

Bandura, A. (1977). *Social learning theory.* New York, NY: General Learning Press.

Baranko, J. (2011). Hear me roar: Should universities use live animals as mascots? *Marquette Sports Law Review, 21*(2), 599–619.

Bem, S. L. (1983). Gender schema theory and its implications for child development: Raising gender-aschematic children in a gender-schematic society. *Signs: Journal of Women in Culture and Society, 8*(4), 598–616.

Bever, M. L. (2011). Fuzzy memories: College mascots and the struggle to find appropriate legacies of the civil war. *Journal of Sport History, 38*(3), 447–463.

Burkley, M., Burkley, E., Andrade, A., & Bell, A. C. (2016). Pride or prejudice? Examining the impact of Native American sports mascots on stereotype application. *Journal of Social Psychology, 157*(2), 223–235.

Burnett, J. W., Anderson, W. P., & Heppner, P. P. (1995). Gender roles and self-esteem: A consideration of environmental factors. *Journal of Counseling & Development, 73*, 323–326.

Coakley, J. J. (2009). *Sport in society: Issues and controversies* (10th ed.). New York, NY: McGraw-Hill.

Dane-Staples, E. (2012). Gendered choices: Mascot interactions in minor league baseball. *Journal of Sport Behavior, 35*(3), 286–299.

Davis-Delano, L. R. (2007). Eliminating native American mascots: Ingredients for success. *Journal of Sport and Social Issues, 31*(4), 340–373.

Deveney, S., & McNeal, S. (2002). They get paid for this? Tired of the daily grind? These five guys have the jobs you only wish you had. *Sporting News, 226*(12), 8–10.

Donnelly, P., & Harvey, J. (2007). Social class and gender: Intersections in sport and physical activity. In K. Young & P. White (Eds.), *Sport and gender in Canada* (2nd ed., pp. 95–119). Don Mills, ON: Oxford University Press.

Eccles, J. S., & Harold, R. D. (1991). Gender differences in sport involvement: Applying the Eccles' expectancy-value model. *Journal of Applied Sport Psychology, 3*, 7–35.

Egan, D. (2002, March 4). A furry flurry. *Canadian Business, 75*(4), 110–111.

Eitzen, D. S., & Zinn, B. M. (1989). The de-athleticization of women: The naming and gender marking of collegiate sport teams. *Sociology of Sport Journal, 6*, 362–370.

Eitzen, D. S., & Zinn, M. B. (1993). The sexist naming of collegiate athletic teams and resistance to change. *Journal of Sport and Social Issues, 17*(34), 34–41.

Eitzen, D. S., & Zinn, M. B. (2001, January). Dark side of sports symbols. *USA Today Magazine, 129*(2668), 48–51.

Freng, S., & Willis-Esqueda, C. (2011). A question of honor: Chief Wahoo and American Indian stereotype activation among a university based sample. *The Journal of Social Psychology, 151*(5), 577–591.

Fryberg, S. A., Markus, H. R., Oyserman, D., & Stone, J. M. (2008). Of warrior chiefs and Indian princesses: The psychological consequences of American Indian mascots. *Basic and Applied Social Psychology, 30*, 208–218.

Giersdorf, J. R. (2006). Why does Charlotte von Mahlsdorf curtsy? Representation of national queerness in a transvestite hero. *GLQ: A Journal of Lesbian and Gay Studies*, 171–196.

Griffin, P. (1998). *Strong women, deep closets: Lesbians and homophobia in sports.* Champaign, IL: Human Kinetics.

Hargreaves, J. (1994). *Sporting females: Critical issues in the history of sociology of women's sports.* New York, NY: Routledge.

Hargreaves, J. (2000). *Heroines of sport: The politics of difference and identity.* New York, NY: Routledge.

Hayden, D., & Dills, B. (2015). Smokey the Bear should come to the beach: Using mascots to promote marine conservation. *Social Marketing Quarterly, 21*(1), 3–13.

Jacobsen, K. (2013). The accidental mascot: How Mr. Celery reached his salad days with the Wilmington Blue Rocks. *NINE: A Journal of Baseball History and Culture, 22*(1), 130–136.

Laveay, F., Callison, C., & Rodriguez, A. (2009). Offensiveness of native American names, mascots, and logos in sports: A survey of tribal leaders and the general population. *International Journal of Sports Communication, 2*, 81–99.

Martin, C. L., & Ruble, D. N. (2004). Children's search for gender cues: Cognitive perspectives on gender development. *Current Directions in Psychological Science, 13*(2), 67–70.

Martin, C. L., & Ruble, D. N. (2009). Patterns of gender development. *Annual Review of Psychology, 61*, 353–381.

Martin, S. B., Richardson, P. A., Weiller, K. H., & Jackson, A. W. (2004). Role models, perceived sport encouragement, and sport expectancies of United States adolescent athletes and their parents. *Women in Sport and Physical Activity Journal, 13*(1), 18–27.

Miller, C., & Swift, K. (1988). *The handbook of nonsexist writing.* New York, NY: Harper & Row.

Morris, S. P. (2015). The trouble with mascots. *Journal of the Philosophy of Sports, 42*(2), 287–297.

NCHS. (2016). Antropometric reference data for children and adults: United States, 2011–2014 [Vital Health and Statistics]. *National Center for Health Statistics, 3*(39). Hyatsville, MA: DHHS. Retrieved from www.cdc.gov/nchs/data/series/sr_03/sr03_039.pdf

Robinson, M. (2003). David Raymond. *Sporting Marketing Quarterly, 12*(2), 69–71.

Stets, J. E., & Burke, P. J. (2000). Femininity/masculinity. In E. F. Borgatta & R. J. V. Montgomery (Eds.), *Encyclopedia of sociology* (Revised ed.). New York, NY: MacMillan Co.

Svoboda, S. A. (1998). There's nothing fish about Billy the Marlin. *Public Relations Tactics, 5*(10), 4–5.

Tomlinson, A. (2007). *The sport studies reader.* London: Routledge.

Wells, S. (2017). Live animal mascots: A tradition of exploitation, not conservation. *Animal Legal Defense Fund Blog.* Retrieved from http://aldf.org/blog/live-animal-mascots-a-tradition-of-exploitation-not-conservation/

Yager, G. G., & Baker, S. (1979, September). *Thoughts on androgyny for the counseling psychologist.* Paper presented at the annual meeting of the American Psychologist Association, New York, NY.

Appendix

To see pictures from each mascot dyad, please visit: bit.ly/gender-and-mascots

Part III

Press Box

Section V

Social Media

18 A Grand Slam

Major League Baseball's Social Media Evolution Through the Expectancy Violations Theory Lens

Alisa Agozzino & Brian Hofman

Digital technologies have led the sports industry to shift its public relations strategy. The brand image can be maintained and establish positive violations of brand expectation for the organization's key publics through social channels. To help readers make a practical connection, the Expectancy Violations Theory (EVT) is explored and applied. Additionally, the multiple dimensions of social media and the various ways both Major League Baseball (MLB) as an organization and its franchised teams integrate social media into operations while understanding and promoting the brand is investigated. How MLB has captured the younger demographic through digital platforms is also examined.

Introduction

As Major League Baseball (MLB) nears its sesquicentennial celebration as America's oldest professional sports league, the game itself has seen a variety of changes over the years to survive and thrive. In its early years, baseball was the only game in town, thus providing baseball a captive audience (Rader, 2008). These attentive fans allowed baseball to become extensively popular with the American public. Today, despite increased competition by other sports, this pastime is an industry with an estimated worth of over $36 billion (Ozanian, 2015) and revenues approaching close to $10 billion annually (Brown, 2016).

Yet, to be the best game in town and attract a younger demographic into the ballpark, MLB must keep up with the digital era. Through careful social media strategy, brand image can be maintained, and fans can come to expect positive brand engagement through social channels. Expectancy Violations Theory (EVT) is discussed and applied throughout this case study to further develop best practices concerning MLB's social media strategy. At the heart of public relations, the quest involves developing and maintaining mutually beneficial relationships. This case study explores and highlights MLB's journey and practice of building those relationships through social media. In an effort to be at the forefront of professional sports via social media, the opportunities and challenges that MLB has undertaken will be reviewed. At the end of the case study we encourage you to make the call. Did MLB strike out or hit a grand slam?

Background

Since its creation, one of the fundamental values of MLB has been the fan experience. According to *Baseball Parks* (2005), early ballparks were relatively small, so when the grandstands were full, fans could sit on the grass in the outfield. Harry Stevens' idea of selling scorecards at the game, as well as the concept of selling food and drink items at games, increased the fan experience. When games began being played at night and under the lights, even more fans were able to attend games after work and in more comfortable weather conditions (White, 1996).

Even with its growth and popularity, the game of baseball has encountered many existential pressures over the decades. These pressures have forced baseball to continually reexamine and reinvent itself to remain relevant. According to Rader (2008), some of the early external challenges included night games being viewed by baseball purists as "un-natural," the loss of talented players to military duty during WWII, and the development of other professional sports leagues. Additionally, the invention of television and the volume of baseball games delivered on a variety of cable programming has presented a challenge to get fans to attend games.

Internally, baseball has also had to overcome some of its own created issues. As documented by Costill (2011), the strike of 1981 was the first time that regular season MLB games were cancelled. The 1994–95 strike scrubbed the remainder of the 1994 season including the post-season. Rader (2008) posits that even before the 1994 strike, baseball had been losing popularity amongst fans. Reasons included multi-purpose stadiums that weren't fan friendly, the perception of player and/or owner greed, the competition from other forms of entertainment, and widespread doping among its players. Despite its unrelenting pressures, the end of the 2016 MLB baseball season demonstrated the sports' resiliency, marking its 14th consecutive season posting record revenues (Brown, 2016).

The difficulty of sustaining a successful business model remain. Two of the biggest issues MLB faces today are the aging demographics of fans and maintaining a connection with fans through technology, both offering the league another opportunity for increased growth in the number of fans and in league revenue. When Rob Manfred became the 10th commissioner of MLB in 2014, his main message focused on addressing MLB's waning connection to youth (Antoniacci, 2016). MLB has the oldest median TV audience at age 56, followed by the NFL at age 49 and the NBA at age 41 (Baysinger, 2016). One goal for Manfred is to get millennials to the ballpark and thus tap into their tremendous buying power.

In an effort to increase participation of the millennial generation, one must understand the importance social media has for this younger generation. A survey conducted by CISCO (2017) reported millennials are inclined to leave sporting events if they are not connected to the Internet, do not have the ability to upload photos, or cannot tweet about their experiences at sporting events. MLB has taken notice, as millennials represent the up-and-coming generation of professional sports fans. The Internet and one's ability to stay connected is now an amenity expectation for young fans (Brousell, 2015).

MLB has attempted to cultivate the millennial market and get younger patrons to attend its parks using a strategic social strategy. The regular season of 162 games is spread out over seven months. Thus, MLB needs a strategic plan to keep fans stay engaged on social platforms. Studies have shown 80% of fans want a more immersive and content-rich experience while attending events, including things like live video, real-time stats, alternative camera angles, and slow-motion replays (Martin, 2016). To address these concerns, MLB's social strategy has included tapping into star players' social media followings, as many of the up-and-coming stars for the MLB are millennials themselves. MLB is also putting together more bite-size content to keep fan interest high. By posting these singular moment highlights on social media platforms, the visuals attract and engage fans from around the globe (Baysinger, 2016).

Expectancy Violations Theory (EVT) was originally developed to explain the impact of personal space violation on interpersonal relationships (Burgoon, 1978). Since then, EVT has been useful in predicting nonverbal and verbal behaviors in online communication (Bevan, Ang, & Fearns, 2014; Fife, Nelson, & Bayles, 2009; McLaughlin & Vitak, 2012). Burgoon (1993) described the expectancy portion of the theory as a "predictable behavior that can be specific to an individual, context, and/or relationship that occurs in a consistent pattern" (Bevan et al., 2014, p. 172). The theory posits that one can experience either positive (favorable) or negative (unfavorable) violations. An example can include when a spouse surprises you with flowers at work. This is an expectancy violation, yet one that most do not view as negative for the recipient.

One of the main tenets of EVT includes the prescriptive and predictive expectancies within the theory. Prescriptive expectancies are based on social norms and behaviors that are appropriate within a specific context of communication. An example of a prescriptive norm violation could include MLB posting too many status updates, as this goes against the norm of having the right amount of communication with its fans. Another violation could be individual MLB players having a heated interaction with fans in public forum posts, as this goes against expected behavior for MLB players. Predictive expectancies, on the other hand, are often determined by the individual's past behavior or unique interaction style and thus can calculate anticipated behaviors that are particularized for said specific individual (Burgoon, 1993). An MLB example could include how quickly MLB responds to a question posted on a social media platform.

Furthermore, online users' (defined as "fans" in the current case study) personal communication and/or relationships on varied social media platforms with companies' extensive promotional and branding efforts can be deemed violations of the users' expectations. Even though some think only of negative expectations, expectations can be both negative and positive. When a company or brand utilizes social media to exceed previous expectations, those expectations are positively violated.

The Case

As social media began to seep into MLB, Rymer (2013) stated, "It's changed the entire baseball experience for good" (para. 5). In the following section, we will discuss the case of MLB's social media evolution.

When social media began a public relations shift throughout every industry, the sports industry was no different. In spring of 2011, MLB's Cleveland Indians announced they were breaking away from the traditional media access approach they had implemented for years. Instead of the more traditional approach, the Indians would allow anyone with a social media account to apply for a single-day credential to access the team's social media suite, the first move of its kind by a major league team (Holton & Coddington, 2012).

As social suites and social media days at parks developed, connectivity became increasingly important. Mark Newman (2013) stated that as early as 2011 fans were demanding the ability for connectivity, mainly, at first, to download data for activities such as checking email but later to conduct the social media activity to which fans had grown accustomed. By 2013 Newman had seen an increase in upstream data. While watching games from their stadium seats, fans were now increasingly uploading content, from tweets to Facebook posts to Instagram pictures. Maddox (2014) emphasized the importance of connectivity, arguing younger fans would leave the stadium if they couldn't get connected, forcing the sports industry to digitalize or be left with less revenue.

Published on the MLB's website (2012), All-Star players were authorized to use social media at the All-Star Game for the first time in 2012. Computer stations were set up to allow players to interact with their fans via social media. Media giants like ESPN and Fox also heavily incorporated social media into their television broadcasts. Fans began to experience a social media shift within professional baseball that would continue to gain momentum.

Hashtag campaigns gained popularity from 2013–2015 and continues to be used daily. MLB saw an increase in social audience engagement with specific hashtags it created throughout these seasons. According to Mendoza (2015), tweets including hashtags #THIS and #OpeningDay saw significant growth in audience engagement. By incorporating a carefully planned hashtag strategy, MLB increased fan engagement and excitement on social media platforms. Washenko (2013) pointed out how the campaign was strategized by providing access to computer stations on the field for the players. Those who had access were able to interact with fans in real time, revolutionizing baseball's social media landscape. Campaigns like this allowed fans to engage by arguing with team rivals, posing questions, or cheering on their favorite players.

In an effort to keep with the ever-evolving digitized world, Snapchat and MLB Advanced Media partnered to feature fan-generated content on Snapchat in 2015. According to Talbot (2015), as of 2015, Snapchat had grown to "100 million daily active users and 400 million snaps per day" (para. 5). Talbot also noted that in 2015 almost three-fourths of its users fell into the 18-to-34 year old age range. For businesses such as the MLB, content can be distributed through Snapchat's stories, which is accessible by all of its followers on the platform. Although this wasn't the first time professional sports appeared on Snapchat's *Our Story*, it was the first time Snapchat featured live sports on a weekly basis (Bergson, 2015). Furthermore, during spring training in 2015, all 30 MLB teams published Snapchat stories to bring fans even closer to the action. Players were granted access to their phones to capture spring training moments on Snapchat for greater fan engagement and to increase fan excitement about the upcoming MLB season.

Roth and Handley (2017) argue that although TV is still widely used to attract and retain viewers of sporting events, social media is vastly under evaluated. Naturally, advertisers in the sports industry are driven to wherever the most eyeballs are attracted. This caused a shift to social media, especially when social platforms can be viewed from mobile devices from almost anywhere. MLB created its online social media clubhouse to attract and retain fan engagement.

MLB's Social Media Clubhouse is housed on its website to connect viewers to its social media platforms and initiatives. Along with your traditional platforms—Facebook, Instagram, Pinterest, Twitter, and Tumbler—MLB also has its own unique platforms. At Bat is an application that allows fans to follow games through live audio. Gameday features video highlights, schedules, and more. For fans attending a game, the Ballpark app allows them to personalize their experience with mobile check-in, social media, player and team music, and exclusive content. These apps and platforms offer other ways to influence fans expectancy value in a positive way. However, they can also become negative when technology fails to work properly or Internet connections are slow.

Facebook Live posts also seem to be gaining in popularity, particularly among the younger demographic. MLB announced in May 2017 it would livestream 20 MLB games nationally with no blackout restrictions throughout the season (Cohen, 2017). Twitter, which has had a livestreaming pact with MLB since July 2016, also livestreams MLB games throughout the season (Cohen, 2017). Schattner (2016) spoke to the real-time interactivity of Facebook Live and its ability to answer fan questions when he claimed that simply watching and listening was no longer sufficient for fan expectation. Within EVT, increased expectations would include fans' desires to personally engage with players, coaches, and staff in real time.

To create a new positive expectation, in June 2017 MLB teamed up with Intel to deliver a live-streaming game of the week virtually for the next three years (Baig, 2017). Although special virtual reality gear is needed to experience the game, MLB administrators believe this advancement in the digital and social industry will bring fans closer to the action. Baig points out this is the first time an entire live game will be streamed in virtual reality.

Baseball fans enjoy watching the game from the comfort of their homes, others from social settings, and yet others from the actual sports stadiums. Ko, Yeo, Lee, Lee, and Jang (2016) studied factors that affect sports viewers' online interactions for a variety of locations. They found that most influential factors affecting chat interactions are closely related to performance records and chat interaction histories of teams, as well as the dynamics of game events. Those fans who are most engaged are those who have the expectations of high interaction on the social platform validated through the EVT framework.

To best connect with those fans who are most engaged, the Major League Baseball Players Association is making strides with player-to-fan interaction. Implemented in 2017, a tool titled Infield Chatter was developed at the request of players who wanted a more meaningful way to connect with fans (Heitner, 2017). When considering EVT, this would help to create a positive expectation violation if the engagement on both ends is upheld.

You Make the Call

There is no magic formula for a guaranteed social media strategy success. If one existed, everyone would implement it. By conducting thorough research and developing a carefully planned strategy based on that research, best practices emerge.

The National Basketball Association (NBA) was the first within the professional sports industry to hit the most followers on Twitter, Facebook, and YouTube (Ortiz, 2011). Early on, the NBA understood it wasn't enough just to engage fans but that the league had to listen to and monitor its social channels in order to meet its fans' wants and needs (expectations) on various platforms. As discussed throughout this case study, MLB has come to the same conclusion. Faced with a multitude of pressures that have made attracting and retaining a loyal following a challenge, MLB realized the opportunity social media presented in more fully engaging, retaining, and creating new fans.

In contrast, the National Football League (NFL) arrived relatively late to the game. Recognizing their industry was also shifting and studying the success MLB has garnered, Smith (2012) explained how the NFL partnered with a marketing company to create effective social media platforms for both the league and its teams. In December 2017 the NFL signed a multi-year agreement with Verizon to carry football games on mobile phones. Fans are now able to stream football games on three apps, including Yahoo Sports, Verizon's go90, and NFL Mobile (Goldman, 2017).

Alongside the National Hockey League (NHL), 2015 saw MLB continuing to take risks that paid high dividends. DiLorenzo (2016) points out that both the NHL and MLB took on digital-rights mega-deals to cultivate their businesses across all things digital, from web to mobile. For MLB this included a one-year Snapchat agreement that helped the league expand into a younger market.

As the social media paradigm shift continues, so do the ethical considerations. According to Pritchard and Burton (2014), one important ethical concern for MLB is to maintain trust. Sport organizations are held to a high standard by fans because fans develop a great attachment to the brand and its teams through following via social media and/or attending games. This attachment is made even greater due to the excitement and the unpredictability of the outcome of the game. MLB players also gain credibility with fans and "inspire [fans] to trust that the [players] will do right by the brand or product, team or sport" (Pritchard & Burton, 2014, p. 91). Violations of this trust through inappropriate uses of social media—such as team media personnel arguing with fans via Twitter or MLB players posting inappropriate comments, photos, or responses on Facebook—will be viewed as a negative expectancy violation. Pritchard and Burton state breaches of trust illicit strong negative emotional responses. To try to alleviate problems caused by inappropriate uses of social media by its players, MLB issued a memorandum regarding its social media policy and has fined or suspended players for inappropriate material or comments posted via social media (Sullivan, 2011) or using social media during the game itself (Fisher, 2015).

As MLB approaches its 150th season it continually strives to build and maintain a mutually beneficial relationship with its fans. Social media has provided myriad ways to enhance the fan experience. MLB has diligently targeted the younger demographic through varied digital platforms through a purposeful social media strategy. From the early quest of Facebook followers, to witty Twitter posts, to special in-park social suites, to a season-long initiative with Snapchat, through the EVT framework, MLB has developed a social strategy within the sport industry that's home-run worthy.

Discussion Questions

1. The many apps MLB has developed to help fans enjoy the in-game experience have also allowed MLB to collect a lot of data on each individual who signs up for the app. What ethical responsibility does MLB have to protect this information from being hacked by an outside group? Does MLB have the right to sell this information to third parties to help generate additional revenues for MLB?

2. Due to fans using technology to purchase tickets, food, drink, etc., MLB is able to track fan behavior and likes and can customize marketing strategies to specific fans through promotions or brand-specific advertising. What are the advantages of this strategy? Are there any potential

pitfalls or ethical concerns related to this ability to segment fans in this manner?

3. Many fans have built an allegiance to a particular team and are highly active on their team's social media platforms. How does MLB as a larger, yet separate, entity build a following and keep baseball fans actively engaged on its platforms to build a professional baseball brand itself? What social media platforms do you think will offer the greatest opportunity to engage a younger demographic? If you had to choose one platform to invest the most time and resources in for MLB, which platform would you choose and why?

4. In an ever-evolving world of social strategy, how is MLB building upon the discussed social media strategies through new applied social media platforms? Can you provide a current example of a new social media strategy currently being implemented by MLB or other professional sports leagues? How would you forecast this new social strategy will impact fan engagement?

References

Antoniacci, M. (2016, June 30). The top 10 social media all-stars of Major League Baseball: MLB players take on technology to engage the next generation of baseball fans. Retrieved from www.inc.com/mandy-antoniacci/the-top-10-social-media-all-stars-of-major-league-baseball.html

Baig, E. C. (2017, June 1). Major League Baseball is about to play ball: In virtual reality. Retrieved from www.usatoday.com/story/tech/columnist/baig/2017/06/01/major-league-baseball-broadcast-live-vr-game-week/102376824/

Baseball parks. [video recording]. (2005). [New York]: A & E Television Networks: Marketed and distributed by New Video, c2005.

Baysinger, T. (2016, March 28). Can social media help Major League Baseball get younger? Commissioner Rob Manfred sets out to the solve the age problem. Retrieved from www.adweek.com/tv-video/can-social-media-help-major-league-baseball-get-younger-170432/

Bergson, Z. (2015, May 15). Snapchat's partnership with MLB has big upside for both companies. Retrieved from www.forbes.com/sites/zachbergson/2015/05/15/snapchats-partnership-with-mlb-has-big-upside-for-both-companies/-2f0dba985381

Bevan, J. L., Ang, P., & Fearns, J. B. (2014). Being unfriended on Facebook: An application of Expectancy Violation Theory. *Computers in Human Behavior, 33,* 171–178. doi:10.1016/J.CHB.2014.01.029

Brousell, L. (2015, September 2). How the Red Sox brought new tech to baseball's oldest park. Retrieved from www.cio.com/article/2979658/wi-fi/how-the-red-sox-brought-new-tech-to-baseballs-oldest-park-video.html

Brown, M. (2016, December 5). MLB sees record revenues approaching $10 billion for 2016. Retrieved from www.forbes.com/sites/maurybrown/2016/12/05/mlb-sees-record-revenues-approaching-10-billion-for-2016/-cce334570882

Burgoon, J. K. (1978). A communication model of personal space violations: Explication and an initial test. *Human Communication Research, 4*(2), 129–142. doi:10.1111/j.1468-2958.1978.tb00603.x

Burgoon, J. K. (1993). Interpersonal expectations, expectation violations, and emotional communication. *Journal of Language and Social Psychology, 12*, 30–48.

CISCO. (2017, June 8). The new fan experience is here. San Jose, CA: CISCO Systems, Inc. Retrieved from www.cisco.com/c/dam/en_us/solutions/industries/docs/sports/cisco_se_brochure.pdf

Cohen, D. (2017, May 18). 20 Major League Baseball games are coming to Facebook Live on Friday nights. Retrieved from www.adweek.com/digital/major-league-baseball-facebook-live/

Costill, A. (2011, June 9). A look back at professional sports labor disputes. Retrieved from www.amog.com/101341-professional-sports-disputes/

DiLorenzo, M. (2016, June 9). Raising a cup to 5 great NHL social media activations. Retrieved from www.adweek.com/digital/michael-dilorenzo-rebel-ventures-guest-post-five-great-nhl-social-media-activations/

Fife, E. M., Nelson, C. L., & Bayles, K. (2009). When you stalk me, please don't tell me about it: Facebook and Expectancy Violation Theory. *Kentucky Journal of Communication, 28*(1), 41.

Fisher, G. (2015, June 19). For the first time, a Major League Baseball player has been punished for using social media during a game. Retrieved from https://qz.com/432830/for-the-first-time-a-major-league-baseball-player-has-been-punished-for-using-social-media-during-a-game/

Goldman, D. (2017, December 11). Verizon will stream NFL games on any network next year. Retrieved from http://money.cnn.com/2017/12/11/media/nfl-verizon/index.html

Heitner, D. (2017, April 8). Here is baseball players' new proprietary social media tool. Retrieved from www.forbes.com/sites/darrenheitner/2017/04/18/here-is-baseball-players-new-proprietary-social-media-tool/-149d8dec2d11

Holton, A., & Coddington, M. (2012). Recasting social media users as brand ambassadors: Opening the doors to the first "social suite". *Case Studies in Strategic Communication, 1*, 4–24. Retrieved from http://cssc.uscannenberg.org/wp-ontent/uploads/2013/10/v1art2.pdf

Ko, M., Yeo, J., Lee, J., Lee, U., & Jang, Y. J. (2016). What makes sports fans interactive? Identifying factors affecting chat interactions in online sports viewing. *PLoS ONE, 11*(2). doi:10.1371/journal.pone.0148377

Maddox, T. (2014, April 11). Stadiums race to digitize: How sports teams are scrambling to keep Millennials coming to games. Retrieved from www.techrepublic.com/article/how-sports-teams-are-scrambling-to-keep-millennials-coming-to-games/

Martin, K. (2016, February 1). Digital fandom: Are you ready? [Web log post]. Retrieved from https://blogs.cisco.com/digital/cisco-sports-and-entertainment-digital-fanom-are-you-ready

McLaughlin, C., & Vitak, J. (2012). Norm evolution and violation on Facebook. *New Media & Society, 14*(2), 299–315. doi:10.1177/1461444811412712

Mendoza, K. (2015, May 28). Social best practices in U.S. sports industries [Web log post]. Retrieved from www.shareablee.com/blog/2015/05/28/social-best-practices-in-u-s-sports-industries/

MLB. (2012). All-Stars to use social media during All-Star Game for first time. Retrieved from http://m.mlb.com/news/article/32793088/all-stars-to-use-social-media-during-all-star-game-for-first-time/

Newman, M. (2013, April 10). MLBAM, Qualcomm to boost mobile access at parks. Retrieved from http://m.mlb.com/news/article/43585514/mlb-advanced-media-qualcomm-partner-to-boost-mobile-ballpark-experience-at-ballparks/

Ortiz, M. B. (2011, April 25). The NBA's social media explosion. Retrieved from www.espn.com/espn/page2/story/_/page/burnsortiz%2F110425_nba_social_media/sportCat/nba

Ozanian, M. (2015, March 25). MLB worth $36 billion as team values hit record $1.2 billion average. Retrieved from www.forbes.com/sites/mikeozanian/2015/03/25/mlb-worth-36-billion-as-team-values-hit-record-1-2-billion-average/-d0a7f19fd590

Pritchard, M. P., & Burton, R. (2014). Ethical failures in sport business: Directions for research. *Sport Marketing Quarterly, 23*(2), 86–99.

Rader, B. G. (2008). *Baseball: A history of America's game.* Urbana, IL: University of Illinois Press.

Roth, C., & Handley, L. (2017, March 22). Sports teams are getting more exposure on social media than they are on TV: Expert. Retrieved from www.cnbc.com/2017/03/22/sports-teams-are-getting-more-exposure-on-social-media-than-they-are-on-tv-expert.html

Rymer, Z. (2013, May 9). How the rise of social media has changed the game of baseball forever. Retrieved from http://bleacherreport.com/articles/1634493-how-the-rise-of-social-media-has-changed-the-game-of-baseball-forever

Schattner, M. (2016, November 9). Facebook Live is driving the next wave of fan engagement. Retrieved from http://digitalsport.co/facebook-live-is-driving-the-next-wave-of-fan-engagement

Smith, C. (2012, September 10). NFL teams turn to social media to connect with fans. Retrieved from www.forbes.com/sites/chrissmith/2012/09/10/nfl-teams-turn-to-social-media-to-connect-with-fans/-148aa7bb70be

Sullivan, J. (2011, April 29). Ozzie Guillen suspended two games for tweeting after ejection. Retrieved from www.sbnation.com/2011/4/29/2334380/ozzie-guillen-suspended-two-games-for-tweeting-after-ejection

Talbot, K. (2015, July 28). 5 ways to use Snapchat for business. Retrieved from www.socialmediaexaminer.com/5-ways-to-use-snapchat-for-business/

Washenko, A. (2013, July 22). 3 Facebook Hashtag Campaigns that have already become hits. Retrieved from https://sproutsocial.com/insights/facebook-hashtag-campaigns/

White, G. E. (1996). *Creating the national pastime: Baseball transforms itself 1903–1953.* Princeton, NJ: Princeton University Press.

19 Witness?

Perceptions of Lebron James' Civic Responsibility

Amy Graban Crawford

This case study examines the #NoJusticeNoLebron social media campaign on Twitter following the 2014 shooting of Tamir Rice by Cleveland police. The campaign lobbied LeBron James to sit out two Cleveland Cavaliers' games as a protest of the grand jury decision to not indict the two police officers involved in the shooting. Attribution theory is used to examine media narratives in this study. The #NoJusticeNoLeBron campaign allows readers to question whether there is a link between sports viewership and civic engagement and explores the role that media narrative has on how a story is framed and how causality, responsibility, and blame are assigned.

Introduction

A person driving into downtown Cleveland, Ohio, encounters several landmarks: an operational steel mill on the edge of town; the Cuyahoga River, which famously caught fire in 1969 and helped inspire the modern environmental movement; and the Gateway district with Progressive Field and Quicken Loans Arena, home to the Cleveland Indians and Cavaliers. Towering over it all is a Nike-sponsored 10-story banner of LeBron James in his iconic "chalk toss" stance, with his back to the viewer. The giant letters on the back of his jersey read "Cleveland." About 40 miles south in Akron, Ohio, the city of LeBron James' birth, there is a similar banner. In this one, James hoists the Larry O'Brien Championship Trophy under a header stating, "I'm Home."

Background

When LeBron James left the Cleveland Cavaliers in 2010 to take his talents to the Miami Heat, the Nike-sponsored banner in Cleveland came down, replaced by one for a local company celebrating city history. In the last decade Cleveland has experienced a renaissance. People moved downtown, investors built new hotels, restaurants, and a casino, and the city is home to a thriving bio-medical industry (Blasky, 2015). To top it all off, LeBron James announced he was "coming home." He eventually fulfilled his promise of delivering a championship to one of the city's success-starved sports

Figure 19.1 This Banner of LeBron James Hangs in Downtown Akron Near the Street
Named for Him, King James Way

Source: Denis M. Crawford

franchises. The LeBron James banner went back up, and Cleveland was
dubbed the Comeback City (Jordan, 2016).

Not all parts of the city experienced this success equally. A recent study by
the Economic Innovation Group called Cleveland "the most distressed large
city in America" (Russell, 2016). The city struggles with high rates of poverty. In a city where 53% of the population is African American, only 27%
of the police force is black. Cleveland police faced a series of misconduct
allegations and a U.S. Justice Department investigation, which concluded
that the Cleveland police department systematically applied excessive force
against civilians (Josefczyk, 2015).

The questions many asked at the time about race and policing practices in Cleveland mirrored those in other cities in America, such as Ferguson, Missouri, and Baltimore, Maryland. Protests and demonstrations across the country and the formation of the Black Lives Matter movement kept the issue of police shootings of unarmed black men in the headlines through 2014 and 2015 ("Protest snarls up major US Freeway", 2014; Smydo, 2016; Somashekhar, 2014). Across the country, high-profile athletes Derrick Rose, Colin Kaepernick, and Reggie Bush joined the debate through on-field and on-court gestures (Campbell, 2014; Ebenezer, 2016; Kang, 2016; Robinson, 2014), continuing the tradition of politically active athletes, such as Muhammad Ali, Tommie Smith, and John Carlos ("Causes worth caring about", 2015).

LeBron James has a history of speaking out on political issues, from donning an "I Can't Breathe" T-shirt in solidarity with civil-rights protesters to supporting NFL players' anthem protests (Lancaster, 2017). Despite his public statements about other high-profile police shootings, James sidestepped speaking out on the shooting death of Tamir Rice, a 12-year-old Cleveland boy killed by police, saying that he didn't have enough information to speak on the topic (Bondy, 2014). Media outlets and activists on social media noted James' silence on violence within the community so closely identified with him, questioning why he chose not to speak out. This chapter uses attribution theory as a conceptual foundation to examine calls from activists, analysts, and journalists for LeBron James to act on behalf of the family of Tamir Rice and asks how the public perceives the responsibility of an athlete to act as a spokesperson for the community.

The Case

On November 22, 2014, a Cleveland police officer shot 12-year-old Tamir Rice while responding to a 911 call. The caller told dispatchers that a guy, "probably a juvenile," at a recreation center was pointing a pistol at bystanders. The caller also said two times that the weapon was "probably fake," but this information was never relayed to the responding officers. Tamir Rice died from his wounds the next day ("Ohio Boy Shot," 2014).

Tamir Rice went to the park with friends on a Saturday afternoon. Surveillance video, released at the request of the family, showed Rice walking in the park and pointing what appeared to be a weapon. The Airsoft replica gun he was carrying did not have its orange safety indicator. A police squad car pulled up next to Rice, and one officer, Timothy Loehmann, a rookie who had been with the force for seven months, fired twice within two seconds of arriving. Within those two seconds, Loehmann, who was less than 10 feet away from Rice, told Rice to raise his hands, and shot him when he touched the pellet gun at his waistband. (Fitzsimmons, 2014).

Tamir Rice was African American, and Loehmann and his partner are white. The shooting death of Tamir Rice was one example in a series of allegations of excessive force leveled against Cleveland police, including the

2012 shooting of two unarmed African Americans following a car chase. Days after the Rice shooting, the U.S. Justice Department issued a report outlining cases of excessive force against civilians by Cleveland police. Rice's death also came two days before a St. Louis grand jury did not indict a white officer in the shooting death of an unarmed black teenager, Michael Brown, in Ferguson, Missouri (Josefczyk, 2015). Nationally, the case became another example of police officers shooting unarmed black citizens and added to the debate about race and policing policies in the United States.

After a six-month investigation, a judge on the Cleveland municipal court found probable cause to charge Loehmann with murder and charge Loehmann's partner with negligent homicide. A grand jury convened on October 16, 2015, and in December declined to indict the two officers (Danylko, 2015). After the grand jury's decision, activists on Twitter called for LeBron James to protest by sitting out two games, under the hashtag #NoJusticeNoLeBron. (Davidson, 2015) When asked about the grand jury decision and the call for a boycott, James expressed reluctance to speak publicly on the issue, saying, "I've always been a guy who's taken pride in knowledge on every situation that I've ever spoken on. I haven't been on top of this issue so it's hard for me to comment" (Hickey, 2015; Jones, 2016). The discussion on Twitter, and the resultant debates on sports talk shows and sports pages, attributed causes for why LeBron, who was willing to speak out on other occasions, was now silent. Why, the pundits asked, won't James take a stand on this issue in his hometown?

You Make the Call

Attribution theory can be used as a lens through which to examine the media coverage of LeBron James' statements on the Tamir Rice shooting. Attribution theory is most often associated with social psychology but can be applied to a wide array of subjects (Kelley, 1973). Based on the writings of Fritz Heider and often associated with Harold H. Kelley, attribution theory explores how people interpret environmental data and use them to make decisions. It is natural to try to make sense of our environment by trying to locate the cause of an event. Attribution theory explores our systematic way of explaining why things happen the way they do (Vishwanath, 2014). This examination process is largely perceptual and subjective. This psychological epistemology looks at how a person learns about the world and determines what is true. Further, attribution theory explores how people answer "why" questions and how people attribute causality (Kelley, 1973).

In Kelley's model of causal attribution (1967), all perceived causes have three dimensions: locus, stability, and controllability. With locus, the observer asks whether the cause is perceived to come from within an individual or from an external source. For example, if a student fails a math exam, this may be attributed to internal causes, such as a lack of motivation, preparation, or aptitude in math. Applying external causes, one could say the student received inadequate teaching, experienced a distracting testing environment, or took a poorly designed exam (Ryan & Boscia, 2003).

For a person to identify an external factor as the cause, several requirements must be met. First, a person or actor must respond differently to different items. Second, the person must respond consistently to the item across time and space. Finally, a consensus is expected from others to an object (Kelley, 1967). To apply this, let's say a researcher enjoys a meal and wishes to study why. She can ask herself, "Is it because it was well made with good ingredients (external)? Or was I just hungry (internal)?" To test whether the enjoyment was due to the meal, she must like this meal but not like all food, enjoy this meal every time she eats it, and others should agree that it is good.

The second dimension in Kelley's model is stability. Is the cause constant or does it vary over time? Personality and ability are stable causes. Unstable causes are luck and effort. Observers often attribute cause to the most stable factor. If the cause is stable, it is often used to predict future behavior as well (Kelley, 1973).

Controllability is the third dimension and examines how much control an individual has to affect an outcome. When an event is perceived as controllable, we assign or attribute more personal responsibility to the individual (Ryan & Boscia, 2003). This is true for awarding praise if the outcome is positive or assigning blame if the outcome is negative. This responsibility may be due to role responsibility, which is when a person is expected to perform certain duties based on his or her role in the system. Usually this is a leadership role or a place of distinction. For example, a teacher is responsible for a classroom, and a commanding officer is in charge of a military unit. The second type of controllability is causal responsibility, where one's action, or failure to act, leads to a result. This is usually ascribed in hindsight, and the effect and cause cannot be swapped. For example, an accident caused the injuries, or the lack of rain caused the drought (Hart, 2008). The third is capacity responsibility, which is based on control and reason. Was a person able to understand the impact of his or her actions? Is the person able to understand the conduct that the law and morality requires? In the case of children, the courts or the law may establish that children do not have the capacity to make informed decisions. The final type of responsibility is liability responsibility. This is responsibility in the moral realm only, where a person may make a statement in good faith that harms another but the harm is indirect. Someone may be assigned a moral responsibility but not blamed. As an example, if two people at work are having an illicit affair and a co-worker gossips to the rest of the staff, this may cause harm, but it will not cause the affair. The gossip had control of his or her behaviors and was not coerced, so there is a level of responsibility, but it is a vicarious responsibility versus a legal or a strict responsibility (Shaver, 1985).

The start of the #NoJusticeNoLeBron campaign is generally attributed to writer and social justice activist Tariq Touré. On December 28, after the grand jury verdict in the Tamir Rice case, Touré posed a question on his Twitter account: "Can we collectively flood @KingJames mentions to remind him not to play?" In subsequent tweets, Touré argued that a protest by LeBron James could bring about real change by drawing attention to a broken system and leveraging his power. By later in the day, the hashtag was trending. On Twitter, several themes began to appear, not only commenting on the boycott call, but also attributing reasons why LeBron should or should not sit out games (Touré, 2016).

One theme in the tweets pointed to external forces that could be driving LeBron's choice. Some commented that LeBron James is a brand ambassador who does not want to hurt his image or marketability. Others pointed to contractual obligations. For those who argued in this camp, the main complaint was that it was unfair to ask him to risk his livelihood. In a commentary on the debate, Tony Jones at the *Salt Lake Tribune* wrote, "Yes, James has more money than you or I [sic]. Still, you can't ask a man to intentionally not show up for work, and then lob criticism at him when he decides that's not the way to go" (Jones, 2016). There were few tweets mentioning internal attributions for his action or inaction. Some commentators and journalists mentioned a quote that James gave in a *Hollywood Reporter* article in February 2015, where he talked about the Tamir Rice shooting and whether he and his wife plan to have "the talk" with their two sons about dealing with the police. In that piece, LeBron James said:

> Absolutely . . . and the talk is, "You be respectful, you do what's asked and you let them do their job, and we'll take care of the rest after. You don't have to boast and brag and automatically think it's us against the police."

He went on to add that they do not allow their sons to play with realistic toy guns. "We have Nerf guns that are lime green and purple and yellow, but I don't even let them take them out of the house" (Guthrie, 2015).

On Twitter and in articles on the social media campaign, the stability dimension seemed to stump observers. Many commented that James had grown increasingly vocal on social justice issues since 2012, when he and his teammates on the Miami Heat donned hoodies to start a conversation about the Trayvon Martin shooting near Orlando. James had also been a vocal supporter of Cleveland and Akron, contributing millions of dollars his own money to education and sending more than a thousand young people from Akron to college. To many commentators, this incongruity was difficult to follow. In his follow-up letter to LeBron James, Tariq Touré wrote:

> The reason I went as far to ask you sit out is because every bit of empathic work you have done makes you the archetype for this sort of leadership. Whether it be hoodies, T-shirts or 4th quarter comebacks, your energy commands allegiance.

(Touré, 2016)

Many who were commenting on the #NoJusticeNoLeBron campaign pointed to James' role responsibility as a celebrity and a spokesperson for Cleveland. Tamir Rice's mother, when asked by a reporter, said that Tamir Rice idolized James and that she found it "quite sad" that James was not more vocal on the topic of her son's death (Moore, 2016). Others felt that being revered as role models put black athletes in a no-win situation in politics, pointing to the double-standard that reporters were not asking Caucasian Cleveland-area professional athletes Johnny Manziel, Jason Kipnis, and Kevin Love or Cavaliers' owner Dan Gilbert about the case (Howard, 2015). Others argued that black athletes have political capital that others lack, and they should spend it to make a difference (Carlson, 2016; O'Neal, 2015).

Some on Twitter also pointed out the causal responsibility, or lack thereof, of LeBron James. Some accused the campaign of putting pressure on LeBron and diverting attention away from faulty systems and institutions that arguably led to the situation. Others accused Touré of shaming LeBron for something in which he had no direct culpability. Touré added a tweet reiterating that the point of the campaign was to raise awareness rather than blame LeBron. Ultimately, it is in terms of liability responsibility that the campaign says it was rooted. The argument, articulated by Dave Zirin in *The Nation*, is that LeBron James has a level of moral responsibility not only as an African-American athlete in Cleveland but because "first and foremost, it is highly disingenuous to pretend that LeBron is just another athlete, especially in Cleveland, and is being asked to boycott solely because of the historic burden foisted upon black athletes to do more than just play. LeBron has asked for this weight, even demanded it" by making political endorsements, stating he would like to be a social leader like Muhammad Ali, and using a provocative Public Enemy song in his Samsung commercial (Zirin, 2016). While no one was attributing direct, legal culpability for the case, Twitter was the site for a lively and complex debate about the role of civic responsibility for athletes and role models. According to Touré, extending this dialogue was a key objective for the campaign.

Many times, the role of sports commentators, media pundits, and social media campaigns is to delve into complex situations and ascribe meaning and identify causes. According to Kelley, this is a natural instinct, which can feel like common sense. The role of attribution theory is not to dismiss what feels like common sense or say that it is wrong. Rather, the goal is to consciously analyze the assumptions people make about responsibility and blame and help explain why these assumptions can often feel so comfortable.

Discussion Questions

1. Many of the attributions made on Twitter looked at possible external causes for LeBron James' reaction. Applying Kelley's model of causal attribution to quotes from LeBron James, can you identify possible

internal causes? Is it valid to make such calls about celebrities and public figures based on their statements in the press?

2. Based on the material on attribution theory and the #NoJusticeNoLeBron campaign, apply attribution theory to statements from Tariq Touré, reporters, and commentators.

3. Athletes are often respected as role models by fans and the press. What level of responsibility in the model of attribution accounts for the tendency? What justifications are used for holding athletes to a higher standard than others in society?

4. Attribution theory is often called an extension of "common sense." Explain why common sense feels so natural.

5. Discuss any new developments in this ongoing issue. Have current events changed the conversation?

References

Blasky, M. (2015, June 3). Oakland and Cleveland: Two cities with much in common, on center stage for NBA finals. *Contra Costa Times.* Retrieved from http://eastbaytimes.com

Bondy, F. (2014, December 5). LeBron finds rare air: King goes where Jordan wouldn't. *Daily News* (New York), 54.

Campbell, M. (2014, December 29). Sports Business: Can the activist and the ambassador co-exist in the same athlete? *The Toronto Star.* Retrieved from www.thestar.com

Carlson, J. (2016, September 21). Stand up? Sit down? This is the time to fight for the right. *The Daily Oklahoman.* Retrieved from www.newsok.com

Causes worth caring about: Athletes have fought racism and racial profiling, and objected to war efforts. *The Toronto Star,* S4 (2015, November 14).

Danylko, R. (2015, November 20). The Tamir Rice shooting and the year that followed: A timeline. *The Cleveland Plain Dealer.* Retrieved from www.cleveland.com

Davidson, K. A. (2015, December 31). No justice, no LeBron? *Bloomberg.* Retrieved from www.bloomberg.com/view/articles/2015-12-31/no-justice-no-lebron-

Ebenezer, S. (2016, September 2). Protests supposed to agitate, Boomer. *Daily News* (New York), 4.

Fitzsimmons, E. (2014, November 27). Video shows Cleveland officer shot boy in 2 seconds. *The New York Times.* Retrieved from www.nytimes.co

Guthrie, M. (2015, February 11). LeBron James reveals ambitious plan to build Hollywood empire: "Winning is the first thing that matters". *The Hollywood Reporter.*

Hart, H. L. A. (2008). *Punishment and responsibility: Essays in the philosophy of law.* London: Oxford University Press.

Hickey, J. (2015, December 30). LeBron James speaks up, but doesn't sit down. *Contra Costa Times.* Retrieved from http://eastbaytimes.com

Howard, G. (2015, December 31). LeBron James doesn't owe you shit. *Deadspin.* Retrieved from www.deadspin.com

Jones, T. (2016, January 2). Wrong to criticize LeBron for Tamir Rice situation. *The Salt Lake Tribune.* Retrieved from www.sltrib.com

Jordan, M. (2016, June 7). Cleveland shakes off rust before Trump rolls in. *The Washington Post.* Retrieved from www.washingtonpost.com

Josefczyk, A. (2015, May 25). Cleveland Police say 71 people arrested overnight in protests. *The Pittsburgh Post-Gazette.* Retrieved from www.post-gazette.com

Kang, J. C. (2016, October 16). How Colin Kaepernick's protest is connecting playing fields to the streets. *The New York Times*. Retrieved from www.nytimes.com

Kelley, H. H. (1967). Attribution theory in social psychology. In D. Levine (Ed.), *Nebraska symposium on motivation* (pp. 192–238). Lincoln, NE: University of Nebraska Press.

Kelley, H. H. (1973). The process of causal attribution. *American Psychologist, 28*(2), 107–128. doi:10.1037/H0034225

Lancaster, M. (2017, September 25). LeBron James on protests: My voice is more important than my knee. *The Sporting News*. Retrieved from www.sportingnews.com

Moore, E. F. (2016, January 6). Black athletes in no-win situation with politics. *The Chicago Tribune*. Retrieved from www.chicagoredeye.com

Ohio boy shot by police over fake gun dies. (2014, November 24). *The Washington Post*. Retrieved from www.washingtonpost.com

O'Neal, L. (2015, December 31). Tamir Rice case shows we must get off sidelines. *The Washington Post*, C1.

Protest snarls up major US freeway. (2014, December 10). *The Star* (South Africa), 12.

Robinson, D. (2014, December 21). Consistency needed in free-speech censorship. *Deseret Morning News* (Salt Lake City). Retrieved from www.lexisnexis.com/hottopics/lnacademic

Russell, K. (2016, February 24). In an improving economy, places in distress. *The New York Times*. Retrieved from www.nytimes.com

Ryan, J., & Boscia, M. W. (2003). Using attribution theory to help frame moral dilemmas: An empirical test of the President Clinton: Monica Lewinski case. *Teaching Business Ethics, 7*(2), 123–137. doi:10.1023/A:1022637518414

Shaver, K. G. (1985). *The attribution of blame: Causality, responsibility, and blameworthiness.* New York, NY: Springer-Verlag.

Smydo, J. (2016, January 17). Cleveland getting ready for 2016 Republican National Convention. *The Pittsburgh Post-Gazette*. Retrieved from www.post-gazette.com

Somashekhar, S. (2014, December 9). Protesters' challenge: Turn anger into results. *The Washington Post*, A1.

Touré, T. (2016, January 1). No justice no LeBron: A last thought. Retrieved from http://muslimmatters.org/2016/01/02/no-justice-no-lebron-a-last-thought/

Vishwanath, A. (2014). Negative public perceptions of juvenile diabetics: Applying attribution theory to understand the public's stigmatizing views. *Health Communication, 29*(5), 516–526. doi:10.1080/10410236.2013.777685

Zirin, D. (2016, January 4). The tactical intelligence of #NoJusticeNoLeBron. *The Nation*. Retrieved from www.thenation.com

20 "I Was Very Intoxicated"

An Examination of the Image Repair Discourse of Ryan Lochte Following the 2016 Olympics

Kevin Hull & Kelli S. Boling

This chapter examines the image repair discourse of swimmer Ryan Lochte following the 2016 Summer Olympics. After alleging that he and three teammates were robbed at gunpoint in Rio de Janeiro, Brazil, Lochte admitted to fabricating the story. Shortly after, Lochte attempted to improve his image through social media posts and television interviews. Lochte's Instagram posts, Twitter posts, and major television interviews were examined using Benoit's Image Repair Theory. Results demonstrate that Lochte used traditional media primarily to express mortification and social media for bolstering. Compared to other athletes, Lochte's strategy is unique in that he takes full responsibility for his mistakes.

Introduction

Despite winning his 12th Olympic medal (only Michael Phelps has more among all American athletes in history), Ryan Lochte's 2016 Summer Olympics will likely be remembered for an incident out of the pool. Just days after completing his final race of the Olympics, Lochte claimed that he and three of his teammates were robbed at gunpoint while riding in a taxi. In an interview with NBC's Billy Bush, Lochte said, "The guy pulled out his gun, he cocked it, put it to my forehead and said, 'get down'" (Today, 2016).

Less than a week after the incident was reported, details regarding Lochte's version of his harrowing escape from the robbery were under attack. A surveillance video from a gas station showed the swimmers breaking into a locked bathroom, and the owner stated that the group vandalized the station (Wright, 2016). On August 18, just days after claiming he was robbed, Lochte posted an apology on Instagram. Two days later, he appeared on both NBC and Brazil's TV Globo, admitting he made the entire incident up, saying that the gun being held to his head "didn't happen" (NBC Sports Group, 2016). While confessing his guilt, Lochte claimed, "I was very intoxicated." Following Lochte's confession, four sponsors dropped him (Perez, 2016), he was ultimately suspended 10 months by USA Swimming (Drehs, 2016), and it was estimated that Lochte cost himself at least $5–10 million in future income due to the damage to his image (Rishe, 2016).

Following his return to the United States, Lochte began work to repair his public perception. The swimmer appeared as a contestant on *Dancing with the Stars*, announced his engagement to his girlfriend, and later revealed that his new fiancée was pregnant. Lochte kept the public abreast of his life through television interviews and his social media accounts. The purpose of this study is to examine, compare, and contrast the image repair strategies Ryan Lochte used on both social media and broadcast media. Using Benoit's (1995) Image Repair Theory as an analytical framework, the study analyzes the image repair efforts of Ryan Lochte following his admission that he falsified the story of being robbed.

Background

While Michael Phelps may get the majority of the headlines in the world of swimming, Ryan Lochte can make a case that he is also one of the greatest American Olympians of all time. Following the 2016 Olympics, only Phelps has more overall medals than Lochte in the history of the United States at the Olympics (Glock, 2017). Lochte has held multiple world records in both individual medley races and the backstroke (Associated Press, 2006, 2011) and was, at one point, making millions of dollars in endorsements based off his successes (Rishe, 2012). However, along with Lochte's swimming history is a less flattering image out of the pool. He's been called "America's sexiest douchebag" and "a joke the size of an Olympic swimming pool" (Clark-Flory, 2012). He even was the focus of a reality television show, *What Would Ryan Lochte Do?*, in 2013, which chronicled his partying ways (Yahr, 2016). With Lochte's social life a well-documented part of his persona, it should come as no surprise that he was out late in Rio after finishing his swimming obligations during the Olympics. However, he remained, at least in terms of his Olympic success, an American icon.

Before the start of the Olympics, Americans were warned about Rio's crime rate and that the city was not safe for tourists, and some Brazilians even told international fans not to come to Brazil because the situation was "ugly" (Berlinger, 2016; Quintana, 2016). Therefore, based on impressions before the Olympics, Lochte's story about being robbed at gunpoint seemed believable to many, as the initial tale was that a famous, rich American was targeted by the very criminals people had been warned about for months. That, of course, proved not to be the real story.

Following Lochte's admission of fabricating the story, many different political, economic, cultural, and social environments were impacted. Perhaps most noticeable was the impact from a combination of all those environments on the country of Brazil (Cuadros, 2016). A Brazilian sociologist said, "People here feel vulnerable and angry when Americans come down here and act like they can do whatever they want, with no respect for rules or regard for the locals" (Flynn & Brooks, 2016). The Rio mayor said he felt "shame and contempt" for Lochte (Fenno & Wharton, 2016). The Brazilian police quickly charged Lochte with making a false report, which could lead to six months in prison and a monetary fine (Domonoske, 2016). Politically, socially, and culturally, Brazilians were angry that Lochte had wantonly damaged their nation's reputation (Cuadros, 2016).

In the weeks after the Olympics, Lochte's personal and professional life took a dramatic hit as sponsors ended their financial partnerships with him, USA Swimming suspended him for 10 months, and he became the punchline for late-night comedians looking for a laugh. In order to flip the narrative, Lochte began the process of repairing his image.

The idea of image restoration theory (IRT) was conceptualized by Benoit (1995, 1997). He stated that when a person's image is threatened, he or she utilizes various strategies in order to repair his or her image. Benoit conceptualized that there were 14 total image repair strategies within five categories. He stated that people used denial (consisting of simple denial or shifting blame), evading responsibility (consisting of provocation, defeasibility, making excuses, demonstrating good intentions), reducing offensiveness (consisting of bolstering, minimization, differentiation, transcendence, attacking the accuser, compensation), corrective action, and mortification (Benoit, 1995, 1997).

Two previous studies have looked at how athletes' image repair strategies varied over traditional and social media. Cyclist Lance Armstrong used competing narratives on the two distinct mediums when addressing allegations he was using performance-enhancing drugs. On Twitter, Armstrong attacked his accusers, while he expressed mortification in a televised interview (Hambrick, Frederick, & Sanderson, 2015). Football player Richie Incognito was accused of bullying a teammate in 2013. Similar to Armstrong, the offensive lineman used opposing strategies on the two outlets. Incognito's Twitter account was used primarily to attack his accusers, while the television interview focused on shifting the blame and bolstering (Schmittel & Hull, 2015).

The Case

In order to help repair his image, Ryan Lochte turned to both the traditional media through television interviews and his own social media accounts. To examine how Lochte used these two distinct mediums, five television interviews and his social media posts from the day of his admission of lying (8/20/16) until the end of 2016 (12/31/16) were collected for a content analysis. This resulted in 136 Twitter posts and 91 Instagram posts. Facebook was not used for this study as Lochte only posted four times during this time period, and all four were duplicates of what appeared on his Instagram feed. The television interviews were from NBC (8/20/16), TV Globo (8/20/16), TMZ (8/22/16), ABC (8/30/16), and *The Ellen DeGeneres Show* (9/12/16). The authors coded the same two interviews, and intercoder reliability using Krippendorff's α determined a high level of reliability for content (α = .88). Based on the acceptable level of initial agreement for intercoder reliability, the remaining sample was divided, and each author coded approximately half.

The unit of analysis was each sentence for the television interviews and each individual post for the social media sample. Each unit was coded into one of 15 categories based on Benoit's 14 strategies outlined in IRT and supplemented with an additional category of providing background on the incident.

For the television interviews, 241 total sentences were coded (M = 48.2, SD = 45.47). Within these interviews, Lochte primarily used the strategy of mortification, in which one admits responsibility and asks for forgiveness. More than half (125 sentences, 51.9%) of Lochte's statements fell into the mortification category. In the interview with TV Globo, Lochte said, "I'm embarrassed. I'm embarrassed for myself, for my family, and for my country."

The second-most frequently appearing category was Lochte providing background information regarding the incident (40 sentences, 16.6%). While many interviewers wanted to get the emotional answers from Lochte, many would preface those questions with attempts to get more information. For example, he was asked on *Good Morning America*, "Would you still characterize what happened that night as a robbery?"

Lochte used corrective action strategies in 31 sentences (12.9%). The goal of this strategy is to demonstrate that the person will make changes so that it will not happen again. When asked in the interview with TMZ about his excessive drinking, Lochte said, "It's definitely something that I'm going to have to be more responsible about. Everything that happened in Rio, I'm definitely going to learn from it. We learn from our mistakes."

In 22 occurrences, Lochte did make an excuse for the incident (9.1%). This happened frequently during his first interview in which he spoke with then NBC anchor Matt Lauer. Lochte said, "We were frightened," and "We wanted to get out of there as quickly as possible."

The remaining strategies used by Lochte appeared in less than 5% of the sample, with defeasibility (a lack of knowledge about factors involved) used 10 times (4.1%), minimization (attempting to convince people that the offense is not as serious as portrayed) used seven times (2.9%), transcendence (placing the act into a broader, less offensive context) used four times (1.7%), and both compensation (offering to redress victims) and provocation (act was in response to another act) used just once (0.4% each).

On social media, Lochte's primary strategy was bolstering. Of the 227 social media posts, 221 fell into the bolstering category (97.4%). Of those 221, 88 were on Instagram and 133 were from Twitter. Benoit (1995, 1997) wrote that bolstering reminds the audience of previous good acts or the person's good reputation. Here, Lochte posted tweets or photos about his athletic accomplishments (pictures of him training), his newfound family-man persona (photos of him and his fiancée), his charitable work, his carefree personality (funny photos), and his newfound celebrity on *Dancing with the Stars*. All these posts were designed to remind his followers about the good he has done in the past or current activities to change his future.

Four total posts (two each on Twitter and Instagram) fell into the corrective action category (1.8% of the sample). Following an incident in which two protestors rushed the stage to confront Lochte live on *Dancing with the Stars*,

Lochte posted a message that thanked everyone involved with the show and added, "I am dedicated to my new family and to working hard to do my best."

Two posts (0.9% of the sample) demonstrated mortification (one from each social network). In one of these posts, Lochte wrote his initial apology about the lie he made up. He wrote, "I want to apologize for my behavior last weekend," and "I accept responsibility for my role in this happening and have learned some valuable lessons."

You Make the Call

Based on the content analysis of Lochte's image repair strategies, it appears as if he was consistent with his message. In the days immediately following his admission of lying, Lochte primarily used the mortification strategy in televised interviews. One of the primary recipients of his apologies was the city of Rio. The city came into the Olympics under a wave of negative publicity, and Lochte's initial lie only added to that. In his interview with NBC, Lochte said:

> The people of Rio or Brazil, the authorities, everyone there, they put on a great Games. And my immature, intoxicated behavior, tarnished that a little. And I don't want that, because they did a great job. The fans were amazing. I know going out into my races they were all cheering for me. So, I mean, they were great. They hosted a great Games. And I'm just really sorry. And I hope they can accept my apology.

In the interview with Brazilian station TV Globo, Lochte said, "I just want the people of Brazil to know how truly sorry I am." This demonstrates that Lochte recognizes the damage his lie caused to the city, the country, and the Olympics as a whole.

Following his admission, Lochte's social media use focused on bolstering his image. The opportunity for the swimming champion to attempt to become a dancing competition champion provided him an outlet to showcase his new attitude. Smiling photos of Lochte and his dancing partner flooded his Twitter and Instagram accounts, reminding the public of the carefree personality that was a large part of his pre-scandal public persona. Additionally, Lochte attempted to bolster his image from a party animal to a family man. Previously known for being a "drunk frat boy," as Lochte described himself in his interview with Matt Lauer, his social media accounts now contained photos of his girlfriend with loving captions such as "I love you @kaylareareid beautiful inside and out," and "My Christmas gift came early this year, can't wait for next year! Best news I've ever received" with a photo of Lochte kissing the stomach of his girlfriend, announcing the two were expecting a baby.

Perhaps surprisingly, Lochte did not go on the offensive—a previously popular image repair strategy among troubled athletes. Lochte did not use the image repair strategies of shifting the blame or attacking the accusers.

Instead, Lochte simply accepted responsibility for his lie and then attempted to repair his image through bolstering. This made for a more ethical image repair quest than had he continued to lie about the events. The Olympic champion accepted fault ("I've done wrong, I know that"), apologized to the city of Rio ("I hope they can accept my apology"), and vowed to improve his image ("I want to be a role model").

Ultimately, Lochte's image repair strategies appear to have been a success. While nearly all of his sponsors left him shortly after the scandal, Lochte picked up new endorsements after his admission of guilt (Johnson & Saliba, 2016). Even with these new sponsorships, Lochte stayed true to his image repair strategy of admitting guilt; however, he now chose to do it in a humorous way. As part of the #CleanStartPledge ad campaign from energy bar manufacturer PowerBar, Lochte remarked in the commercial how he wanted to put "questionable hairstyles and stuff that happened" behind him (Birkner, 2017). The "stuff that happened" is an obvious reference to his problems in Rio. A cough drop company (Pine Bros.) hired Lochte to be the face of their "in the season of forgiveness" holiday campaign, a reference to both the forgiving nature of the drops on a sore throat and Lochte's quest for forgiveness (Birkner, 2016). In an ad for a crime prevention detection device, Lochte said, "I've been traveling a lot lately. We all like to have fun, but it's a good idea to stay safe" (Wattles, 2016).

While Lochte's initial response to his transgression was obviously unethical, he did quickly admit fault, saying, "I'm taking full responsibility for my actions." During the immediate time following his admission, it appeared as if repairing his image was something with which he was concerned. In an interview with Ellen DeGeneres, he relayed the advice given to him by fellow swimmer Michael Phelps: "It's not what you did, it's what you do now that will shape who you are." This implied that he was already thinking about how he could improve himself in the future. He would later add, "I don't want little kids to look at me for what I did just that one night. I don't want that. I want to be a role model for those little kids. And I know I can change that." While Ryan Lochte's image took a hit during the time immediately following the Olympics, his image repair strategies both on traditional media and social media appeared to put him back in a positive light. Months after the outrage of Rio had subsided, and Lochte had a successful run on *Dancing With the Stars*, became a father, and signed agreements with new sponsors, an article in *ESPN The Magazine* may have summed up the success of Lochte's image repair with the title, "Do you really still hate Ryan Lochte?" (Glock, 2017).

Discussion Questions

1. Discuss any new developments in this ongoing issue. As of this writing, Lochte's charges in Brazil are still outstanding. Have the Brazilian police pushed forward with the charges? If not, what impact (if any) do you think Lochte's image repair played in the case?

2.   Immediately following the Olympics, Lochte was a contestant on *Dancing With the Stars*, a television show that allowed him to showcase a different side of his personality and possibly change the way the public viewed him. Despite the fact that Lochte's appearance on the show was booked before the Olympics started, do you think the show played a greater role in his image repair than any of his own strategies? Why or why not?
3.   Lochte was considered by some to lack a great deal of intelligence before the Olympics. Do you think the fact that many already had a negative impression of his intelligence played a factor in how quickly he was able to repair his image? Why or why not?
4.   Ryan Lochte admitted that he had fabricated the story after he was done swimming in the 2016 Olympics. If Lochte still had events remaining, how do you think the narrative surrounding the alleged robbery would have changed?

References

Associated Press. (2006, April 9). Lochte sets 200m backstroke world record. Retrieved from www.espn.com/olympics/news/story?id=2402516

Associated Press. (2011, July 28). Ryan Lochte sets world record in 200 IM. Retrieved from www.espn.com/olympics/swimming/story/_/id/6811637/ryan-lochte-beats-michael-phelps-200-meter-im-sets-world-record

Benoit, W. L. (1995). *Accounts, excuses, and apologies: A theory of image restoration strategies.* Albany, NY: State University of New York Press.

Benoit, W. L. (1997). Image repair discourse and crisis communication. *Public Relations Review, 23*(2), 177–186.

Berlinger, J. (2016, May 11). Former Brazilian soccer star: Don't come to the Rio Olympics. Retrieved from http://edition.cnn.com/2016/05/11/sport/rivaldo-brazil-olympics-2016/index.html

Birkner, C. (2016, December 15). Ryan Lochte promotes "forgiving" throat drops in intentionally weird Pine Bros. ad. Retrieved from www.adweek.com/brand-marketing/ryan-lochte-promotes-forgiving-throat-drops-intentionally-weird-pine-bros-ad-175135/

Birkner, C. (2017, January 19). Ryan Lochte seeks fresh start from his drama-filled past in PowerBar campaign. Retrieved from www.adweek.com/brand-marketing/ryan-lochte-seeks-fresh-start-his-drama-filled-past-powerbar-campaign-175664/

Clark-Flory, T. (2012, August 6). Ryan Lochte: So sexy, so dumb. Retrieved from www.salon.com/2012/08/06/ryan_lochte_so_sexy_so_dumb/

Cuadros, A. (2016, August 18). Why Brazilians are so obsessed with the Ryan Lochte story. Retrieved from www.newyorker.com/news/news-desk/why-brazilians-are-so-obsessed-with-the-u-s-swimmers-story

Domonoske, C. (2016, August 26). Brazilian police charge Ryan Lochte with making a false report. Retrieved from www.npr.org/sections/thetwo-way/2016/08/26/491469384/brazilian-police-charge-ryan-lochte-with-making-a-false-report

Drehs, W. (2016, September 8). Swimmer Ryan Lochte reportedly suspended 10 months. Retrieved from www.espn.com/olympics/swimming/story/_/id/17493633/ryan-lochte-suspended-10-months-united-states-olympic-committee-usa-swimming

Fenno, N., & Wharton, D. (2016, August 19). Ryan Lochte apologizes but will the Brazilian people accept it? *Los Angeles Times*. Retrieved from www.latimes.com/sports/olympics/la-sp-oly-lochte-apology-20160819-snap-story.html

Flynn, D., & Brooks, B. (2016, August 19). U.S. swimmers' tall tale touches a raw nerve. Retrieved from www.reuters.com/article/us-olympics-rio-lochte-brazil-idUSKCN10U28C

Glock, A. (2017, June 6). Do you really still hate Ryan Lochte? ESPN the Magazine. Retrieved from www.espn.com/espn/feature/story/_/id/19506033/will-hate-ryan-lochte-end-story

Hambrick, M. E., Frederick, E. L., & Sanderson, J. (2015). From yellow to blue: Exploring Lance Armstrong's image repair strategies across traditional and social media. Communication & Sport, 3(2), 196–218.

Johnson, A., & Saliba, E. (2016, August 30). Ryan Lochte dives back in with alarming new endorsement deal. Retrieved from www.nbcnews.com/news/us-news/ryan-lochte-dives-back-alarming-new-endorsement-deal-n640266

NBC Sports Group. (2016, August 20). Transcript: Matt Lauer exclusive interview with Ryan Lochte. Retrieved from http://nbcsportsgrouppressbox.com/2016/08/20/transcript-matt-lauer-exclusive-interview-with-ryan-lochte/

Perez, A. J. (2016, August 22). Speedo, three other sponsors drop Ryan Lochte. Retrieved from www.usatoday.com/story/sports/olympics/rio-2016/2016/08/22/speedo-ends-sponsorship-ryan-lochte/89099284/

Quintana, A. (2016, August 4). Forget Zika, urban crime is the real threat to Rio's Olympic Games. Retrieved from http://dailysignal.com/2016/08/04/forget-zika-urban-crime-is-the-real-threat-to-rios-olympic-games/

Rishe, P. (2012, July 28). Ryan Lochte swims towards larger endorsements with 400 IM gold medal at 2012 London Olympics. Retrieved from www.forbes.com/sites/prishe/2012/07/28/ryan-lochte-swims-towards-larger-endorsements-with-400-im-gold-medal-at-2012-london-olympics/

Rishe, P. (2016, August 19). Ryan Lochte sinks future endorsement potential with actions worthy of an Olympic gold for stupidity. Retrieved from www.forbes.com/sites/prishe/2016/08/19/ryan-lochte-sinks-future-endorsement-potential-with-actions-worthy-of-an-olympic-gold-for-stupidity/

Schmittel, A., & Hull, K. (2015). "Shit Got Cray #MYBAD": An examination of the image-repair discourse of Richie Incognito during the Miami Dolphins' bullying scandal. *Journal of Sports Media, 10*(2), 115–137.

Today. (2016, August 15). Ryan Lochte talks to Billy Bush about being held up at gunpoint. *Today* [Video file]. Retrieved from www.youtube.com/watch?v=IxrYj0yCyLE

Wattles, J. (2016, August 30). Ryan Lochte's new endorsement deal is for crime prevention device. Retrieved from http://money.cnn.com/2016/08/30/news/ryan-lochte-robocopp-endorsement/index.html

Wright, B. (2016, August 18). Ryan Lochte robbery update: Video shows "US Swimmer" "fighting", "breaking down" Rio gas station restroom door. Retrieved from www.ibtimes.com/ryan-lochte-robbery-update-video-shows-us-swimmer-fighting-breaking-down-rio-gas-2403576

Yahr, E. (2016, August 19). Now you can watch Ryan Lochte's gloriously terrible reality show. Retrieved from www.washingtonpost.com/news/arts-and-entertainment/wp/2016/08/19/now-you-can-watch-ryan-lochtes-gloriously-terrible-reality-show/?utm_term=.8b37501caa2f

Appendix

Table 20.1 Image Repair Strategy Used

Strategy	Number of Times Used	Percentage Within Medium
Television Interviews		
Mortification	125	51.9
Background	40	16.6
Corrective action	31	12.9
Making excuses	22	9.1
Defeasibility	10	4.1
Minimization	7	2.9
Transcendence	4	1.7
Compensation	1	0.4
Provocation	1	0.4
Social Media		
Bolstering	221	97.4
Corrective action	4	1.8
Mortification	2	0.9

21 Swimming Against the Tide

Lessons in Public Image Management From Competitive Swimmers

Erin E. Gilles & Mary Beth Reese

Olympic gold medalists Michael Phelps, Ryan Lochte, and Lilly King used social media and interacted with the news media to manage their reputations during their public relations crises. Professional athletes sometimes attain celebrity status, and often with little or no media training. Social media connects the athlete, the media, fans, and the public while also shaping an athlete's personal brand. Without advice from PR counsel, athletes may damage their image, lose corporate sponsors, or be stripped of eligibility or titles. This case study will recommend strategies to handle crises using situational crisis communication theory, reputation management, and apologia theory.

Introduction

High-profile competitive swimmers face many challenges in navigating the media environment. From social media to media interviews, there are many opportunities to enhance or damage their reputations. Celebrity athletes face more ethical decision-making challenges than athletes competing at a lower level. Simply based upon their visibility in the media, these athletes are often considered to be role models for aspiring athletes. When these athletes make mistakes, the repercussions are amplified on a global scale. Without counsel from experienced public relations practitioners, athletes are often left to their own devices to manage the fallout. Throughout this chapter, key examples from the careers of three Olympic athletes—Michael Phelps, Ryan Lochte, and Lilly King—highlight how media communications often have far-reaching implications for athletes. Specifically, principles from three major PR theories and concepts (situational crisis communication theory, reputation management, and apologia theory) are applied to these athletes' situations.

Background

Competitive Swimming and the Olympics

Competitive swimming was one of the original nine sports in the Olympics in 1896 (swimming.org, 2016). Today, the competition is a pool event for people of all ages and backgrounds who meet the multitude of eligibility rules that are continually refined by the Fédération Internationale de Natation (FINA), the international regulatory body that oversees the sport. Competitive swimming begins at an early age for most high-level swimmers, and young swimmers must learn rules imposed by FINA regarding such things as stroke techniques, codes of conduct, pool requirements, and appropriate swimwear.

Athletes have unprecedented access to the mainstream media, social media, and their fans by creating personal websites, hosting podcasts, using social media, posting swim-meet videos, uploading race times, and sharing swim details. On Twitter, each of the three swimmers has an active profile with numerous followers: Michael Phelps (2.25 million), Ryan Lochte (1.2 million), and Lilly King (37,004) (Twitter.com, 2017).

Olympians are often young; Phelps and Lochte were high school students during their first Olympics, and King had just graduated from high school. Fresh celebrity status may be burdensome for novices. Thrust into a media spotlight, and often in a foreign country, few athletes receive media coaching prior to competition. Yet, athletes are expected to be increasingly media savvy as they negotiate interviews, press conferences, represent their country through public appearances, and monitor and communicate with their fan base.

Athletes as Brands and Corporate Ambassadors

Celebrity endorsements have been used in promotions for more than a century, and selection of the right athlete can enhance the brand and generate profits. In 2015, North American companies spent $21.4 billion on brand endorsements (IEG, 2016). On Forbes.com's annual list of the 100 highest-earning athletes, the highest endorsement earners are Roger Federer ($58 million), LeBron James ($55 million), and Phil Mickelson ($40 million) (Badenhausen, 2017). In many cases, the Olympians also may represent a brand for one or more companies. Corporate sponsors of Olympians must gain prior approval for all promotional materials (ads, marketing materials, public appearances, websites, and so on) from the U.S. Olympic Committee (USOC, 2015). In addition, during the blackout period, which is generally when the Olympic Village is open, no ads featuring individual athletes may be aired or distributed unless a waiver is granted.

Consumer connections with athletes can engender emotional attachments, increase athlete/team-related merchandise sales, and spike viewership levels of particular teams or athletes (Carlson & Donavan, 2013). Other research indicates that three primary characteristics of athletes that impact brand image are: skilled athletic performance, an attractive appearance, and a marketable lifestyle (Arai, Ko, & Ross, 2014). Miller and Laczniak (2011) suggest that companies should perform prerequisite character evaluations of athletes prior to signing them as endorsers and should have a defined exit strategy to quickly break ties from the athlete should their actions threaten the brand.

Public Relations Theories

Reputation management is an important component of maintaining corporate sponsorships, without which many athletes would be unable to compete. Reputation management includes a wide range of tactics used in public relations, including "research, strategic planning, deliberate implementation of that plan, and continual monitoring and evaluation" (Smith, 2017, p. 449). For corporations, the opportunity to sponsor a celebrity-status athlete can dramatically increase sales and brand visibility. And, going after top-notch athletes increases this pay-off (Elberse & Verleun, 2012). Because many U.S. brands portray a wholesome image, corporations often avoid athletes who are perceived as high-risk or who are prone to scandal. Negative associations with celebrity behavior can transfer to the brands they endorse (Carrillat, D'Astous, & Christianis, 2014; Miller & Laczniak, 2011), which may result in the loss of revenue from the buying public. If the athlete does garner negative attention or incur a damaged reputation, apologia theory can be useful. "Corporate apologia is a communicative effort to defend the corporation against reputation/character attacks" (Coombs, Frandsen, Holladay, & Johansen, 2010, p. 337). While an actual apology may be part of the strategy, apologia theory more widely encompasses the efforts that an organization or individual makes to explain or deny the action.

Social media can play a strong role in an athlete's communication strategies. A study found that athlete endorsements (tweets) could increase visibility for unknown brands (Brison, Byon, & Baker, 2016). This strategy is likely effective due to the sheer number of athletes using social media; top athletes can have a global following numbering from the hundreds of thousands to more than 50 million (Fan Page List, 2017). Managing a crisis for professional athletes often takes place in a public forum, such as social media. One useful theory is situational crisis communication theory (SSCT), which dictates that the organizational response to a crisis should be in proportion to the magnitude of the threat of the crisis (Coombs & Holladay, 2002).

The Case

Michael Phelps

Michael Phelps, born in Towson, Maryland, in 1985, has earned 28 Olympic medals, 23 of which were gold. His Olympic successes earned him two additional records—the most-decorated Olympian in history along with being the first swimmer to win a gold medal in the same event in four consecutive Olympic Games. Now retired from swimming, Phelps participated in five Olympic Games, although he did not medal in his first showing in Sydney, Australia, at the age of 15 in 2000. Phelps may be best known for his butterfly stroke, buoyed by his impressive 80-inch fingertip to fingertip span, but he is also skilled in freestyle, backstroke, and individual medley (Swimswam.com, 2017).

Despite continuous success in the pool, Phelps struggled with a tarnished image due to a few episodes in his personal life. In 2004, Phelps was arrested for driving under the influence. This arrest resulted in probation, a fine, and community service. In 2009, a British tabloid published a picture of a then 23-year-old Phelps smoking marijuana from a glass pipe at a party. Phelps admitted the picture was authentic and apologized for his behavior. USA Swimming suspended Phelps for three months, and Kellogg's—one of his paid endorsers—removed his image from its Corn Flakes and Frosted Flakes boxes (Macur, 2009). After a second DUI arrest in 2014, Phelps posted on Facebook that he would attend a treatment program. As a result of the DUI, Phelps was banned from competitions for six months by USA Swimming, which included the 2015 World Championships. After pleading guilty to the charges, Phelps was not sentenced to jail time, but instead was given a probation of 18 months during which he was required to remain sober (swimswam.com, 2017).

Ryan Lochte

Lochte was born in New York state in 1984 but grew up primarily in Florida. Coached by both parents, Lochte began swimming at a young age. Although he also pursued basketball and skateboarding, Lochte chose competitive swimming as his sole sport in high school. While in college, Lochte competed in his first Olympic Games in 2004, earning a silver and gold medal. Competing in both the 2008 and 2012 Olympic Games, Lochte earned five medals in each. In 2013, his boisterous and flashy personality earned him a short-lived sitcom on E!, *What Would Ryan Lochte Do?* Lochte earned another gold medal in the 2016 Olympic Games in Rio de Janeiro, Brazil, which was Lochte's 12th medal (Swimswam.com, 2017).

Lochte has fought for years to escape Phelps' shadow, despite Lochte's admirable record of medals and world records. In 2016, Lochte did just that when his bizarre and inconsistent tale of a robbery at gunpoint captivated the world. Lochte claimed that, while returning intoxicated from a party, he and three teammates were held at gunpoint after their cab was stopped by robbers. The next morning Lochte told Billy Bush, then with *The Today Show*, that his wallet and money were stolen after a gun was held to his forehead. Later, an eyewitness and security camera footage from the gas station disproved Lochte's story. The video showed Lochte and his teammates returning from a party and exiting their cab at a gas station. The gas station attendant said the men broke the door lock of a restroom and urinated on some bushes on the premises, and then Lochte tore down a framed advertisement on the building. Armed security guards detained the swimmers and demanded they pay for damages before leaving (Auerbach, 2016a). A witness claimed that no guns were drawn during the episode, and that he served as translator for the swimmers (Prengaman, 2016).

The story gained momentum quickly, especially after discrepancies in Lochte's story emerged throughout his multiple interviews. Lochte returned to the US, but the other men were detained at the airport and had their passports confiscated. Lochte posted on Twitter twice about dying his hair back to brown from the bluish white he sported during the Olympics. Then, he posted a birthday video for a friend. Two out of three of these social media comments were removed amid criticism and negative comments because his teammates were still in Brazil facing charges (Auerbach, 2016b). As it became evident that Lochte had fabricated the robbery, his sponsors, including Speedo, Ralph Lauren, Gentle Hair Remover, and Air-weave, quickly dropped him. The cost of losing these sponsors is estimated at $1 million (Associated Press, 2016). Lochte was suspended for 10 months, stripped of $100,000 in Olympic earnings, sentenced to community service, and excluded from the official Olympic White House visit.

Lilly King

King, who began swimming at age 7 because it calmed her down, was born in Evansville, Indiana, in 1997. Her parents were both college athletes, and her mother swam for two university teams. King swam at Indiana University. Known for her breaststroke, King earned her first gold medal at the 2016 Olympics in Rio, where she set a new world record (swimswam.com, 2017).

In Rio, King made headlines as much for her gold medal as for her run-in with Russian swimmer Yulia Efimova, who finished second. Efimova had been banned and then reinstated for testing positive for a recently banned substance, which Efimova claimed was due to usage preceding the ban. King stated that getting to number one clean was the ultimate victory. In this context, when the media captured King wagging her finger at Efimova's on-screen image while King waited for the announcement of the final breast-stroke swim event, King's action went viral. It generated conversations about doping in the sport, as well as hyped the final swim for King and her competitors. King's sportsmanship was questioned when she wagged her finger again at Efimova, refused to shake Efimova's hand after the race, and told a reporter that she was proud that she earned her gold medal racing clean (Maine, 2016). King quickly racked up more than 60,000 retweets of her interview within minutes of her race. Others praised King as the consummate American, Olympian, and competitor. "I hope I did [make a statement about doping]," said King (Kurtenbach, 2016, para. 9).

You Make the Call

When an Olympic athlete behaves inappropriately or becomes engaged in a scandal, it can be treated as a public relations crisis. Specifically, employing the principles of the SCCT would be beneficial in aligning the response to the severity of the crisis. Due to the typically unexpected nature of these events, individuals may be less than prepared. While specific preplanned protocols may be applicable, there are general guidelines that should dictate the handling of many public relations crises. This final section outlines several recommendations for managing an athlete's reputation during challenging times.

1. **Be honest and transparent.** As Lochte demonstrated by lying, his media attention might have blown over more quickly if he had simply been honest at the outset. Instead, his lies became the story. This strategy is in contrast to Phelps' approach, in which he favored transparency when discussing his DUIs and the picture of him smoking marijuana. Unlike other sports in which the athletes receive more consistent media attention, and thus have more opportunity to rebuild a strong public image after a scandal, swimmers are most visible to the public during the Olympics. This also means that any scandal is likely to be revisited by the media at the next Olympic games in which the athlete competes. And while these athletes receive little media attention between games, their status as Olympians will make them instant news should they misbehave.

2. **Respond quickly.** When responding to a crisis, public relations research shows that athletes should address the issue quickly to maintain control of the situation. In 2009, after his marijuana photo surfaced, Phelps brought up his 2004 DUI during an interview (Walsh & McAllister-Spooner, 2011). Knowing that these events would be compared, Phelps was able to use the information first and thus control the message, which illustrates his use of the apologia theory. In Phelps' case, in responding to both of his DUIs and his snapshot with the glass pipe, Phelps quickly addressed the issue before the journalist could surprise him with it.

Regarding Lochte's experiences in Rio, he was unable to control the story partly because Billy Bush and his producer ran into him on the street and conducted an impromptu interview recorded on a smartphone. Although Lochte responded quickly, he had no advance warning to craft an appropriate message. Compounding the situation, he was still intoxicated during this morning-after interview (Glock, 2017).

3. **Be accountable, but careful.** Olympians are considered national heroes and role models for youth. They are often held to a much higher standard than non-public figures. When King received negative attention for her response to Efimova, she took accountability in a large dose. Amid assertions that King's finger wagging was due to youthful inexperience, King indicated that it was purposeful and strategic. She stated the plan was to get in her competition's head. King was even blamed for reinvigorating Cold War tensions between the US and Russia (Howard, 2016). While some degree of competitiveness is expected, King's reactions bolstered the media's representation of it being a feud. A later press conference by King attempted to reign in the situation, stating that she

was not making sweeping statements about any particular country having a reputation for doping. But, it was too little, too late to control the story. King's gentler moments with the media in Rio, when she showed a childhood picture of herself with former Olympic breaststroker Janet Evans, were overshadowed by the conflict with Efimova.

4. *Monitor social media.* During Lochte's 2016 Rio gas station scandal, his irresponsible social media behavior escalated the situation. In a nation already plagued by street crime and poverty, some considered Lochte to have further humiliated Brazil (Jenkins, 2016). King's vocal behavior surrounding her conflict with Efimova also garnered online attention. King asserted that she [King] was not "a sweet little girl," which caused her Twitter followers to jump by 10,000 people (Howard, 2016). This assertion led to online denunciations of King as a bully.

The public relations reputation management concept promotes the continuous monitoring of media messages for changes in organizational reputation. This process is further complicated for athletes, who must understand the social media policies of the governing bodies of their sport. There may be guidelines, policies, or both across various social media outlets.

For instance, some universities may prevent their athletes from using social media during the season. Another consideration is in managing negative social media posts. Should these posts be left up and, if so, for what duration? Ott and Theunissen (2015) suggest that removing negative posts is acceptable if a clear policy exists (which is more relevant to a company than to a celebrity athlete) but that removing negative posts can be considered censorship and further inflame angry posters. Once a post is removed, it is difficult to rescind or control. For instance, Lochte's superficial posts immediately after the Rio incident were taken down amid backlash. However, this was not before screenshots had been taken. While athletes can delete their controversial posts after the fact, this does not mean they are truly gone.

It is critical to provide media training to athletes before they enter the spotlight. Athletes need preparation for media interviews and coverage and training on social media etiquette, brand, image and reputation management, and adherence to their contractual obligations for their performance in and out of the pool. The Olympics offers a global stage on which athletes display their athletic prowess, but the global audience watching also sees any potentially embarrassing behavior.

Discussion Questions

1. Find a current and similar public relations reputation or crisis sports example in the media. Discuss this example using the theories presented in the case study.

2. Are athletes their own personal brands, or are they extensions of the companies/products that they represent? How does this influence how they should act on social media? Does an athlete have an expectation of privacy?
3. Discuss the apologia theory used by Phelps as a PR crisis communications strategy following his three transgressions. Would you handle a second and third offense in the same way as a first? Why or why not?
4. If you were on the International Olympics Ethics Committee, what would your statement to the media have been regarding Ryan Lochte? Do you agree with his 10-month suspension and other penalties? Research the IOEC guidelines to support your answer.
5. Using a search engine, find videos of Lilly King's response to her competitor before and after the race and her formal statement at the news conference following the races. Has King's reputation changed in the media? Now, acting as her PR counsel, write the script that you would have provided for King at the news conference.

References

Arai, A., Ko, Y. J., & Ross, S. (2014). Branding athletes: Exploration and conceptualization of athlete brand image. *Sport Management Review, 17*(2), 97–106.

Auerbach, N. (2016a, August 16). Ryan Lochte: "We were afraid we'd get in trouble". *USA Today.* Retrieved from www.usatoday.com/story/sports/olympics/rio-2016/2016/08/16/ryan-lochte-robbery-gunpoint-rio-taxi-security/88865556/

Auerbach, N. (2016b, August 18). Amid controversy, Ryan Lochte has been active on social media. *USA Today.* Retrieved from www.usatoday.com/story/sports/olympics/rio-2016/2016/08/18/ryan-lochte-social-media/88951310/

Badenhausen, K. (2017, June 7). The world's highest paid athletes 2017: Behind the numbers. *Forbes.* Retrieved from www.forbes.com/forbes/welcome/?toURL=www.forbes.com/sites/kurtbadenhausen/2017/06/07/the-worlds-highest-paid-athletes-2017-behind-the-numbers/&refURL=www.google.com/&referrer=www.google.com/

Brison, N. T., Byon, K. K., & Baker, T. A., III. (2016). To tweet or not to tweet: The effects of social media endorsements on unfamiliar sport brands and athlete endorsers. *Innovation: Management, Policy & Practice, 18*(3), 309–326. doi:http://dx.doi.org.ezproxy.uky.edu/10.1080/14479338.2016.1237304

Carlson, B. D., & Donavan, D. T. (2013). Human brands in sport: Athlete brand personality and identification. *Journal of Sport Management, 27*(3), 193–206.

Carrillat, F., D'Astous, A., & Christianis, H. (2014). Guilty by association: The perils of celebrity endorsement for endorsed brands and their direct competitors. *Psychology & Marketing, 31*(11), 1024–1039.

Coombs, W. T., Frandsen, F., Holladay, S. J., & Johansen, W. (2010). Why a concern for apologia and crisis communication? *Corporate Communications, 15*(4), 337–349. doi:http://dx.doi.org/10.1108/13563281011085466

Coombs, W. T., & Holladay, S. J. (2002). Helping crisis managers protect reputational assets: Initial tests of the situational crisis communication theory. *Management Communication Quarterly, 16*, 165–186.

Elberse, A., & Verleun, J. (2012). The economic value of celebrity endorsements. *Journal of Advertising Research, 52*(2), 149–165. doi:10.2501/JAR-52-2-149-165

Fan Page List. (2017). Top athletes on Twitter. *Fanpagelist.com*. Retrieved from http://fanpagelist.com/category/athletes/view/list/sort/followers/

Glock, A. (2017, June 6). Do you really still hate Ryan Lochte? In consideration of fireworks, massages, Olympic gold, reality TV, marriage, fatherhood—and that incident in Rio. *ESPN*. Retrieved from http://www.espn.com/espn/feature/story/_/id/19506033/will-hate-ryan-lochte-end-story

Howard, J. (2016, December 12). Rio, revisited: Lilly King has no regrets. *ESPN.com*. Retrieved from www.espn.com/olympics/swimming/story/_/id/18265121/2016-rio-olympics-lilly-king-no-regrets-finger-wag-rivalry-yulia-efimova

Independent Evaluation Group [IEG]. (2016). *What sponsors want and where dollars will go in 2016*. Retrieved from www.sponsorship.com/IEG/files/71/711f2f01-b6fa-46d3-9692-0cc1d563d9b7.pdf

Jenkins, S. (2016, August 19). Ryan Lochte's apology is clear: He doesn't realize what has done wrong. *The Washington Post*. Retrieved from www.highbeam.com/doc/1G1-461301587.html?refid=easy_hf

Kurtenbach, D. (2016, November 15). Trash-talking, finger-wagging Lilly King is the perfect Olympian. *FOX Sports*. Retrieved from www.foxsports.com/olympics/story/trash-talking-finger-wagging-lilly-king-is-the-perfect-olympian-080916

Macur, J. (2009, February 5). Phelps disciplined over marijuana pipe incident. *NYTimes.com*. Retrieved from www.nytimes.com/2009/02/06/sports/othersports/06phelps.html

Maine, D. (2016, August 11). Lilly King, congrats on your gold medal, but you get no points for sportsmanship. *EspnW.com*. Retrieved from www.espn.com/espnw/sports/article/17266191/lilly-king-congrats-your-gold-medal-get-no-points-sportsmanship

Miller, F., & Laczniak, G. (2011). The ethics of celebrity-athlete endorsement: What happens when a star steps out of bounds? *Journal of Advertising Research, 51*(3), 499–510. doi:10.2501/JAR-51-3-499-510S

Ott, L., & Theunissen, P. (2015). Reputations at risk: Engagement during social media crises. *Public Relations Review, 41*(1), 97–102.

Pells, E. (2016, September 8). Ryan Lochte banned through June 2017, loses $100,00 in bonuses. *Associated Press*. Retrieved from https://apnews.com/0d687aecc0984c9c9885716c70c739c1/lochte-banned-through-june-2017-loses-100000-bonuses

Prengaman, P. (2016, August 20). Gas station translator, swimmer disagree on gun pointing. *Associated Press*. Retrieved from https://apnews.com/035d22222733446493e01ef8a018363b/gas-station-translator-says-gun-wasnt-pointed-swimmers

U.S. Olympic Committee [USOC]. (2015). Olympic and paralympic athlete endorsement guidelines. Retrieved from www.teamusa.org/Athlete-Resources/Athlete-Marketing/Athlete-Endoresement-Guidelines

Smith, R. D. (2017). *Strategic planning for public relations* (5th ed.). New York, NY: Routledge.

Swimming at the Olympics: Facts about competitive swimming. (2016, June 17). Retrieved from www.swimming.org/sport/swimming-at-the-olympics/

Swimswam.com. (2017). Retrieved from https://swimswam.com

Twitter.com. (2017). Retrieved from https://twitter.com/MichaelPhelps?lang=en

Walsh, J., & McAllister-Spooner, S. M. (2011). Analysis of the image repair discourse in the Michael Phelps controversy. *Public Relations Review, 37*(2), 157–162.

Section VI

Social Justice and Ethics

22 Taking a Knee or Not Taking a Stand

A Lesson in Contingency Theory of Accommodation, the National Football League, and Social Justice

Jack V. Karlis

The media pounced when Colin Kaepernick of the San Francisco 49ers took a knee during the U.S. national anthem in August 2016 to protest law enforcement agencies' killing of black suspects that summer. After Kaepernick's initial protest, a number of NFL players followed suit and also physically displayed their displeasure of the systemic racial injustice of African Americans. The NFL, a self-described trade association financed by its 32 teams and more than 185 million viewers (NFL.com, 2016 A), faced pressure from its key publics to take a stance on the growing protests and would use the Contingency Theory of Accommodation.

Introduction

In July 2016, Philando Castile and Alton Sterling, two unarmed black men, were shot by law enforcement personnel in Minnesota and Louisiana, respectively (Associated Press, 2016). The two killings were within days of each other and added to an already tempestuous national discussion on social justice (Rawls, 1971), racial profiling, and systemic oppression of black people in the United States through the #blacklivesmatter movement (blacklivesmatter.com, 2017).

The conversation would enter the realm of sports on August 26, 2016, during a preseason game between the San Francisco 49ers and the Green Bay Packers. During this game, an innocuous photo shared on social media by a beat writer for a 49ers fan site (https://twitter.com/jenniferleechan, 2016) depicted a lone San Francisco player sitting on the bench while his teammates stood for the U.S. national anthem. Despite it being the third time Kaepernick had refused to stand for the anthem at a preseason game (https://twitter.com/MikeGarafolo, 2016)—he wasn't dressed in uniform—the photo was distributed to and scrutinized by both the sports and mainstream media, which led people to analyze the definition of true patriotism. The National Football League was unwillingly pulled into a national conversation of First Amendment freedoms, racial equality, and social justice. The league was left the unenviable task of mediating a tense situation between crucial key publics while minimizing the damage and negative publicity to its organization.

Kaepernick, a one-time Super Bowl runner-up but now a backup quarterback for a rebuilding San Francisco 49er team, was firmly at the center of the controversy when he explained his actions after that preseason game: "I am not going to stand up to show pride in a flag for a country that oppresses black people and people of color" (Wyche, 2016). A well-publicized controversy and dialogue would ensue.

Background

Founded in 1920, the National Football League is currently the most popular sports league in the United States, with the No. 1 fan base of 185 million fans, 32 million viewers of its self-produced NFL Network, and 67 million unique visitors to its website (NFL.com, 2016 A). The average NFL team is worth $2.34 billion, and the average NFL player earns $2.1 million (Ozanian, 2016).

Most people would agree that professional football is the "nation's pastime."

According to the NFL, its mission and values are as follows (NFL.com B, 2017):

Our Mission:

- To provide our fans, communities and partners the highest quality sports and entertainment in the world, and to do so in a way that is consistent with our values
- Responsibility
- Respect
- Integrity
- Responsibility to Team
- Resiliency

In the NFL, 69.7% of its players identify as African American (TIDES, 2016). Given the racial make-up of its players, the NFL has taken special care to address issues of diversity by creating the "Rooney Rule," a process mandating at least one minority candidate be interviewed for a vacant head coaching position. The company also has a separate section on its employment website entitled "Commitment to Diversity" (See Appendix). With a statement emphasizing the league's commitment to be "a culturally progressive and socially reflective organization," Kaepernick's protest fell well within league guidelines—even in a very conservative culture where players have been fined for not wearing the right color socks with their uniforms. Yet, Kaepernick's protests grew into something else entirely: a full-blown controversy that gained steam while the NFL avoided definitively addressing the matter.

This was hardly the first time the NFL and Commissioner Roger Goodell faced enduring public controversy. The NFL continues to be scrutinized for its mishandling of concussions (Fainaru-Wada, 2017), performance enhancing drugs (SI.com, 2015), domestic violence (Macur, 2016), and other controversies involving league and player conduct (Marvez, 2016).

The NFL avoided an immediate explosion as its publics waited for the NFL to either condone or condemn the protests. Its silence was deafening. On one side was the large number of the league's black players and the

National Football League Players Association and on the other was the vocal conservative fan base and the league's partnership with the U.S. military (Lamothe, 2016). Also watching were the apolitical or indifferent NFL fan base, the league sponsors, player endorsers, and the casual public observer.

Socially, the #blacklivesmatter movement was gaining momentum through social media. Social justice had risen to the forefront of a national debate in the media. Dating back to the 1840s, Rawls (1971) defined social justice as the basic liberties every society should guarantee. Under Rawls' (1971) operationalization of social justice, guaranteed liberties included:

- Freedom of thought
- Liberty of conscience as it affects social relationships on the grounds of religion, philosophy, and morality
- Political liberties
- Freedom of association
- Freedoms necessary for the liberty and integrity of the person
- Rights and liberties covered by the rule of law

The disparate rate of African Americans shot and killed by law enforcement agencies compared with other racial groups is a clear violation of Rawls' notion of social justice. Colin Kaepernick decided to take an individual stance by silently protesting. What happened afterwards was anything but silent. Someone was going to be negatively affected in the oncoming storm.

The Case

Despite it being his third time sitting during the national anthem, once the image of Kaepernick on the bench circulated on social media, major news outlets picked up on the story and opinions were formed. Some felt it was Kaepernick's right to protest as an individual, while others felt it was blatantly unpatriotic and disrespectful to the U.S. military—a big money partner of the NFL (O'Connell, 2016). While players debated Kaepernick's methods, he gained supporters for the next week (Breech, 2016). The NFL remained silent on the protests.

During the last week of the preseason, the media's spotlight was on Kaepernick, but he wouldn't be alone in his protests. Teammate Eric Reed joined Kaepernick in protest by taking a knee during the national anthem. Kaepernick began to kneel rather than sit after consulting former NFL player and Green Beret Nate Boyer so as to not dishonor the U.S. military (Fucillo, 2016). That same week, Seattle Seahawk Jeremy Lane also sat during the national anthem, making him the first non-teammate to join the protest (Sandritter, 2016). Kaepernick, in an effort to display his sincerity, pledged to donate $1 million of his 2016–2017 salary to various organizations committed to helping communities in need (Wagner-McGough, 2016). In an effort to support its player, the San Francisco 49ers organization pledged $1 million to charities that focus on racial issues brought into focus by Kaepernick (Loumena, 2016).

The NFL regular season opener was approaching on a day associated with patriotism in the United States, September 11, and the NFL's various publics waited for the league's response. Finally, four days before the start of the regular season, Roger Goodell, the chief public figure for the NFL responded to the protests publicly for the first time (Usatoday.com, 2016):

> Well my personal thoughts are . . . I support our players when they want to see change in society, and we don't live in a perfect society. We live in an imperfect society. On the other hand, we believe very strongly in patriotism in the NFL. I personally believe very strongly in that. I think it's important to have respect for our country, for our flag, for the people who make our country better; for law enforcement, and for our military who are out fighting for our freedoms and our ideals.
>
> These are all important things for us, and that moment is a very important moment. So, I don't necessarily agree with what he is doing. We encourage our players to be respectful in that time and I like to think of it as a moment where we can unite as a country. And that's what we need more, and that's what I think football does—it unites our country. So, I would like to see us focusing on our similarities and trying to bring people together.
>
> Players have a platform, and it's his right to do that. We encourage them to be respectful and it's important for them to do that.
>
> I think it's important if they see things they want to change in society, and clearly we have things that can get better in society, and we should get better. But we have to choose respectful ways of doing that so that we can achieve the outcomes we ultimately want and do it with the values and ideals that make our country great.

While Goodell tried to distance his personal feelings in the matter, his position as the key public figure of the NFL would be interpreted as the organization's voice. While he did not condemn Kaepernick outright, Goodell also did not give Kaepernick unfailing support either (Schilken, 2016). The NFL was caught in a very precarious position with its publics (Table 22.1).

The NFL had taken reactive steps to address the crisis facing the validity of its commitment to diversity and First Amendment freedoms. Through the lens of the Contingency Theory of Accommodation (Cancel, Cameron, Sallot, & Mitrook, 1997), it can be inferred that the NFL delayed addressing the situation.

The Contingency Theory of Accommodation uses the accommodation continuum ("pure advocacy to pure accommodation") for public relations practitioners' stances during crisis situations or "what is going to be most effective method at a given time" (Cancel et al., 1997, p. 35) by considering a total of 87 different internal and external variables within the theoretical framework for identifying why and how an entity's stance change depending on the scope of the crisis. According to Cancel et al. (1997), threats are deemed external (threats; industry and environment; general political; social

Table 22.1 NFL Key Publics in Colin Kaepernick Controversy

Internal	External
NFL players The majority of which are black, and the issue affected them	**U.S. military** Strong corporate partners
NFL season ticket holders How would they react to players protesting based on their own values	**The media** Both liberal and conservative leaning
NFL as a league Goodell and the NFL work for the individual teams, teams didn't want to lose revenue due to offending external publics	**The television viewing audience** Would they tune the NFL out in light of the NFL's stance on the protests?

environment; and external culture) or internal (characteristics of the organization; characteristics of the public relations department; characteristics of top management or the dominant coalition; internal threats; the individual characteristics of the public relations practitioner or managers; and characteristics of organization-public relationships).

This application of this theory has already been applied in the realm of sports (Mitrook, Parish, & Seltzer, 2008) when the Orlando Magic moved all the way across the continuum from advocacy to accommodation in securing a new arena. In another case that involved the 1996 Summer Olympics in Atlanta and a conflict between gay activists and local politicians, the stance of the Atlanta Committee of the Olympic Games shifted from accommodation to advocacy (Yarbrough, Cameron, Sallot, & McWilliams, 1998). In an NFL-related case on concussions, Wilbur and Myers (2016) found that the NFL's publics developed a hostile stance on Twitter towards it because of the movie *Concussion*.

The NFL's silence or "avoidance" in the immediate period following the discovery of Kaepernick's protest magnified the issue. When Kaepernick's actions became a topic of conversation in the following days, the NFL was likely allowing Kaepernick to express his First Amendment rights, taking a "compromise" stance towards "pure accommodation" from August 27 (Day 2) until September 6 (Day 11). The NFL initially miscalculated how big the controversy would get, hoping the issue would resolve itself or simply fade away. By September 7 (Day 12), Goodell's statement indicated that the NFL would take a stance of "compromise." By neither condoning nor condemning Kaepernick's actions, the NFL shifted toward the other end of the spectrum, "pure advocacy."

You Make the Call

During the regular season, other NFL players and teams joined Kaepernick in solidarity with various displays of protests (taking a knee, sitting, locking arms, raising a fist, refusing to take the field until after the anthem) (see Figure 22.1).

As the movement began to gain momentum in the early weeks of the season, scheduled bye weeks and injuries would lessen the number of protests as well as a few other factors:

- A photo of Colin Kaepernick emerged of him wearing socks depicting police officers as pigs during the preseason (Nadkarni, 2016).
- NFL ratings for the season would drop by an average of 8%for the regular season (Rovell, 2017).
- Other protests in the world of sports at different levels would appear making it less than an NFL–exclusive issue.
- Studies by the Sharkey Institute (2016) and Rasmussen Reports (2016) indicated that people were tuning out of NFL games due to the protests.

Kaepernick did not play in the NFL during the 2017 season and, at this printing, remains unsigned by any NFL team. He has publicly vowed to stop protesting for the upcoming season (Rafferty, 2017). Other players' protests continued throughout the 2017 season and even drew critical comments from the White House (ESPN, 2017).

Due to its inability to address the issue immediately and effectively, the National Football League, mired in other ongoing negative publicity issues,

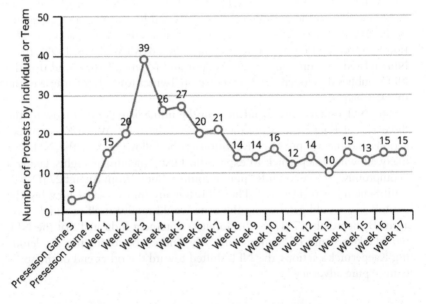

Figure 22.1 Number of Public Sideline Anthem Protests by NFL Players or Team (2016 Regular Season)

Source: www.espn.com/blog/nflnation/post/_/id/227095/nfl-players-who-protested-during-the-national-athem-in-week

lost precious television ratings that they can show off to television networks during contract negotiations. An 8% ratings drop meant that the NFL had decreased revenue and negotiating power in future televisions contracts. Investors may be reticent to pay top dollar for fear of another crisis leading to another ratings drop. Roger Goodell, already unpopular with the NFLPA over labor negotiations and player suspensions, further alienated himself from his largely black player base with his public comments.

Even though Kaepernick was an uninfluential, backup player prior to the crisis, his jersey was one of the best-selling in the 2016 season. While the NFL took a less than supportive approach to Kaepernick, the organization could have diminished the impact and severity of the crisis by employing the following tactics:

- Immediately supporting Kaepernick by respecting his First Amendment rights and recognizing his "social awareness" and "courage"
- Installed a moment of silence at season openers across the league in honor of those who lost their lives during the summer of 2016
- Reinforced its "commitment to diversity" while respecting the contributions of veterans and the U.S. military and recognizing every citizen's First Amendment right to peaceably protest
- Awarded Colin Kaepernick the Walter Payton Man of the Year Award, an honor given annually to a player for his excellence on and off the field
- Created a new award for the player who supports the U.S. armed forces
- Used its power as the top sporting league in the nation by recognizing the growing need for social justice in the United States

By waiting too long and shifting positions on the accommodation continuum, the NFL faced uncertainty in its television ratings, created player uneasiness with the NFL administration, and compromised the confidence of stakeholders for future crises. Instead of arriving at a solution that was amicable to all stakeholders, the league and its stakeholders lost. Any company would be wise to pay attention to issues of social justice and react quickly and decisively in the future.

Discussion Questions

1. What did and didn't work in the NFL's use of Contingency Theory of Accommodation?
2. What can other sports leagues or organizations learn from the NFL's example?
3. If you were Roger Goodell, given the nature of your relationships with your stakeholders, what would you have done differently?
4. What place, if any, does social justice have in the world of sports?
5. What variables in the Contingency Theory of Accommodation were taken into account or ignored in this situation?

References

Associated Press. (2016). A look at recent police shootings involving Black men. Retrieved from http://bigstory.ap.org/article/1c5658f4b50e49ff8ce6c79d6de1d3c7/look-recent-police-shootings-involving-black-men

Blacklivesmatter.com. (2017). The Black lives matter network advocates for dignity, justice and respect. Retrieved from http://blacklivesmatter.com/

Breech, J. (2016). NFL players react to Colin Kaepernick protesting the national anthem. *NFL*. Retrieved from www.cbssports.com/nfl/news/nfl-players-react-to-colin-kaepernick-protesting-the-national-anthem/

Cancel, A. E., Cameron, G. T., Sallot, L. M., & Mitrook, M. A. (1997). It depends: A contingency theory of accommodation in public relations. *Journal of Public Relations Research, 9*(1), 31–63.

Chan, J. L. (2016). This team formation for the national anthem is not Jeff Fisher approved. *#HardKnocks*. Retrieved from https://twitter.com/jenniferleechan/status/769354272735531009

ESPN. (2017). NFL players who protested during national anthem in Week 16. *NFL Nation*. Retrieved from www.espn.com/blog/nflnation/post/_/id/263318/nfl-players-who-protested-during-national-anthem-in-week-16

Fainaru-Wada, M. (2017). Lawyers, others vie for pieces of NFL concussion settlement. Retrieved from www.espn.com/espn/otl/story/_/id/19029607/billion-dollar-nfl-concussion-settlement-turns-nasty-lawyers-others-vie-pieces-payouts-player

Fucillo, D. (2016). Colin Kaepernick, Nate Boyer meet in San Diego, discuss national anthem controversy. *San Francisco 49ers News*. Retrieved from www.ninersnation.com/2016/9/1/12761112/colin-kaepernick-nate-boyer-meet-in-san-diego-national-anthem-controversy

Garafolo, M. (2016). He's actually done it all preseason: No one noticed. *First Time in Uniform Was Last Night*. Retrieved from https://twitter.com/MikeGarafolo/status/769498231243993088

Institute, T. S. (2016). National anthem protest a "turn off" for NFL fans. Retrieved from www.shu.edu/sports-poll/upload/Nove-21-NFL-viewing.pdf

Lamothe, D. (2016). The Colin Kaepernick flap highlights the NFL's complex history with the military and patriotism. *Checkpoint*. Retrieved from www.washingtonpost.com/news/checkpoint/wp/2016/08/29/the-colin-kaepernick-flap-highlights-the-nfls-complex-history-with-the-military-and-patriotism/?utm_term=.f6d758d22068

Loumena, D. (2016). 49ers to donate $1 million to charities that focus on racial issues cited by Colin Kaepernick. *NFL*. Retrieved from www.latimes.com/sports/nfl/la-sp-colin-kaepernick-49ers-donation-20160908-snap-story.html

Macur, J. (2016). N.F.L. shows it doesn't really care about domestic violence. *Pro Football*. Retrieved from www.nytimes.com/2016/10/22/sports/football/nfl-domestic-violence-josh-brown-new-york-giants.html?_r=0

Marvez, A. (2016). Notable scandals that have hit the NFL over the years. Retrieved from www.foxsports.com/nfl/gallery/deflategate-notable-nfl-scandals-bountygate-bullygate-ray-rice-ray-lewis-012315

Mitrook, M. A., Parish, N. B., & Seltzer, T. (2008). From advocacy to accommodation: A case study of the Orlando Magic's public relations efforts to secure a new arena. *Public Relations Review, 34*(2), 161–168.

Nadkarni, R. (2016). Here's what we know about the Colin Kaepernick sock controversy. Retrieved from www.si.com/extra-mustard/2016/09/01/san-francisco-49ers-colin-kaepernick-anthem-protest-police-pigs-socks

NFL.com A. (2016). *NFL.com media kit*. Retrieved from www.nfl.com/static/content/public/photo/2016/08/09/0ap3000000682159.pdf

NFL.com B. (2017). Mission and values. Retrieved from www.nfl.com/careers/about

NFL.com C. (2017). Commitment to diversity. *NFL.com*. Retrieved from www.nfl.com/careers/diversity

O'Connell, R. (2016). Did Colin Kaepernick really insult the troops? *Culture*. Retrieved from www.theatlantic.com/entertainment/archive/2016/08/colin-kaepernick-nfl-patriotism/498014/

Ozanian, M. (2016). Confirmed: NFL losing millions of viewers. Retrieved from www.forbes.com/sites/mikeozanian/2016/10/05/confirmed-nfl-losing-millions-of-tv-viewers-because-of-national-anthem-protests/#453e6d0c226c

Rafferty, S. (2017). Colin Kaepernick's national anthem protest comes to an end. Retrieved from www.rollingstone.com/sports/colin-kaepernick-ends-national-anthem-protest-w470204

Rawls, J. (1971). *A theory of social justice*. Cambridge, MA: Belknap.

Reports, R. (2016). Are Americans tuning out the NFL over protests? *Politics*. Retrieved from www.rasmussenreports.com/public_content/politics/current_events/social_issues/are_americans_tuning_out_the_nfl_over_protests

Rovell, D. (2017). NFL TV viewership dropped an average of 8 percent this season. *NFL*. Retrieved from www.espn.com/nfl/story/_/id/18412873/nfl-tv-viewership-drops-average-8-percent-season

Sandritter, M. (2016). A timeline of Colin Kaepernick's national anthem protest and the athletes who joined him. *NFL*. Retrieved from www.sbnation.com/2016/9/11/12869726/colin-kaepernick-national-anthem-protest-seahawks-brandon-marshall-nfl

Schilken, C. (2016). Roger Goodell on Colin Kaepernick: "I don't necessarily agree with what he is doing", but "it's his right". Retrieved from www.latimes.com/sports/nfl/la-sp-roger-goodell-colin-kaepernick-20160907-snap-story.html

SI.com. (2015). Former NFL RB Eddie George: PEDs "very rampant" in NFL today. Retrieved from www.si.com/nfl/2015/01/08/former-nfl-running-back-eddie-george-steroids-very-rampant-nfl-today

TIDES. (2016). The 2016 racial and gender report card: National Football League. Retrieved from http://nebula.wsimg.com/1abf21ec51fd8dafbecfc2e0319a6091?AccessKeyId=DAC3A56D8FB782449D2A&disposition=0&alloworigin=1

Today, U. (2016). Roger Goodell on Colin Kaepernick: "We believe very strongly in patriotism in the NFL". *Sports*. Retrieved from www.usatoday.com/story/sports/nfl/2016/09/07/goodell-doesnt-agree-with-kaepernicks-actions/89958636/

Wagner-McGough, S. (2016). Colin Kaepernick to donate $1 million to charities that aid communities in need. *NFL*. Retrieved from www.cbssports.com/nfl/news/colin-kaepernick-says-hell-donate-1-million-to-charities-that-help-communities-in-need/

Wilbur, D., & Myers, D. (2016). The NFL and its concussion crisis: Adapting the contingency theory to examine shifts in publics' stances. *Journal of US-China Public Adminstration, 13*, 181–188.

Wyche, S. (2016). Colin Kaepernick explains why he sat during national anthem. Retrieved from www.nfl.com/news/story/0ap3000000691077/article/colin-kaepernick-explains-why-he-sat-during-national-anthem

Yarbrough, C. R., Cameron, G. T., Sallot, L. M., & McWilliams, A. (1998). Tough calls to make: Contingency theory and the Centennial Olympic Games. *Journal of Communication Management, 3*(1), 39–56.

Appendix

NFL Statement on Diversity (NFL.com C, 2017):

Diversity is critically important to the NFL. It is a cultural and organizational imperative about dignity, respect, inclusion and opportunity. Accordingly, diversity has been incorporated into the League Values and Strategic Constants and is therefore an integral element in establishing the League's strategic initiatives. Diversity is the right thing to do both for moral and ethical reasons as well as for the long-term business success of the League. To speak effectively to the broad society externally, the NFL must represent and celebrate a broad society internally. We must overcome the existing cynicism by making progress in both the culture and composition of the NFL organization.

- To be effective in embracing and supporting diversity as an organization, every individual must take ownership of the diversity initiative and strive to make a difference in the culture and behaviors of the NFL while impacting workforce composition and advancement whenever possible, as described below:
- To cultivate an organization and community representing a wide variety of individuals at all levels, all of whom respect, honor and celebrate the broad range of human differences among us, while also embracing the commonalities we share, and to provide each individual with the opportunity to achieve his or her full potential as organizational goals are pursued.
- The overall objective of the diversity effort is to create a culturally progressive and socially reflective organization that represents, supports and celebrates diversity at all levels.
- The NFL strives to be a model of diversity and inclusion. The NFL defines diversity as the respect and appreciation of race, skin color, gender, nationality, religion, sexual orientation, gender identity, physical abilities, age, parental status, work and behavioral styles. Accordingly, it is the goal of the NFL to honor and celebrate the

broad ranges of human difference among us, while also embracing the commonalities we share, and to provide each individual with the opportunity to achieve his or her full potential as organizational goals are pursued. To achieve organizational success each individual must take ownership of the diversity initiative.

23 The Offensive Line

Journalists' Use of Words Considered Disparaging

David P. Burns & James A. Rada

The First Amendment provides wide latitude in matters of freedom of speech and freedom of the press. What then should journalists make of a word that even the courts agree is disparaging to those whom it represents? And when that word is the nickname of a billion-dollar sports franchise in a multi-billion-dollar sport, does it create a journalistic paradox between profit and principle? This chapter applies agenda setting and framing theories to the controversy surrounding the NFL's Washington football team. The case study suggests journalists consider this issue as it impacts every aspect of the industry and society.

Warning: This article contains words that some may find offensive.

Introduction

The headlines set the stage for conflict: The owner of a National Football League team, citing tradition and community support, vows never to change the controversial name of his sports franchise—the Washington Redskins. Meanwhile, Major League Baseball's Cleveland Indians quietly takes the advice of the league's commissioner and begins to phase out the use of its controversial Chief Wahoo logo. How and when does a word or image become so offensive or controversial that mainstream society stops using it? And who determines when the mainstream media should stop using the term?

Words have power (rape vs. sexual assault). Words create images ("television is a vast wasteland"). Words can transcend their original symbolic representation and become the dominant, iconic, and symbolic representation of that thing (some use Xerox to describe any photocopying). Words can be renegotiated over time. And when they are, their meaning changes.

Journalists adapt their writing to reflect society's current and accepted usage of words or risk offending the audience. But when a word some members of society consider offensive—like redskin—exists as a proper noun for a billion-dollar NFL sports franchise, journalists face a difficult decision. Knowing the controversy, should reporters covering the Washington football team "stick to the facts" and cover the team using its actual nickname? Or, should reporters seek out an ethics-based framework to guide them in referring to the team? Using the NFL Washington Redskins name controversy as a case study, this chapter endeavors to investigate the legal/political, economic, cultural, and social implications of this issue by drawing upon the frameworks of second-level agenda setting and framing theories.

Background

Agenda Setting

Researchers use the term agenda setting to describe the media's role in social discourse. First-level agenda setting occurs when the media highlight *the what:* issues for a community to think about—such as unemployment, opiate abuse, etc. (Kim, Scheufele, & Shanahan, 2002). Second-level agenda setting allows journalists to provide social context and perceptions on *how* to think about social issues (see Moon, 2013; Huck, Oliver, & Brosius, 2009). Kessler and Guenther (2017) found that journalists provide these social contexts through the construction of cultural themes or frames in their storytelling.

When an issue challenges the status quo—like a movement to eliminate a controversial team name—it can polarize a community. Here a powerful and popular social entity—an NFL team—is challenged by a minority group of social outliers wishing to redefine a cultural norm.

Tuchman (1978) found society's less advantaged "are cut off from the media as a resource unless they recruit middle-class supporters who have routinized media contacts, attack those who attract media coverage, or (p. 133) recruit reporters to join their cause as 'advocate journalists'" (p. 134). Journalists prefer to cover events, not issues, since events are linear (have a beginning, middle, and end) as opposed to issues, which Freeman (2000) says requires modifying the way people think. Thus, a disenfranchised group must seek counter-public spheres to voice opposition, create social buzz about their issue, and influence socio-political decision-making (Choi & Cho, 2017).

At the same time, corporations work to maintain a positive reputation within the community and with the press. Corporate representatives—called *news promoters* by Tuchman (1978)—develop a long-term relationship with the press and sometimes reach tacit agreements regarding coverage of stories. Corporate owners buy advertising space from the media and expect their views to be represented in the news when an issue arises (Entman, 1993, p. 55). News promoters, like NFL team owners, understand second-level agenda setting and story-framing techniques and use them to strengthen their positions in the public sphere (Meijer & Kleinnijenhuis, 2006).

A city's professional team loyalties run deep, and Washington DC is no exception. But a cursory look at bumper stickers, car magnets, car flags, and pennants reveals a nuance especially pronounced in the fall—the number of Dallas Cowboys fans in the DC area. One online site tracking team followers via Twitter found that in 2014, the Cowboys were one of the three most popular teams in the DC region (#NFL2014, 2014).

While some of that loyalty can be attributed to the Cowboys' self-proclaimed title as "America's Team," and some can be tied to transplanted Texans, there may be another explanation. A common narrative in the DC region is that loyalties do not extend to the hometown football team due to its racist past (see Monkovic, 2009; Morrissey, 2012). George Preston Marshall, the team's owner from 1932 until his death in 1969, was on the record opposing integration and was often seen as a virulent racist (Monkovic, 2009; Gildea, 2002). The team was purposely and proudly the last in the NFL to integrate—and even then, their integration was not by choice but under the threat of government intervention (Gildea, 2002). Conversely, the Dallas Cowboys signed their first African-American player in 1960. This disparity provided Washington fans with an opportunity to make a political statement through their allegiance (Monkovic, 2009).

Imagine the irony, then, when in 1988 the Washington football team was the first to win a Super Bowl with an African-American quarterback. While the team may have overcome its racist past on the field, it still finds itself at the center of controversy as it relates to the team's nickname[1]—the Redskins. The team owner claims—and some fans agree—the name is a sign of honor and respect and should invoke pride among Native Americans. Others—including some Native Americans—say it is a vestige of a racist past and painful reminder of a genocidal government policy directed toward a powerless minority (Riley & Carpenter, 2016). As the issue of Native American imagery has gained attention, many colleges, universities, and high schools with Native American nicknames reconsidered their team name and either altered it to be less inflammatory or abandoned it altogether. But the Washington football team's owner, Daniel Snyder, has held fast—citing tradition, the onerous cost of a name change, research ostensibly indicating Native American support of the name, and political correctness coverage in the press run amok.

The Case

The National Football League is a financial and societal powerhouse. In 2016, the league generated $13 billion dollars in profits (Belzer, 2016), $3.5 billion of that on advertising revenue (Badenhausen, 2017). A 2015 Harris Poll lists professional football as America's favorite sport (Harris Poll, 2016). Some say the NFL enjoys a culturally hegemonic position, and thus media coverage in support of the social status quo generally portrays the league favorably. Johnson-Cartee (2005) says cultural hegemony exists when reporters adopt a purely American ideological perspective where "the views, beliefs, and ideas expressed in news accounts . . . reflect the dominant ideology operating in the United States at that particular time in history" (p. 175).

Professional Conduct by Journalists

To assist professional editors and reporters, independent organizations publish codes of ethics and news organizations institute style books (see Tuchman, 1978), which establish ethical standards of conduct for journalists to utilize when constructing news stories. A few examples from major media make the point. The *New York Times* trains its journalists at all levels to avoid "tendentious language in news stories, features and analysis" and expects an analysis of past news stories to identify "lapses that look like favoritism" ("Preserving Our Readers Trust," May 9, 2005).

The *Washington Post* encourages reportorial skepticism: "The motives of those who press their views upon us must routinely be examined and it must be recognized that those motives can be noble, ignoble, obvious or ulterior." It also stresses the need for sensitivity regarding language:

> A word offensive to the last generation can be part of the next generation's common vocabulary. But we shall avoid prurience. We shall avoid profanities and obscenities unless their use is so essential to a story of significance that its meaning is lost without them.
>
> ("The Washington Post Standards and Ethics").

NPR's policy on potentially offensive language is clear:

> Use of such language on the air has been strictly limited to situations where it is absolutely integral to the meaning and spirit of the story being told . . . We follow these practices out of respect for the listener.
>
> ("This is NPR").

At the time of this writing, these three media organizations still use the word to refer to the Washington football franchise in their news reporting; however, some individual journalists and policy makers avoid using the term. The *New York Times* columnist William C. Rhoden says "I've committed to stop using the nickname in public and in private, except in columns addressing the debate" (Beaujon, 2014). The *Washington Post* editorial board policy states in its editorials: "[W]e have decided that, except when it is essential for clarity or effect, we will no longer use the slur ourselves" (Beaujon, 2014).

Corporate Influence Over Second-Level Agenda Setting

Gans (1980) identified several recurring cultural themes—what he called enduring news values—that journalists use in constructing their news stories. They are *small-town pastoralism* (traditionalism must be supported), *ethnocentrism* (the American way is best), *individualism* (underdog/hero worship), *moderatism* (support status quo, eschew extremism), *altruistic democracy* (majority needs over minority), and *responsible capitalism* (the marketplace of ideas is sacrosanct and noble).

The NFL Washington football franchise and its surrogates routinely use these cultural themes to frame their arguments in support of retaining the team name against its opposition and are rewarded with media attention. But more recent societal changes have empowered the oppositional base to challenge the name on several legal and historical levels.

Challenging the Ethnocentrism Theme

In 1992, Suzan Harjo was the lead plaintiff in *Harjo v. Pro Football, Inc.* The lawsuit alleged the team's nickname violated the Lanham Trademark Act (*Harjo v. Pro Football, Inc.*, 1994). The Act states:

> No trademark . . . shall be refused registration . . . unless it . . . (a) Consists of or comprises immoral, deceptive, or scandalous matter; or matter which may disparage or falsely suggest a connection with persons, living or dead, institutions, beliefs, or national symbols, or bring them into contempt.
>
> (U.S. Government Publishing Office, 2016)

The Trademark Trial and Appeal Board (TTAB) ruled in favor of Harjo; however, the verdict was overturned on a technicality by a district court in 2003. The cause was revived in 2006 in *Pro Football, Inc. v. Blackhorse* (*Pro Football, Inc. v. Blackhorse*, 2014). In 2014, the TTAB definitively ruled the name was disparaging and not protected under the Lanham Act, thus rescinding the team's right to trademark protection. In its ruling, the TTAB referred to a resolution passed by the National Council of American Indians wherein the Council noted the disparaging nature of the nickname (Rasul, 2014). The Council cited several studies that showed significant numbers of members of recognized Native American Nations and Tribes found the nickname offensive (Angle, 2016).

Without trademark protection, any person or organization could legally produce and sell goods using the team's trademark name and logo—thus cutting into the team's revenues. In an unrelated case, the Supreme Court in 2017 unanimously ruled that the Lanham Act infringes on free speech: thus even offensive trademarks enjoy First Amendment protection (*Matal v Tam*, 2017). Although the case did not involve the Washington football team, the ruling resulted in the Justice Department abandoning its case against the NFL team just weeks after the Supreme Court decision (Associated Press, 2017).

But is a legally disparaging name an inappropriate name? Indeed, what constitutes an offensive word? American media routinely used the term "Japs" during World War II. American newspapers decried "Japs Bomb

Pearl Harbor" to begin the US participation in the war and concluded with the headline "Japs Surrender." In 1941, the newly named Redskins team was not yet 10 years old but already a popular and dominant football presence. While the redskin term is still used, today, the term "Jap" is considered disparaging and is not routinely used by the media or even displayed in public in a historical context (Winn, 2009). In looking at the concept of disparagement, another element comes to the fore: impact.

Angle (2016) found exposure to stereotype-ridden Native American mascots—like the Cleveland team's Chief Wahoo—is correlated with an increased likelihood that subjects will hold stereotypes about Native Americans. In 2005, the American Psychological Association recommended banning all Native American mascots, saying they had a deleterious effect on Native Americans (Rasul, 2014).

However, those defending the name refer to their own research that shows not *all* Native Americans find the term offensive (Post, 2016). While the Washington football team's nickname may be legally disparaging, there is no legal recourse to force the team to give up the nickname.

Challenging the Small-Town Pastoralism Theme

Lacking any specific guidelines or legal framework, many teams are choosing to keep their Native American nicknames but cleaning up the imagery associated with them. Here, the Washington football team is the outlier, having kept their nickname and the images associated with it. Riley and Carpenter (2016), among others, trace the term's roots to colonial times and the era of westward expansion where it promoted violence against Native Americans through advertising offering money for bringing in "red-skins."

The team's owner, Daniel Snyder, often invokes the *honor through history* frame regarding the team's name. He says the name was chosen to honor its first coach, William Dietz. However, there was a great deal of uncertainty and controversy as to whether Dietz actually was Native American, or whether he used that as a ruse to get out of military service and enhance his coaching career (Barr, 2014; Leiby, 2013; Messbauer, 2016).

Messbauer (2016) poses an alternative explanation for how the team got its nickname. During that time, as a practical matter, professional sports teams in major cities often looked for similar nicknames. Since the team was based in Boston—home of the Braves baseball team—the fledgling football team would obviously seek a similar nickname. Thus, the *honoring through history* argument may not hold water.

Challenging the Individualism and Responsible Capitalism Themes

The team administration, the local community, and team fans say the nickname should stand because it honors Native Americans. But if it is socially acceptable and noble to select a nickname to honor a population, why are there no other populations—African Americans, Asian Americans, Jews, the disabled, etc.—being used as mascots (see also Rasul, 2014)? To be sure, there are mascots that represent specific groups of people (Vikings, Trojans, Spartans) but these mascots represent groups that do not exist in present-day representations.

When considering teams like the Utah Utes, the Chicago Blackhawks, or the Florida State University Seminoles it is important to consider that these mascots represent specific Native American groups that still exist. As such, those tribes have often taken an active role in crafting the imagery that represents them. Messbauer (2016) refers to this as *authorized out-group propagation*. Riley and Carpenter (2016) refer to the case of the Seminole Tribe and Florida State University where, after consulting with tribe members, the university altered its mascot's attire to be more culturally accurate and changed the name of the booster club from "Scalp Hunters" to "Spirit Hunters."

But the Washington football team has taken no such steps to alter or otherwise clean up its image. Regarding whether the imagery *honors* those being portrayed, an underlying current of entitlement must be addressed. Namely, can members of a socially dominant group dictate to members of a minority outgroup how they should feel about imagery pertaining to that outgroup? Messbauer (2016) calls this *unauthorized out-group propagation*, where issues of cultural appropriation and misappropriation dovetail. Here, it is not just the team's name—they are also incorporating elements of the Native American culture such as attire and rituals.

In words and actions, Snyder and his supporters reframe the issue from the team's perspective. They view the cultural trappings as theirs; thus, the team, its fans, and the team's history and traditions are under attack by the mainstream. A name change would upset the marketplace and cost his team millions in rebranding. In effect, a name change would challenge the team's and the fan's collective identity. Thus, in their view, it is a justifiably noble gesture to oppose the name change and a heroic act by its "underdog" owner and loyal fans to rail against the politically correct media establishment, the legal system, and even the National Football League.

You Make the Call

Journalists consciously consider their word choices every time they construct a story. They consider how every word impacts the audience. Industry ethics codes and organizational policies hold journalists responsible for considering the audience when producing stories. The audience relies on the media to identify important social issues, present the stakeholders involved in a balanced way, and provide a comprehensive report on the issue that is free from outside coercion.

Should more media outlets abandon the use of the word "redskin" in their coverage of the NFL football franchise? Maybe the real question is, why have they not done so already? It is not a First Amendment issue. Journalists are free to choose which words they use in stories. There are plenty of examples of the media discontinuing the use of words that become offensive and/or derogatory over time, making this particular change suspiciously late in coming. Societal pressure to maintain the status quo is ever present. There is also corporate pressure from the NFL and its Washington franchise, which have lucrative broadcast and advertising deals with the media. After all, media companies are in the business to turn a profit, and advocates of the Native American tribes possess little more than grassroots-level clout. Since writing policies are easy to change, the media's failure to adjust to lexical changes may be more about financial principal than ethical principle. John Grogan (2010) once said, "the English language . . . all comes down to this: Twenty-six letters, when combined correctly, can create magic. Twenty-six letters form the foundation of a free, informed society." Journalists simply need to consider the whole community when combining those letters and selecting their words.

Discussion Questions

1. The Society of Professional Journalists, the National Press Photographers Association, and the Radio Television Digital News Association all publish codes of ethics to guide journalists. Find these codes of ethics and look for items listed which help direct a journalist when covering a team with a controversial name like the Washington NFL football franchise. In what specific ways do these codes encourage societal inclusion and warn against dominant social ideologies?
2. You Make the Call: If you were a journalist, would you use controversial team names in your coverage? In what ways could you push your media organization's management to establish/amend editorial policy/standards and practices regarding coverage of teams with controversial names? If you continue to use the term, in what ways could you defend your decision?
3. Discuss any new developments in this ongoing issue. What has occurred lately to change the editorial coverage or the tenor of the conversation? Choose and defend a side on whether teams with controversial names and/or images should adopt new ones. Justify your stance in terms of the financial, political, and social ramifications of your position. Discuss the publics you might call upon to support your position.
4. Analyze and evaluate the survey administered by the *Washington Post* in regard to the name controversy (www.washingtonpost.com/page/2010-2019/WashingtonPost/2016/05/19/National-Politics/Polling/release_424.xml?tid=a_inl). Apply what you know about survey construction and validity to the survey and discuss the instrument's strengths and weaknesses.
5. This chapter presented a specific example of a term that was deemed acceptable in the 1940s but is now deemed derogatory and offensive

and no longer in use. Find another specific example of a word that was accepted and commonly used in the past but is viewed differently today. What factors led people to look at this word in a different light? Discuss how some words may only be acceptable within a given group and are considered derogatory when used by members outside the group. What social purpose does that serve? How must journalists navigate these language issues?

Note

1. In this chapter, we use the term 'nickname' to also include the team's mascot.

References

Angle, J. (2016, September 15). Sorry Redskins fans: Native American mascots increase racial bias. *The Washington Post*. Retrieved from www.washingtonpost.com/news/speaking-of-science/wp/2016/09/15/sorry-redskins-fans-native-american-mascots-increase-your-racial-bias/?utm_term=.55a0079ff300

Associated Press. (2017, June 29). Justice Department gives up Washington Redskins name fight. Retrieved from www.csnne.com/new-england-patriots/justice-department-gives-washington-redskins-name-fight

Badenhausen, K. (2017, March 1). NFL TV ad revenue hits record $3.5 billion despite drop in ratings. Retrieved from www.forbes.com/sites/kurtbadenhausen/2017/03/01/nfl-tv-ad-revenue-hits-record-3-5-billion-despite-drop-in-ratings/#39b7e1f7525b

Barr, J. (2014, September 2). Was Redskins' first coach a fraud? *ESPN.com*. Retrieved from www.espn.com/espn/otl/story/_/id/11455467/was-washington-redskins-first-coach-fraud

Beaujon, A. (2014, June 19). Here's a list of outlets and journalists who won't use the name "Redskins". Retrieved from www.poynter.org/2014/heres-a-list-of-outlets-and-journalists-who-wont-use-the-name-redskins/256258/

Belzer, J. (2016, February 29). Thanks to Roger Goodell, NFL revenues projected to surpass $13 billion in 2016. Retrieved from www.forbes.com/sites/jasonbelzer/2016/02/29/thanks-to-roger-goodell-nfl-revenues-projected-to-surpass-13-billion-in-2016/#2ddc87e81cb7

Choi, S. Y., & Cho, Y. (2017, April). Generating counter-public spheres through social media: Two social movements in neoliberalised South Korea. *Javnost-The Public, 24*(1), 15–33. doi:10.1080/13183222.2017.1267155

Entman, R. M. (1993). Framing: Toward clarification of a fractured paradigm. *Journal of Communication, 43*(4), 55. doi:10.1111/j.1460-2466.1993.tb01304.x

Freeman, J. (2000). *The politics of women's liberation: A case study of an emerging social movement and its relation to the policy process.* Lincoln, NE: IUniverse.com.

Gans, H. J. (1980). *Deciding what's news: A study of CBS Evening News, NBC Nightly News, Newsweek, and Time.* Evanston, IL: Northwestern University Press.

Gildea, W. (2002, June 5). Integrating the Redskins: George Preston Marshall vs. the U.S. government. *The Washington Post*. Retrieved from www.washingtonpost.com/archive/politics/2002/06/05/integrating-the-redskins-george-preston-marshall-vs-the-us-government/b8b82386-4cf0-498c-8a5a-e0498b8d5884/?utm_term=.8963d0f70f89

Grogan, J. (2010). *Bad dogs have more fun: Selected writings on family, animals, and life.* New York, NY: Vanguard Press.

Harjo v. Pro Football, Inc. (1994). Trademark Trial and Appeal Board 1994 TTAB LEXIS 9; 30 U.S.P.Q.2D (BNA) 1828.

Harris Poll. (2016, January 26). Pro football is still America's favorite sport. Retrieved from www.theharrispoll.com/sports/Americas_Fav_Sport_2016.html

Huck, I., Oliver, Q., & Brosius, H. (2009). Perceptual phenomena in the agenda setting process. *International Journal of Public Opinion Research, 21*(2), 139–164. doi:10.1093/ijpor/edp019

Johnson-Cartee, K. S. (2005). *News narratives and news framing: Constructing political reality.* New York, NY: Rowman & Littlefield Publishers.

Kessler, S. H., & Guenther, L. (2017, March). Eyes on the frame. *Internet Research, 27*(2), 303–320. doi:10.1108/IntR-01-2016-0015

Kim, S., Scheufele, D. A., & Shanahan, J. (2002). Think about it this way: Attribute agenda-setting function of the press and the public's evaluation of a local issue. *Journalism & Mass Communication Quarterly, 79*(1), 7–25. Retrieved June 20, 2017, from Academic Search Complete.

Leiby, R. (2013, November 6). The legend of lone star Dietz: Redskins namesake, coach– and possible impostor? *The Washington Post.* Retrieved from www.washingtonpost.com/lifestyle/style/the-legend-of-lone-star-dietz-redskins-namesake-coach-and-possible-imposter/2013/11/06/a1358a76-466b-11e3-bf0c-cebf37c6f484_story.html?utm_term=.6e060ac5a561

Matal v Tam. (2017). No. 15–1293. Supreme Court of The United States 2017 U.S. Lexis 3872 Certiorari to The United States Court of Appeals for The Federal Circuit No. 15–1293.

Meijer, M., & Kleinnijenhuis, J. (2006, September). Issue news and corporate reputation: Applying the theories of agenda setting and issue ownership in the field of business communication. *Journal of Communication, 56*(3), 543–559. doi:10.1111/j.1460-2466.2006.00300.x

Messbauer, I. (2016). Beyond "redskins": A source-based framework for analyzing disparaging trademarks and native American sports logos. *The Federal Circuit Bar Journal, 25*, 241–270.

Monkovic, T. (2009, January 25). Readers point to race as reason for Cowboys fans in Redskins land. *The New York Times N.F.L. Blog.* Retrieved from https://fifthdown.blogs.nytimes.com/2009/01/25/readers-point-to-race-as-reason-for-cowboys-fans-in-redskins-land/?_r=1

Moon, S. J. (2013, October). Attention, attitude, and behavior: Second-level agenda-setting effects as a mediator of media use and political participation. *Communication Research, 40*(5), 698–719. doi:10.1177/0093650211423021

Morrissey, A. (2012, January 27). Why are there so many Cowboys fans in D.C.? *Washington City Paper.* Retrieved from www.washingtoncitypaper.com/news/article/13042042/why-are-there-so-many-cowboys-fans-in-dc

#NFL2014: Where are your team's followers? (2014). Retrieved from https://interactive.twitter.com/nfl_followers2014/#?mode=team&team=all

Post, D. (2016, May 23). Poll shows Native Americans don't care that much about the name "Redskins". *The Washington Post.* Retrieved from www.washingtonpost.com/news/volokh-conspiracy/wp/2016/05/23/poll-shows-native-americans-dont-care-that-much-about-the-name-redskins/?utm_term=.415db3dae7cd

Preserving Our Readers' Trust. (2005, May 9). Retrieved from www.nytimes.com/2005/05/09/business/media/preserving-our-readers-trust.html?_r=0

Pro Football, Inc. v. Blackhorse. United States District Court for the Eastern District of Virginia, Alexandria Division 62 F. Supp. 3d 498; 2014 U.S. Dist. LEXIS 166889; 113 U.S.P.Q.2D (BNA) 1749.

Rasul, H. (2014). Fourth and long: The time is now for the "Washington Redskins" to punt the name. *University of Maryland Law Journal of Race, Religion, Gender & Class, 14*(2), 338–355. Retrieved February 22, 2017, from http://search.ebscohost.com/login.aspx?direct=true&db=a9h&AN=103635194&site=ehost-live

Riley, A. R., & Carpenter, K. A. (2016). Owning red: A theory of Indian (cultural) appropriation. *Texas Law Review, 94*(5), 859–931. Retrieved February 22, 2017, from http://search.ebscohost.com/login.aspx?direct=true&db=a9h&AN=114886639&site=ehost-live

This is NPR. (n.d.). Retrieved June 20, 2017, from http://ethics.npr.org/

Tuchman, G. (1978). *Making news: A study in the construction of reality.* New York, NY: The Free Press.

U.S. Government Publishing Office. (2016). 15 U.S. 1052 (Section 2 of the Lanham Act): Trademarks registrable on principal register: Concurrent registration. Retrieved from www.bitlaw.com/source/15usc/1052.html

The Washington Post Standards and Ethics. (n.d.). Retrieved June 20, 2017, from http://asne.org/content.asp?contentid=335

Winn, P. (2009, March 10). VA hospital pulls "Japs Surrender" headline from historical display. Retrieved June 20, 2017, from www.cnsnews.com/news/article/va-hospital-pulls-japs-surrender-headline-historical-display

24 Paradigm Repair and the Hero Myth in Sports Journalism
An Analysis of Lance Armstrong Coverage

Sada Reed

When journalism routines result in erroneous reporting, journalists often engage in paradigm repair by demonstrating that the rules of the paradigm are reliable but were violated. When cyclist Lance Armstrong confessed to Oprah Winfrey that he used PEDs, his confession came after years of sports journalists framing him as a hero for being a cancer survivor and a Tour de France winner. An analysis of sports journalists' reactions to Armstrong's confession show that despite the role sports journalists had perpetuating Armstrong's hero narrative, sports journalists did not see Armstrong's fall from grace as threatening to their professional paradigm.

Introduction

In a two-part interview beginning on January 17, 2013, American cyclist Lance Armstrong confessed to Oprah Winfrey that he won his record-breaking seven Tour de France titles with the help of performance enhancing drugs. The confession came after years of denials—and support from American sports journalists like Pulitzer Prize–winner and *Friday Night Lights*–author Buzz Bissinger. "The country has a right to at least one [hero]," Bissinger wrote in a June 15, 2012, column in *The Daily Beast*. "Armstrong embodies all the attributes, his dominance in the sport of cycling, his successful battle against testicular cancer, the work of his foundation" (Bissinger, 2012).

Bissinger, like many sports journalists, composed narratives since the late 1990s about Armstrong's humble beginnings, battle with cancer, and comeback career. This narrative is referred to as a *hero myth*, one of several myths news-content creators use to build stories (Lule, 2001). American sports journalists traditionally use the hero myth to craft narratives about elite athletes and coaches. In order to create and sustain this myth, however, sports journalists need to look past, or at least minimize, athletes' and coaches' vices.

Objectivity is a hallmark of journalism in which reporters are to use objective, as opposed to subjective, methods for interpreting events and messages around them. When journalists make mistakes, for example, the Society of Professional Journalists' Code of Ethics recommends a media organization acknowledge "mistakes and correct them promptly and prominently.

Explain corrections and clarifications carefully and clearly" (SPJ Code of Ethics, 2014). When journalism routines, like the practice of covering subjects objectively, lead to shattered narratives, journalists often engage in *paradigm repair* (Berkowitz, 1997). Journalists engage in paradigm repair by demonstrating that the written and unwritten rules of the American journalism paradigm really are reliable, but due to a particular reason or person, the paradigm's rules were violated (Berkowitz, 1997). The following chapter explains the concept of paradigm repair in American journalism and how sports journalists' use of the hero myth complicates how they engage in paradigm repair when the heroes their narratives helped create come tumbling down.

Background

Lance Armstrong was born Lance Edward Gunderson on September 18, 1971, in Plano, Texas, to 17-year-old Linda Mooneyham Gunderson. Armstrong's biological father was "a non-factor" in Armstrong's life, and Armstrong was legally adopted by his stepfather, Terry Armstrong. By 16 years old, he was making $20,000 a year in triathlon competitions and turned pro. Though his reputation as a hothead preceded him, sponsors in the sports world sensed his promising future and wanted to work with him (Macur, 2014). Armstrong collected victories throughout the early 1990s, but this success was temporarily halted in 1996: He was 25 years old when he was diagnosed with stage four testicular cancer, which spread to his brain and lungs. Following treatment, he was declared cancer-free in February 1997. From 1999 to 2005, Armstrong won seven consecutive Tour titles. He retired after the 2005 win, then returned, finishing third and 23rd in the 2009 and 2010 Tours, respectively, before retiring again in 2011.

Paradigm Repair

Paradigms are systems that shape how members of a collective—or in this case, sports journalists—learn the profession's rules (Kuhn, 1962). These rules may be written or unwritten; members learn these rules through regulation and/or socialization (Hindman & Thomas, 2013).

Paradigm repair, on the other hand, is "a process that attempts to show that, despite [the occurrence of] an isolated instance . . . the professional practices incorporated into the journalistic paradigm really do work to provide an objective rendering of reality" (Berkowitz, 1997, p. 500). When journalists engage in paradigm repair, they affirm the value of professional norms and distance themselves from the threat that the rogue journalist represents (Hindman, 2005).

An example of paradigm repair is Hindman and Thomas' (2013) examination of mainstream journalists' reactions to the late White House correspondent Helen Thomas after she made anti-Semitic remarks in a 2010 interview with New York rabbi David Nesenoff. Thomas was a long-time correspondent, covering the administrations of 10 U.S. presidents. Her 57-year career was renowned; she was the first female winner of multiple press honors and authored six books.

Thomas' comments in the 2010 interview, however, challenged journalism's paradigm as an objective, ethical media system. Members of the media singled out Thomas as unrepresentative of the field (Hindman & Thomas, 2013; vanden Heuvel, 2013). An analysis of commentators' op-ed essays about the incident showed that journalists' paradigm repair could be categorized into four themes: suggestions that her career should end, that her remarks were caused by senility, that her remarks were racist and privately held for a long time, and that there is a blurred line between acceptable and unacceptable speech (Hindman & Thomas, 2013).

This notion of distancing oneself from the journalist who erred is a common occurrence in paradigm-repair research. In an analysis of the *New York Times'* reaction to the 2003 Jayson Blair plagiarism and fabrication scandal, the *Times* initially cast Blair as a renegade and then announced the formation of a committee that would "address what went wrong" (Hindman, 2005, p. 235). This committee's findings, posted as a PDF on the corporate website, cited management style and intra-newsroom communication problems and made recommendations that were implemented, like the creation of a "public editor" position (Hindman, 2005).

Hero Narrative

The hero myth is a traditional, prominent aspect of mainstream American sports media narrative construction. The use of the term "myth" can be misleading: These are not stories that have been simply made up. Myths reflect humankind's values and vices (Lule, 2001; Oates & Pauly, 2007). Journalists' presentation of people and events can be categorized into one of seven myths: the victim, the scapegoat, the hero, the good mother, the trickster, the other world, and the flood (Lule, 2001).

The hero became a dominant myth in sports journalism directly after the Civil War during journalism's Gilded Age, "the first period in American history when sports and games moved away from casual amateurism in the direction of organization and professionalism" (Isenberg, 1988, p. 206). Elements needed for the hero myth "formula" include an athlete of humble birth who is on a quest—a quest laced with adversity and of social significance—that the athlete either triumphs or dies while attempting (Lule, 2001). In an examination of the 1998 home-run race between Major League Baseball sluggers Sammy Sosa and Mark McGwire, Butterworth (2007) argued that sports journalists' construction of McGwire as a hero was a way of embodying him with values prized by the wider society. Sports media used this hero myth to structure Lance Armstrong's narrative, most prominently from Armstrong's initial 1999 Tour victory. An example of this can be seen in Rick

Reilly's December 16, 2002, *Sports Illustrated* Sportsman of the Year article about Armstrong:

> What's the deal with that name, anyway? Lance Armstrong. Is that a comic-book hero or a bendable action figure? Once somebody gives you a name like that, how hard can life be? Lance Armstrong. Wasn't he the star of those 1950s boys' sports books?
>
> This is his third hour on the bike today, and the Tour de France isn't for seven months. This is not natural. No other racer in the world is doing this.

Sports journalists often *believe* the myths they craft, too. A love of sport and admiration for athletes' abilities is what draws many sports journalists to the field (Walsh, 2012). Younger, less experienced sports journalists experience vicarious achievement through the athletes they cover, whereas their older, veteran counterparts experience it much less (Reed, 2015).

The Case

Reed's (2014) study examined whether American sports journalists' use of the hero myth may have bound them to unwritten paradigm rules that would have inhibited more critical reporting earlier on in Armstrong's career and shaped how sports journalists engaged in paradigm repair upon Armstrong's confession. The study had two parts: First, it examined if American sports journalists engaged in paradigm repair when Armstrong confessed to doping. This was done by examining American sports journalists' columns from October 9, 2012, when the United States Anti-Doping Agency released its report on Armstrong's history of doping, to January 31, 2013, the month following Armstrong's confession to Oprah Winfrey. This was done through a LexisNexis search of major American publications, as well as a search of *ESPN*, *Sports Illustrated*, *Deadspin*, and *The Daily Beast*'s archives. This resulted in 54 stories from 32 sports journalists.

Altheide's (1996) ethnographic content analysis, a method also known as qualitative content analysis, was used to examine these columns. According to Altheide (1996, p. 16), "The aim is to be systematic and analytic but not rigid. Categories and variables initially guide the study, but others are allowed and expected to emerge throughout the study." Columns were first read to establish familiarity and context. They were read a second time, with portions of the text that specifically discussed Armstrong's confession highlighted and any references sports journalists made to themselves and any role they take credit for having in building Armstrong's hero narrative. Common themes that spanned the columns were identified.

Second, the study determined whether sports journalists had *reason* to engage in paradigm repair by examining the content produced by sports journalists in the first sample to see if they used a hero narrative in their work between January 1, 1999, the year Armstrong won his first Tour, and December 31, 2010, Armstrong's final year on the Tour. This was done through another LexisNexis and advanced Google search of all the stories the 32 authors in the above sample wrote about Armstrong. This resulted in 109 articles from 22 authors. Ten authors were missing. A search through Academic Search Premier and LinkedIn determined the authors were either working for a broadcast company, were still university students, or were not writing for sports beats before 2011.

Paradigm Repair

Of the 32 sports journalists in the first, post-confession sample, eight of them wrote about their professional or personal interactions with Armstrong. ESPN columnist Rick Reilly, for example, engaged in paradigm repair in a January 17, 2013, article, speaking about his professional interactions with Armstrong and his personal anger toward Armstrong for making Reilly "look like a chump" after defending Armstrong for 14 years. He cited Armstrong's record of passing drug tests and that Armstrong consistently told Reilly he was clean—both on and off the record. Reilly said it's "partially" his fault because he let himself admire Armstrong. "When my sister was diagnosed, she read his book and got inspired. And I felt some pride in that. I let it get personal. And now I know he was living a lie and I was helping him live it." He ended the article with an apology to his readers.

Bissinger took a similar route in a January 14, 2013, *Daily Beast* article. He said he believed Armstrong for as long as he did because he told himself competitive cycling was rife with doping; Armstrong had passed more than 500 drug tests; Armstrong overcame a *heroic* battle with cancer; Armstrong founded an organization, Livestrong, that benefited cancer patients; and the cyclists cooperating with USADA against Armstrong were "rogues" with "proven credibility problems." He said he previously did not realize how serious the allegations against Armstrong were, or about Armstrong's former teammates' statements taken under oath, or the elaborate ways Armstrong beat the testing system.

Other sports journalists were less direct. One person, however, stood out from the sample. Sally Jenkins of the *Washington Post* (Dec. 16, 2012) defended Armstrong, saying she "searched high and low for [her] anger at Lance, and [she] can't find it." In her co-authored book about Armstrong, *It's Not About the Bike* (2000), Jenkins described Armstrong as the hardest working cyclist in the world and how she developed long-standing questions about the "wisdom and fairness" of the anti-doping effort.

Jenkins' column received critical feedback from the *Washington Post's* audience, but her reputation as a journalist was defended by Patrick Pexton, who was the *Post's* ombudsman in 2012. "I understand that *Post* readers are angry at sports columnist Sally Jenkins' long-standing defense of cyclist Lance Armstrong," Pexton wrote on December 23, 2012. However, he goes on to say that Jenkins did not violate *Post* ethics rules or journalistic standards. He highlights her career at the *Post* and the wide range of events she has covered; her lack of participation in *Post* Tour coverage; and her openly close relationship with Armstrong. Thus, she has never claimed to be objective.

Besides these examples, responses from other journalists fell into four categories: 1) Armstrong's poor character and disingenuous apology; 2) the world of sports' widespread dysfunction; 3) weighing the good Armstrong did against the bad; and 4) acknowledgement of a collective role in myth-making. This final category is of note because it isn't clear if sports journalists, airing collective feelings of betrayal, were talking about "we" as sports journalists or "we" as sports enthusiasts.

Hero Myth

A hero narrative was present in 44 of the 109 articles (40.4% of sample), or from 15 of the 22 sports journalists (68.2%). This hero narrative was evident by the adjectives sports journalists used to describe Armstrong: Besides using the word "hero," sports journalists described him as a "virtual saint," "the best ever," "godlike," "icon of hope and inspiration," "saintly," "supergenes," "America's greatest untarnished sports icon," "aberration," "sustained excellence," "greatest cyclist in history," "all-time great," "true greatness," "different from competitors, most mere mortals," and "product of a miracle," among others. Of the eight sports journalists who wrote about their professional or personal interactions with Armstrong, six of them used a hero narrative in at least one of their stories between 1999 and 2010. The earlier the story was published, the more likely it had a hero narrative. The hero myth and Armstrong's status as a cancer survivor were intertwined. Armstrong's battle against cancer was also mentioned in 44 stories (40.4%) from 14 different sports writers. The earlier the story was published, the more likely the sports journalist mentioned Armstrong's status as a cancer survivor.

This does not mean doping allegations and rumors were not mentioned, but they were dispelled. Sports journalists' most common retort to these accusations were that Armstrong had yet to fail a drug test. This was mentioned in 15 stories from 10 sports journalists. The second-most common defensive theme was French anti-Americanism for the root of Armstrong's doping accusations. This was mentioned in 14 stories from seven journalists, including statements about the French not liking Armstrong or Americans in general, and that the French were disgraced from previous doping scandals. Poor testing or bad USADA leadership were mentioned in 13 stories from eight journalists.

You Make the Call

Whereas past research suggests journalists will isolate and label the journalist who erred (i.e., Jayson Blair, Helen Thomas) as the "rogue," make them a scapegoat, and distance themselves from him or her (see Hindman & Thomas, 2013; Hindman, 2005), sports journalists in this study painted Armstrong as the rogue and scapegoat, *not* members of their own profession and rarely themselves. In the month after Armstrong's confession, no one in the sample suggested paradigm changes or a review of specific routines sports journalists could or should do differently to avoid deception in the future.

Discussion Questions

Numerous sports journalists used Armstrong's clean history of testing as a reason for disregarding doping accusations. However, Armstrong did not have a clean history. In 1999, he tested positive for traces of corticosteroids (see Ziegler, 2013). Armstrong said at the time that he was using cream for saddle sores (Gibney, Marshall, & Tolmach, 2013).

1. The Union Cycliste Internationale allegedly accepted the saddle sore cream explanation when Armstrong produced a therapeutic use exemption certificate, though this medical certificate was later determined to be backdated (Ziegler, 2013). What other sources could sports journalists have consulted in order to find the truth?
2. Denham and Duke (2010, p. 114) found distinctions between how American and non-American publications approached Armstrong's success—particularly where he "may have come to symbolize perceived U.S. arrogance, self-assuredness, and hypocrisy abroad." Consult U.S. and non-U.S. news articles from this time period. How did this anti-American perception play a role in how U.S. and non-U.S.-based sports journalists created their narrative about Armstrong?
3. According to Gibney et al. (2013), widespread doping was already prevalent before Armstrong won the 1999 Tour de France. It was so common, riders didn't necessarily see it as cheating. "You weren't trying to beat the system; you were trying to be *in* the system," said George Hincapie, Armstrong's former teammate. "Nobody made me dope. I just knew I had to dope in order to do the sport I loved to do" (Gibney et al., 2013). How might mainstream American sports journalists' relative unfamiliarity with this sport's culture contribute to the hero myth surrounding Armstrong and influence any objective reporting?
4. Besides sports journalists, who else was responsible for creating and perpetuating Armstrong's hero narrative? Did their narrative influence sports journalists as content creators?
5. Discuss any new developments or cases in this ongoing issue. What has occurred lately to impact the tenor of the hero myth practice?

References

Altheide, D. (1996). *Qualitative media analysis*. Thousand Oaks, CA: Sage Publications.

Armstrong, L., & Jenkins, S. (2000). *It's not about the bike*. New York, NY: G. P. Putnam's Sons.

Berkowitz, D. (1997). *Social meanings of news*. London: Sage Publications.

Bissinger, B. (2012, June 15). Leave Lance Armstrong alone. *The Daily Beast*. Retrieved from www.thedailybeast.com/articles/2012/06/15/leave-lance-armstrong-alone.html

Bissinger, B. (2013, January 14). I was deluded to believe Lance Armstrong when he denied doping. *The Daily Beast*. Retrieved from www.thedailybeast.com/articles/2013/01/14/buzz-bissinger-i-was-deluded-to-believe-lance-armstrong-when-he-denied-doping.html

Butterworth, M. L. (2007). Race in "the race": Mark McGwire, Sammy Sosa, and Heroic constructions of whiteness. *Critical Studies in Media Communication, 24*(3), 228–244.

Denham, B. E., & Duke, A. (2010). Hegemonic masculinity and the rogue warrior: Lance Armstrong as (symbolic) American. In H. L. Hundley & A. C. Billings' (Eds.), *Examining identity in sports media*. Thousand Oaks, CA: Sage Publications.

Gibney, A., Marshall, F., Tolmach, M. (Producers), & Gibney, A. (Director). (2013). *The Armstrong Lie* [Documentary]. Santa Monica, California: Kennedy and Marshall Productions.

Hindman, E. B. (2005). Jayson Blair, *The New York Times*, and paradigm repair. *Journal of Communication, 55*(2), 225–241.

Hindman, E. B., & Thomas, R. (2013). Journalism's "Crazy old aunt": Helen Thomas and paradigm repair. *Journalism & Mass Communication Quarterly, 90*(2), 267–286.

Isenberg, M. T. (1988). *John L. Sullivan and his America*. Urbana, IL: University of Illinois Press.

Jenkins, S. (2012, December 16). I'm not angry at Armstrong. *The Washington Post*. Retrieved from http://articles.washingtonpost.com/2012-12-15/sports/35846813_1_usada-report-tour-de-france-victories-lance-armstrong

Kuhn, T. S. (1962). *The structures of scientific revolutions*. Chicago, IL: University of Chicago Press.

Lule, J. (2001). *Daily news, eternal stories: The mythological role of journalism*. New York, NY: The Guilford Press.

Macur, J. (2014). *Cycle of lies: The fall of lance Armstrong*. New York, NY: Harper & Row.

Oates, T. P., & Pauly, J. (2007). Sports journalism as moral and ethical discourse. *Journal of Mass Media Ethics, 22*(4), 332–347.

Pexton, P. (2012, December 21). Sally Jenkins's steadfast support of Lance Armstrong. *The Washington Post*. Retrieved from http://articles.washingtonpost.com/2012-12-21/opinions/35950282_1_lance-armstrong-columns-armstrong-books

Reed, S. (2014). *Who is to Blame? An examination of American sports journalists' Lance Armstrong hero narrative and post-doping confession paradigm repair*. Presented at Association for Education in Journalism and Mass Communication Conference, Montreal.

Reed, S. (2015). *Conflicting loyalties: An examination of the role community membership and sports fandom have on sports journalists' interactions with whistleblowers* (Unpublished doctoral dissertation). University of North Carolina, Chapel Hill.

Reilly, R. (2002, December 16). Lance Armstrong: For his courage and commitment-not to mention his fourth straight Tour de France victory: SI salutes the ultimate road warrior. *Sports Illustrated*. Retrieved from www.si.com/vault/2002/12/16/8110566/lance-armstrong-for-his-courage-and-commitmentnot-to-mention-his-fourth-straight-tour-de-france-victorysi-salutes-the-ultimate-road-warrior#

Reilly, R. (2013, January 17). It's all about the lies. *ESPN*. Retrieved from www.espn.com/espn/story/_/id/8852974/lance-armstrong-history-lying

Society of Professional Journalists. (2014). *SPJ code of ethics*. Retrieved from www.spj.org/ethicscode.asp

vanden Heuvel, K. (2013, July 23). Helen Thomas's legacy. *The Nation*. Retrieved from www.thenation.com/blog/175397/helen-thomass-legacy#

Walsh, D. (2012). *Seven deadly sins: My pursuit of Lance Armstrong*. New York, NY: Atria Books.

Ziegler, M. (2013, April 17). Cycling: Lance Armstrong failed four drug tests in 1999, UCI admits. *The Independent*. Retrieved from www.independent.co.uk/sport/general/others/cycling-lance-armstrong-failed-four-drugs-tests-in-1999-uci-admits-8577491.html

25 "Don't Say"

The Use of Identity Communication in Sport to Advance Positive Social Change

Kara A. Laskowski, Ashley Grimm, & Carrie Michaels

Against a backdrop of a social climate featuring strong condemnation of "political correctness," social activism in professional sports, and increasing focus on and concern about abuses perpetrated by athletes at all levels, this case study assists readers who endeavor to leverage the power of sport for positive social change. Through the lens of the Communication Theory of Identity, this case study interrogates the efficacy of strategic sport communication in a successful campus campaign and asks readers to challenge the authors' assertions and problematize alternative outcomes.

Introduction

From the preschool to the professional level, sports play an oversized role in contemporary American culture. Despite the magnitude of importance allocated to sport in terms of time, attention, and economic spending, many fans—and perhaps more critically, many organizations and owners—have rejected athletes' use of their public positions for messages deemed too political or controversial. From the 1968 banishment of Olympians Tommie Smith and John Carlos to the 2017 failure to sign National Football League quarterback Colin Kaepernick, athletes who have spoken out on the issues of the day have been forcibly excluded from sport, even when their positions have resonated with a majority of Americans.

This dual construct of athlete identity as both public and silent, together with the visibility afforded athletes, has created a backdrop against which activism on the part of athletes invokes multiple identity concerns. Athletes who employ strategic sport communication to challenge social injustices and leverage the power of sport for positive social change engage in personal, relational, and communal identity messages.

Despite the risks presented in a complex political climate, athletes from all levels have increasingly used the platform afforded them by sport to speak out on social issues. Professional athletes have taken on pay equity and police brutality; youth league participants have engaged in more mainstream anti-bullying and public health campaigns. The ongoing employment of athletes in anti-drug and anti-violence campaigns nationwide demonstrates the importance of both the 'role model effect' and sustained public attention to sport.

Paradoxically, collegiate athletes had not traditionally been among those using their positions to advance social change (Wolken, 2017). Although colleges are often the incubators of social change, and traditionally aged students are the vanguard of social progress, collegiate athletes across all divisions have been notably absent in recent activist sport communication; for instance, Kaepernick's protest of the national anthem was not widely shared by collegiate athletes even while it was replicated by high school teams across the country. Instead, when college athletes make the news for conduct off the field, it is often for engaging in antisocial behavior. That behavior includes bullying, rape and sexual assault, and hazing, often with elements of racism, ableism, or other forms of privilege, perpetuating the stereotype that athletes are less progressive and more abusive than the general body of students (a sentiment reflected in Donald Trump's dismissal of his description of committing sexual assault as "locker room talk").

Background

Collegiate athletes are largely bound by codes of conduct, scholarship requirements, and other university athletic department, conference, or national governing body policies. While team culture may perpetuate hazing and abuses, the potential personal loss of playing time, funding, or positive recruitment reputation may serve as impediments for collegiate athletes who may consider engaging in political or social action in a manner that is connected to their athletic identity.

This changed abruptly in 2014 when an alliance between student organizations at Duke University resulted in the creation of the "You Don't Say" campaign. Initially launched by non-athletes, student leaders soon realized the power of high-profile student-athletes, and the combined effort led quickly to a publicly recognized campaign. The photo project drew attention not only to the effect of slurs used against gay, lesbian, and transgendered students, but was later expanded to include language considered demeaning or offensive on the basis of sex, gender identity, race, and ethnicity.

The power of "You Don't Say" was quickly apparent. Duke University athletes who participated in the campaign were simultaneously lauded for the risks they took and ridiculed on social media. Despite the downsides, the campaign gained traction—and began to spread. Students at Duke saw the power of the campaign, and despite some derisive online comments, student-athletes continued to volunteer to participate, leading organizers to label it as a success (Kort, 2017). The campaign was subsequently adopted at multiple universities, including first at Shippensburg University, an NCAA Division II regional comprehensive university, where the campaign was implemented in 2015 by the Student-Athlete Advisory Committee (SAAC). The full campaign is available for viewing at http://shipraiders.com/sports/2016/4/20/dontsay2016.aspx.

The adoption (with permission) of the "Don't Say" campaign by the student-athletes at Shippensburg University was done with the support of the Department of Athletics, with emphasis on educating the campus community and broader public regarding inappropriate language directed towards various constituent groups both in and out of the realm of sport. The implementation of the campaign demonstrates the complex dynamic of sport within an organizational context, as offices and administrators from all levels of campus provided permissions and production assistance. More significantly, the campaign reflects the multiple structures of identity communication employed by the student-athletes featured in the "Don't Say" posters and digital products.

Select student-athletes who volunteered to serve as ambassadors on behalf of the campaign were featured on posters and social media graphics produced by the Department of Athletics. Each poster featured student-athlete(s) standing next to an offensive or demeaning word or phrase along with an explanation as to why individuals might choose to refrain from using that language. The graphics were produced as social media images and the posters unveiled at the university's campus-wide Day of Human Understanding, an annual event orchestrated by the Office of Social Equity and supported by the campus Women's Center—offices designed to emphasize diversity and promote inclusion. The images were subsequently shared widely, including on the university's Department of Athletics official website; on social media feeds; and in classroom, administration, and student-housing buildings across campus.

The purpose of the campaign is not to censor words or phrases but instead to provide a justification for the choice to eliminate marginalizing language. The success of the campaign can be understood in the frames of identity theorized by Hecht (1993) and applied most extensively to the creation of health message campaigns. Hecht (1993) and others (notably, Jung & Hecht, 2004) describe identity as a social construct composed of multiple layers. These layers include the personal, enacted, relational, and communal levels of identity, each of which is reflected in the SAAC Shippensburg University "Don't Say" campaign.

The Case

As described by Hecht and Choi (2012), the Communication Theory of Identity, or CTI, "posits that individuals internalize social interactions, relationships, and a sense of self into identities through communication" (p. 139). Identities are realized and expressed as a sense of self, through performance, in relationship with another, and as a consequence of group membership. Accordingly, the creation of graphics and posters featuring student-athletes asserting that they "Don't Say" particular words or phrases itself can be understood to be the enactment of identity—the use of communication to express, in a persuasive and performative manner, some aspect of the self. Through further application of CTI, the "Don't Say" campaign provides student-athletes with the capacity and the channel to assert identity at all levels in a manner that challenges stereotypical views of athletes, and invites the campus and broader community to take part in the campaign.

The SU SAAC deliberately constructed the campaign in a manner that makes use of powerful identity messages, including personal frame 'I' and 'we' statements. Each student-athlete was empowered to select the verbiage deemed marginalizing or offensive, and to construct a statement of rationale. The terms selected, and the stories relayed, convey specific meaning for the student-athlete. In this way, the personal layer of identity provides an immediate lens into understanding the "Don't Say" campaign. CTI provides an "understanding [of] how individuals define themselves in general as well as in particular situations" (Hecht, Collier, & Ribeau, 1993, pp. 166–167). In general terms, when an individual asserts (or thinks) that she is a good pitcher or that she is strong, she is engaging in the personal frame of identity communication.

Several of the posters produced by the SAAC featured messages from student-athletes that challenged stereotypes based on individual identity characteristics, most notably gender. Figures 25.1 and 25.2 are two such message examples.

As described by the student-athletes in these images, stereotypical messages about what they should or should not do based on gender are rejected by their participation in sport. In the accompanying text in Image 25.1, Tara Bicko asserts:

I DON'T SAY
HIT LIKE A GIRL
BECAUSE MY GENDER
DOESN'T LIMIT MY
ATHLETIC ABILITY

TARA BICKO, SOFTBALL

shipraiders.com/dontsay

Figure 25.1 Identity Communication & Gender

Source: Student-Athlete Advisory Committee, Shippensburg University

I DON'T SAY
MAN UP
BECAUSE IT IMPLIES
WOMEN ARE WEAK

BAILEY DAVIS, WOMEN'S TRACK & FIELD

shipraiders.com/dontsay

Figure 25.2 Identity Communication & Gender

Source: Student-Athlete Advisory Committee, Shippensburg University

Ever since I was a little girl, I've always been engaged in sports. From the age of 5–12, I played baseball since my town did not have a softball team.

As you read this, you're probably thinking, "isn't baseball a boy's sport?" Yes, baseball is predominantly played by males, but that does not limit females from participating. I have been approached by many people throughout the years saying, "What are you doing?" or "You don't belong."

My athletic ability is not hindered because I am a female; therefore, it is not appropriate in any circumstance to discriminate based on gender.

The student-athletes depicted in images that reflect the personal frame of identity are not only engaging in the expression of a message about who they are—they are also actively countering a message about who others perceive or expected them to be. In this manner, they ask (and perhaps, in some instances, challenge) the campus and larger community to problematize messages about (student-athlete) identity based on stereotypical conceptions of individual characteristics.

The "Don't Say" campaign also provides student-athletes a platform from which to enact identities that are predicated upon, or based in, relationships. The relational frame of identity is composed of three parts—the messages we receive from others about who we are, the roles we play in relationship to another, and the identity of a relationship with another (Hecht & Choi, 2012). For instance, being a good brother involves being recognized for behaviors in relation to a family member with whom one shares a close relationship; by contrast, being a bad friend may mean divulging secrets and betraying the trust of a confidant with whom one is close. For many student-athletes who participated in the "Don't Say" campaign, relational identity provided motivation. Among these student-athletes whose message is reflective of the relational frame is Erin Doherty, a member of the women's track and field team, who participated in the 2016 "Don't Say" campaign and stated:

> When people say "retarded," in sports or in everyday settings, it is used to insult someone's intelligence or to demean someone who is socially awkward or different.
>
> Ever since I was born, I knew my brother was different. Having low-functioning Autism, my brother has never been able to speak or do simple tasks alone, like reading or writing. But he is just as intelligent as anyone else.
>
> He has made me into a better athlete and person. He has taught me patience and kindness. He exhibits how to cherish the little things in life and to be accepting of everything and to not judge a book by its cover.
>
> No one should feel victimized by the use of this word to insult their intelligence because people with handicaps are intelligent. Let's stand together to rid society of this disgusting word.

Additional messages in the "Don't Say" campaign that reflect the relational frame of identity challenge conventional views of male athletes and sexual relationships. Multiple male student-athletes, including football players Schuyler Harting and Ryan Zapoticky, have used the "Don't Say" campaign as a means to speak out against sexual assault. This poster both sends a powerful message about how language conveys responsibility in sexual assault and challenges the stereotype that male athletes, and especially football players, routinely and reflexively use such language (and commit such crimes), and do so from the players' relational identities. As the student-athletes explain:

SCHUYLER HARTING: Sexual assault is also becoming more prominent in collegiate and professional sports. As a football player, it is frustrating go see men with enormous size and strength, using it in malicious ways off the field. Sexual assault needs to end.

RYAN ZAPOTICKY: Over the past few years, I have noticed that many professional athletes have been involved in sexual assault crimes. Some of the same athletes that I have looked up to, growing up, have been accused and convicted for this offense. It is time to put an end to sexual assault.

Student-athletes are readily recognized as members of a communal identity frame; both their team membership and inclusion in the broader category of student-athlete provide ample points for analysis.[1] Student-athletes frequently encounter the perception that they enrolled in college only to continue to play a sport, casting doubt on their qualification for admission. It is worth noting that Shippensburg University student-athletes consistently have a collectively higher GPA than the student body at large (Serr, 2017). Unfortunately, this fact does not counter the "dumb jock" stereotype that persists on most college campuses, and several student-athletes—including Jimmy Spanos (Figure 25.3)—chose to speak out on this aspect of their communal identity.

In some instances, student-athletes chose to tackle broader communal messages, speaking to social categories, sport, and their futures. Included among these are Max Barkley and Julia Wise, who said:

MAX BARKLEY: I've always been the type of person to work hard for what I want, because that's how I was raised.

You have to be willing to push yourself and others along the way. Perseverance and hard work are nothing to be ashamed of, ever.

JULIA WISE: As a determined female leader in academics and athletics, I am presented with a conflict that questions my integrity. I have found there's a fine line between what can be described as a strong leader or "bossy."

We need to encourage females to be strong, ambitious, and to get rid of the negative word that holds us back.

Here, student-athletes demonstrate that the language used to communicate expectations about gender as a communal frame of identity are limiting

I DON'T SAY DUMB JOCK BECAUSE STUDENT-ATHLETES ARE STUDENTS TOO

JIMMY SPANOS, BASEBALL

shipraiders.com/dontsay

Figure 25.3 Identity Communication & Stereotypes of Student Athletes

Source: Student-Athlete Advisory Committee, Shippensburg University

not only to student-athletes and their performance in their sport but also to women in the classroom and workplace. In much the same way, Shaneice Jackson and Bernard England reject language that defines them as (only) their racial/ethnic characteristics.

As highly visible members of a campus community, student-athletes are often the locus of magnified stereotypes. Student-athletes face assumptions by others that they are only admitted to college because of their athletic skills, they lack academic prowess, and they are only interested in sport. In addition, they are frequently viewed as exemplars of groups to which they are ascribed. Through the "Don't Say" campaign, SU student-athletes challenge the campus and broader community to reconsider the stereotypes underpinning language before engaging in its use and speak out against assumptive norms based on their communal identities.

Unpacking identity frames means recognizing that aspects of identity are interpenetrated—our self-concept (personal frame) and behaviors (enacted frame), the relationships we have and how we communicate to others in them (relational frame), and the groups we belong to (communal frame) are most often related and interdependent. However, on occasion, there can be disconnect between two or more frames, a dissonance known as an identity gap (Jung & Hecht, 2004). Identity gaps occur when an individual's personal frame (for instance, the belief in oneself as a tolerant person) comes into conflict with another aspect of their identity (for example, laughing [enactment frame] at a racist joke told by a friend [relational frame]). Identity gaps can be the source of significant stress, leading to depression and other negative outcomes for individuals (Jung & Hecht, 2008). One student-athlete expressed the difficulty created by an identity gap that originated in sport culture.

In LeQuan Chapman's explanation of his poster, he writes:

> Not only in sports-culture, but in our everyday lives, the word "fag" is tossed around to insult and humiliate any man or boy when displaying "non-masculine" behavior.
>
> I have personally been a victim of the verbal abuse of this word and believe that it has no rightful place in society, as it only serves to oppress gay men.
>
> It's time to stop joking around and realize that, to gay men, this isn't funny.

Collectively, the messages from the student-athletes who voluntarily participated in the "Don't Say" campaign reflect the power of sport to highlight messages about social issues and social justice. The poster campaign enacts identity messages that are reflective of the personal identities of student-athletes, originate in the relationships that comprise student-athletes' relational level identities, and take positions on the attributes ascribed to the communal identities based on their team, athlete status, and larger social roles. The application of CTI provides a lens to better understand how and why these messages work and to illustrate how identity messages help student-athletes *make the call* about identity, language, and communication.

You Make the Call

Student-athletes in the Shippensburg University "Don't Say" campaign comprise a powerful collection of voices that, when analyzed through the lens of the Communication Theory of Identity, are shown to be reflective of the personal, relational, and communal frames of identity through enactment of identity messages on graphics and posters shared with the campus community and broader public. In this manner, student-athletes took a stand against language that is demeaning and hurtful. While the long-term effects of "Don't Say" at Shippensburg University remain to be seen, the high visibility on campus and the enthusiasm expressed by students and student-athletes signal the power of sports and communication to make positive social change. Now it's time for you to *make the call*.

Discussion Questions

1. Imagine that you are an administrator at the university, and you have been asked to approve a poster in which a student-athlete opts to use a particularly offensive term (e.g., "I don't say n_____"). How would you respond to this request?

2. How would this kind of campaign, and the student-athletes who participated in it, be received on your campus? What message would you pick if you were to be asked to participate in a "Don't Say" campaign? Which of your identity frame(s) would that message reflect?

3. What responsibility, if any, do the student-athletes who have opted to be in the poster campaign have to speak up when they (over)hear demeaning or offensive language in the locker room—or elsewhere? What would happen if a student-athlete who was featured on a poster didn't speak up—or was observed or reported to have engaged in behavior that she disavowed?

4. What impact do the actions of athletes have, if any, on those outside of their sport? On those coming up in their sport? Specifically, what impact do you think the "Don't Say" campaign would have on your college campus? How would having the posters displayed in residence halls and classrooms effect students and communication on campus?

5. Discuss any new developments in this ongoing issue. What has occurred lately to impact the tenor of the conversation?

Note

1. For instance, Ron Jackson, author of *Cultural Contracts Theory*, often points to this stereotype of student-athletes, and in particular student-athletes of color, to illustrate how communal identities become 'contracts' that set expectations for performance and achievement, largely in negative and limiting ways.

References

Hecht, M. L. (1993). A research odyssey: Towards the development of a communication theory of identity. *Communication Monographs, 60*, 76–82. doi:10.1080/03637759309376297

Hecht, M. L., & Choi, H. (2012). The communication theory of identity as a framework for health message design. In H. Choi (Ed.), *Health communication message design: Theory and practice*. Newbury Park, CA: Sage Publications.

Hecht, M. L., Collier, M. J., & Ribeau, S. A. (1993). *African American communication: Ethnic identity and cultural interpretation*. Newbury Park, CA: Sage Publications.

Jackson, R. L. (2002). Cultural contracts theory: Towards an understanding of identity negotiation. *Communication Quarterly, 50*, 359–367. doi:10.1080/01463370209385672

Jung, E., & Hecht, M. L. (2004). Elaborating the communication theory of identity: Identity gaps and communication outcomes. *Communication Quarterly, 52*, 265–283. doi:10.1080/01463370409370197

Jung, E., & Hecht, M. L. (2008). Identity gaps and level of depression among Korean immigrants. *Health Communication, 23*, 313–325. doi:10.1080/10410230802229688

Kort, D. (2017, December 06). Duke athletes speak out on the power of language. *Huffington Post: The Blog*. Retrieved from https://www.huffingtonpost.com/daniel-kort/duke-studentathletes-spea_b_6440866.html

Serr, R. (2017, June 23). *Report to the council of trustees*. Shippensburg, PA: Shippensburg University.

Wolken, D. (2017, August 29). What if college athletes follow Kaepernick's lead? They might find they have real power. *USA Today*, https://www.usatoday.com/story/sports/college/columnist/dan-wolken/2017/08/29/college-football-players-kaepernick-protest/612864001/

26 The Bathroom Bill and the Basketball Game

The Role of College Sports in Political Arbitration

Ryan Rogers

This chapter outlines the communication related to the controversy surrounding Marist College's decision to send their men's basketball team to North Carolina in place of the University of Albany. Some faculty, employees, and community members criticized this decision as a lack of moral leadership in the face of anti-LGBT legislation, while the school defended its decision to attend the game. This issue is as timely as ever and raises important questions related to sports organizations and their role in political arbitration. The communication from Marist College's president will be analyzed with special attention to the Elaboration Likelihood Model and framing.

Introduction

A variety of major events were cancelled in North Carolina in protest of House Bill 2, more commonly known as the "bathroom bill" (ESPN.com, 2016; Kludt, 2016), which, among other regulations, required people to use the bathroom that corresponded to their birth sex. Despite this, Marist College administrators decided to send its men's basketball team to Duke University as part of the Hall of Fame 2016 Tip-Off Tournament. The college's attendance drew criticism, as some viewed the decision as a lack of moral leadership in the face of anti-LGBTQ legislation (Hogan, 2016; Appendix A). The decision came under increased scrutiny when New York governor, Andrew Cuomo—Marist's home state—banned all nonessential state travel to North Carolina in response to the enactment of the bill and its impact on the LGBTQ community (governor.ny.gov, 2016). The president of Marist College, David Yellen, issued a statement defending the decision to have the men's basketball team travel to North Carolina and play Duke (Yellen, 2016). Ultimately, Marist played at Duke University on November 11, 2016. The game has been heralded by the Marist athletics department as an achievement in exposure and recruiting for the institution while criticized by others for its insensitivity toward the LGBTQ community.

Background

North Carolina's legislature passed a law that reversed existing ordinances that provided perceived protections for the LGBTQ community (Gordon,

Price, & Peralta, 2016). This law became known as the "bathroom bill" because of reasons detailed above. In doing so, the law defined which individuals were protected against discrimination—sexual orientation was not included among them. The bathroom bill was initially enacted but later repealed in March of 2017 (Hanna, Park, & McLaughlin, 2017). Notably, Marist's decision to play and the game itself was played before the repeal and while the debate was, perhaps, at its most prominent.

Supporters of the law, such as the conservative Christian Action League's Reverend Mark Creech, argued that the law was common sense and protected "the safety of our women and children" (Bonner, 2016). The law has also been described as a move against forced political correctness (Valencia, 2016). Critics of the law said that it was discriminatory and bigoted against the LGBTQ community as well as stigmatizing for transgender people (Valencia, 2016). In response, many events and plans were altered in protest of the law. For example, the 2017 NBA All-Star Game was moved from Charlotte to New Orleans (Espn.com, 2016), Bruce Springsteen canceled a concert in North Carolina (Kludt, 2016), and PayPal canceled plans to expand into the state, costing jobs (Bonner, 2016).

The law became part of a national conversation, and the issue became polarizing between those in support of the law and those against it. More specifically, travel to North Carolina during this period became politically divisive in noteworthy ways. Consequently, examining the communication of Marist College's president on this topic through two theoretical lenses is valuable. Media framing and the Elaboration Likelihood Model help to contextualize and understand the message. Media framing describes how a sender "defines" and "constructs" a topic (Nelson, Clawson, & Oxley, 1997). In other words, framing helps the communicator to control the meaning that a recipient perceives (Fairhurst & Sarr, 1996). In the same way that an artist might carefully present work to ensure that audiences experience a piece in a certain way, other messages often do the same thing through word selection and omission (Tewksbury & Scheufele, 2009). Framing has also been closely related to agenda-setting theory (McCombs & Ghanem, 2001). Agenda-setting theory suggests that the presentation of messages will instruct audiences on what to think about such that people will perceive more frequently received messages as more important than ones that are not received as frequently. Framing, on the other hand, suggests that media messages tell people how to interpret a message. Though contested, framing might be understood as **second-level agenda setting** (McCombs, Llamas, Lopez-Escobar, & Rey, 1997). There are many types of frames that are useful for constructing effective, coherent, persuasive messages. They include gain or loss frames, thematic or episodic frames, metaphors, jargon, contrast, spin, and stories (Fairhurst & Sarr, 1996; Iyengar, 1991; Kahneman & Tversky, 1979), though it has been argued that firm typologies such as these are too rigid (Tewksbury & Scheufele, 2009). To provide an example of framing, a study by Nelson and colleagues (1997) showed that when a news story framed a Ku Klux Klan (KKK) rally as a demonstration of free speech, the audience was more tolerant of the KKK than when the rally was framed as a disruption. This is an example of a spin frame, or one that presents the content in a positive or negative light in order to influence the audience. For another example, a story on food products impacted audiences based on the terminology used (Chung, Runge, Su, Brossard, & Scheufele, 2016). When referring to food products as "pink slime" audiences were more concerned than audiences that encountered the industry term "lean finely textured beef." Thus, the word choice of a message can help to frame a topic. A similar pattern can be found with the HB2 controversy. Those who support the law frame it in terms of safety and choose words related to safety. Those who do not support the law frame it as discrimination and use words that lend to that interpretation. In short, the way in which a message is presented influences the way in which people interpret it. Consequently, this is a useful tool in examining persuasive messages as it can indicate how a message appeals to audiences.

The Elaboration Likelihood Model (ELM) describes how someone may be persuaded by a message. Petty and Cacioppo (1986) describe two routes of persuasion: the central route and the peripheral route. The central route is used when a person spends a lot of cognitive energy on a topic and elaborates upon the message. In short, a person thinks about the topic. If the message is persuasive, the effect on the recipient will be more predictable and consistent. For the peripheral route, people do not engage in much thought regarding a message but instead rely on cues to give them a positive or negative impression of the message. On the central route, a strong argument is likely to convince a recipient, while a weak argument would not. On the peripheral route, the strength of the argument is irrelevant. To be clear, a cue is not an argument. A cue, instead, is something akin to the aesthetic appeal of a message instead of the content of the message itself. In other words, a person might like the way a message looks and develop a positive impression of the issue regardless of the message's content. In the case of the bathroom bill, one factor that is particularly important to consider is relevance. That is, whether the recipient can personally relate to the message's topic. When a message is more relevant to a person, he or she is more likely to process the message through the central route. When a message is less relevant to a person, he or she is more likely to process the message through the peripheral route.

Petty and Cacioppo (1986) detailed a series of experiments that demonstrated how the ELM functions. In one experiment, the number of arguments served as a cue for those who were not involved in the topic. In addition to the number of arguments, the strength of the arguments provided also enhanced agreement with the message. In another experiment, source expertise served as a cue. Here the results indicated the expert had an impact on those who were not involved in the topic, while an expert source did not impact those who were involved—they still were mainly persuaded by strong arguments. In yet another, repetition of the message helped to strengthen strong messages and weaken weak messages regardless of relevance of the topic. Based on these dimensions, the ELM provides a meaningful way to assess the message from Yellen.

The Case

In 2016, the Naismith Memorial Basketball Hall of Fame Tip-Off Tournament scheduled the University at Albany Great Danes to play against the Duke University Blue Devils in North Carolina on November 12. However, since the University at Albany is part of the State University of New York (SUNY) system, they complied with Governor Andrew Cuomo's travel ban of state employees and dropped out of the game against Duke (Wilkin, 2016).

Tournament organizers altered the schedule so that the University at Albany would then play Penn State University at a venue in Connecticut and Marist College would play Duke in North Carolina. Marist, a private institution, was not beholden to the same travel ban as the University at Albany. Marist College had, per college president David Yellen (2016), agreed to play in the Tournament in 2014, before the controversial HB2 law was enacted, and thus Marist "did not seek this game."

The original press release announcing the decision to play the game is no longer available on Marist's website despite several news sources linking to it (Amodeo, 2016; Stiles, 2016). After this press release, criticism came from the Marist community (Haynes & Strum, 2016). One Marist alum penned an open letter to Yellen on the Huffingtonpost website, stating that the decision maintained the status quo and lacked courage (Amodeo, 2016). The alum also requested Marist's withdrawal from the game and an apology to those hurt by the decision. Timmian Massie, Marist's former director of public affairs, offered this statement (Hogan, 2016):

> How disappointing for me, a gay man, former long-time employee and major donor, to know Marist College doesn't care about #LGBT rights . . . here's Marist saying . . . We don't care about discrimination. I hope LGBT and straight students, faculty, staff and alumni express their displeasure.

One faculty member offered a statement saying that playing the game sent the wrong message (Appendix A), while another claimed that the individuals on the team, not outside parties, should make the decision (Appendix B).

In response to the controversy, Yellen (2016) released a formal statement in the *Chronicle of Higher Education*. The full text can be found by following the cite below. Ultimately, Marist lost the game 94–49, and no other major controversies or criticisms have emerged. Yellen's statement in the *Chronicle* is the focus of the analysis in this chapter. To assess the efficacy of this statement, the outcomes of the game are explored within the context of Yellen's statement as related to the ELM and framing.

You Make the Call

The main questions that emerge from this event is: How should issues like these be handled, and how effective was Yellen's statement? The remainder of this chapter will assess the successes and failures of Yellen's statement.

Yellen's statement can be examined for strengths in terms of the ELM and framing. Yellen's statement utilized a loss frame to discuss the issue. Mainly, he argued that if Marist did not participate in this game, then there were many other things at stake beyond just a basketball game. For example, "If we boycott North Carolina, should we boycott other states with laws discriminating against the LGBT community?" and "Which other issues of social justice should lead us to boycott various states? . . . The list of such questions is endless." In short, Yellen argued that there was much to be lost if Marist did not participate in this event, and Marist would have entered a "slippery-slope" where the core tenets of a higher learning institution might be risked.

In terms of frames, people tend to be more persuaded by messages that use loss frames when the outcomes are uncertain and more persuaded by gain frames when the outcomes are certain (Toll et al., 2007). With a scenario like this one, which featured considerable political complications and unpredictable developments, the outcomes were likely more uncertain than certain. As a result, this was an effective frame for Yellen to utilize.

Beyond that, using a gain frame that detailed how the school would benefit might come across as opportunistic or callous toward the LGBTQ community. On top of this, the Yellen statement utilized spin and contrast frames (Fairhurst & Sarr, 1996). Spin refers to presenting the subject positively or negatively—like the KKK example used earlier in this chapter. In this case, Yellen presented going to the game as positive and boycotting the game as negative.

Contrast frame refers to how a message defines itself by what it is not. Yellen did so quite explicitly: "our opposition to boycotting North Carolina should not be read as a lack of commitment to LGBT rights." Yellen was also careful to use terminology such as "discrimination," "rights," and "struggle," which helped present his message as sympathetic and thoughtful. In light of the outcomes, Yellen's statement appears effective. Nearly all of the comments from the community that came afterward focused on the positives, which would have been lost had Marist not played the game. Here, the game was treated as an opportunity for outreach rather than discrimination (Hogan, 2016).

After the game, the individuals involved in this process claimed it a success, which indicates that Yellen's message was effective. Marist students who attended the game, the players involved in the trip, and some students from

Duke expressed that the trip was a positive experience (Hogan, 2016). An article written by a student and published on the Marist Media Hub clearly put the game in a positive light such that it offered an opportunity for discussion on the topic and personal growth (Hogan, 2016). Students from Marist wore shirts to the game stating "Love is love," and the team wore rainbow tie-dyed socks during the game (Hogan, 2016).

From the perspective of the ELM, many of the comments examined as outcomes were from stakeholders invested in this decision, like members of the student body and the president of Marist's Lesbian Gay Straight Alliance (LGSA) club.

An editorial by a Marist student published several weeks after the game stated that Marist was justified in traveling to Duke for the game (Rzodkiewicz, 2016). The editorial revisited many of the arguments outlined by Yellen but with more blunt examples than Yellen had employed. Much of the student's argument focused on the benefits to the basketball program. For Marist, "a rebuilding team with a young roster, this game offers exposure" (Haynes & Strum, 2016). Dr. Geoff Brackett, the executive vice president of Marist, supported this sentiment (Rzodkiewicz, 2016).

Brother Michael Flanigan, head of the Marist Men's Spirit Group for gay men, saw "no reason" that the game should have been boycotted (Belmonte & Derario, 2016). Even the president of Marist's Lesbian Gay Straight Alliance (LGSA) club, Hannah Sayers, said that Yellen's reasons for going "made a lot of sense" (Belmonte & Derario, 2016).

Notably, the magnitude and benefit of the exposure the game had on the college's athletic program specifically and the college in general is difficult to measure. The financial benefits of playing in this game are not publicly available but routinely alluded to as an important factor. There were two reader comments on Yellen's article, neither of which were negative. Given the emphasis on the positive and the lack of controversy or criticism after either Yellen's statement or the game, any major issues for Marist dissipated. Critics largely fell silent after the game, perhaps because the "damage had been done."

Regardless, it appears the Marist community moved on from the controversy after Yellen's statement. Thus, one could conclude that Yellen's statement was effective. Since this decision was relevant to the people who made positive statements after the game, one could infer that Yellen made strong arguments in his statement. Since the message was relevant to these parties, these parties were more likely to elaborate on the message. Messages tend to be more convincing to audiences involved in the topic when the arguments are strong. In other words, the central route was likely employed by these people. Indeed, Yellen's points tended to be more substantive than a cue would be and thus would serve as arguments. Even if all parties, like those who might have commented in web posts, did not process the message centrally, there is reason to believe that the message would have been processed favorably on the peripheral route.

Yellen presented multiple arguments, and the number of arguments can serve as a cue. Likewise, it was probable that Yellen, as the president of the school, had a large degree of source expertise, which is another cue, making the message more effective than if it came from someone who might have been less prominent or credible. Finally, Yellen's statement presented several arguments which were repeated by other Marist officials. This repetition served to strengthen his message.

One student-media article interviewed several Marist school officials, and many of them echoed statements in support of Yellen's piece in the *Chronicle of Higher Education* (Belmonte & Derario, 2016). The officials even suggested that the controversy was perhaps overblown such that only those who were disappointed in the decision were vocal about it. They insinuated that the issue stemmed from longtime former director of public affairs Tim Massie's critical comments about the decision, but that even those dissenting views had since "died down" (Belmonte & Derario, 2016).

Of course, this assessment is theoretical, and the long-term outcomes of this decision are yet to be determined. Based on the outcomes used here, Yellen's statement seemed effective, but using other unforeseen outcomes, the question might remain whether Yellen convinced critics that this was an acceptable decision. Beyond that, critics remained largely silent after they had made their voices heard. Without more meaningful data points, a definitive conclusion remains elusive, but regardless, this event provides an opportunity to think about how sports teams and their institutions might approach issues like this.

Discussion Questions

1. What are some other frames used in Yellen's statement? What about in Appendix A and B? How effective are they?
2. What additional communication could Marist (the college/the team) have made before, during, or after the game? Why?
3. Describe other events that might be comparable to this. What are key differences? Similarities? Were the outcomes the same or different?
4. Considering Appendix A and B in terms of the ELM, what are the other arguments and cues used? Are they effective? Why or why not?
5. Discuss any new developments with this issue. What has occurred lately to impact the tenor of the conversation?

References

Amodeo, J. (2016). Marist college should withdraw from Duke game because of North Carolina's Anti-LGBT HB2. Retrieved from www.huffingtonpost.com/entry/president-yellen-marist-college-should-withdraw-from_us_57b5bb87e4b04c609978aad0

Belmonte, A., & Derario, G. (2016). Marist sees educational opportunity in playing Duke. Retrieved from http://maristmediahub.com/2016/11/08/marist-sees-educational-opportunity-in-playing-duke/

Bonner, L. (2016). Rally to support HB2 Monday. *Newsobserver.com*. Retrieved from www.newsobserver.com/news/politics-government/politics-columns-blogs/under-the-dome/article70015127.html

Chung, J., Runge, K., Su, L. F., Brossard, D., & Scheufele, D. (2016). Media framing and perceptions of risk for food technologies: The case of "pink slime". In *Food futures: Ethics, science and culture* (pp. 219–227). Wageningen, the Netherlands: Academic Publishers.

Espn.com. (2016). NBA moves 2017 all-star game from Charlotte over HB2 bill. Retrieved from www.espn.com/nba/story/_/id/17120170/nba-moving-all-star-game-charlotte-north-carolina-bill

Fairhurst, G. T., & Sarr, R. A. (1996). *The art of framing: Managing the language of leadership* (Vol. 50). San Francisco, CA: Jossey-Bass.

Gordon, M., Price, M., & Peralta, K. (2016). Understanding HB2: North Carolina's newest law solidifies state's role in defining discrimination. *CharlotteObservor.com*. Retrieved from www.charlotteobserver.com/news/politics-government/article68401147.html

Governor.ny.gov. (2016). Governor Cuomo Bans non-essential state travel to North Carolina. Retrieved from www.governor.ny.gov/news/governor-cuomo-bans-non-essential-state-travel-north-carolina

Hanna, J., Park, M., & McLaughlin, E. C. (2017).North Carolina repeals "bathroom bill".*CNN.com*. Retrieved from www.cnn.com/2017/03/30/politics/north-carolina-hb2-agreement/index.html

Haynes, S., & Strum, P. (2016). Marist defends decision to play Duke, criticizes North Carolina law. Retrieved from www.poughkeepsiejournal.com/story/news/2016/08/17/marist-issues-statement-decision-play-duke/88913556/

Hogan, B. (2016). Marist travels to Duke HB2 law. *Maristmediahub.com*. Retrieved from http://maristmediahub.com/2016/11/21/marist-travels-to-duke-despite-hb2-law

Iyengar, S. (1991). *Is anyone responsible? How TV frames political issues*. Chicago, IL: University of Chicago Press.

Kahneman, D., & Tversky, A. (1979). Prospect theory: An analysis of decision under risk. *Econometrica, 47*(2), 263–291.

Kludt, T. (2016). Bruce Springsteen cancels North Carolina concert over "bathroom law". *CNN.com*. Retrieved from http://money.cnn.com/2016/04/08/media/bruce-springsteen-north-carolina-show-canceled/index.html

McCombs, M., & Ghanem, S. I. (2001). The convergence of agenda setting and framing. *Framing Public Life: Perspectives on Media and our Understanding of the Social World*, 67–81.

McCombs, M., Llamas, J. P., Lopez-Escobar, E., & Rey, F. (1997). Candidate images in Spanish elections: Second-level agenda-setting effects. *Journalism & Mass Communication Quarterly, 74*(4), 703–717.

Nelson, T. E., Clawson, R. A., & Oxley, Z. M. (1997). Media framing of a civil liberties conflict and its effect on tolerance. *American Political Science Review, 91*(3), 567–583.

Petty, R. E., & Cacioppo, J. T. (1986). The elaboration likelihood model of persuasion. In *Communication and persuasion* (pp. 1–24). New York, NY: Springer-Verlag.

Rzodkiewicz, M. (2016). Marist Justified in Pursuing NCAA Tournament. Retrieved from http://maristmediahub.com/2016/11/28/marist-justified-in-pursuing-ncaa-tournament-2/

Stiles, A. (2016). Marist college rebuffs calls to Cancel Duke basketball matchup over NC bathroom law. Retrieved from https://heatst.com/culture-wars/marist-duke-basketball-bathroom

Tewksbury, D., & Scheufele, D. A. (2009). News framing theory and research. In J. Bryant & M. B. Oliver (Eds.), *Media effects: Advances in theory and research*. Hillsdale, NJ: Lawrence Erlbaum Associates, Inc.

Toll, B. A., O'Malley, S. S., Katulak, N. A., Wu, R., Dubin, J. A., Latimer, A., & Salovey, P. (2007). Comparing gain-and loss-framed messages for smoking cessation with sustained-release bupropion: A randomized controlled trial. *Psychology of Addictive Behaviors, 21*(4), 534.

Valencia, J. (2016). Hundreds rally for HB2 and the GOP lawmakers who approved it. Retrieved from http://wunc.org/post/hundreds-rally-hb2-and-gop-lawmakers-who-approved-it#stream/0

Wilkin, T. (2016). UAlbany's game at Duke is off. *Timeunion.com.* Retrieved from www.timesunion.com/sports/article/UAlbany-s-game-at-Duke-is-off-8376947.php

Yellen, D. (2016). Why we are going to Duke. *Chronicle of Higher Education.* Retrieved from www.chronicle.com/article/Why-We-Are-Going-to-Duke/237540?cid=trend_right_t

Appendix A

Statement From Marist Faculty Member

I understand the practical reasons for wanting our young basketball team to play Duke BUT I find the decision tone deaf to human rights, social justice and the underlying morality and values that have girded Marist.

The NC law also goes beyond the common transgender bathroom issue—it also restricts all NC municipalities from passing anti-discrimination legislation to give Lgbtq persons equal rights necessary in public accommodations, housing, health and employment. Not all laws are just.

Public accommodations and employment nondiscrimination are the cutting edge in equal rights for Lgbtq persons. Someone may be fired /not hired in many states because the employer THINKS that person is Lgbtq. People are not being served in businesses because of their gender identity or expression. There are recent two cases of such discrimination in Ulster County; and Ulster county has a Gender Identity Non Discrimination in Public Accommodations bill in front of them. (I just wrote the letter of support for this for the Ulster County Human Rights Commission.)

As for our students on campus, what message are we sending them? Is this the civil society we want to live in—where fellow citizens are discriminated against while we pledge "liberty and justice for all"?

And, one final thought: as my hero Eleanor Roosevelt said "where do human rights live, in those small places close to home" (1958). States can pass both just and unjust laws—it is up to citizens to have the moral courage to act on them or oppose them (acts of civil disobedience).

Appendix B

Statement From Marist Faculty Member

It seems to me this discussion has left out a group of stakeholders. The players and coaches might argue they are participating in athletic competition, not engaging in politics, and that their presence does not necessarily endorse discriminatory laws.

Each player and coach should have the option of staying home without penalty. If a high-level decision is made that Marist will boycott as an institution, the players and coaches are not allowed to act according to their individual consciences.

This reminds me of the case many years ago when it was announced an ROTC program was coming to Marist. One member of the community tried to organize the faculty against this, in protest of the foreign policy of then President Bush. If he had succeeded, it would have removed the right of each individual Marist student to participate in ROTC or not.

Taking away choices of individuals does not seem to fit Marist's values, nor the progressive agenda as published.

It is significant that Duke has denounced the law, as have many other institutions in the NC system. If Marist declines, does it punish Duke, or North Carolina? Duke can't pick up their campus and move to a neighboring state.

Index